FALSE WITNESS

FALSE WITNESS

THE REAL STORY OF JIM GARRISON'S
INVESTIGATION AND
OLIVER STONE'S
FILM *JFK*

Patricia Lambert

M. Evans and Company, Inc.
New York

M. Evans and Company, Inc.
216 East 49th Street
New York, New York 10017

ISBN 0-87131-879-2

Book design and typesetting by Rik Lain Schell

Printed in the United States of America

9 8 7 6 5 4 3 2 1

For Bill and for Terry

To bear false witness is, of course, nothing new. But the number of instances found in this story—their variety, motivations, transformations, impact, and lingering presence—is extraordinary. It was done for money, notoriety, advancement, reward, revenge, loyalty; it was done intentionally, maliciously, nonmaliciously, accidentally; it was done in public, in private; it was done to subordinates, supporters, skeptics, audiences, and media representatives; and it was done at a lectern, in a magazine, in legal proceedings, in state court, in federal court, in a book, in a movie, and in silence by insiders who always knew the truth.

CONTENTS

PHOTO SECTION

PART TWO: Fraud Perpetuated

PREFACE

Thirty-two years ago, when New Orleans District Attorney Jim Garrison was investigating President Kennedy's murder, I was one of those excited by Garrison's rhetoric, one of those convinced he *had something*. My thinking seemed logical enough. He was an elected official. Such men want to be reelected. If he weren't telling the truth, he wouldn't be. Therefore, he must be telling the truth. I was wrong on both points, but it was two full years before I realized that. I still doubted the official version of the assassination, but by then I knew Garrison had none of the answers.

So it was easy to turn away from him with little thought about my earlier misguided enthusiasm, though even then I experienced a twinge of discomfort about it. Over the years, on the rare occasion when his name came up or something occurred to remind me of that time, the memory was always accompanied by that twinge. Once or twice I even engaged in some minor soul-searching about it. The small personal insights this yielded were overshadowed by the larger mystery that remained. What on earth was Jim Garrison all about? If he didn't have *something*, what then did he have?

In the aftermath of Oliver Stone's film JFK, I witnessed history repeating itself. Garrison's spirit, his thinking, and his certitude were loose in the land once more. I felt as though my past had overtaken me. To those other riddles, I now added another. How had Garrison managed to do it again?

In June 1993, I suddenly realized I had to have the answers. Moved by a surprising sense of urgency, I began studying the earliest available records and a few months later was on an airplane headed for that beguiling city where it all happened.

I would return to New Orleans four more times in the next two years and, in between, visit the National Archives. I would read thousands of pages of documents and interview many of the principals involved.

This book tells what I learned.

INTRODUCTION

UPROAR: FRAUD IN THE ARTS

Who owns our "history"? He
who makes it up so that most
everyone believes it.[1]
                    —Oliver Stone, 1992

One day in December 1988, Hollywood's self-styled guerrilla film-maker Oliver Stone was in Cuba, attending a Latin American film festival when he stepped onto an elevator in Havana's old Nacional Hotel. There, an obscure New York publisher named Ellen Ray thrust a book into his hands.[2] The unlikely convergence of Ellen Ray and Oliver Stone in that Havana elevator would beget, three years later, the most controversial film ever created about an American historical event and provoke a thunderous media uproar that is unresolved even now. The cause of it all was the book Ray pressed upon Stone that day. It was On the Trail of the Assassins, the story of President Kennedy's assassination as told by former New Orleans District Attorney Jim Garrison.

Stone later told an interviewer that he had been doubtful about Ellen Ray at first, thinking she was just another "advocate of a cause." But he took Garrison's book with him to the Philippines where he was shooting Born on the Fourth of July. (Like Platoon, it excoriated the Vietnam War and it, too, would win an Academy Award.) Stone ended up reading the book three times.

The relaxed and intimate first person narrative, which is almost seductively easy to read, described Garrison's 1960s investigation and how he discovered the plot that had taken the president's life. According to him, it was a CIA operation, with a contingent in New Orleans run by a local businessman named Clay Shaw, a prominent figure in the community and a closet homosexual. Arrested by Garrison on March 1, 1967, and charged with conspiring to murder the presi-

·xiii·

dent, Shaw was the only individual ever tried for the crime. He was quickly acquitted, but Garrison blamed the verdict on a prosecution witness he said gave lunatic testimony on cross-examination and his own failure to establish Shaw's connection with the CIA.

Garrison told a plausible-sounding story that transported the crime from the narrow boundaries of Dealey Plaza to a larger, more appropriate stage; and he cast as villains an organization many Americans had come to believe was capable of anything. Assassination books tend to be grim and unreadable, but Garrison had written an interesting one. In the process, he transformed his prosecution of Clay Shaw, which the New York Times called "one of the most disgraceful chapters in the history of American jurisprudence," into a righteous enterprise.

Stone later said he was "deeply moved and appalled" by Garrison's story. Until then, he had thought little about the assassination and had accepted the conclusion of the Warren Report that Lee Harvey Oswald, acting alone, shot the president. Garrison, Stone said, opened his eyes. It was through Garrison's book that Stone first learned the "facts" of the case. More important was its Vietnam theme, Garrison's claim that President Kennedy's plan to withdraw from there triggered the assassination. For Stone, a twice-wounded Vietnam veteran, that war was the watershed experience of his adult life. In Garrison's story, Stone had found his own personal Rosetta stone, an explanation for why he had ended up in the jungles of southeast Asia. He embraced it all as gospel. Over the next twenty-four months, he traveled to New Orleans three or four times each year, slipping into the city quietly and meeting secretly with Garrison. Like others before him, Stone fell under Garrison's spell.

"Anyone who has experienced the six-hour lecture from Garrison," wrote columnist Max Lerner after a visit to Garrison's home at the height of his assassination celebrity, "knows that, like a Merlin, he draws you into his never-never land world where everything is upside down, and you get the magical sense of a total reversal of reality." Lerner was enthralled for awhile, he recalled, until his "sanity" was restored.

Oliver Stone's reality reversal was permanent. He stepped into Garrison's magic web and never stepped out. He saw in Garrison's experience material for a film that would reveal what he described as "the untold story" of the assassination. Stone optioned the book himself. "I wanted to get this story out," he said. And so he did. Stone proceeded to create a movie energized by the passion he felt about the Vietnam war that turned the history of the Garrison investigation upside down and pulled fifty million moviegoers into Garrison's "never-never land world."

The process was not easy. Along the way, Stone encountered a major bump in the road. During the summer of 1991, while he was still shooting the film, the media erupted with stories challenging his intentions.

The instigator was Harold Weisberg, an aging and ill first-generation assassination investigator, best known for his *Whitewash* series of books. Weisberg, part of that loose-knit community of writers and researchers originally known as the critics of the Warren Report, had acquired first-hand knowledge of Garrison's shortcomings back in the sixties when he had traveled to New Orleans and for a time assisted him. Stone was in Vietnam most of that period and had missed the Garrison phenomenon. Appalled that a film glorifying Garrison was being planned, Weisberg tried to enlighten Stone in a letter. Stone's response, which came from his assistant, was entirely unsatisfactory to Weisberg, who then took a dramatic step that struck at the heart of Stone's operation.

From the outset, Stone had engaged in extraordinary security precautions. Even the name of the film, known only as "Project X," was a secret. Crew members were required to sign nondisclosure statements. Stone had his office swept for bugs, and drafts of the screenplay were numbered and locked away. Nevertheless, Weisberg obtained a copy of the script and leaked it to columnist George Lardner, Jr., at the *Washington Post*.[3] This ignited what would eventually become a firestorm of criticism from journalists who had covered Garrison's investigation and retained strong opinions about him.*

The *Dallas Morning News* led off with an article that labeled Stone's plan "morally repugnant." Lardner followed that with a scathing attack on the "errors and absurdities" in the screenplay and on Stone himself. Stone, Lardner wrote, was "chasing fiction." Lardner also called Garrison's investigation "a fraud." Stone fired off a response defending his film, and, in a disquieting echo of Garrison's reaction to criticism a quarter century earlier, implied that Lardner was working for the government's intelligence

---

* It also, understandably, infuriated Oliver Stone, who reportedly considered filing a lawsuit.

community. Lardner threatened to sue, but reportedly accepted instead a complete retraction from Stone. Before long, others were expressing their opinions both pro and con, sometimes passionately, occasionally with a good deal of wit, mostly in letters to the editor and newspaper editorials around the country. Stone seemed genuinely wounded by this unprecedented barrage of media criticism before his film was even finished. But he benefited from all that free press coverage. As one observer noted once the film was released, Stone was riding a wave of negative publicity.

JFK, a three-hour-and-seven-minute marathon, premiered in Los Angeles on December 17, 1991, at Mann's Village Theater in Westwood and opened nationwide on Friday, five days before Christmas.* Audience reaction was intense. A writer for the Los Angeles Times reported "gasps" and "tears" during the Abraham Zapruder film sequence showing the moment the president died. "Nobody left to get popcorn," he wrote. What made the movie such a powerful experience was its apparent authenticity.

Actual film footage, some of it quite moving (Walter Cronkite fighting for composure after announcing President Kennedy's death and the wrenching images captured on Zapruder's home movie), was woven together so seamlessly with recreations that it is difficult at times to separate the two. Stone's blurring of that line intensified the movie's documentary-like quality, the sense that this is the real thing. But the chief reason for that impression is its real-life protagonist. Stone tried to deflect criticism about his choice there by claiming the man on the screen was "a fictional Jim Garrison who is dealing with facts. And, sometimes, speculation."[4] But audiences experienced the screen version as an accurate portrayal, or a close facsimile. The movie wouldn't have worked otherwise. The American people didn't want some screenwriter's fantasy about the assassination. They wanted the truth. Stone understood that, for it was what he, too, wanted. He couldn't deliver it but whether or not he realized that initially, or if he ever did, is unclear. What is clear is that he knew how to make a film that appeared to deliver it.

Those who had not spoken up beforehand weighed in now.

---

* In that holiday "sweeps" weekend the big winner was Hook, followed by Father of the Bride. Early reports placed JFK third, but (though the numbers were close) it trailed The Last Boy Scout and Star Trek VI.

INTRODUCTION

"Stone went too far," said former Texas Governor John Connally, who was wounded in the Dallas shooting. "This was a national tragedy. [Stone] mixed fact and fiction in such a way that he's going to convince practically every young person that the federal government, their own government, conspired to kill an American president. And I think that's evil, frankly." Connally ridiculed the sheer size of Stone's conspiracy, which he called "ludicrous." President George Bush, on tour in Australia, responded to a question by saying he had seen "no evidence" that the Warren Report was wrong but didn't think Stone should be censured for putting his own spin on the assassination. *Newsweek* published an eight-page cover story that labeled the film "propaganda." Two former aides to President Lyndon Johnson joined the fray. Joseph A. Califano, Jr., writing in the *Wall Street Journal*, said that JFK was "a disgraceful concoction of lies and distortions." Jack Valenti, now president and chief executive of the Motion Picture Association of America, waited until after the Academy Awards balloting* to denounce the film as a "smear" and "a hoax" on the order of Leni Riefenstahl's Nazi propaganda film *Triumph of the Will*.

The most serious objection was voiced by Brent Staples in the *New York Times* who pointed out that "historical lies are nearly impossible to correct once movies and television have given them credibility." Echoing Governor Connally, Staples predicted that "the children of the video age will swallow JFK whole." He noted that policing art "for inaccuracies" was an impossible task and the best that society could do was to "denounce" such history as "bogus."[5] The harshest words came from Washington columnist George Will. Stone, he said, was "an intellectual sociopath, indifferent to truth" who combined "moral arrogance with historical ignorance." The film he called "execrable history and contemptible citizenship."[6]

As debate on the subject inundated the country, talk radio and television commentators jumped into the fray; university symposiums and town hall meetings were held to discuss the controversy, and it quickly escalated into the most extraordinary war of words ever exchanged over a movie. What was missing in that great debate was *Clay Shaw*. Except for a few muffled voices in New Orleans, virtually no one spoke

---

* The film, nominated in eight categories, including Best Picture and Best Director, won for editing and cinematography.

in his defense. No national figure uttered his name. Everyone was focused on the grand conspiracy. No one seemed to care about Shaw's reputation, his fate, or how it came to pass. No one was more indifferent than Oliver Stone. He felt "[no] responsibility to Clay Shaw because he was [acquitted]," Stone told one interviewer.

Forty-four at the time, Stone is a brawny man with a round boyish face, a gap between his front teeth, thinning black hair and an energy level said to verge on the demonic. He admitted he had "made Garrison better" than he was and proudly referred to himself and others like him as "sons of Jim Garrison." At the National Press Club, Stone staunchly defended his mentor. He had heard "all the horror stories" about Garrison, he said, but none of them held up on investigation, and he challenged Garrison's detractors to show him their evidence.

This book does that.

Its focus is not Dallas and Washington but New Orleans and Hollywood, not the death of the president but the destruction of an ordinary citizen, who could have been anyone. That is what makes what happened in New Orleans more threatening in one sense than what happened in Dallas. The man who went gunning for Shaw didn't do it from a hidden position. Garrison struck Shaw down publicly with assistance from many, using bureaucratic procedures. Writer Nicholas Lemann noted that Stone often referred to Kafka and Orwell but that the essence of their vision was that no government could do anything worse than "turn its powers against an innocent individual in order to advance a larger cause." Garrison did exactly that. His was a wholly societal act that involved some of our most important institutions: the district attorney's office, the local judiciary, the grand jury, the business community, one of the largest news organizations of its time and, later, the publishing world and entertainment industry all played a role in it. Stone and the others who dismiss "the Shaw business" as inconsequential necessarily ignore its implications and monstrousness.

The labyrinthine story that follows is not about the president's assassination. It is about what really happened in New Orleans. What Jim Garrison was really like. How he got away with it in the first place, and how he managed on four separate occasions to rise phoenixlike from his own ashes.[7]

PART ONE
FRAUD IN NEW ORLEANS

CHAPTER ONE

MARCH 1, 1967: THE ARREST

> I went out to the D.A.'s office
> with a perfectly clear conscience.
> I didn't take a lawyer with me. To
> my mind, I was in the position
> of a good citizen making himself
> available to give information to
> these people, which might or
> might not be useful.[1]
>
> —Clay Shaw *(regarding his arrest), 1969*

It happened on a Wednesday. A television announcer broadcast the first news of it. The New Orleans district attorney's office had issued a subpoena for Clay Shaw to appear for questioning. Shaw, the fifty-three-year-old retired director of the International Trade Mart, was visiting the office of a friend that morning. He learned of the subpoena from someone who had heard about it on television. Shaw wondered what it was all about. Why didn't District Attorney Jim Garrison just telephone and say he wanted to speak to him? Shaw had given Garrison all the information he had when he was interviewed back in December and had thought no more about the matter. Now this. Shaw recalled hearing on television last night that Garrison's office had asked a former neighbor of his, James Lewallen, to come in for questioning. Perhaps they wanted to ask him something about Lewallen.

Shaw immediately called the district attorney's office. He asked to speak to Garrison, but he wasn't there. So he spoke to one of Garrison's investigators, Louis Ivon. Yes, Ivon said, a subpoena had been issued. That was "entirely unnecessary," Shaw said. He "would be glad" to come in and talk to them—when did they want him? Since he hadn't had lunch, they agreed on one o'clock. But when Shaw, on his way to a restaurant with a friend, stopped by his house to pick up his mail, he found three deputy sheriffs and a detective waiting on his patio, subpoena in hand. Because it was almost noon, Shaw accepted the detective's offer to drive him to the D.A.'s office. They arrived around 12:15. Garrison wasn't there and didn't show up until 4:00 that afternoon.[2]

They kept him waiting about two hours, Shaw later said, while they moved him from one room to another and he listened to the detective's life story. "What is the holdup?" he asked. No one seemed to know. At one point they shifted him to Garrison's office, which Shaw noted was "quite large and impressive" with a "beautiful desk, comfortable chairs," a "handsome chess board" in one corner, and the complete works of Shakespeare "in small red leather-bound volumes" on the desk. By now Shaw was irritated and hungry, having missed lunch, and he let the detective know it. Soon afterwards, they took him into a different type of room, plain and utilitarian, where Asst. D.A. Andrew Sciambra and Ivon were waiting. They gave him a sandwich and a Coke and waited until he finished eating. Then, with Sciambra sitting directly across from Shaw, and Ivon sitting on the edge of the desk, they began to question him. To Shaw's surprise, his neighbor wasn't the topic. They showed him several pictures of boys, none of whom Shaw knew, and they reeled off a list of names, none of which he recognized. Sciambra soon turned to the real subject at hand. What did Shaw know about a man named David Ferrie? Had he ever been to Ferrie's apartment on Louisiana Parkway? Had he visited a service station Ferrie owned on Veterans Highway? Did he know Lee Harvey Oswald? Shaw told them he had never in his life seen Ferrie, had never been to his apartment, or his service station, and he didn't know Oswald. "What would you say," Sciambra said, "if we told you we have three witnesses who could positively identify you as having been in Ferrie's apartment and in Ferrie's gas station?" Their witnesses, Shaw replied, "were either mistaken or they were lying."[3]

Sciambra asked him to take a truth-serum test to prove he didn't know Ferrie. "Why on earth should I take a truth-serum test?" Shaw said. "If you don't," Sciambra replied, "we're going to charge you with conspiring to murder the president of the United States." Describing that moment later, Shaw conveyed his astonishment by flinging his arms outward. "You've got to be kidding," he said, "you've got to be kidding!"

Sciambra assured him they weren't. "In that case I want a lawyer and I want one now," Shaw said. They agreed, and he began trying to reach his attorney. Shaw quickly discovered that Edward F. Wegmann, the civil attorney who had represented him since 1949, was out of town. Shaw tried his brother, William J. Wegmann, but he, too, was unavailable. He finally reached thirty-three-year-old Salvatore Panzeca, an associate working in William Wegmann's law office, who said he would be there in about thirty minutes. Sciambra and Ivon then left the room, locking the door behind them. Shaw sat alone, a "storm [raging] inside" him, awaiting the arrival of Salvatore Panzeca.[4]

He had never seen "a more welcome sight" than Panzeca's "stocky little form coming through the door."

"I am Sal Panzeca," he said, "you are now my client, I must advise you this room is probably 'bugged,' that the mirror on the wall is a two-way mirror, and therefore, from this moment on you communicate with no one, absolutely no one, except me." This "aggressive, bantamcock attitude" Shaw found "strengthening." Panzeca, whose size and manner call to mind actor Danny DeVito, recently recalled that tense situation. Since he was certain the room was bugged, the two at first communicated by writing notes. Finally, Panzeca asked Sciambra for an office to use, but Sciambra claimed they were all occupied. So Panzeca told Sciambra that he was going to talk to his client in the men's room.[5]

Panzeca led Shaw into a tiny bathroom off the hallway leading into the district attorney's office. Even there, Panzeca didn't feel safe. It, too, might be bugged. As a precaution, they would forgo English. He asked Shaw if he spoke Spanish. Shaw said he did and made some additional comment in Spanish. Something about his inflection or the use of his hands triggered an intuitive insight on Panzeca's part. "Esta maricón?" ("Are you queer?") he asked. "Si," Shaw replied. Until that moment, Panzeca had been unaware of Shaw's sexual orientation. For the defense, this was the first note sounded of that sexual theme that would run throughout the prosecution of this case.[6]

Panzeca spoke to Shaw at length and was "totally convinced" he was innocent. The question was, what to do about the truth-serum test. Shaw had no objection to the test per se, but he was afraid that personal questions might be asked that would expose his private life. Panzeca eventually worked out a counterproposal. Then he asked to speak to Jim Garrison. Ushered into Garrison's office, Panzeca found himself in the midst of an ongoing meeting. Confronting him was a phalanx of assistants and investigators (among them Warren Report critic Mark Lane). Panzeca recounted his conversation with Garrison: "'Well, Sal,' Garrison said, and he starts giving me [a] litany about how important all this was. Then he said, 'Will Clay Shaw take a truth-serum test?' And I thought about it and I said, 'No, I don't think that is something I could recommend to my client.'" Then Panzeca made his counteroffer. "'Maybe I could talk to Ed Wegmann tomorrow and have Clay Shaw take a polygraph,' I said. But there were certain conditions. One would be that Shaw have a night's rest to get over all this trauma. Two, that we wanted to see the questions before they were asked, even though we wouldn't review them with our client. And I said it was all predicated upon the approval of Mr. Ed Wegmann, Shaw's lawyer." Garrison exploded. "'That's bull shit,' he said, 'We're not going to do that. I'll charge him.' I said, 'With what?' And he said, 'Conspiracy to kill Kennedy.' Well, I almost fell off the chair. I asked Garrison what the bond would be and he said, 'Oh, it'll be hundreds of thousands of dollars.' I said, 'Is that it?' He said, 'Yes, we're going to charge him.'"[7]

Feeling as though he had been "hit by a two-by-four," Panzeca left to inform his client. Jim Garrison was known to be impulsive but neither Panzeca nor Shaw had expected such an outcome. Shaw, especially, felt "that surely this was all some mistake which could still be cleared up." Panzeca went into the anteroom and told Shaw he was going to be arrested. "I don't think he responded except to listen to me," Panzeca said. "The man was totally obedient." Shaw and Panzeca now assumed the arrest was inevitable. But two key members of Garrison's staff made an effort to prevent it. Asst. D.A. James Alcock and private investigator William Gurvich had been out of town and returned in the midst of this. Surprised to find Shaw there, they were dismayed to learn his arrest was "imminent." They decided to object "vehemently" and requested a meeting with Garrison. The three convened in the office of First Assistant District Attorney Charles Ward. Garrison told them about a new witness who incriminated Shaw. Garrison was persuasive. Gurvich and Alcock backed down. The arrest would proceed.[8]

Panzeca called Criminal District Judge Thomas Brahney, who knew

Shaw, to arrange for bail. Judge Brahney was aware of what was happening—he was watching it on television. Garrison requested $25,000 but Brahney later reduced it to $10,000.[9]* William Wegmann arrived with a bail bondsman around 5:00 P.M. Some thirty minutes later, Louis Ivon entered the room where Shaw was waiting and formally placed him under arrest "for conspiracy to murder the president, John F. Kennedy." Shaw listened in "a state bordering on shock," and later referred to those words as "unbelievable and outrageous." A short time later, one of Garrison's investigators announced Shaw's arrest to the 200 or so media representatives waiting outside Garrison's office. Garrison himself soon emerged and told reporters he had "no doubts about the case."[10]

Unaware of the momentous events taking place at the Criminal District Court building, Edward Wegmann had returned home from his business trip to Atlanta. His daughter, herself an attorney today, described how her father learned about his client's dilemma. The telephone rang just as he entered the front door. "He was still wearing his hat and coat when he answered it," Cynthia Wegmann said. The caller was a friend of Shaw who told Wegmann that Shaw was being charged with conspiracy to murder the president. "I'm in no mood for jokes," Wegmann said, and hung up the phone. It rang again immediately. This time Shaw's friend convinced Wegmann he wasn't joking. Wegmann left at once for the district attorney's office.[11]

Shaw later wrote "how happy" he was to see Wegmann "and the flame of indignation surrounding him as he came into the office." "What the hell is this all about?" Wegmann asked. "Your guess is as good as mine," Shaw replied. It was now about 7:00 P.M. A long conference followed. Their immediate concern was the search warrant on Shaw's home, which they had learned about only a short time before.† Edward Wegmann decided to stay with Shaw. Panzeca and William Wegmann (who had left and was summoned from a social event) headed for Shaw's house to handle the search. When they arrived on

---

* A reporter on the scene that day recently remarked that a mere $10,000 bail for plotting to assassinate the president caused considerable comment among his colleagues in the media and injected a note of unreality into the proceedings.
† The application for that warrant contained information that Garrison's statement to the press did not contain. It identified the other alleged conspirators: David Ferrie and Lee Harvey Oswald.

the scene, the process was already underway. About a dozen of Garrison's men had descended on Shaw's red-door carriage house at 1313 Dauphine and were photographing and boxing up material. An irate William Wegmann, doing what he could to protect Shaw's rights, demanded that Shaw's private papers be inventoried before they were removed. One of Garrison's assistants threatened to arrest him. Garrison's men would leave that night with five cardboard boxes filled with Shaw's possessions.[12]

Meanwhile, Garrison's aides prepared to transfer Shaw to the police department's Central Lockup for booking. Louis Ivon insisted on hand-cuffing Shaw. Edward Wegmann objected, angrily and loudly. "He isn't going anywhere," Wegmann said. Ivon clamped on the handcuffs. Shaw was then transferred. That scene was captured on television. Shaw later recalled being "led forward into the dazzling glare of the TV cameras and the stacatto flash of flashbulbs." He was guided down a corridor full of jostling reporters and camera crews. Wegmann, trying to shield the handcuffs from view, told Shaw to stay behind him, but Shaw found it impossible to do so. Dressed in a conservative brown suit with a green and light-orange striped tie, Shaw remained silent and stoic as he walked "what seemed an interminable distance" to the elevator. It deposited him and his contingent of "guards" on the ground floor at approximately 8:30. From there, sitting between Edward Wegmann and investigator Lynn Loisel in the back seat of a car, he rode the short distance to the recently opened Central Lockup. To Shaw "it looked very clean and efficient, all gleaming white and yellow tile." He emptied his pockets, removed his tie and belt, and was booked for conspiring to murder John F. Kennedy.* Then he was fingerprinted and photographed. Released on bail, he left with Wegmann at 9:20 that night.[13]†

Clay Shaw was a commanding figure. His curly white hair was clipped short, his face was square, features strong, and his eyes a remarkable shade of blue. Like Garrison, he was huge, six feet four

---

* Louis Ivon, Lynn Loisel, Al Oser, John Volz, and James Alcock were listed on the Register as the arresting officers.
† They went to Wegmann's office, where Shaw revealed to Wegmann (a deeply religious, conservative man) the facts about his personal life. "None of these problems," Shaw later wrote, "made any difference in Eddie's attitude" (Shaw Journal, p. 19).

inches, 225 pounds, with broad shoulders and a deep chest. That morning his physical stature was more than matched by his stature in the community, which he had served for almost two decades. He entered Garrison's office at noon a respected civic leader. He left some nine hours later accused of the American equivalent of regicide.

In the high emotion of that time, many people were convinced of his guilt by the charge alone. After all, no district attorney would bring such a charge unless he had substantial evidence to back it up. Only a few of those closest to Garrison knew the truth, that Shaw was arrested on the basis of statements made by a single witness while he was in a drugged and semi-conscious condition.

That witness and his statements were the end point of certain unlikely events set in motion at the time of President Kennedy's death. But Shaw's arrest was primarily the consequence of the strange and complex character of the man who ordered it, New Orleans District Attorney Jim Garrison.

CHAPTER TWO

THE JOLLY GREEN GIANT

> My office may not be a popular
> office in the next four years. But
> it will be honest and efficient.
> No favors will be granted. A little
> old lady with a problem will
> receive as much attention as the
> mayor of the city.
>
> —Jim Garrison (after being elected district
> attorney of New Orleans in 1962)

Jim Garrison gave no sign in his early years that he would later emerge the central figure in an international controversy of historical importance involving the political crime of the century. Born Earling Carothers Garrison on November 20, 1921, in Denison City, Iowa, he was the first child and only son of Jane Ann Robinson and Earling R. Garrison. His parents divorced when Garrison was two and he and his younger sister, Judith, were raised by their mother, a former school teacher, and a woman of large physique, a Robinson-family trait (her father and two uncles were seven feet tall), and reportedly of a domineering nature. His maternal grandfather, Garrison wrote in his memoir, was successful in coal and real estate and one of the leading citizens of Knoxville, Iowa, where his mother was born.

The great mystery about Garrison's life has been his father.* When Garrison was thirty, according to his military medical records, he had seen his father only once. Even his name was unknown until the release recently of Garrison's FBI file. Prior to that the only public reference to

---

* A father-son snapshot, recently discovered in one of Garrison's old office files, shows a well-dressed and handsome young man supporting a sturdy-looking infant standing on a porch railing.

him was a single sentence Garrison wrote in his memoir that described him as "an attorney."[1] He was also a convicted felon.

Earling R. Garrison, alias Waldo Morrison, born June 2, 1898, in Denison City, Iowa, was arrested seven times. He was first picked up on May 16, 1928, in Des Moines for mail fraud,* and served two years in the federal penitentiary at Leavenworth, Kansas. On April 26, 1930, he was convicted of larceny† and received a five-year sentence in the penitentiary at Anamosa. How much time he actually served is unclear, but only three years later he was arrested again in Des Moines for "uttering [a] forged instrument," disposition unknown. After that he was arrested at various times for drunkenness, and for selling liquor to Indians in the southwest. On April 8, 1943, he applied for a "storekeeper" job in Fort Huachuca, Arizona. What became of him afterwards is not known.[2] How all this affected his son is unclear.

The year after his father was sent away for larceny, Garrison's mother moved her family to New Orleans. Garrison was ten. He attended several different elementary schools and graduated from Fortier High. He joined the U.S. Army on January 12, 1941, almost a full year before Pearl Harbor thrust the country into World War II. Garrison first served in an artillery company, along with another young man from New Orleans named Pershing Gervais, and the two formed a close relationship that would endure for more than two decades.

They were separated on June 23, 1942, when Garrison was appointed a First Lieutenant and began to pilot observation aircraft, but Garrison stayed in touch by writing Gervais long letters, some of which have survived.[3] Garrison liked the military. "It became a surrogate family for me," he later wrote, and he recalled his wartime experiences with nostalgia. In addition to flying thirty-five combat missions and receiving the European Theater Campaign Medal with two battle stars, he attended American University in England for eight weeks where he studied the history of philosophy, business law and play writing prior to his discharge on March 1, 1946. Less than four months later he tried

---

* He was sending fountain pens to dead people C.O.D.; relatives, believing they had been ordered, paid the charges.
† He stole a cashier's check in the amount of $1198, and bought a car, a typewriter, and clothes.

to reenlist but his "efficiency index" was too low and the Army declined his request. Garrison apparently was trying to rejoin the military about the time of his mother's marriage to Lyon Gardiner, later described in an FBI report as being "from probably the wealthiest family" in Laurel, Mississippi.[4] Rebuffed by the Army, Garrison returned to school, studying law at Tulane University. In 1949, because of his veteran status, he was automatically admitted to the Bar without taking the examination. The following year at the age of thirty, Garrison, who had been a student and a soldier but had never held a job, applied to the FBI.

In filling out the employment application, Garrison omitted his father's criminal history and took the added precaution of listing him as "deceased." Believing he was dead, the FBI failed to run the usual background checks on the name and didn't learn the truth about him for many years.[5] Garrison also kept the FBI in the dark about his psychiatrically troubled sibling, Judith, who had been placed in a Mississippi state mental hospital suffering from schizophrenia.[6] On his FBI application he indicated that no family member had been treated for mental illness or confined to a mental institution. After brothers and sisters, Garrison wrote "none." He had now erased two family members.

In his interviews he made a strong impression. He was "of large, athletic physique," one interviewer wrote. He dressed well and spoke well, they noted, possessed the right credentials, and could write a proper report. He inspired high hopes. They recommended him. The following year he was accepted by the FBI.

After eight weeks of training, Garrison traveled west to a field office assignment in Seattle, Washington. But after less than four months, he abruptly resigned, supposedly because his Army reserve unit had been called to active duty in Korea.* Over the next few months, Garrison behaved in a strangely erratic manner. On July 24, 1951, after completing his first day's routine back in the Army, he realized he "just couldn't make it." He reported to sick call. Twenty-four days later he wrote Hoover, asking to be reinstated with the FBI. Hoover said no. Garrison was transferred to Brooke Army hospital in September and treated for exhaustion.

---

* A former FBI deputy director under J. Edgar Hoover recently told this writer that "there are other facts to be known" regarding Garrison's sudden departure from the FBI.

No organic cause was found for his complaints. He was diagnosed as suffering from chronic anxiety with hypochondriasis, functional bowel symptoms and psychogenic allergic manifestations, in addition to exhaustion syndrome. A "marked mother dependency" was diagnosed as well and under "past history" it was noted that "there has always been a close relationship between the patient and his mother. She was oversolicitous and made every effort to monopolize his affections." The report further stated that Garrison had "a severe and disabling psychoneurosis of long duration" that had "interfered with his social and professional adjustment." Garrison's "illness," the report concluded, "existed long before his call to active duty" and was "of the type that will require long-term psychotherapeutic approach."[7] On the basis of those findings, Garrison was discharged October 31, 1951, for "physical disability."

Back in New Orleans, Garrison joined the district attorney's office.[*] In 1957 he was a losing sacrificial candidate for the office of Assessor. In 1958, when the incumbent D.A. was defeated, Garrison lost his job and was forced to turn to private practice. He was not a success on his own and the years that followed were difficult. Yet, by one account, he maintained his sense of humor, joked about his financial troubles and kept up appearances. In 1959, as a reward for past political assistance, Garrison was appointed assistant city attorney, a part-time job with a minimal salary. In 1960 he mounted a campaign for criminal district judge and suffered his second defeat at the polls. Along the way, he married a lovely blonde from New Orleans, Leah Elizabeth Ziegler, and eventually would father five handsome children.

Garrison first emerged from obscurity on Sunday night, January 14, 1962, during the Democratic primary for district attorney when he and the other candidates took part in a round-table discussion carried live on all four of the city's local television stations. The main topic was the "part-time" incumbent district attorney, Richard Dowling, the entrenched Democratic machine politician who had declined to appear on the show. Like many D.A.'s back then, Dowling maintained a civil practice on the side to supplement his modest salary. Most of the guests on the program criticized that custom in general and Dowling in particular, and pledged

---

[*] Sometime prior to this, he legally changed his name to "Jim Garrison."

to work full time in their public post if elected. The lone exception was F. Irvin Dymond, who five years later would help defend Clay Shaw. Once a merchant seaman, Dymond had attended college on a boxing scholarship and fought in World War II, receiving five medals, including the Purple Heart.* One of the most respected criminal lawyers in the state, he was considered Dowling's major opponent. Of the five, only Dymond had a flourishing practice and would have been relinquishing something of value, but the viewers didn't know that. He made it clear he wouldn't consider living on the salary the office paid. "If the voters are looking for a sixteen-thousand-five-hundred-dollar-a-year district attorney," he said, "I'm not their boy." Watching the program from his living room was William Wegmann, a friend of Dymond and another attorney who would later assist in Shaw's defense. "There goes the election," said Wegmann.[8]

Candidate Garrison, with nothing to lose, took the politically wiser position. The people, he said, "expect a full-time district attorney, and I believe they deserve one." He was relaxed and articulate, exhibiting what one local writer called a "beautifully modulated self-assured voice."[9] That television appearance transformed Garrison's life and rearranged the political landscape of New Orleans for years to come. It was the first step on the road to political power that would culminate in Garrison's eccentric investigation of the president's assassination five years later. Garrison's darkly handsome presence and easy way with words were perfectly suited for television. A mysterious bonding occurred that evening and a political star was born. "New Orleans fell in love with him," one reporter later wrote. "He looked like Perry Mason and sounded like Eliot Ness."[10]

Garrison, an enthusiast of Ayn Rand, the novelist who glorified individual initiative unhampered by government authority, had entered the race running as an independent. He had practically no money and no political backing. But he was supported by the city's two newspapers, the *New Orleans States-Item* and the *Times-Picayune*,[11] both owned by the same organization, and his television appearance had made him the talk of the town. He launched his campaign with preemptive strikes at the

---

* A Division Gunnery Officer on the *Bismarck Sea*, the last carrier sunk in the war (off the coast of Iwo Jima), Dymond was knocked unconscious when the first of two Japanese Kamikazes crashed into the deck. Thrown over the side by a friend, he survived four hours in the water and was wounded by a strafer.

opposition, what is today called negative campaigning, and he made ample use of the most powerful tool of modern communication. Television was his medium and he understood what it could do for him. He bypassed the old-fashioned rallies, still the mainstay of politics in those days, and carried his message directly to the voters. In the primary held on January 27, Garrison garnered enough votes to force a runoff with Dowling.

Before the second primary, the two debated on television. Garrison did poorly, unable to handle "hard facts" well or the one-on-one exchange. When it was over, he reportedly "looked as though he had been hit with a wet mop."[12] This single setback had no impact on the campaign but Garrison had learned a lesson—he never again engaged in such a confrontation.

Garrison's oversize stature—six feet seven inches, 240 pounds—and glad hand soon earned him the nickname the Jolly Green Giant. He took the primary in April and went on to defeat the Republican candidate by almost 73,000 votes.[13] With no obligation to anyone, he had won a mandate from the citizens of New Orleans. Unencumbered by political ties, he had a free hand to pick his people and run his office as he saw fit. As his chief investigator, Garrison named his old army buddy and former policeman Pershing Gervais, described by one fan as an "investigative genius" with "a scarifying face, enormous physical strength" and unsettling candor. Gervais had been fired from the police department in the late fifties for alleged "infractions" and before joining Garrison's staff had managed a bar "that had the reputation of being a gathering place for homosexuals."[14] His appointment angered some, particularly in the police department, and would lead to future difficulties.

As district attorney, Garrison's new headquarters was a sprawling suite of interconnected rooms on the second floor of the massive, gray stone Criminal District Court building. This grim fortresslike structure stretches from one block to the next and everyone in New Orleans calls it by the two streets that intersect at its location: Tulane and Broad. Garrison's private office, with wood-paneled walls and deep blue carpet, was handsomely appointed, unusually large and remotely situated. Its most unique feature was an elevator concealed inside a closet, enabling the D.A. to come and go in secret. Garrison, who was in the habit of arriving late for work and leaving early, had developed the reputation of being lazy, and many now feared that he would be a do-nothing D.A.

Early in his first term though, Garrison grabbed the city's attention and its headlines and never let go of either, as he publicly attacked virtually everyone in sight: the police department, the mayor, the state legislature and bail bondsmen. Described by one close friend as "exhilarated by conflict,"[15] he also developed a slash-and-burn, take-no-prisoners approach to his opponents that continued throughout his tenure as D.A. His counterattacking technique was brute-force simple. He crushed anyone who resisted him. Nor was he shy about using the power of his office. When Pershing Gervais came under investigation during a police probe of gambling payoffs, Garrison ordered nine policemen arrested and charged with brutality.[16] The charges were quickly dropped and, eventually, so was the police investigation of Gervais.*

Soon after taking office, Garrison targeted French Quarter homosexuals, arresting "gay kids on the streets" and raiding "gay bars." After one such sweep, a curious reporter discovered that the formal charge lodged against them was "being a homosexual in an establishment with a liquor license." In time Garrison's drive against the gay community died down.

Another of Garrison's early targets was Bourbon Street, the French Quarter's "sin strip," which has been described as "one peel parlor after another." Garrison instigated a series of padlocking raids against establishments where prostitution, gambling and B-drinking (hiring women on a commission to solicit drinks from customers) were rampant. Garrison kicked up a ruckus with this assault on Bourbon Street, a major tourist attraction. New Orleans relies heavily on the tourist trade, and many felt Garrison was hurting business and giving the entire Quarter a bad name.

In a region with a high tolerance for outlandish, even felonious behavior by public officials, an attitude best described by the resident who said "somehow our outrage gland got stunted," what happened next was extraordinary even by New Orleans standards. In an effort to curtail Garrison's attack on Bourbon Street, the city's eight criminal court judges eliminated the source of the funds he was using to finance his undercover activities. Garrison retaliated by claiming that justice was being

* But Gervais resigned his post prior to Garrison's next election.

impeded by the number of holidays the judges were taking. He also suggested they might have been affected by "racketeer influences." The judges charged Garrison with criminal defamation of character. Garrison, exercising his power as district attorney, dismissed the charges against himself. State Attorney General Jack Gremillion reinstituted them. Then he traveled to New Orleans and personally tried the case and won a conviction. Garrison (fined $1,000 or four months in jail) appealed, and his conviction was overturned in a landmark decision by the U.S. Supreme Court that upheld the right to criticize "public figures."

Garrison had won a major victory that greatly enhanced his political leverage. He also managed to replace two of the judges who had opposed him with two candidates he supported, and after that "the rest of the bench [fell] into line."[17] The importance of this triumph in future events cannot be overemphasized. Garrison had flexed his muscles against the judiciary and won in the most chilling way possible. The rest of the judges in New Orleans and the other officeholders beholden to the election process for their bread and butter understood the message: *opposing Garrison meant risking their jobs.* Adding to Garrison's prestige was the record of his office. His assistants had not lost a single murder case. These successes and his popularity made Garrison seem invincible and he may have felt that he was. Even the governor would one day remark on the folly of challenging him. One of Garrison's opponents ordered a survey seeking his political weak spot and discovered Garrison had none; he was strong across the board.[18] No one seemed to mind that his initial charges against the judges were never proved. Or that the crackdown on Bourbon Street put a few B-girls out of work but was of no lasting value.

Garrison, who studied, admired, and emulated Huey P. Long, Louisiana's late demagogic governor and U.S. senator, seemed made to order for the Mardi Gras spirit of New Orleans. Whether he was issuing his dictums from his second-floor suite at Tulane and Broad or enjoying nightlife at the Playboy Club, he kept most of the citizenry startled, entertained, and satisfied. In the next governor's contest, he went against the local tide, campaigning for John J. McKeithen over Ambassador de Lesseps Morrison. McKeithen's victory gave Garrison a powerful connection in Baton Rouge and made him a major state political force.

But Garrison didn't rely solely on the free flow of news to convey his image as "an incorruptible crusader for justice." He cultivated newsmen. A former assistant district attorney remarked recently that Garrison always had some reporter under his sway, that Garrison was good at that. A local journalist admitted that some of the reporters were much too close to Garrison and mentioned David Chandler, who was one of Garrison's best friends for awhile.[19] Recently described by a colleague as "lively and nice looking, about five-nine, with a full head of brown hair, a round face and a pleasant aspect about him that women liked," Chandler would be the first to openly break with Garrison later. But at first this twenty-seven-year-old Pulitzer Prize–winning newsman was a strong Garrison advocate and Garrison was best man at his wedding. Chandler was so taken with the Garrison charisma and his slugfest with the judges that he suggested an article about the battling D.A. to *The Saturday Evening Post.* The editor liked the idea and sent one of his staff writers to New Orleans.

James Phelan spent ten days there, much of it in Garrison's company, and concluded that Garrison *was quite a guy.* "The Vice Man Cometh" was published in June 1963, and Garrison couldn't have asked for anything better.[20] Phelan penned a valentine of sorts. He tagged Garrison "Sir Galahad" and depicted him as a reformer and a frustrated writer, with a knack for colorful speech and literary allusions. "Not since Hamlet tried to decide whether or not to stab the king of Denmark," Garrison said about the mayor's waffling on an issue, "has there been so agonizing a political decision." Phelan was the first to quote Garrison referring to Lewis Carroll's famous classic (a favorite later in his celebrity period). "When I was elected I fell down the rabbit hole and landed smack in the middle of Wonderland," Garrison said. "Nothing I've seen since has surprised me." As for the skepticism about his reform effort, Garrison insisted that he was "going to end the rackets here and the only way anyone can stop me is to kill me." His motive was simple, Garrison claimed. "I just want to run the best D.A.'s office New Orleans ever had."

Phelan captured Garrison's appeal—his eloquence, his belief in the individual, his maverick streak, magnetism, and his political promise. But Phelan also sensed Garrison's other side, his tendency toward excess and his enigmatic core. "Garrison himself remains something of a puzzle," Phelan wrote. The existence of that *puzzle* would become more apparent in the years to come and Phelan would be one of those pondering it up close. The suggestion was barely noticeable though in this light-hearted tribute, which was Garrison's first significant national publicity and started a trend. Soon readers of *Pageant, Time, Newsweek*, and the *New York Times* were seeing items about the battling New Orleans D.A.

Later on, a New Orleans writer, attorney Milton Brener, who had worked for Garrison in the D.A.'s office, observed that there was "a quality about Garrison incapable of definition that renders an abiding dislike of the man virtually impossible upon personal contact." Brener said the quality was something close to "charm," though that word didn't quite convey it. Brener called Garrison's sense of humor "delicious" and said it permeated all of Garrison's conversations, both private and public; Garrison's general attitude Brener described as "casual and unhurried." But Brener also noted that Garrison tended "to make snap judgments on insufficient facts" and to "oversimplify." His ego was "abundant" and "in his humor there could at times be detected traces of cruelty." Yet overall, these flaws seemed relatively minor.[21]

Brener, Phelan, Chandler, and earlier the FBI interviewers found in Garrison the same attractive qualities that would soon draw to him an extraordinary array of supporters once he became involved in the Kennedy assassination.

That began on November 22, 1963.

About 12:30 that day, Garrison was sitting at his desk when First Asst. D.A. Frank Klein ran into the office. "The president has been shot!" Klein shouted. Stunned, like the rest of the world, the two men left the building and headed for Tortorich's, a restaurant in the French Quarter with a television set in the dining room. On the way there they listened to the bulletins on the car radio.

The radio is how most Americans first learned about the shooting. *We interrupt this program for a report from Dallas, Texas: Just minutes ago something happened in the presidential motorcade in downtown Dallas ... shots were fired ... it's believed that President Kennedy was hit.*

For the next hour, the country held its breath, hoping. Even when the news came that he was wounded in the head, the country continued to hope, while fearing the worst. That hour served as a sort of psychological buffer, blunting the shock when the announcement finally came. *Ladies and Gentlemen, the president of the United States is dead.*

The assassination occurred on a Friday and the funeral took place the following Monday, a time span of four days, an overlong long weekend. Ordinary activity ceased. Life didn't merely revolve around the television set; life it seemed *was* the television set. In the days and nights that followed, millions of tearful Americans sat in their living rooms fixated on the screen even after they had seen it all over and over and over again.

But not everyone became permanently attached to their sofas that weekend, overwhelmed by it all, anguished and passive. A few reached out and thrust themselves into the flow of events. Jack S. Martin and Dean Adams Andrews, Jr., a couple of oddities in New Orleans, were two such volunteers. They could be called the First Fathers of Jim Garrison's case. Martin and Andrews heard the news everyone else heard that Friday. They watched the television programs everyone else watched, but separately and independently of each other they saw something others did not. They saw *opportunity*.

Their individual efforts to make the most of that opportunity over the next few days would become permanently embedded in the record of the Kennedy case. Among the many would-be witnesses whose names appear in the Garrison files, none was more responsible for what ensued than Martin and Andrews. What they did that weekend laid the groundwork for Garrison's later investigation and all that followed.

Yet, surprisingly, the complete story of what actually occurred with Martin and Andrews over that long November weekend in 1963 has never before been told.

CHAPTER THREE

FIRST FATHERS:
THE TIPSTER AND THE LAWYER

I ruin everything I get my hands
on.[1]
—Jack Martin, 1956

Once you make a fool out of
yourself, that is it, you are stuck
with it.[2]
—Dean Andrews, 1969

Two days after the president was shot, First Asst. D.A. Klein telephoned
Jim Garrison at home concerning a tip the office had just received about
a possible New Orleans link to the assassination. What Klein didn't know
was that the tipster, forty-eight-year-old Jack Martin, a thinnish, sometimes private investigator "with the red blotchy face of an alcoholic," had
been on a two-day binge. It had started the evening of the assassination.

That night Martin boozed it up in a neighborhood bar called Katz &
Jammer. He was with Guy Banister, whom Martin had worked for "from
time to time." Banister, a twenty-year veteran of the FBI, former assistant
superintendent of the New Orleans Police Department and dedicated anti-
communist, anti-Castro activist, was the owner-operator of Guy Banister
Associates, an extremely modest New Orleans investigative firm.[3] He and
Martin left Katz & Jammer together and went to Banister's nearby office.

There they began discussing various "personal and political subjects," which led to the topic of some "unauthorized" long-distance
telephone calls that Banister accused Martin of making. Martin denied
it. The conversation "became heated," with Banister warning Martin
not to call him "a liar" and Martin claiming he wasn't. At that point
Banister "became enraged" and struck Martin on the head "five or six

times" with the barrel of a .357 Magnum. When he began to bleed, Banister stopped.* Martin washed up in the rest room and left.[4]

Twice that night he received treatment for his injuries, "three small lacerations on the forehead" and "one on the rear of his head," first at Charity Hospital, where he took himself, and later at the Baptist hospital, where a police lieutenant drove him after he reported the attack. Twice Martin refused to file charges, both times saying that Banister was "like a father" to him (which may explain Martin's troubled psyche) and remarking that the attack "was nothing to get irritated about." But he claimed he couldn't understand why Banister had walloped him with the gun. Banister explained it later to the owner of his office building. He "had warned Martin to stay out," Banister said, "and he didn't."[5]

Martin had had a busy day—a presidential assassination, drinks at Katz & Jammer, a pistol-whipping, high-level police attention, and trips to two different hospitals. For most that would have been ample excitement for one weekend. But for Martin the events of that Friday were only the beginning.

The following day, he and a close friend, W. Hardy Davis, a New Orleans bail bondsman, like everyone else were discussing the president's assassination. But their conversation was unique. It focused on a local man, a former Eastern Airlines pilot with a hairless body (due to the disease alopecia) and a checkered past. His name was David Ferrie, and Martin harbored a simmering hostility toward him. He and Davis both agreed that Ferrie was a "gun fancier." Martin thought the rifle allegedly used to kill President Kennedy was "similar" to one Ferrie owned "several years ago." And, Martin recalled, Ferrie once mentioned a short story plot about a presidential assassination. With nothing more than that, the two "speculated on the possibility" that Ferrie "might have had something to do with killing President Kennedy."[6] This flimsy gossip would propel David Ferrie into a principal figure in this case; he would become Jim Garrison's favorite suspect and a stepping stone to Clay Shaw.

That evening, after Hardy Davis left, Martin watched a television program about the life of accused assassin Lee Harvey Oswald. One of Oswald's classmates told an interviewer that while they attended

---

* This incident, vastly reshaped, will later be retold by Garrison in his book and prominently featured in Stone's film.

Beauregard Junior High School he had persuaded Oswald to join the Civil Air Patrol (CAP).* When Martin heard that, he completely "flipped," as he later put it. For he knew that David Ferrie had once been active in the CAP. Here was a connection—as Martin saw it—between the man he and Davis had been speculating about and the accused assassin of the president.

Martin spent the rest of that long weekend drinking and making one telephone call after another, spreading the word about Ferrie's involvement in the assassination. Many in New Orleans heard from Martin in the next two days; and many others heard his escalating accusations from the grapevine. Ferrie had taught Oswald "to fire foreign weapons." He "had flown Oswald to Dallas." He was "communicating with Oswald" and had been with Oswald in Dallas "within the last ten days." Ferrie had said "Kennedy should be killed." He had "outlined plans" to accomplish it, and he had given Oswald a posthypnotic suggestion to do the deed. Martin also claimed that when Oswald was arrested, he had in his possession Ferrie's library card.† And he told virtually everyone he spoke to that Ferrie was homosexual. Except for the latter, all of Martin's information was fabricated.[7]

Two of Martin's first targets were the New Orleans Police Department and television station WWL-TV.[8] As Martin's stories about Ferrie ricocheted like a hockey puck around the New Orleans telephone system, several of those he spoke to reacted by calling the local office of the Secret Service.‡ One misdirected telephone call Martin made resulted in three separate individuals contacting that agency. Special Agent-in-Charge John Rice responded by driving to Ferrie's home that same evening, hoping to interview him. He crossed paths there with a representative of television station WDSU, who had learned of Martin's charges secondhand. Jack Martin's humming telephone line turned David Ferrie's doorstep at 3330 Louisiana Avenue Parkway into the busiest spot in New Orleans. But Martin wasn't satisfied. His main objective, the police department, refused to take him seriously.

* The classmate later told the FBI that Oswald attended only two or three meetings, "four at the most" (Edward Voebel, FBI interview, Nov. 25, 1963).
† This story has had a long life (see chapter 13).
‡ This prompted Secret Service inquiries about David Ferrie that weekend, which have prompted some students of this case to conclude that the government possessed legitimate information of his involvement in the crime.

So he telephoned one of Jim Garrison's assistant district attorneys. Martin didn't go directly to the top because Garrison, like the police, was acquainted with him.[9] Instead, he called Herman Kohlman, a cunning choice, for Kohlman had once worked as a newspaper reporter and written some articles about Ferrie; so Kohlman knew more about Ferrie than most, and less about Martin than some. Kohlman passed on Martin's information to First Asst. D.A. Klein, who called Jim Garrison.[10] This was when Garrison first heard of David Ferrie's alleged connection to the assassination. Garrison ordered the police to join the hunt. Martin finally had accomplished his goal. Ten officers were soon "scouring" the streets for David Ferrie.[11] He was the most wanted man in New Orleans. The media, the FBI, the Secret Service, the district attorney's office, and the police were all beating the bushes, looking for him.

Unaware of his notoriety, Ferrie was on a vacation with two friends. They had gone to Texas, but to Houston not Dallas, and then on to Galveston, traveling by car. And the timing of their trip had nothing to do with the assassination in Dallas. Ferrie had been assisting Attorney G. Wray Gill in his defense of New Orleans mafia boss Carlos Marcello on immigration charges. On the day the president was shot, the jury returned a verdict in favor of Marcello, which meant Ferrie (who was sitting in the New Orleans federal courtroom at the time)[12] was free for awhile. His work on the case had been intensive and he had planned that as soon as it concluded "he would take a trip for the purpose of relaxing" with his friends. Their original plan was to go ice skating in Baton Rouge, but when they learned the rink there was closed they switched to Houston.[13] This remarkably mundane journey will later assume near-mythic dimensions.

The trip began with a telephone call about six hours after the assassination. Ferrie spoke to the manager of Houston's Winterland Skating Rink and obtained its schedule. Then he, Alvin Beaubouef and Melvin Coffey set out in Ferrie's blue '61 Comet station wagon. They arrived in Houston Saturday around 4:30 A.M. This was sixteen hours after Kennedy had been shot. They slept a few hours at the Alamotel, shopped at Sears for warm clothes, then showed up that afternoon at the skating rink. Ferrie skated for a while, "looking the situation over." But he wasn't enthusiastic and went onto the ice only briefly to show Beaubouef "he could do it." Ferrie was considering the "possibility of opening a rink in New Orleans," and discussed "the cost of installation and operation" with the manager. The trio stayed about two hours. Back at their motel, Ferrie tried twice to reach attorney Gill to find out if he was needed for a trial scheduled to begin the following Monday. Ferrie failed to reach him.[14]

That night, after a stop at the Manned Space Craft Center, the three drove to Galveston. This was the same evening Jack Martin launched his telephoning enterprise. By the time Ferrie and his friends arrived at their motel, Martin had already placed the first of his calls. Ferrie fell asleep that night unaware that television newsmen and an agent of the Secret Service were hammering on his apartment door in New Orleans.

Intending to visit relatives of Beaubouef, they drove north the next day. Ferrie again tried unsuccessfully to reach Gill. Then he telephoned his own apartment and temporary house guest Layton Martens answered.* It was from Martens that Ferrie first learned he was being accused "of being implicated in the assassination of President Kennedy." "Very much disturbed," Ferrie turned his station wagon south and headed home. He had learned what was being said about him, but he didn't know the source of the accusations, nor the extent of them. At another telephone at another service station along the way, he at last managed to reach attorney Gill and discovered the initiator was Jack Martin. It was early Sunday evening.[15]

When they arrived in New Orleans, Ferrie drove to the vicinity of his apartment and dropped Alvin Beaubouef off so he "could check to see if anyone was waiting"—to act, as Beaubouef described it, as "a decoy," though he wasn't expecting what occurred. Ferrie and Coffey then drove to a nearby grocery store. When they returned, they saw a "bunch" of cars and "a lot of people." Figuring it was the police, Ferrie telephoned his apartment. "Some dumb ox," he later said, answered and tried "to sucker" him into a conversation. Ferrie hung up.[16]

It *was* the police. Five of them had arrived after Beaubouef entered. They "burst through the door," Beaubouef said recently, with warrants, looking for Ferrie. Beaubouef told them he didn't know where Ferrie

---

* Martens, who was dealing with a difficult home situation, stayed at Ferrie's apartment only about two weeks until he rented a place of his own (Martens, interview with Jim Garrison's assistants, March 12, 1967).

was and they arrested him. They arrested Layton Martens as well and charged him with "vagrancy, under investigation of subversive activities." They also confiscated a batch of embarrassing photographs. (Three years later these pictures would reappear in one of the mini-dramas in Jim Garrison's investigation.)[17]

The police staked out the apartment and waited for Ferrie to show up. But after dropping Coffey off, he headed north again, at Gill's suggestion, and spent the night with a friend at Southeastern Louisiana College in Hammond. The following day, he returned to New Orleans and, accompanied by Gill, surrendered at the district attorney's office. Ferrie was questioned by a police officer and two of Garrison's aides. Then he was booked, oddly, with "vagrancy, pending investigation of being a fugitive from the State of Texas." How he could have been a fugitive from a state where no charge was filed against him is unclear.[18]

That evening Ferrie was interviewed by agents of the Secret Service and FBI. Ferrie acknowledged that he had criticized President Kennedy "both in public and in private" over his failure to provide "air cover" during the Bay of Pigs invasion and may have used the expression "he ought to be shot." But he said he had "never made any statement that President Kennedy should be killed with the intention that this be done" and had "never at any time outlined or formulated any plans or made any statement as to how this could be done or who should do it." To everyone who questioned him that day and into the evening, and on November 27, and still again on December 13, David Ferrie rejected all the charges Martin had made against him. Among others, Ferrie emphatically denied being in Dallas in the last eight to ten years, or knowing Lee Harvey Oswald in the CAP* or any capacity. He also denied ever loaning Oswald his library card. Or being implicated in the assassination of President

---

* Though Ferrie had no recollection of it, on at least one occasion, perhaps two, his path crossed with Oswald's. (See notes, pp. 44 and 61.) But he and Oswald were never concurrent members of the CAP. Oswald joined on July 27, 1955. That was six months after CAP officials denied Ferrie's membership renewal— a reaction to his political lectures to cadets. Nevertheless, for a period of time that year Ferrie continued "to work with the squadron" unbeknownst to CAP officials, who "found out" in "late" 1955 and put a stop to it. Ferrie was reinstated in 1958, and permanently terminated in 1960. For awhile afterwards he operated a "spurious" CAP squadron. (Joseph Ehrlicker, CAP Commander, Louisiana Wing, FBI interview, Nov. 26, 1963; John Ciravolo, telephone conversation with author, July 9, 1997.)

Kennedy in any manner. Ferrie said his four-passenger monoplane hadn't been airworthy since 1962 (which was later confirmed by the FBI) and that he hadn't flown it to Dallas since 1949.[19]

The FBI, as well as the New Orleans police, quickly verified Ferrie's movements that weekend. They checked registers, interviewed motel clerks and the manager of the skating rink,[20] and they obtained a record of the telephone numbers Ferrie called from Houston. At the request of Garrison's office, the Texas Rangers investigated Ferrie's trip as well and "were unable to implicate" him in the assassination. The Houston police also corroborated Ferrie's visit to their city and to Galveston the following day. The New Orleans police reported that they were "unable to uncover any evidence which would link Ferrie to the assassination." There was no reason to hold Ferrie and he and his friends were released.

The instigator of all this chaos, Jack Martin, recanted his tales about Ferrie to the FBI and two days later made an even more sweeping disavowal to the Secret Service. Martin, who the Secret Service agents noted in their report had "every appearance of being an alcoholic," admitted suffering from "telephonitis" when he drank. He said "that it was during one of his drinking sprees" that he telephoned the D.A.'s office and told his "fantastic story" about Ferrie being involved with Oswald. Yet even in this confession Martin didn't tell the truth. He reduced his manic exercise with the telephone to a single ill-advised call.[21] It is often reported that Ferrie was linked to the assassination that weekend by *various* reports, the sheer number lending credibility to the charges. What few seem to realize is that all of them originated from a single source, Jack Martin's red hot telephone line.

The missing element was his motivation.[22] That was rooted in something personal. The most likely possibility is that Martin's pistol whipping by Banister Friday night was unwittingly triggered by Ferrie. Ferrie told the FBI he had discovered that Martin, when "moving around" the United States, was making long-distance telephone calls and charging them to Gill's and Banister's offices. Ferrie probably passed that information to Banister, prompting the quarrel that escalated into the beating. So when Martin was sitting at home nursing his cranial "lacerations" and speculating about Ferrie's crimes, the crime

Martin had in mind wasn't the assassination in Dallas. It was closer to home, right there on his head in fact. And the word for what motivated Martin that weekend, as he strove to link David Ferrie to the president's murder, was *revenge*.[23]

Jack Martin—who always wore a black hat and a black trench coat, apparently to enhance his "private eye" image—was clearly a world-class troublemaker. Many in New Orleans recall his excessive drinking and "big talk." But few knew the truth about him. Martin was born in 1915 in Phoenix, Arizona. His real name was Edward Stewart Suggs. An FBI rap sheet on Suggs lists a string of arrests and charges dating from 1944, the most serious being a 1952 murder charge in Dallas, Texas, which somehow was cleared up the following year. The subject of Martin's psychological health is a recurring theme in his government records. "Several sources have reported Martin is a mental case," reads an Informative Note in his FBI file. He was confined to a mental hospital in 1956 and diagnosed as having a "sociopathic personality disturbance, antisocial type." Given Martin's prominent role in Jim Garrison's later investigation, whether or not he belonged in a rubber room is no minor issue.* Martin was not just ornery, irresponsible, and vengeful. He was exploitative, malicious and cunning, and he knew how to work the system.[24]

His relationship with David Ferrie had been a troubled one since they met in the fall of 1961. Ferrie had assisted Martin in an investigation of ecclesiastical certificate frauds in the so-called diploma mills. Ferrie claimed that Martin had defrauded him of one of his fees and that Martin, himself, "was dealing in phony certificates." Martin, Ferrie told the FBI, was an "unethical and dangerous person."[25]

The short-term upshot of all that tumult in 1963 was negligible. Ferrie was cleared and Martin humiliated. That should have been the end of it. Of course, it wasn't. For this episode was now lodged in Jim Garrison's memory bank.

◆　◆　◆

* Pershing Gervais said Martin was "absolutely crazy." On one occasion Gervais physically threw Martin out of his office and "hit him on the head" with his telephone. Guy Banister used his gun. Martin seemed to drive people to strike out at him with whatever happened to be handy.

Jack Martin drew Garrison into his conniving almost immediately. But Dean Andrews's scheming, which eventually would spark Garrison's interest in Clay Shaw, escaped Garrison's attention that weekend.

At the time of the assassination, the five-foot-seven-inch, 240-pound Andrews, a colorful small-time lawyer with a deep thirst for the limelight, was in a New Orleans hospital being treated for pneumonia. He had been there three days, would remain seven more, and was seriously ill. He was so feverish and heavily medicated that later he was unable to recall much of what had taken place that weekend. But his condition failed to dampen his passion for talking, which he did in an idiom all his own. Unfortunately, his room was equipped with a telephone and a television. The absence of either would have altered the history of this case. The television brought the assassination and related information into Andrews's realm of consciousness. The telephone enabled him to exploit it.

On Saturday Andrews had a visitor. R. M. Davis, U.S. Army Sgt. retired, worked as an investigator for Andrews in his New Orleans law practice, later described by the forty-three-year-old Davis as "a Damon Runyon-type operation" made up of "pimps, prostitutes, and two-bit hustlers." Andrews slept on and off, and the main topic of their discussion was the progress of his political campaign. Andrews, a part-time assistant district attorney in neighboring Jefferson Parish, was running for a judgeship there and the election was only two weeks away. The visit was quiet and uneventful and Davis left sometime between 3:30 and 4:00 P.M.[26]

Shortly after that the phone rang, waking Andrews from a sound sleep. The caller, another man with the surname "Davis," Eugene C. Davis, was the thirty-eight-year-old part-owner of a bar in the French Quarter. He and Andrews had known each other for some fifteen years, having met while Andrews was still a student. Davis had sent Andrews clients from the gay community, and Andrews had represented Davis in some minor legal matters. His call that Saturday dealt with the sale of an automobile.[27]

Before long the conversation turned to the tragedy being piped into Andrews's room on television. That's when Andrews indulged in the fantasy that would alter his life. He said to Gene Davis, "Man, I would be famous if I could go to Dallas and defend Lee Harvey Oswald; whoever gets that job is going to be a famous lawyer."[28] For Andrews that idea proved to be irresistible. He locked onto it like an iron filing onto a magnet. The world's spotlight was focused on Dallas, just 500 miles away, where that "gravy train" was waiting for some lucky lawyer to "hop aboard" and ride it to fame and fortune.

At this point, the notion of representing Oswald was only a fanciful idea mentioned to an old friend who understood and sympathized with Andrews's yearning for attention and riches. Gene Davis dropped the matter after he hung up the telephone. Andrews concentrated on it. Almost immediately the idea mutated into a possibility. Perhaps it was the fever that did it, or the bug in his system, or the oxygen, the medication, or the excitement pulsating from the proximity of Dallas. For the idea was basically absurd—no reasonable person would have considered Andrews for the job. No one facing even an ordinary murder charge (much less the assassination of the president) would have sought out this small-time, jive-talking attorney with a clientele of "pimps, prostitutes, and two-bit hustlers." Accused assassin Lee Harvey Oswald was trying to contact New York attorney John Abt, who represented American Communist party chiefs Gus Hall and John Davis, to act in his defense.[29] Unaware of that, Andrews's imagination took flight on the telephone. He was under such heavy sedation that his doctor later said he did not believe Andrews "capable of using the telephone" that weekend.[30] The doctor was wrong.

To implement his plan, Andrews had to inform his secretary, Eva Springer. She was the first person he telephoned. It was about four o'clock and Springer had just returned from doing her marketing. She was surprised to hear from Andrews; he didn't ordinarily call her at home. His news was astonishing: "I'm representing Lee Harvey Oswald in Dallas, Texas," he said. Her response was immediate and unequivocal. "I'm not going to Dallas with you. I want nothing to do with the case." Then she asked the logical question, the one that would bring on disaster. "Who hired you?" The question put Andrews in a bind. No one had hired him, but he couldn't tell Springer that. So he blurted out a one-word fictitious name. "Bertrand," he said. Bertrand? The name meant nothing to Eva Springer and she quickly ended the conversation.[31]

Her reaction temporarily halted his telephoning. For the rest of the evening, his physical condition and the routine of the hospital took over. At six he "was treated with nose drops and cough medicine." At eight he was given a sedative and "complained of pains in the chest." At nine he received antibiotics. At ten he was "quiet again." Quiet but not entirely idle. Watching television that evening, he learned about Oswald's life: his defection to Russia, his Russian wife, his return to America, and the fact that Oswald was born in New Orleans and had lived there the previous summer while engaging in pro-Castro activity. Andrews heard too that Oswald was upset about his undesirable discharge from the Marine Corps and wanted it changed.[32]

Andrews awoke Sunday morning with his scheme to finagle a piece of the Dallas action still percolating. The Bertrand story he had told his secretary the day before was taking on a life of its own. In his feverish and doped-up condition, as he later said, "I might have believed it myself."[33] The idea had obvious flaws—logistics, for instance. In his incapacitated state he needed help, someone he trusted to go to Dallas and act in his stead. He knew the man to ask, a local attorney and close personal friend named Sam "Monk" Zelden. Andrews also knew where to find him—the posh New Orleans Athletic Club where the two usually played racquetball Sunday mornings.

He reached Zelden there about eleven and nudged the Bertrand fantasy a notch further. "I've been approached to defend Oswald," Andrews said. Zelden, too, was surprised, but unlike Eva Springer he didn't ask any questions. "Would you be interested in helping in Oswald's defense?" Andrews asked. The idea didn't appeal to Zelden. "I'll have to think about it," he replied. Zelden's lack of enthusiasm didn't matter. While the two men were speaking on the phone, Dallas night club owner Jack Ruby shot and killed Lee Harvey Oswald in the basement of the Dallas County Jail, an event Zelden and much of the country witnessed live on television. Said Zelden, "Don't worry about it. Your client just got shot."[34]

In Dallas the spotlight Andrews sought had gone out.

But the shooting of Oswald that Sunday was for Andrews both good news and bad news. The bad news was the "client" was dead and Andrews had no one to defend. The good news was the "client" was dead and Andrews could fabricate any story and Lee Harvey Oswald couldn't deny it.[35] The next day, which was President Kennedy's funeral, the faithful R. M. Davis again visited the hospital. He found Andrews "disturbed" about a news report that Oswald had fired three shots in three seconds from a bolt action rifle, a feat Andrews understandably believed was impossible. He wanted to call the FBI and Secret Service and give them his opinion but Davis talked him out of it. Andrews also wanted to call a local television station to make some "announcement." Davis dissuaded him from that as well. But eventually Davis left.

Andrews then placed calls to the local offices of the FBI and Secret Service. He didn't talk about Oswald's marksmanship, however, but the scenario evolving in his imagination. To his Bertrand story, he now added what might be called *an earlier act*. Andrews said that Lee Harvey Oswald had actually visited his office on three occasions the previous summer seeking legal advice. Drawing on information from local television reports, Andrews told the government agents that Oswald had consulted him about reversing his undesirable discharge, the immigration status of his wife, and whether he had lost his American citizenship while in Russia.[36]* The Oswald visits, Andrews said, began "late in the month of June" and continued in July. Oswald was accompanied by "approximately five persons," all of them homosexual. Twice Oswald was with a young man "of Mexican extraction."[37] Andrews claimed he never opened a file on Oswald because he never provided the necessary information, or a fee for Andrews's services. Andrews had mentioned none of this to anyone until *after* Oswald was shot and killed. Nevertheless, this earlier act gave his Bertrand story *legs*.[38]

Andrews told the FBI and Secret Service agents about that call as well, and provided his caller with a first name, "*Clay.*" This Clay Bertrand might have contacted him previously on another matter, Andrews said, and Bertrand could have been one of those who accompanied Oswald to his office, but Andrews could provide no information to help locate his mysterious caller. Andrews described Bertrand as "youthful," twenty-two to twenty-three years of age, five feet seven inches tall, weighing 160 pounds, with blonde crew cut hair, and said he "believed that

---

* What Andrews didn't know was that Oswald's careful handling of citizenship and immigration matters while in Russia, and his returning home with U.S. government help, indicated he knew exactly where he stood on those issues.

Bertrand was homosexual." Even that first day, what Andrews told the two agencies was contradictory in some ways.[39]

After he hung up the phone, Andrews dozed off, only to be awakened a short time later by FBI Agent Regis Kennedy standing at his bedside. Agent Kennedy "appeared before me like a myth," Andrews later said. The pressure was on. The FBI agents, in particular, became a thorn in Andrews's side. Over the next ten days they would interview him five times, the Secret Service agents three. They also interviewed his friends and employees and contacted all agencies that might have provided a lead to the mysterious Clay Bertrand, launching an all-out effort to find the man. Andrews, using only his telephone and operating from a hospital bed, diverted FBI and Secret Services agents in the midst of the most important investigation of the century. Their search yielded nothing. They could find no Clay Bertrand.

The day after Andrews returned to work, FBI agent Kennedy visited him at his office. In this session, the first conducted when Andrews was free of medication, he didn't recall telephoning the FBI or Secret Service, and said that "since leaving the hospital" the call from Bertrand "seems like a dream."[40]

Andrews made his final statement to the FBI two days later, and it was a clear-cut *mea culpa*. Maneuvering skillfully to extricate himself, Andrews said he had no memory of calling his secretary and was "unable to account for the name 'Bertrand,'" which he used in their conversation. He ticked off numerous shortcomings of the story, and pointed out that it lacked the basic details he would have obtained from any prospective client. These defects led Andrews to conclude that the Bertrand call "was a figment of his imagination."

This allowed Andrews a graceful withdrawal from an embarrassing situation. In wriggling off the hook, Andrews even managed to salvage a bit of self-respect by retaining the part about Oswald visiting his office. Admitting the truth about the call from Bertrand was necessary to dislodge the FBI from his doorstep. But he had no reason to admit he fabricated this other complex back-story with its elaborate supporting cast. No one could refute him and it no doubt seemed harmless enough. It also softened the humiliation by lending some face-saving substance to the whole god-awful mess. So Andrews repudiated Bertrand but clung to *the earlier act.*[*]

That should have been the end of it.

But then the Warren Commission, appointed by President Johnson to investigate President Kennedy's assassination, issued Andrews a subpoena. The spotlight was back and Andrews was in it. A command performance ordered by the United States government. The compulsive talker was compelled to talk.

Warren Commission Assistant Counsel Wesley Liebeler conducted the interview in the Old Civil Courts Building in New Orleans on July 21, 1964. Andrews arrived sporting his trademark dark glasses. As irrepressible as ever, he immediately embellished further the Oswald visits and exhumed the Bertrand story. Responding irreverently to Liebeler's pointed questions, Andrews referred to all the "gay kids" who accompanied Oswald to his office on the first visit as "Mexicanos," and he said they were "swishers"; "what they call here queens."[41]

Andrews referred to Bertrand as "a lawyer without a brief case" and a bisexual, "what they call a swinging cat." He said that prior to the call he had seen Bertrand "probably a couple of years [ago]" and had seen him again more recently, or as Andrews put it: "Oh, I ran up on that rat about 6 weeks ago and he spooked, ran in[to] the street. I would have beat him with a chain if I had caught him." Andrews provided a third physical description of Bertrand, which resembled the other two in gender only. He wasn't trying to mislead anyone. He simply didn't remember what he had said previously. Over time he complained bitterly that the FBI and Secret Service agents refused to provide him with any information about his first statements to them.[42]

Liebeler walked Andrews through the numerous conflicts in his various interviews but Andrews blithely waved them off or explained them away. When asked about his statement to the FBI that the Bertrand phone call was a figment of his imagination, he said, they wrote that did they? Well he knew that the "Feebees" [FBI] were "going to put

---

[*] When he began retreating from the "Bertrand" story, Andrews began shoring up this *Oswald-was-my-client* tale. He increased the *Oswald visits* from "three" to the possibility of as many as "five" and claimed that Oswald arrived *after* 5 P.M., *after* his secretary had left for the day. That explained why there was no record of Oswald in the appointment book and why the secretary had no knowledge that he was a client.

these people on the street looking, and I can't find the guy, and I am not going to tie up all the agents on something that isn't that solid." Then, reacting to his recent less-than-felicitous experience with that agency (in remarks that will later be used against him by Oliver Stone), Andrews pursued the thought further in his own special way. "They were running on the time factor, and the hills were shook up plenty to get it, get it, get it. I couldn't give it to them. I have been playing cops and robbers with them. You can tell when the steam is on. They are on you like the plague. They never leave. They are like cancer. Eternal."[43]

Andrews was a complex man, deliberately outrageous, funny and fun-loving, unusually verbal and imaginative, and desperate for attention. But the last word anyone would associate with him is *malevolent*. One who knew Andrews would later write that he seemed to view the world "as a huge joke." In New Orleans his name usually evokes a smile. Everyone, they say, liked him, even Garrison, who became his nemesis. In his last two interviews with the FBI, Andrews had managed to bury his Bertrand tale and escape with a modicum of dignity. Yet seven months later, performing for the Warren Commission, he resurrected it. He couldn't resist being a player, albeit a minor one, in this national drama, which anointed him with a kind of celebrity status.[44] That compulsion would bring about more than his own downfall.

Those with access to Andrews's FBI documents knew about the hospital, the drugs, how ill Andrews was the weekend of the assassination, and about his quick recantation. But few paid any attention to that. The focus was on Andrews's backsliding testimony to Wesley Liebeler. That was published by the Warren Commission in its Hearings and Exhibits, those twenty-six blue bound books bearing the presidential seal destined for libraries nationwide. Even the Warren Report, while emphasizing its tenuous nature, gave Andrews's testimony a paragraph.[45] That's where Jim Garrison would discover it three years later.

CHAPTER FOUR

THE "SMITH" CASE

To me [Garrison has] always been
a man of imagination who set out
a broad plot at the very beginning
. . . but hadn't yet decided on his
characters, and how they were
going to act. When the public
bought his rough script, he then
started to write his book. And
permitted each character, as he
reacted, to write the next page for
him. The mistake, of course, was
that he sold the book as . . . an his-
toric text. But actually he was
writing fiction.[1]

—*Aaron Kohn, managing director, New Orleans Metropolitan Crime Commission, 1969*

On a humid evening in late October 1966, the upscale New Orleans
restaurant Broussard's was the scene of a significant meeting. That night
Jim Garrison took his old Tulane law school classmate Dean Andrews
to dinner there. Garrison had just discovered that Andrews was a witness before the Warren Commission and he wanted to know all about
it. Andrews was flattered to be invited out by this powerful man. The
office, Garrison told him, thinks very highly of you. The two shared a
skepticism about the Warren Report that created a common ground,
and the occasion was a pleasant social affair. Andrews had no idea an
investigation was in the offing. He thought Garrison merely wanted to
compare notes with him about the assassination.[2]

Garrison, listening attentively, accepted without question what

Andrews said about the Oswald visits and the mysterious Clay Bertrand, and prodded Andrews for everything he could recall about Oswald. Once again the compulsive talker was compelled to talk. Andrews repeated what he could remember of what he had told Liebeler. They kicked around some theories about the assassination, discussed the weapon, and Harold Weisberg's book *Whitewash*, which Garrison had with him. Then Garrison "mooched" Andrews's copy of the Warren Report.[3]

That congenial get-together was Garrison's first move on the case; soon he was talking to Jack Martin. Searching for access to the crime of the century, Garrison had found his on-ramp. Yet exactly *when* he turned his attention to the assassination and *why* are unclear. There are two accounts of how it came about. Garrison claimed his interest was kindled sometime in the fall of 1966 on a plane trip to New York with U.S. Senator Russell B. Long of Louisiana.[4] During that flight, Long expressed doubts about the Warren Report's lone-assassin theory, especially Oswald's ability to fire so accurately in such a brief time.* This troubled Garrison, who had accepted the Warren Commission's conclusions, and prompted a reexamination of the Report, which turned him 180 degrees in the other direction. So goes the official version.

The unofficial one involves a stripper convicted of lewd dancing, a pardon Garrison engineered for her, and the allegation that her case was linked to elements of "organized crime." That charge triggered a classic Garrison counterattack. "Organized crime," Garrison proclaimed, didn't exist in Orleans Parish (an untenable position that he never altered) and he had his principal critic subpoenaed by the Grand Jury "to put up or shut up." A newspaper editorial followed reproaching Garrison. He reacted by turning his guns on the newspaper as well.† Then Garrison's good friend, writer David Chandler, published an article in *New Orleans* magazine implying that some individuals in the district attorney's office were taking bribes. Garrison, the article said,

---

* Sen. Long's family history may have made him especially vulnerable to conspiracy theories. In 1935, his father, the legendary Louisiana political figure, Huey P. Long, was assassinated by a lone gunman, and the assassin was then shot and killed by Long's bodyguards.

† "Garrison just can't stand [criticism]," an aide later said. "It drives him crazy. He forgets everything he's doing" (William Gurvich, Conference with defense team, Aug. 29, 1967 [hereinafter Gurvich Conference], tape #2, p. 3).

had lost his way. No longer the shining knight of old, Garrison had "touched off" what Chandler called an "organized crime donny-brook." Word quickly "got back" to Chandler that his charges had put Garrison "into a complete tailspin"—that he had virtually "gone crazy" over them.[5] In the midst of this escalating furor, Garrison turned his attention to the Kennedy assassination. Some believe he did so in an effort to regain his earlier hero's image and to draw attention away from the corruption and organized crime charges. If so, Garrison selected the right issue. The assassination was the topic of the day.

Stirred by a series of critical books and articles, people everywhere were debating the accuracy of the Warren Report. Mark Lane, in his 1966 bestseller *Rush to Judgment*, presented a serious challenge to the government's conclusions. But Lane's book was an advocate's brief. Harvard graduate student Edward Epstein published *Inquest* that same year and it had no such down side. Impressed by its balance and scholarly cachet, management at a number of leading news organizations (among them *Time* magazine, the *New York Times* and the *Wall Street Journal*) sent their own investigative teams into the field to see what they could find.[6]

While Epstein influenced the members of the news media, it was the nation's most popular magazines, those familiar and trusted publications found on coffee tables everywhere, that swayed middle America. In November 1966, a milestone article appeared in *Life* written by Richard Billings. Using frames from the Zapruder film and citing John Connally's testimony disputing the single-bullet theory, "A Matter of Reasonable Doubt" raised the possibility of a second shooter and called for a new inquiry.[7] No single piece published had more impact. It may have played a greater role in turning the majority of Americans away from the conclusions of the Warren Report than any book written. In those days most of the country still relied heavily on the print media for its news. *Life* (then part of one of the largest news organizations in the world) was still an entrenched and honored part of the American scene. For an institution as conservative and important to endorse such an idea seemed, in itself, to validate the notion of conspiracy. And *Life* was not alone.

Two months later, *The Saturday Evening Post*, a magazine of heartland values and Norman Rockwell sentiments, asked on its cover, "Do we need a new investigation?" and the article said yes.[8] As with the management at *Life*, those at *The Post* had turned away from the official lone-assassin version and were cautiously exploring the idea of conspiracy. Questioning the government's conclusions was in vogue, and the questioning was being done by the people at the nation's most venerable and prominent publications. Many today believe Garrison went out on a limb with his Kennedy investigation; that isn't true. By the time he launched his boat, a news media flotilla had already left the dock. Garrison wasn't bucking the tide, he was moving with it, and so was the rest of the country. Contrary to today's conventional wisdom, it wasn't a handful of cranks that drew the country into the conspiracy camp. It was the mainline media.

But for Garrison it was Senator Long. He shaped to a surprising degree Garrison's thinking on the case during that airborne conversation. Long speculated that the assassins used Oswald as "a fall guy," "a decoy" whose shots from the Texas School Book Depository drew the attention of everyone "while another man fired the fatal shot." Garrison would make those ideas the backbone of his own theory about the mechanics of Dealey Plaza. Long also triggered Garrison's recollections of the flurry of activity in his office when tipster Jack Martin named David Ferrie as Oswald's accomplice. Around the time of the assassination, Garrison told Long, his office had arrested and released "a very unusual type of person who made a very curious trip at a very curious time." Garrison said he might now take another look at all that.[9]

While his motives are obscure, the course Garrison pursued from then on is clear enough. He began by studying the Warren Commission Report and its twenty-six volumes, as well as the writings of some of its critics. Primarily because Oswald had studied Russian while in the Marine Corps, Garrison became convinced that he was linked to the U.S. intelligence community and that he had been engaged in undercover activities the summer before the assassination. Whatever Oswald had been up to, he had spent that summer in Garrison's jurisdiction. With that tenuous justification, Garrison opened his own investigation into the case.

In the weeks that followed, Garrison assembled a small staff to work in secret on the project, which he called "The Smith Case," after Winston Smith, George Orwell's *Nineteen Eighty-Four* protagonist. He also dreamt up code names to identify the principals involved. Oswald was "Patsy,"

Ferrie "Blackstone," and Banister "Barney." This pseudo-clandestine game playing suggests that Garrison, at least for a time, was having fun. He was also busy. He instigated a reunion with David Chandler that would bring about Garrison's deep but short-lived involvement with *Life* magazine. He had numerous sessions with Jack Martin, and he took Dean Andrews to dinner a total of three times, with conversations in between.

Garrison told few outside the secret team that he was "reopening" the Kennedy case. But he confided in Andrews. This was after their initial dinner at Broussard's. Garrison asked for Andrews's help. He named three people he wanted to know about. One was David Ferrie, "whom Garrison called the 'getaway pilot.'" Another was the Mexican Andrews claimed accompanied Oswald to his office. The third was Clay Bertrand. But Andrews couldn't help. He had had contact with Ferrie only once, he told Garrison, in connection with a parole he arranged for a friend of Ferrie.* Regarding the Mexican ("Oswald's shadow") and Bertrand (a "voice on the phone"), Andrews had nothing new to add.[10] Garrison wasn't satisfied, but it would be several weeks before Andrews heard from him again.

Meanwhile, Garrison spoke to the loquacious Jack Martin. Disregarding his recantation to the Secret Service, Martin enlarged and embellished that 1963 story, shaping it to fit the new situation. He told Garrison about the pistol-whipping the night of the assassination. But now he claimed it was sparked by a comment he made about the men he saw in Guy Banister's office that summer. Whom did he see? A "bunch" of Cubans, David Ferrie (who "practically lived there"), and Lee Harvey Oswald.[11] These "revelations" intensified Garrison's interest in all manner of Cuban activities. He concluded that Oswald's pro-Castro public stance was a pretense, that he was actually anti-Castro and working as an *agent provocateur* for Guy Banister. Supporting this idea was the address "544 Camp Street"† that Oswald stamped on some of the literature he handed out on the streets of New Orleans. Banister's office was in the same building (though located around the corner at 731 Lafayette

---

* His actions in that parole, Andrews admitted, had not been "a strictly legal move for an assistant D.A. to make," a damaging admission that Garrison tucked away for future use.
† Oswald's use of the Camp Street address may mean nothing (see chapter 13).

Street), and Garrison found that conclusive. Guy Banister now became central to his thinking. Oswald, Garrison decided, was working out of Banister's office. Nefarious doings, Garrison believed, transpired there.

At Garrison's urging, Martin now told Garrison *everything*, though what that amounted to is unclear. In a series of secret conversations, Martin led Garrison inside "the *sanctum sanctorum*," Garrison later called it, "that secretly had harbored Lee Harvey Oswald."[12] Garrison rewarded Martin by making him part of the investigative team.[13]

Garrison was now convinced that his suspicions about Ferrie's Texas trip were justified. In addition to the timing, there was the weather, which had been stormy and dreadful. Garrison found it unbelievable that Ferrie, though eccentric and unpredictable, would drive all night through a rain storm to go ice skating. Ferrie's friend Alvin Beaubouef recently acknowledged that the weather was terrible but *so what?* he said. He and Ferrie were accustomed to *flying* though storms and "driving through one was no big deal."[14] It was for Garrison and he never budged from that opinion. He obsessed on that trip the rest of his life. Ferrie, he believed, had been assigned to fly Lee Harvey Oswald to safety. It stuck in Garrison's craw that his office had had Ferrie in custody right after the assassination and released him. Though Ferrie was cleared by the Texas Rangers, the Houston Police, and the New Orleans Police Department, Garrison was soon claiming that the FBI let Ferrie "get away."

In mid-December Garrison ordered Asst. D.A. John Volz to interview the villain of Martin's story. As he had three years earlier, David Ferrie denied everything* and told Volz he knew he was being questioned because of Jack Martin. Martin, Ferrie said, "somehow gets to be near the bride at every wedding and the corpse at every funeral." When asked if he would be willing to take a polygraph, Ferrie replied "certainly" and he volunteered to take truth serum. "I have no hesitation at all," he declared.[15] Yet Garrison never gave these tests to Ferrie, his key suspect who eagerly sought them. (If Ferrie had taken them and passed, Garrison would have been left empty-handed, with no suspect,

---

* Ferrie informed Volz that the CAP cadet who introduced Oswald to that organization, Edward Voebel, had said that he and Oswald, along with some other cadets, once stopped by Ferrie's house. But, Ferrie said, he didn't remember the visit (Ferrie, interview with Asst. D.A. John Volz, Dec. 15, 1966).

no link to Dallas, and nowhere for his investigation to go.)

Unmoved by Ferrie's denials and his request to be tested, Garrison immediately began harassing his friends. Layton Martens, Alvin Beaubouef, Morris Brownlee, Melvin Coffey, and others were contacted on the job, called at home at night, embarrassed in front of their employers and families, and interrogated in the district attorney's office, some of them repeatedly. Layton Martens was questioned by the grand jury and soon charged with perjury. Morris Brownlee, Ferrie's godson, was rearrested on an old drug charge previously dropped for insufficient evidence. Ferrie was brought into the jail, given a look at Brownlee in his cell, and told he would be released if Ferrie would "cooperate."[16] But Ferrie had nothing to tell Garrison. Nor did any of his friends. There was nothing to tell.*

Unwavering in his certitude that Ferrie was guilty, Garrison instituted surveillance of him, which was eventually a twenty-four-hour watch. One of those Garrison asked to help with this was his estranged friend, David Chandler. Garrison reached out to Chandler through a mutual acquaintance who telephoned Chandler one night late in November. He said that Garrison was secretly reopening the Kennedy case and asked if Chandler was interested in meeting with Garrison and talking about it. Mindful of Garrison's visceral reaction to his *New Orleans* article, Chandler was surprised by this invitation, but happy at the opportunity "to mend fences,"† which also promised a great story.[17]

The two men met the next day. Sitting in Garrison's comfortable office, Chandler listened as Garrison presented his view of the assassination. Basically Garrison said "the CIA did it" and he identified the two CIA operatives involved. One was Clay Bertrand; the other, David Ferrie. "The case would be broken," Garrison told Chandler "by cracking David Ferrie, 'a very unusual type of person who made a very curious trip at a very curious time about the date of the assassination.'"[18]

Chandler was working as a stringer for *Life* magazine, which already

---

* Ferrie's friends got the message—being around him was an invitation to trouble. They stopped calling and dropping by, leaving him isolated (Beaubouef Interview).

† Garrison's contacting Chandler, who had written the most negative report published about him to date, was a peculiar move. He was using his Kennedy investigation to regain his previous stature in Chandler's eyes, an odd priority.

had begun its own inquiry into the assassination. He immediately contacted its New York office, described his meeting with Garrison, and requested that "a senior editor" be sent to New Orleans. A few days later, Richard Billings, author of "A Matter of Reasonable Doubt," arrived. "We just might have the scoop of the century," Billings said. The two went directly from the airport to a meeting in Garrison's office.[19]

There "a secret deal" was worked out. It was agreed that Life and Garrison would "share all information" they might gather on the assassination. "It was a powerful alliance," Chandler later wrote, "Garrison had the prosecutorial and subpoena powers" while Life had "a worldwide network of correspondents." The arrangement was unorthodox and of arguable impropriety. Yet, theoretically, it could benefit all. Life would give Garrison free assistance and information on a global scale and in return obtain the inside story of his investigation, to be written by Richard Billings.* Chandler and Billings set up headquarters in the Richelieu apartment building in the French Quarter where they rented a suite of rooms. They formed the two-man core of the operation, which was supplemented by "a variety of reporters and photographers" who were "shuttled" in and out of New Orleans on a regular basis. On hand at any given time over the next few months were at least four additional Life reporters and as many photographers.[20] Life's management was investing heavily in Garrison's effort.†

The morning after the deal was struck, Chandler arrived at Garrison's office and received his first assignment: He was to make "undercover contact" with Ferrie. Chandler and a Life photographer drove to the lakefront airport, where Ferrie was working as a charter pilot, and wasted two days trying to bump into him "accidentally." He wasn't what Chandler expected. From Garrison's description Chandler was prepared for a sideshow freak with false eyebrows and a homemade

---

* Garrison boasted to some on his staff that his picture was going to be on the cover of Life (Gurvich Conference, tape #2, p. 12).

† Life provided Garrison a variety of assistance. In Miami a Life researcher investigated the alleged Latin assassins supposedly hiding there; Life's lab provided photographic enlargements and prints (whatever Garrison requested); and wherever Garrison went he was trailed by a Life photographer recording his activities for posterity. In return, Life received a copy of Garrison's master file, which was mailed to New York "as things were printed," and the possibility of the biggest journalistic coup in recent memory.

red wig. But "up close" Ferrie "didn't seem all that garish" to Chandler. It's an opinion some others shared.

On the third day, they had an early-morning conversation with him in the airport coffee shop. Ferrie astonished them with what he had to say. He had a tip for them about what he called "a big secret": The local district attorney, "Big Jim" Garrison "had hot leads to the Kennedy Assassination." His information, Ferrie said, came from one of Garrison's own men, who was sitting in a booth at the far end of the room "doing his best to disappear." But the real shock came when Ferrie chuckled and said, "Garrison had *me* pegged as the getaway pilot in Dallas." This knocked Chandler for a loop; he was still laughing about it years later. "Here we were working on the scoop of the century, a major secret," he said, "and the *suspect* . . . was telling us all about it." David Ferrie "just didn't act like a CIA assassin," Chandler said. Ferrie invited them for a ride in his plane, the first of many such flights. Chandler found him "harmless, even likeable,"[21] another observation others shared.

This "undercover" work with Ferrie stirred Chandler's first doubts about Garrison's case and he began "taking a hard look" at what was going on in the D.A.'s office. He didn't like what he saw or what he was hearing about abuses by Garrison and his aides. Before long Chandler decided that what Pershing Gervais had told him was true, that Garrison *had* "gone nuts" over the assassination. A few days before Christmas, Chandler and Billings were summoned to Garrison's office. What happened there left a lasting impression. As soon as they were seated, Garrison announced that he had "deduced" the identity of Clay Bertrand. "One, Bertrand is homosexual," he said. "Two, Bertrand speaks Spanish. Three, his first name is Clay." Then he triumphantly flipped up a photograph that was lying face down on his desk. It was a picture of Clay Shaw.* Shaw fit these criteria; therefore, Shaw was Bertrand. Chandler was astonished.[22] Clay Shaw, a well-known and respected New Orleans businessman and civic leader, was the last person anyone would suspect of par-

---

* Garrison's "insight" was inspired by notes scribbled in the margin of a paperback copy of the Warren Report by Asst. D.A. Frank Klein. Ruminating on Dean Andrews's Warren Commission testimony, Klein had asked himself who he knew with the first name "Clay" who lived in the French Quarter and was gay, and dashed off the name Clay Shaw and a "question mark" (Gurvich Conference, pp. 13–14; Bethell Diary, p. 11).

ticipating in the president's assassination.

Modest and well-liked, Shaw moved in the city's wealthiest social circles. Among his friends were playwright Tennessee Williams and Sears Roebuck heiress Edith Stern. He was regarded as one of the city's most eligible bachelors and was often seen in the company of women, but he was gay, though discreet and in the closet. Some knew, but no one seemed to care; those who did turned a blind eye. A dedicated supporter of the arts, especially music and theater, and a linguist, at ease in several languages, Shaw was basically self-taught. After graduating from Warren Easton High School, he worked for Western Union as a local manager. As with Garrison, writing was Shaw's long-range lifetime goal,* but as a young man he found it a poor source of the income needed to sustain a life. In his early twenties, he moved to New York City, took some courses at Columbia University, and supported himself by again working for Western Union, this time as a district manager in mid-Manhattan. He turned his writing skill into free-lance work in public relations and advertising, and eventually headed one of the country's leading lecture bureaus. What successes Shaw might have enjoyed in those fields or in New York's theatrical world died a-borning on December 7, 1941, when the Japanese bombed Pearl Harbor. He enlisted at the age of twenty-nine, a private in the Army Medical Corps. He was discharged in 1946 a major with a chest full of decorations from three countries. He had served with distinction as Deputy Chief of Staff to General Charles Thrasher, commander of United States Forces in Northern France and Belgium. Shaw later said that coordinating supplies for three armies as they fanned out across Europe had developed his organizational skills.[23]

With the fighting over, he returned not to New York but to the city where he grew up. He never again left New Orleans except on business trips and vacations. The pivotal moment in Shaw's career occurred in 1947 when a group of prominent local businessmen asked him to help create a center for international trade. To them he was a "highly decorated war hero," and one of their own, Louisiana-born. A native of

---

* By the time Shaw was nineteen he had co-written and published three one-act plays (one of them, Submerged, has been staged thousands of times) and in 1948 his first full-length play, In Memoriam, was produced in New Orleans.

Kentwood, Shaw had lived in New Orleans since he and his parents moved there when he was five years old. His grandfather was a turn-of-the-century sheriff in Tangipahoa Parish and one of the state's best-known lawmen. Shaw later said he had no qualifications for the job the businessmen offered him but realized no one else did either, "because the mart idea had never been attempted before in this country." So he gladly accepted. The city's original Trade Mart, which opened in 1948, was Shaw's creation—he directed its financing, its construction and its operation. When he retired nineteen years later, on October 1, 1965, the legacy he left behind included the thirty-three-story International Trade Mart building at the foot of Canal Street, which was Shaw's idea. One of his friends said recently that Shaw did everything but build it himself.[24]

He could have lent a hand there as well. For years he worked restoring structures in the city's famous but run-down French Quarter—it was his principal avocation.* Others followed his lead and today it is one of the most highly prized areas of the city. A carriage house (with a bright red door) that Shaw restored at 1313 Dauphine Street became his home. Often seen at cultural affairs, Shaw also liked to hang out at the Press Club and drink with the newsmen. Politically a lifelong registered Democratic, Shaw described himself as a Wilsonian-Franklin-Delano-Roosevelt "liberal." He supported John Kennedy's campaign for the presidency in 1960 and thought he was "a splendid president."† Kennedy's "youth, imagination, style and elan" appealed to Shaw, and so did his political programs, especially Kennedy's Alliance for Progress for Latin America. Shaw believed it would benefit all concerned economically, and be a boon to the shipping business in New Orleans. "If there was one person in New Orleans who believed in John F. Kennedy," a friend later said, "it was Clay Shaw."[25]

When Garrison held up Shaw's picture and proclaimed him "Clay Bertrand," it wasn't just Shaw's stature in the community that aston-

---

* Shaw rehabilitated and restored sixteen structures, including a house where naturalist John James Audubon lived in 1921, and the so-called Spanish Stables.
† Clay Shaw met the president once. When the former mayor of New Orleans de Lesseps Morrison was appointed Ambassador to the Organization of American States, Shaw was one of those who accompanied Morrison to Washington for the swearing-in ceremony.

ished David Chandler. It was Garrison's rationale for selecting him, what Chandler called "Garrison's silly syllogism." Chandler found it ridiculous. Garrison cited no evidence whatever. No district attorney in his right mind would make such a leap on that basis. Chandler wasn't the only one to think so. Dean Andrews, who had given "Clay Bertrand" life, shared that sentiment.

Around the time Garrison staged his photographic revelation for Chandler and Billings, he treated Andrews to another dinner at Broussard's and informed him, too, that he believed Clay Shaw was Bertrand. Andrews, as amazed as Chandler had been and alarmed, tried to dissuade Garrison, but he had made up his mind. Now he wanted Andrews to corroborate it. Andrews refused. Garrison continued to press the idea at later meetings, trying to coax Andrews into admitting it, and Andrews began to wonder about Garrison's tactics. "[Garrison] wanted to shuck me like corn, pluck me like a chicken, stew me like an oyster," Andrews later complained. "I wanted to see if this cat was kosher." To test Garrison's integrity, Andrews invented a fictitious Cuban guerrilla fighter, whom Andrews called "Mannie Garcia Gonzales," after a client of his named "Manuel Garcia," to which he added "Gonzales." Not long afterwards, Garrison announced that the "triggerman" in the assassination was "Manuel Garcia Gonzales." Garrison charged this fictitious person with selling narcotics and informed Andrews that Gonzales had been arrested. Dismayed, but with his suspicions confirmed, Andrews told Garrison that he had the wrong Gonzales. Or as Andrews put it, he had "the right ha-ha but the wrong ho-ho."[26]

Andrews regarded the "Gonzales" caper as amusing and harmless but it was worse than that. He had provided Garrison with additional false information about a Latin connection to the crime. To his credit, Andrews had not embellished his Warren Commission testimony. Most importantly, he had refused to falsely identify Clay Shaw as Clay Bertrand. There he stood firm. He would not do it. Garrison wasn't through trying but for now he had to look elsewhere for help. He turned to the man in question.

Early in the morning the day before Christmas, Garrison had one of his detectives telephone Clay Shaw and ask him to come down to the

D.A.'s office to answer some questions. Shaw agreed, having no idea that Garrison suspected him of being the mysterious "Clay Bertrand." Shaw assumed they wanted to ask him about the incident that occurred on August 16, 1963, when Lee Harvey Oswald had distributed Fair Play for Cuba leaflets in front of Shaw's place of business, the Trade Mart building at Camp and Common Streets.

The detective picked Shaw up and drove him to Tulane and Broad where he was "questioned extensively" by Andrew Sciambra. Lee Harvey Oswald knew a man named "Clay" who lived in the French Quarter, Sciambra said, and we wondered if you were that man. Shaw said he was not, that he had not known Oswald. He had "almost" met him, Shaw said, the day he passed out leaflets in front of the Trade Mart. Oswald had come to his office that day but had spoken to his assistant, asking permission to distribute them. The assistant denied the request. Later that afternoon, Shaw was on a long-distance telephone call when a "commotion" occurred downstairs. Oswald, distributing his leaflets, had attracted police and television cameras. When Shaw finished his conversation, he went outside, but by then Oswald and the police were gone and the television crews were packing up. Shaw told Sciambra that was all he knew about the incident. Most of Sciambra's questions focused on the Cuban consulate that had been housed in the Trade Mart and Shaw's contacts with the people there.[*] It was Shaw's understanding that the consulate was the reason Oswald chose the site. Had Shaw ever joined any anti-Castro group? Shaw had not. Did he know David Ferrie? Shaw did not. Had he ever heard of a Clay Bertrand? Shaw had not.[27]

Garrison entered the room and Shaw briefly repeated what he had told Sciambra. Then Shaw left and went to City Hall where a Christmas party was underway. Before he departed the D.A.'s office, Shaw later said, Garrison "thanked me profusely for being a good citizen, for being cooperative and coming in." Shaw thought that was the end of

---

[*] After Castro severed relations with the United States and fired consulate officials abroad, Shaw had agreed to the request of the aging and ill Cuban consul (Carlos Marquez) and allowed the office to remain open for three months (rent free) in the hope that diplomatic relations might be restored (Shaw Journal, pp. 4, 5).

the matter. Temporarily it was. The Jolly Green Giant had been favorably impressed by Clay Shaw, an impressive man. Garrison told his aides to "forget Shaw." Earlier Garrison had mentioned Shaw's name to two newsmen; he now told them that Shaw had "absolutely nothing to do with it."[28]

Garrison would shortly change his mind.

CHAPTER FIVE

A TIGER BY THE TAIL

> This is not a city prone to know-
> ing what it's doing before it
> arrests people. . . .
>
> —*David Ferrie* (to *George Lardner, Jr.*),
> February 22, 1967

As 1967 began, Garrison had his men on the move. Armed with the tools of the sleuthing trade and Garrison's instructions,* they boarded planes to Dallas, Houston, Chicago, and Miami, seeking Cubans who had known David Ferrie. Finding them, Garrison believed, would provide the link to the conspiracy that had killed President Kennedy. Expecting to land the fictional Manuel Garcia Gonzales, Garrison himself joined investigator Louis Ivon in Miami. When the capture failed, Garrison concluded that his presence had been a mistake that had "flushed" their quarry and sent him fleeing to Cuba or Puerto Rico. "Things," Garrison said, were "moving too fast."[1]

This manic scurrying about was prompted not only by the misinformation from Dean Andrews and Jack Martin but also from a Martin protégé—David F. Lewis. Martin and Lewis were so close they ended up living together. A dark-haired twenty-six-year-old in square, horn-rimmed glasses, discharged from the Navy for "psychiatric" reasons, Lewis was a baggage handler at a bus station. Working briefly in 1961 as a "leg man" for Banister, he had bolstered his image of himself as a private eye by wearing a plastic gun in a $17 shoulder holster purchased from F. W. Woolworth. Lewis claimed he met Lee Harvey

---

* James Alcock, dispatched to Houston, was told to "bring Ident Kit" with "photos"; and "Minox camera with enlargement attachment and flashlight" (Jim Garrison, memorandum, "Investigative Assignments," Jan. 7, 1967).

Oswald in Mancuso's coffee shop and later saw him in Banister's office with Ferrie and two anti-Castro Cubans.* He came forward with his story at Martin's urging. Martin had dug up a "witness" to corroborate his own testimony. Garrison embraced Lewis as enthusiastically as he had Martin. David Ferrie was now plagued by a new source of incriminating "information" about him.[2]

Lewis was first certain that Ferrie was present at the meeting in Banister's office but unsure about Oswald. Later he was positive about Oswald but denied Ferrie was there. Then he switched again and said both were present. He first said his sightings occurred in the summer of 1963. Then he said they occurred in the summer of 1962, when Oswald was in the Soviet Union or Texas. Later still, he moved them back to 1963.[3] Lewis told members of the press he knew the names of five people who plotted the assassination and tried to peddle a tape recording he made with Martin "naming names" to a UPI reporter for $1,000. The reporter declined. In January Lewis was Garrison's primary witness. Soon afterwards, Jack Martin bragged that Garrison's investigation "was based on information 'made up'" by himself and David Lewis. No one else supported it and the three accused who were still living—the two Cubans (Sergio Arcacha Smith and Carlos Quiroga) and David Ferrie—vehemently denied it. But their denials fell on deaf ears. Garrison continued to pursue Cuban conspirators, supposedly linked to Ferrie, while exercising tight control over his men. Their trips were closely managed, down to the precise time of their daily telephone reports. Alcock was to call from Houston at 11:00 A.M. "sharp." In Dallas, John Volz was scheduled at "12:00 Noon sharp." But they produced nothing.[4]

One Cuban Garrison did locate, Miguel Torres, ended up being an embarrassment. He claimed, among other things, that the district attorney's office had tried to bribe him. Garrison found Torres by employing his "propinquity theory," the odd notion that the conspirators would be found living near each other, a geographical twist on guilt-by-association.† Miguel Torres fit Garrison's criteria: he was

---

* On January 20, Lewis faked a drive-by shooting in which he was the "target" and anti-Castro Cuban Carlos Quiroga was the "gunman." After doing poorly on a lie-detector test, Lewis admitted making the story up because he thought it would please Garrison.

† See note, page 206.

Cuban and he once lived only a block from Oswald on Magazine Street. "Garrison always said that he was going to solve the assassination with an Esso road map and the city directory and that's all he did all day long," investigator William Gurvich later remarked. "I know; I got him the five city directories." Garrison and his aides invested enormous time and energy chasing this eccentric idea but it was all for naught.[5]

William Gurvich was given the job of proving that on the day of the assassination David Ferrie was in Dallas, sitting in a plane at the end of a runway, engines running, waiting to fly Oswald to safety. Gurvich was supposed to find the airfield. A pilot himself, Gurvich rented a plane and flew from one small field to another, examining records, talking to workers, and showing Ferrie's picture. No one recognized him. When Garrison focused on a tiny airport called White Rock, Gurvich obtained its gasoline receipts for September, October, and November—4,000 of them, which Garrison ordered photocopied and checked. Again, no one found anything. From the outset Gurvich was troubled by the conspicuousness of a "waiting getaway pilot."[6] His doubts were confirmed when he discovered that Ferrie was telling the truth about his whereabouts on the day of the assassination. But when Gurvich first told Garrison he had learned from a federal marshal that Ferrie had been sitting in a federal courtroom in New Orleans, Garrison dismissed the idea. You know who they work for, he said.

The failure of Garrison's men to uncover any evidence against David Ferrie wasn't the only problem on Garrison's horizon. Since the day Garrison had recited his "silly syllogism" identifying Clay Shaw as Clay Bertrand, David Chandler had been heading off the reservation. Chandler didn't conceal his skepticism, and Billings and Garrison began regarding him with suspicion.[7] They had reason to worry. So did Chandler.

On January 25 he was served with a grand jury subpoena. At Tulane and Broad the next morning, he discovered that an investigation he was conducting into an alleged bribe in Garrison's office had prompted it. He was running the risk of being charged with perjury, he was told. "Get yourself a lawyer," Asst. D.A. Charles Ward said. The meaning was clear, "Shut up or go to jail." "For the next six months," Chandler later recalled, "I was never more than a phone call away from a *Life* lawyer." Chandler's disillusionment marked the beginning of a schism at *Life* over

Garrison. "There was the Billings faction," Chandler said, "that was proceeding with a positive Garrison story, and there was my faction" that was urging withdrawal of the magazine's support, believing that Garrison had become sort of a "monster" abusing his power. "We were both filing [separate reports] to New York," Chandler explained. But for the time being, Life's management put their trust in their senior man in the field, and Richard Billings's view prevailed.[8]

Life personnel continued to flow in and out of Tulane and Broad. This alerted members of the local press, who didn't want to be scooped by Life. Garrison's investigation was supposed to be a closely guarded secret, but rumors of it had circulated for some time. Veteran New Orleans States-Item police reporter Jack Dempsey even referred to it once in his column. No one paid any attention to him until the rumblings grew too loud to ignore. How the story finally broke is of more than passing interest, for even as it was happening Garrison was rewriting what was occurring. Later he would revise it even more, as he blamed the press for a self-inflicted wound. Garrison's paranoia about the media was born in these events.

States-Item city editor John Wilds set them in motion when he decided to find out if there was anything to the rumors he was hearing. He assigned Dempsey and Rosemary James (who everyone agrees was not only a fine reporter but one of the prettiest in town) to see what they could learn from Garrison's office. Wilds also sent David Snyder, a tall, clean-cut investigative reporter who hailed from Iowa, to examine the district attorney's expense vouchers at City Hall.

Rosemary James tried to make an appointment with Garrison. When he claimed to be too busy, she asked the question on the phone. "Are you investigating the Kennedy assassination?" "I will neither confirm nor deny that," he replied. To a reporter, she later wrote, that was tantamount to saying yes but "you'll have to get your information somewhere else." Snyder meanwhile had hit a paper trail detailing the expenses of Garrison's aides on all those fruitless trips. On February 16 the three reporters pieced together their information and wrote their story. At ten o'clock the next morning, James went to Garrison's office and handed it to him. After glancing at the first page, he handed it back. She asked for a reaction and he repeated, "I will neither confirm nor deny it." She said later if Garrison had asked her to withhold the story they would have. "All he had to do was say no," she said. "He wanted us to print it." The newspaper's management told Garrison they were going to publish the piece. "Go ahead," Garrison said.[9]

It appeared that afternoon, Friday, February 17. The story centered on the hard information Snyder had dug out: the money, $8,000 that the district attorney's office had spent so far. DA HERE LAUNCHES FULL JFK DEATH "PLOT" PROBE, the headline shouted. MYSTERIOUS TRIPS COST LARGE SUMS, informed the subhead. The article itemized thirty-two expenditures chronologically between November 25, 1966, and February 13, 1967. Garrison wasn't interested in suppressing this news. Public disclosure was inevitable and he was plainly relishing the idea. What he didn't expect was the unflattering slant, riveting attention not on the historic or heroic implications, but on the petty issue of grubby old money. When a reporter from the Times-Picayune asked about "the trips," Garrison understandably "bristled" and used "an unprintable phrase." But that same afternoon, he called the paper's news desk and said the article "was substantially correct."[10]

Despite his role in breaking the story, Dave Snyder thought it was "nothing special." He soon learned otherwise. He was working late that day when the phones began to ring with inquiries from all over the world about Garrison's "probe." The first call was from Scotland, he later said, "and that made me realize what we had." What they had was a story with international sizzle. About 5:30 P.M. a call came in that gave it local sizzle. It was from David Ferrie, and Snyder took it, but he had no idea that he was speaking to Garrison's primary suspect. Ferrie said he had read their article and that their story was true, that Garrison was investigating the assassination. Garrison, he said, had "staked out" his apartment, and he offered to tell Snyder about it. Ferrie said, too, that he was physically ill and his voice was barely audible, his breathing "unsteady."[11] He also expressed his fear of being arrested, which would become the principal theme of his last days. He lived close to the newspaper and told Snyder to hurry over before he changed his mind. Snyder did. As they climbed the stairs to his second floor apartment, Ferrie's "steps were feeble" and he said he had encephalitis. He didn't mention it then but he had also been having severe headaches. Without knowing it, he had suffered one, perhaps two, "small bleeds," minor ruptures in a blood vessel at the back of his head.[12] That evening Ferrie was living on borrowed time.

The two talked for the next four and a half hours. Ferrie laid out what he knew about Garrison's case and the role Garrison thought he had played. Ferrie felt persecuted and angry about his harassment and that of his friends. He poured out his bitterness. He was thinking about filing a lawsuit against Garrison and Jack Martin. And, he told Snyder, as he had all those before him, that he did not know Lee Harvey Oswald. Garrison's investigation, Ferrie said, was "an utter waste of time."[13]

The next day, the interview dominated the front page of the *New Orleans States-Item*: "Definite" JFK Death Plot in New Orleans, DA Aide Quoted: Eyed as Pilot of "Getaway" Craft—Flier. Accompanying the story was a large picture of David Ferrie. In back was an editorial questioning the $8,000 in "unexplained" expenses and asking "has the District Attorney uncovered some valuable additional evidence or is he merely saving some interesting new information which will gain for him exposure in a national magazine? Mr. Garrison, it seems, should have some explanation."

When Garrison arrived at his office, he found the newspaper on his desk. Here was David Ferrie, of all people, stealing his thunder by publicly confirming, before Garrison himself did, that his investigation was indeed underway, and terming it "an utter waste of time." Garrison's chief suspect had upstaged him in the most demeaning way possible. Garrison reacted typically and in accord with his oft-stated belief that "the best defense is an offense." He held his first Kennedy assassination press conference and attacked both local newspapers for publicizing his investigation. He responded to the editorial and to Ferrie's insult. He also officially confirmed Friday's story. Garrison said his office had established that the Warren Commission erred in its conclusion that President Kennedy was murdered by Lee Harvey Oswald acting alone, and that the plot was developed in New Orleans. "We already have the names of the people in the initial planning," Garrison declared. "We are not wasting our time and we will prove it. Arrests will be made, charges will be filed, and convictions will be obtained." Garrison still had nothing but the testimony of Jack Martin and David Lewis, but with those remarks he crossed the Rubicon. While he would make an even more outlandish claim six days later, this was the preemptive first strike with no possible retreat. He would spend the next four years trying to fulfill, and the rest of his life trying to justify, the note of prosecutorial certainty he sounded that day.[14]

The article published Friday had stirred the world's interest, but when Garrison's Saturday proclamations flashed around the world, expectations soared into the stratosphere and representatives of the international media descended on Tulane and Broad. "Does District Attorney Jim Garrison really have a solid investigation brewing into the alleged New Orleans plot which led to the assassination of President Kennedy in Dallas?" asked one newspaper. "The world was waiting for an answer Sunday."[15] The worldwide reaction surprised Garrison and also presented him with a problem. All those newspeople in town were clamoring for his next utterance but he had nothing to tell them. All he had was a theory based on linkages provided by a prevaricator* and his protégé. Garrison solved this dilemma by staging some theatrics at the Fontainebleau Motor Hotel where he held another press conference on Monday. The representatives from the two local newspapers he specifically uninvited. Garrison chose a private facility to avoid the legal implications of barring them from a public building.

Act One of Garrison's show was performed at his office. At about 1:30 P.M., the dozens of press representatives waiting for him since 10:00 that morning were asked to list their names and news affiliations. Then, except for those from the New Orleans States-Item and the Times-Picayune, they were called a few at a time into a small room and given the location of the press conference. This they were asked not to reveal to others, meaning those from the offending newspapers. Six of them showed up at the motel anyway, but were barred from the room. "Remove 'em by force," Garrison shouted, "throw them out if necessary." One reporter who tried to enter was shoved out the door and into the corridor by a Garrison aide.[16] Garrison spent most of his time complaining about the premature disclosure of his probe. Arrests, which before had been "just a few weeks away," were now "months away," he said. As for his investigation, he added nothing to what he

---

* Garrison himself told Richard Billings that Jack Martin invented stories and that he harbored intense hostility toward David Ferrie (Billings Personal Notes, Dec. 29, 1966, p. 4).

had said on Saturday. One reporter said afterwards that Garrison had delivered an "hour-long no comment." The feud Garrison had manufactured between himself and the local newspapers served its diversionary function, giving him something to talk about.[17]

Before Garrison could devise something further to say, he was freed of that burden by David Ferrie's death.

On February 22, sometime after four o'clock in the morning, the already weakened blood vessel at the base of Ferrie's brain ruptured for the last time. At 11:40 Wednesday morning, he was found dead in his bed.[18] Everyone, even Garrison skeptics, found the timing of his death ominous. Oswald had been arrested and promptly murdered; Ferrie came under suspicion and promptly died. No single event gave Garrison a greater credibility boost than David Ferrie's untimely demise.

He died of natural causes from a congenital condition, a berry aneurysm, according to doctors Nicholas J. Chetta, the Orleans Parish Coroner, and Ronald A. Welsh, the pathologist who conducted the autopsy.[19] But Garrison, adept at exploiting circumstances, declared Ferrie's death an "apparent suicide," and anointed him "one of history's most important individuals." "Evidence developed by our office," Garrison said, "has long since confirmed that he was involved in events culminating in the assassination of President Kennedy." Other suicides by other conspirators might be forthcoming, he suggested. With Ferrie's death, the district attorney's "unexplained" expenditures vanished permanently from the news. More significantly, the individual who would have been a far more dangerous adversary than anyone left on Garrison's playing field was gone for good.

Who was this man whose death was such a windfall for Garrison?

In a case cluttered with peculiar characters, David Ferrie was unique. His failure as a young man to become a priest was a great disappointment to him, and in later years he joined a sect known as the Orthodox Old Catholic Church of North America.[20] Early pictures, before the disease alopecia left him hairless—and he began resorting to homemade reddish-brown wigs and eyebrows sometimes carelessly constructed— show an intense-looking dark-haired man with pleasant features. He taught high school in Ohio but soon turned to flying. He was an aviator of considerable skill, active and popular in the Cleveland Civil Air

Patrol, his chief avocation and the hub of his social life. When he moved to New Orleans, he continued to work with the organization there.[*]

In 1953 Ferrie's flying talent caught the eye of famed aviator-industrialist and hero of two world wars, Eddie Rickenbacker. He was president of Eastern Airlines when he wrote in Ferrie's file, "This man's efforts bear watching and his qualifications justify his being used and helped whenever possible in line of duty—and even beyond."[21] Ferrie began working at Eastern in 1951, but he was out of step almost from the beginning. He resisted authority and, as one writer later put it, he had an aversion to soap. There were cumulative infractions and complaints. Then on August 11, 1961, he was arrested in New Orleans for a "crime against nature" involving a fifteen-year-old boy and indecent behavior with three others. Though the charges were dropped, the damage had been done. Eastern fired him.[22] He appealed, and began working as an investigator-researcher for attorney G. Wray Gill and Guy Banister in return for a small salary and the help of both men in his case against Eastern.

Although critical of President Kennedy's handling of the Bay of Pigs invasion, Ferrie approved of Kennedy's civil rights and fiscal programs. He was anti-Communist and anti-Castro, but the rumors of his participation in the Bay of Pigs invasion have never been proved. He claimed he had never been to Cuba, and once remarked that Castro could be a friend of the United States.[23] In 1961 he participated with anti-Castro Cuban leader Sergio Arcacha Smith in the so-called "raid" of an ammunition bunker in Houma, Louisiana.[†] Since they had a key to the bunker and no report of theft was ever made by the company that owned it, this incident was more like a transfer. Martin's stories and Garrison's theories are

---

[*] The discovery in 1993 of a photograph taken at a Civil Air Patrol cookout with Ferrie and Oswald both in it, though not together, was heralded as a major breakthrough by Garrison advocates, who believe it established a definitive link. But it *established* only an overlap of association with that organization, which from the outset was a possibility David Ferrie never denied, but didn't recall. (See note p. 28, and chapter 15, note 10). The owner of the picture, John Ciravolo, attributes no historical importance to it because, he said, it proves nothing. "I'm in the picture," Ciravolo pointed out, "and I'm sure David Ferrie wouldn't remember me either" (Ciravolo, telephone conversation with author, July 9, 1997).

[†] Ferrie also built a miniature "submarine" out of a B-25's reserve gas tank, with the quixotic notion of attacking Cuban harbor installations with it. It ended up in a garbage dump.

predicated on Ferrie's involvement with Smith and his group extending into the summer before the assassination. But it ended almost two years earlier, in October 1961, because of disapproval in the Cuban community over Ferrie's friendships with young boys.[24] During the summer in question, Ferrie was fighting for his professional life and fulfilling his duties to Banister and Gill. His appeal of Eastern's firing, which prompted an exhaustive investigation by the FAA and two hearings in Miami, was not resolved until August 1963, when it was finally rejected.

The stroke that killed Ferrie may have been precipitated by the extraordinary stress he experienced in the last months of his life.[25] His declining physical condition was obvious the Saturday before he died when two of Garrison's aides arrived at his apartment to interview him. He let them in, then "moaned and groaned with each step he took up the stairs" and told them "he had not been able to keep anything on his stomach for a couple of days." Throughout the interrogation he was stretched out on the living room sofa. Nevertheless, he was relieved to see them. He had been calling their office, he explained, because he was worried about the rumors "that he was going to get arrested."* Garrison's men were not encouraging; when they left, he was still frightened.

Ferrie expressed that fear repeatedly after Snyder's interview with him was published, which turned out to be the last five days of his life. On each of those days, Ferrie telephoned either Snyder or his wife, Barbara. Some days more than once. The calls, usually long, were baffled monologues in which Ferrie tried to figure out the reason for Garrison's campaign against him and sought reassurance that he wasn't going to be arrested. If that happened, he asked Snyder to arrange for him to take a lie-detector test. Snyder and his wife both agree about Ferrie's state of mind. "Ferrie was scared to death," they say, "scared to death of Garrison, scared of being arrested."[26] Ferrie was frightened because of the newspaper reports of his 1961 "crime against nature" charge. His predilection for teenage boys was a matter of public record. Many would regard him

---

* Twice during this interview Ferrie asked Asst. D.A. Andrew Sciambra to arrange for him to meet with Garrison personally. Sciambra countered by offering to relay to Garrison whatever Ferrie had to say. Ferrie replied that he wanted to talk to Garrison himself and "look him in the face" (Andrew Sciambra, memorandum dated Feb. 28, 1967, regarding David Ferrie interview with Sciambra and Louis Ivon on Feb. 18, 1967).

as a child molester, and they are not dealt with kindly in prison. Those last days, Ferrie was terrified by that, not (as Garrison and later Stone depicted) the fear of being murdered because of his knowledge of the assassination. He had no such knowledge.

In good spirits on Sunday, Ferrie called Dave Snyder and said he was going to meet with an attorney about his lawsuit. Reporters were continuing to pester him though and that evening he asked Louis Ivon (with whom he was friendly) for help to escape from them. Garrison said okay, hoping the favor might encourage Ferrie's cooperation, and Ivon put him up for the night at the Fontainebleau "to give him some rest."[27]

Ferrie called Snyder the next day from an attorney's office. He asked for the dates that Oswald had been in New Orleans, which Snyder supplied. Afterwards, Ferrie visited Carlos Bringuier, who had scuffled with Oswald in 1963, and inquired about Oswald's associates and the date the alleged conspiracy supposedly began. But Bringuier, who later would recall Ferrie's difficulty in walking, was unable to help him. That same day, Ferrie stopped by the FBI office. He later told Snyder that the agents were laughing about Garrison's "investigation."[28]

He was at the New Orleans Public Library on Tuesday "perusing" the Warren Report, looking for facts to fill in the blanks. Talking to Barbara Snyder that evening, he spoke again of his fear of arrest and his bewilderment over Garrison's targeting him. He also complained of headaches. Meanwhile, Snyder had heard from *Washington Post* reporter George Lardner, Jr.; he wanted to interview Ferrie, who was balking. Snyder agreed to help and that evening he, too, had his final telephone conversation with Ferrie, assuring him Lardner was okay. Ferrie, "oozing good-natured confidence," agreed to speak to him.[29]

Lardner, the last man to see Ferrie alive, arrived at his apartment about midnight, stayed until almost 4:00 A.M., and found him "in a good mood." Ferrie impressed Lardner as an "intelligent, well-versed guy [on] a broad range of subjects."* Garrison's probe, Ferrie told

---

* Ferrie spoke several languages, owned 3,000 books and many, including Garrison, considered him brilliant. To the CAP cadets he was "charismatic": When he spoke about flying they forgot about his appearance. "It was like being children," one said recently, "at the foot of Christ" (John Ciravolo, telephone conversation with author, July 9, 1997).

Lardner, would end up being a "witch hunt." One last time, Ferrie declared that he "never knew Oswald and had no recollection of ever having met him." Twice Ferrie voiced his concern about being arrested. He asked Lardner to withhold most of what he said for fear of antagonizing the district attorney, which might "trigger" his arrest. Lardner later said they parted on "a cheerful note."[30]

Ferrie was found the next morning lying on his back in bed naked with a sheet pulled up to his chest. The first Garrison aides on the scene were Asst. D.A. Alcock and Louis Ivon, who had been watching the apartment all night from across the street.[31] The notion that he committed suicide was based solely on two typewritten messages found among his belongings, which were undated and unsigned. One was a bitter criticism of society, especially its judicial system; the other, an aggrieved statement about a ruined relationship.[32] These communiqués were written by a tormented man, but when he wrote them, and to what end is unknown. Had Ferrie shot, hanged, or poisoned himself, thrown himself beneath the wheels of a moving vehicle, or fallen on a sword, they might be properly interpreted as "suicide notes." But Ferrie had died of a ruptured blood vessel, sleeping in his bed. When last seen, he was cheerful. Despite the debilitated condition of his body, he spent his last two days on earth dragging himself around the city, gathering information for the $500,000 lawsuit he intended to file against his enemies. He was a man with a mission, with a reason to live.

Though no evidence supported it, Garrison theorized that Ferrie had deliberately overdosed on his thyroid medication, Proloid, a medical improbability due to the slow-acting nature of the drug. One doctor recently said that Ferrie could have swallowed an entire bottle of it without an immediate effect. Garrison persisted in his contention, however, and pressured the coroner to return a suicide verdict. Dr. Chetta refused. The autopsy pathologist, Dr. Ronald Welsh, in a 1993 interview with me, said he had been outraged by Garrison's campaign to make something out of nothing and corrupt the scientific process.[33]

But that was only part of it.

With David Ferrie dead, Garrison could do what he couldn't do while Ferrie was alive: brand him a conspirator in the president's murder without fear of legal repercussions.

Garrison immediately announced that he and his aides had made the decision that very morning "to arrest" Ferrie "early next week." That was not true. But for twenty-seven years, no one in the Garrison camp admitted it publicly. In 1994 James Alcock went on record with the truth. "To my knowledge," he told me, speaking each word deliberately, "there was no intent to arrest David Ferrie." Alcock should know. He was one of those Garrison said was present when the "decision" was made.[34]

Alive, Ferrie had required careful handling. As he told George Lardner that last night, Garrison realized he had "a tiger by the tail."[35] Ferrie had endured arrest by Garrison in 1963, knew it had been triggered by a hostile alcoholic who was at it again, and this second time around Ferrie was preparing to strike back with legal action. His death removed that threat. And the blinking neon conspirator's sign that Jack Martin had hung around Ferrie's neck would now glow brighter from the grave.

Had Ferrie lived, Garrison's case against Clay Shaw might have died before its birth in Garrison's imagination. Not only did Garrison have no evidence against Ferrie,* he had no witness linking Ferrie and Shaw. The loss of his principal suspect should have signaled the end to Garrison's case. He had had nothing to begin with, and now he had a way out. Many expected him to take it. Instead, he elevated Ferrie into a key figure in the Kennedy assassination, which paved the way for the first of Garrison's four miraculous recoveries. For it flushed out a former friend of Ferrie, a pliant and crucial witness who would soon provide a legal foundation for a case against Clay Shaw. At the time he proclaimed David Ferrie "one of history's most important individuals," Garrison was wholly unaware of this man. His name was Perry Raymond Russo.

---

* Garrison staffer Tom Bethell was worried about the impression Ferrie's innocuous file made on outsiders who read it. Bethell explained his concern to Mark Lane, who suggested Bethell tell people that all the significant data in it had been moved to a secret file (Bethell Diary, p. 17).

CHAPTER SIX

THE FRIEND

... it was like a big roller coaster.
I couldn't get off.[1]
—Perry Russo, 1971

The death of David Ferrie was heralded in banner headlines around the globe and new additions to the world's press poured into New Orleans: two reporters from the Soviet Union; teams from *Paris-Match*, the BBC, and Canadian Broadcasting Company; journalists from the three television networks, the U.S. wire services, most major American newspapers, and a few minor ones. This media circus cluttered the halls of the courthouse, tracked Garrison's every move, and encouraged his garrulousness.

Two days after Ferrie died, Garrison attended a luncheon at the Petroleum Club with fifty local businessmen who pledged to privately finance his investigation.* The idea was Garrison's own. After the press revealed his expenditures, he vowed to maintain secrecy by using donated or borrowed money that wouldn't require a public accounting. The founding members of this group, which named itself "Truth and Consequences, Inc.," were three prominent, wealthy New Orleanians. Membership was meant to be secret but a writer for a local magazine soon identified some of them.[2]

Both before and after the luncheon, Garrison held impromptu press conferences for a horde of newsmen. In the one *after*, he dropped a bombshell. "My staff and I solved the case weeks ago," Garrison declared. "I wouldn't say this if we didn't have evidence beyond a shadow of a doubt. We know the key individuals, the cities involved, and how it was done." Arrests, though not imminent, would be made; and other

---

* Private financing of the public prosecutor is today prohibited by the American Bar Association's rules of ethics (Posner, *Case Closed* [New York: Random House, 1993], note at page 432).

suicides were to be expected. "The only way they are going to get away from us, is to kill themselves," he said. "We are going to be able to arrest every person involved—at least every person who is still living. I'm sure that there will be convictions"; "we're now building a case," he said, and "it's a case we will not lose."[3] Garrison had no evidence to support his new allegations. But his timing (on the heels of Ferrie's seemingly mysterious death) was exquisite. Many assumed he must have some mighty trump up his sleeve. Some on his staff, who already believed they were engaged in a righteous endeavor, now exhibited an alarming hubris. Anything that advanced Garrison's cause seemed justified.

It was at this moment, in this overwrought atmosphere, that Perry Russo, a twenty-five-year-old insurance trainee living in Baton Rouge, stepped from obscurity to center stage. He had once known David Ferrie and read with interest the newspaper articles about his death, in particular Garrison's labeling him one of history's most important individuals.

That morning Russo called a Baton Rouge newspaper and told reporter Bill Bankston that he had once been a friend of David Ferrie.[4] Bankston questioned him on the telephone and then in person at the newspaper for about an hour. Russo said he called to "get the whole story down with somebody." In view of the remarkable ballooning of his tale the following week, Russo's first account of the "whole story" is revealing. Bankston found it simple, believable, and innocuous.

Russo said he met Ferrie in New Orleans around April 1962 through a friend in the Civil Air Patrol. He described Ferrie as "screwy but sharp." He and Ferrie had a number of general political discussions, initiated by Russo (who was majoring in political science). Ferrie talked frequently about how easy it would be to assassinate a president but had not initially mentioned Kennedy. About a month before the assassination, however, Ferrie had said, "We will get him, and it won't be long." Russo didn't take Ferrie seriously. He knew the South teemed with people who detested Kennedy, and had heard others make similar remarks. "I imagine a lot of people would say, I'd like to get the president, or something to that effect," Bankston later said, and since Ferrie was "a strange individual," he might be more likely to say it than most.[5]

Russo made no mention to Bankston of a plot to kill the president, no mention of knowing or encountering Oswald, no mention of Ferrie knowing Oswald, and nothing about Clay Shaw, by name, alias, or description. Yet Russo's rapidly escalating recollections would shortly precipitate Shaw's arrest. In a brief five days, the essentially innocent tale Russo told at the newspaper burgeoned into *the plot that killed the president*. It began that afternoon when Bankston's piece recounting Russo's experiences with Ferrie appeared on the front page of the *Baton Rouge State-Times*, bringing Russo to Garrison's attention.[*]

"Has anyone talked to Russo yet?" Garrison asked Asst. D.A. Andrew Sciambra. It was eight o'clock the next morning, a Saturday, and Garrison had telephoned him at home. Practically the forgotten man in this case, despite his prominent role, Sciambra, known by his childhood nickname Moo Moo, was a handsome thirty-one-year-old recent law school graduate who "had had a hard life" and gone to law school later than most. He was surely grateful to Garrison for taking him on board, and the sentiment flowed both ways. Garrison treated Sciambra like the fair-haired boy. Yet when Garrison called that morning, he had no way of knowing how important this assignment would turn out to be.

Sciambra was soon on his way to Baton Rouge with a briefcase full of photographs, including one of Clay Shaw. After tracking Russo down at an LSU practice baseball game, Sciambra spent much of that day with him. It was several hours later when they returned to Russo's apartment and Sciambra commenced the interview, reportedly making sketchy notes on a legal-size pad. Russo, an articulate young man with dark hair and a trim physique, did most of the talking. During this three-hour session, the first tentative but important changes occurred in Russo's story.

He haltingly identified a picture of Lee Harvey Oswald as David Ferrie's roommate shortly before the president's assassination. But the roommate Russo described was "a typical beatnik, extremely dirty, with his hair all messed up," a "bushy" beard and "dirty blond hair." Oswald was clean-shaven and almost compulsively neat about his personal grooming. As Milton Brener first pointed out, Russo's description seems to fit Ferrie's known roommate, James Lewallen, a thirty-eight-

---

[*] That evening Russo repeated his innocuous story to three radio and television reporters. When asked if he had known Lee Harvey Oswald, he added a remark that would come back to haunt him. Russo stated that he never heard of Oswald until he saw his picture on television after the assassination (*Chicago Tribune*, March 16, 1967).

year-old former Air Force pilot who worked as a mechanic at the near-by NASA space facility and lived with David Ferrie in September 1963. Lewallen was often unshaven and because of his work his clothes were often dirty. A picture of him published at the time shows a narrow face and bone structure not unlike Oswald's. Russo didn't identify the roommate as "Oswald" but said "the name Leon really rings a bell." Lewallen was sometimes known as "Lou" or "Lee."[6]

When shown a picture of Clay Shaw, Russo thought he had glimpsed him twice in New Orleans, once with David Ferrie at a service station he owned, and once at a Kennedy rally at the Nashville Street Wharf. But that man wore "tight pants" and ogled young boys, while Clay Shaw dressed conservatively and behaved in a dignified manner. Here, again, Russo did not identify him by name.

If Russo was trying to accommodate his dedicated interrogator, he sure-ly succeeded where Ferrie was concerned. He described him talking about the slow speed of the presidential car, the need for "availability of exit," and how he "could jump into any plane under the sun and fly it out of the country to a place that would not extradite, such as Cuba or Bra-zil."[7] Russo had mentioned none of this to Bill Bankston the day before.

Russo's information was tentative and questionable but it fit Garrison's theory about David Ferrie's involvement in the assassination. And by placing Clay Shaw in Ferrie's circle, Russo had provided Garrison with a live suspect to pursue. Garrison instructed Sciambra to *get Russo to New Orleans.* Early Monday morning, Sciambra telephoned Russo and he agreed to come, unaware that he was embarking on a sort of Twilight Zone journey and that his life would never again be the same. He was about to undergo a series of procedures called "objectifying" by Garrison, who touted them as the ultimate truth-seeking tools. First, he was questioned after being injected with sodium Pentothal. Two days later, he submitted to the first of several interviews under hypnosis.

Russo arrived at Tulane and Broad about 11:00 that morning and quickly agreed to take the sodium Pentothal.[8] Before it was adminis-tered, though, he and Sciambra worked several hours (perhaps as many as six) with an artist on a sketch of the roommate. The difficulty arose, Sciambra later claimed, because the figure wasn't "dirty and disheveled" enough to suit Russo. Russo told it differently. All day, he later said,

Sciambra kept asking him about the roommate. "You sure this is not the same guy?" Sciambra said, referring to a picture. "Well, I don't know," Russo replied, "it looks a lot like him . . . but I know that's Oswald. Lee Oswald." Sciambra then asked the artist to "touch up the photograph" to make it fit Russo's dirty beatnik.[9] So the sketch that resembled Oswald actually began with a picture that Russo knew to be him, which was altered to fit Russo's recollections. Once they finally finished with that, they moved to Mercy Hospital for the first "objectifying" step.

Contrary to popular belief, sodium Pentothal does not elicit "the truth." It only "suppresses inhibitions," including those against fantasizing. If a person is trying to hide something, he may be more likely to reveal it because he is more relaxed. But if a person is inclined toward fantasizing, the drug may encourage that. As Dr. Donald Gallant, a professor of psychiatry at Tulane University Medical School, stated at the time, the drug is "quite unreliable" in establishing a person's truthfulness. A person can still lie, Dr. Gallant pointed out, while under the drug's influence. Moreover, as with hypnosis, suggestibility is a problem, meaning great caution and professionalism must be employed in the questioning, which was not the case here.[10]

The procedure took place in the emergency ward operating room. Coroner Nicholas Chetta administered the drug, while Asst. D.A. Alvin Oser reportedly took notes. Moo Moo Sciambra conducted the interview. Dr. Chetta first injected a dose of glucose into Perry Russo's arm. Then, at 3:28 P.M., he began the sodium Pentothal and continued for about forty minutes, ending the session at 4:10 P.M. Russo was semiconscious during the entire time and remembered none of the questioning that occurred. The only record is the memorandum prepared by Sciambra the following day.[11]

According to it, Russo again described the roommate as "very dirty." Though this was still wildly off the mark, Russo added a smattering of details that fit Oswald.* He did not know Clay Shaw, Russo said. But when Sciambra asked if he knew "Clay Bertrand," Russo replied he did,

---

* He was "around 25 years old"; wore a "wedding band"; "was a bug on history" and "read a lot." He was also a "nut about guns," owning, as Oswald did, both a pistol and a bolt action rifle (with a telescopic sight), which, Russo said, he saw him cleaning one day.

that "he is a queer" and described him, providing some facts that fit Shaw. ("A tall man with white kinky hair, sort of slender.") But Russo had not recalled the name "Clay Bertrand" independently. Sciambra brought it up. Nor was this the first time Russo had heard it. Sciambra "first voiced" the name Bertrand, Russo later said, sometime prior to the sodium Pentothal interview, when Sciambra told him Bertrand was "the name [Shaw] went as."[12]

In addition to the other two sightings, Russo now said he met "Bertrand" at Ferrie's apartment. This paved the way for Russo's crucial recollections about the assassination plotting session.* Sciambra put that on the last page of his report and described it in a single, strangely hollow paragraph. David Ferrie is in his apartment talking. Present and presumably listening are Russo, Ferrie's "roommate," and "Clay Bertrand." Ferrie's first words are almost straight from the Bankston article: "We are going to kill John F. Kennedy . . . it won't be long." Ferrie said he could plan the perfect presidential assassination and repeated his earlier comments about his flying skills providing "availability of exit out of the country."[13] This borrowed and skimpy David Ferrie monologue is the sum total of *the plot that killed the president* at this point. At dinner that evening, Russo denied that he ever met anyone named "Bertrand."[14] Garrison dismissed this as a by-product of the drug.

Sciambra wrote a fairly cut-and-dried account of the sodium Pentothal interview. But Russo later described the experience in dramatically different terms. He recalled lying on a table, the needle inserted into his right arm, as "a clear substance" was administered, which he thought took about ten minutes, and he felt nothing out of the ordinary. Then the Pentothal bottle was attached and Russo reacted instantly. "My head started spinning round and round—things started closing in on me and tightening up and I started getting violent and upset." "I knew I was upset," he said. "I recall being bothered—I didn't want to be bothered, didn't want anybody to touch me and I didn't want anybody close to me." At first "the doctors were holding me down." Then "I felt like I was kicking at them." He became violent and had to be physically restrained. "It seemed like they strapped my whole body, they strapped the right

---

* It was Sciambra's prodding for "details about Clay Bertrand being up in Ferrie's apartment" that led Russo to "remember" the plotting session.

arm down and they held the left arm . . . and they strapped me around the waist and around the legs." "I just kept swinging and twisting and squirming away" and "the needle came out once, at least, maybe more." "That's when they strapped me down." "Oser . . . was holding me down right at the waist. He's big!" "He just physically got on top of me and I kept saying, I remember saying 'Get away you mother fuckers, get away,' and I kicked at them and I was swinging at them." After the session was over, Russo was unstrapped. But when he tried to stand up, he couldn't. "I started to fall down," he said. He was "dizzy"; "had to hold on to something" and was "sick" for "a couple of hours." He also felt abandoned by Sciambra and the others. "Everybody was interested in going," Russo said. "They all left." "I felt like I was dropped like a coot."[15]

Considering Russo's reaction, it seems remarkable that Sciambra managed to question him. But he did, and Garrison was tremendously impressed by the results. At last he felt he had evidence he could use to make an arrest. The following day he instructed Sciambra to arrange for Russo to see Clay Shaw. "We got Shaw," Sciambra told Russo, "we need you to make a positive identification . . . [then] we're gonna take it from there." Sciambra withheld their intent to arrest Shaw and minimized Russo's importance. "Then you will have done your duty," Sciambra said, "[and] we're probably not even gonna use you in the courtroom."[16]

Russo made the first identification from the back seat of a car parked outside Shaw's residence where he, Sciambra and Oser "waited and waited and waited" for Shaw to appear. Later, Russo described the thoughts passing through his mind as he sat there. "Shaw was anti-Kennedy," Russo said, and "enjoys being beat by whips . . . Kennedy represented youth to him" and since there would never be "a set of circumstances where [Shaw] could get whipped by Kennedy," Shaw was driven to "kill him." Someone in Garrison's office told him that, Russo said.[17] Shaw finally opened his front door for a friend and Russo said, "Yeah, that's him." But Garrison's men weren't satisfied. They sent Russo to knock on Shaw's door.* Shaw opened it. Using a false name,

---

* This was a peculiar move. For if Russo really did recognize Shaw from the evening they shared at Ferrie's plotting session, Shaw should have recognized Russo too. (Shaw later said he had never laid eyes on Russo until he knocked on his door.)

Russo introduced himself as an insurance salesman and handed Shaw a business card. Shaw told him he didn't need any insurance, and Russo went back to the car and confirmed the identification.[18] He had now *done his duty.* Garrison wanted to arrest Clay Shaw immediately after Russo's doorstep identification of him. But Asst. D.A. Charles Ward and Louis Ivon objected, and Garrison agreed to wait.[19]

Russo later said that when he first arrived in New Orleans "he made it clear" to Sciambra and the others "that there was grave doubt in his mind as to the identity of Clay Shaw but the representative[s] of the DA's office," Sciambra in particular, "kept telling him that he was positive." "The real culprit," Russo insisted, was Sciambra, who "continually" implanted "the identification in his mind." Sciambra, he said, would show him a picture of Shaw and say, "That is the man you saw there." Russo called this "a complete brainwashing job,"[20] which may be more accurate than he realized. For the information elicited by Sciambra's leading questions while Russo was drugged was fed back to him afterwards to persuade him of its validity. This information also guided the upcoming first hypnosis session, which, in turn, reinforced and expanded Russo's information. Garrison meant for these "objectifying" procedures to convince the public that Russo's story was true. But the one they convinced was Russo himself. *The plot that killed the president* was transferred like a virus from Garrison's imagination to Sciambra's and, from there, to Russo's recollections. Afterwards, as Russo would eventually admit, he could no longer distinguish what was real from what was not.[21]

During the frenetic five days after Russo first emerged and before Shaw's arrest, Garrison took Dean Andrews to dinner one last time. But this was no social occasion. Garrison had used all his wiles over the past few months trying to entice Andrews to identify Shaw as Bertrand. He had minimized the importance of the identification by falsely claiming he had "other witnesses" who could do it. And he had played the ego card. "We will ride to glory together," he told Andrews. Nothing had worked. Now Garrison took a different tack. If Andrews wouldn't cooperate, he would at least keep quiet. If he didn't, Garrison made it clear he would end up in "the Bastille." A deal was struck. Andrews agreed that although he would not say Shaw was Bertrand, he wouldn't deny it either. Or, in Andrews's words, "I won't say he is and I won't say he ain't." Andrews told writer Edward Epstein that he had no choice, that had he refused, "the Jolly Green Giant would pounce on me like a thousand-pound canary."[22] He was going to pounce anyway but Andrews had no way of knowing that. He thought he was saving his hide.

Garrison had deftly neutralized the only man alive who could have rained on his parade. Only Andrews knew with certainty that Clay Shaw was not "Clay Bertrand," that there *was* no such person. Garrison could now arrest Clay Shaw confident in the knowledge that Andrews would not call a press conference and contradict his scenario. For an agonizing time, Andrews respected the deal he had made but the increasing sense of guilt eventually caused him to speak out. By then, it was too late to save himself, and almost too late to help Clay Shaw. For once Perry Russo surfaced, Garrison had moved swiftly.

Sciambra first interviewed Russo in Baton Rouge on February 25. Russo arrived in New Orleans February 27, and Garrison ordered the sodium Pentothal questioning that same day. Russo knocked on Clay Shaw's door and identified him February 28. The next day, March 1, Garrison issued the subpoena for Shaw to appear for questioning at the district attorney's office and had him arrested.

Three days earlier, NBC reporter Walter Sheridan had told Shaw about the "rumor" that he was the "mysterious Clay Bertrand." Shaw had replied that it would be absurd for him to assume an alias, that he was too well-known. His picture had been in the local newspapers and on television, he said, and his "size alone" made him conspicuous. The idea was so ridiculous Shaw didn't connect it to the subpoena when he heard about it.[23]

That afternoon, as he sat in the interrogation room trying to reach his attorney, Shaw was unaware of what was happening a few feet away. In addition to hidden microphones, the room he was in was equipped with a viewing "mirror" that allowed people in an adjacent room to see inside. From there a Life magazine photographer was snapping pictures of him. Others joined the photographer from time to time, among them Perry Russo and Andrew Sciambra. Shaw, unsuspecting, was seated at a desk facing what looked to him like an ordinary mirror. On the other side, Russo stood up close to what he later referred to as "the window," observing Shaw. Russo later said that Sciambra told him, "That is the man you saw." Russo agreed. Then Sciambra took him back into his office and Russo left the building by climbing down the fire escape.[24]

He went down alone. Garrison didn't want anyone to see Russo with his aides for fear someone might discover the identity of his new witness. The media learned of his existence from the application for the search warrant on Shaw's home. But he was referred to only as a "confidential informant." Speculation was intense and the news representatives made every effort to identify him, but only Garrison and his top aides knew it was Perry Russo.

The following day Garrison released to the press a list of some of the articles seized at Shaw's home. Included were a black gown, a net hat, a black hood and cape, a chain and five whips.* (Though none of these articles had any bearing on the assassination, a *Life* photographer took pictures of them that evening at Garrison's home.)[25] † Shaw's homosexuality was now public knowledge. Garrison had accomplished that part of his goal.

As a veteran of World War II, Shaw had experienced the madness of war. He had joined the U.S. Army as a private and risen to the rank of major. He had served in France and received that country's Croix de Guerre, the U.S. Legion of Merit, and Bronze Star. But nothing in his past prepared him for the bolt of legal lightning that struck him that day. It was the beginning of an ordeal that he said made him "feel like a character in a Kafka novel."

About two hours before Shaw was booked and released on bail, at seven o'clock that same evening, Perry Russo was further "objectified," this time by hypnosis. The hypnosis had been scheduled for the evening hours to minimize the possibility that someone would spot Russo and identify him.[26] It went forward despite the unexpected arrest of Clay Shaw. Al Oser and Andrew Sciambra again took Russo to the office of Coroner Nicholas Chetta. Also on hand were Russo's friend Steve Derby, a stenographer, and the New Orleans family physician who performed

---

* Shaw later explained that the unusual items were all "residue" from old Mardi Gras costumes. He noted that Garrison's men left behind Greek and Japanese outfits, which, if taken, would have indicated the context of the others (Shaw Journal, March 1, 1967, p. 19).
† Garrison also showed them to some reporters and researchers.

the hypnosis and conducted the interview, Dr. Esmond Fatter.

Dr. Fatter didn't set out to "plant a story" in Russo's mind. But he posed his questions in a way that virtually guaranteed that a story would be planted. Using hypnosis to elicit information is not the same as using it in medical treatment. A different technique is required. Dr. Fatter seemed unaware of that. The problem is the phenomenon of heightened suggestibility, that is, the inclination of the subject "to believe what others desire [him] to believe." The very definition of hypnosis is "a trance-like state of altered awareness that is characterized by extreme suggestibility."[27]

In recent years the public has learned much about this in the controversy over recovered memories. But even in 1967 the medical community was aware of the nature of the hypnotic state. "False ideas and beliefs can be implanted upon the mind of a subject who is in a trance without any intent on the part of the questioner to implant such beliefs," Dr. Herbert Spiegel, an expert on the subject, wrote in 1967, "if the subject thinks that the examiner or hypnotizer desires him to entertain such beliefs or if such beliefs seem to him to be necessary to support other beliefs or to please the hypnotizer or whomever he represents."[28] How the questioner interacts with the subject is clearly a tricky business, requiring finesse and a high degree of awareness. Dr. Fatter exhibited neither.[29]

A later report from the American Medical Association's Council on Scientific Affairs, which dealt with the use of hypnosis on "witnesses" of crime, warned that hypnosis "leads to an increased vulnerability to subtle cues and implicit suggestions that may distort recollections in specific ways." Simply "the manner in which a question is framed can influence the response and even produce a response when there is actually no memory." The "transformation" of a "suspicion" into a "vivid pseudomemory" during hypnosis, the report concluded, may result in "serious consequences to the legal process."[30]

Dr. Fatter followed a line of questioning that leaves little doubt about what he was told to explore.* He also had in hand a copy of Sciambra's report on the sodium Pentothal session and used it as a guide. Dr. Fatter

* The discussion that follows is based on the transcript of that March 1, 1967, interview, labeled by Clay Shaw's defense team: "First Hypnotic Session"— "Exhibit F," for presentation at the trial, but never admitted into evidence.

had been well-briefed and the cues and suggestions he communicated to Perry Russo were far from subtle. Fatter was quite explicit.

The visual image he used throughout the interview was "the television screen." He invoked it in his opening sentence and referred to it fifteen times. It turned out to be a powerful device. Russo quickly pinpointed a date, September 16, 1963, when a beer party was underway. The place was Ferrie's apartment but Russo didn't volunteer that, Dr. Fatter told him the location. Fatter also placed the "white-haired man" there with him. And it was Fatter who put the "white-haired man" inside an automobile at a "service station." Russo then obliged him by saying, "He is sitting with Dave." But Fatter had difficulty eliciting the man's name. He referred to him six times before Russo said, "That is a friend of Dave's." Fatter then asked for his name and Russo said, "Clem [not Clay] Bertrand." It was once again Dr. Fatter who first mentioned the name "Clay."

It was also Fatter who interjected "the rifle" into Russo's television program, saying, "I wonder who that is sitting on the sofa with the rifle?" Russo, predictably, said "Leon," Ferrie's roommate, whom Russo earlier in the interview had described, as he had consistently and repeatedly in the past, as "dirty, dirty, dirty." It was Fatter who conjured up the assassination conversation. "See that television screen again," he said, "there will be Bertrand, Ferrie, and Oswald and they are going to discuss a very important matter and there is another man and girl* there and they are talking about assassinating somebody. Look at it and describe it to me." Not too surprisingly, Russo did. "They planned to assassinate President Kennedy," he said. "Dave paced the floor back and forth and he talked and talked and told them if they were to get the president they would fly to Mexico or Cuba [and] on to Brazil and Clem said they could not go to Mexico and Brazil—it involved too much gas expense and the cooperation of Mexican authorities and that wouldn't be possible." Russo then described a bit of squabbling that occurred between "Leon" and "Bertrand."

At the end of the interview, Dr. Fatter urged Russo to provide more details about "how they were going to assassinate the president" and

---

*This was a reference to Russo's friends, Lefty Peterson and Sandra Moffett, who later denied being there. Moffett signed a sworn affidavit stating she did not meet David Ferrie until 1965 (Sandra Moffett McMaines, deposition, June 24, 1968, p. 11).

Russo replied that Dave "said there would be a cross fire and a mob in between and if everybody was looking at the guy who is the diversionary and made the diversionary shot, the other guy could make the good shot." And who was going to take which shot? "They never said," Russo stated.

Russo had finally provided a more fully developed assassination plot. Yet the process that spawned it was grossly flawed.* And why hadn't Russo remembered any of it before? As one writer would later point out, it was difficult to believe Russo's life was so filled with intrigue and high adventure that he had to be drugged and hypnotized to recall a plot to kill the president.

Russo was no tabula rasa when he was put into that trance. Shortly after he arrived in New Orleans, he "had picked up a lot of information from Garrison's people just from the way they asked questions," he later said. "I'm a pretty perceptive guy and besides, when they got through asking me questions, I asked them a lot of questions—like 'Why is this man important?' and so on. I also read every scrap the papers printed about the case before the Shaw hearing."[31]

Only days before he was hypnotized, Russo had attended a dinner at the Royal Orleans Rib Room where his knowledge was substantially advanced. "Eight or ten people" were present, among them Garrison (who arrived late, about ten o'clock), his wife, Sciambra, Russo's friend Steve Derby and Richard Billings. Russo met Garrison for the first time that night. The two spoke "privately for ten or twenty minutes." Garrison asked Russo to put his life on hold "for six months," stay in New Orleans, and come under his "protection." Russo agreed. After they joined the others, he quickly discovered that he was the star of the evening. Garrison "seemed charged up," Russo later said. "He started introducing me to Billings as his prize, his secret weapon." Russo was baffled by this. "Garrison kept offering suggestions of what to tell Billings. I never did understand why he was giving this to a magazine reporter." The dinner turned into a grilling for Russo. "It was pressure, boy," he said, "I felt like I had to convince Billings of things I hadn't even convinced myself of yet."

---

* As noted earlier, suggestibility is also a problem with sodium Pentothal, and Andrew Sciambra, who conducted that interview, was even less cautious than Dr. Fatter.

Billings didn't know what questions to put to him, Russo said, "until Garrison showed him how it all worked." Of course, in explaining how it all worked to Billings, Garrison was also explaining how it all worked to Russo. "Actually," as Russo put it, "I found out more facts about the case that night than I'd ever been told before." The conversation was "all about Clay Shaw and Oswald, stuff like that."[32]

So two nights later, when Russo sat down in Dr. Chetta's crowded office to have his memory refreshed by Dr. Fatter, Russo probably knew as much about Garrison's thinking on the case as anyone.

Perry Russo didn't come to New Orleans expecting to end up being Jim Garrison's "prize" or "his secret weapon." Nor was he an innocent lamb entangled merely by coincidence. He was an eager participant, at least in the beginning, seduced by the attention, the opportunity to be a player in this high-stakes historical event, and the promise of money. "Every time that I stayed here at one of the fancy motels [I] was told that there was no limit on what I could spend," he later said. "I was permitted to invite all of my friends there for dinner and on more than one occasion had dinner checks in excess of one hundred dollars. This was always done in someone's name other than my own." And though he never received it, Garrison guaranteed him "thirty dollars a day for all the days the investigation went on." In addition, Russo said *Life* had promised Garrison $25,000 and he was told that he would be receiving "a lot" of that for his "trouble." "They made me feel like I was the most important guy in the whole world," Russo would later say, and "it all seemed so 'right,' that we should punish these killers."[33]

Before Russo appeared on the scene, Garrison was relying on the testimony of Jack Martin and David Lewis, an alcoholic mental case bearing a grudge and a private eye wannabe wearing a plastic gun. Russo, on the other hand, was young, athletic, attractive, a college man working for a large New York–based insurance company. Stepping forward in the footsteps of those two, Russo must have looked like a dream come true to Jim Garrison. But he was never the boy-next-door that he appeared to be.

Russo later revealed just how far removed he was from that wholesome image he projected. He referred to himself as a "sexual freak" who liked "sadism and masochism" and was "particularly enthused about bondage and submission and domination and the role playing associated with it." He explained that he preferred men but not exclusively. A former girlfriend, he reminded his interviewer, publicly had claimed she bore a child fathered by him.[34].

Another friend of his had said Russo turned that same girlfriend over to his friends. "It didn't cost you anything," he explained, "it was free." Russo enjoyed taking pornographic pictures of her with various men, pictures he kept "in a big shoe box" and showed to visitors.[35] Russo, himself, later admitted to a police interviewer "that he considered all of his sexual activity to be of a perverted type," that he "liked to engage in group sex" and "had a large collection of pornographic movies" that he exhibited at "sex parties."[36] The friend who knew about the girl and the porno pictures said he once entered Russo's apartment and found him with another man discussing basketball. Russo suddenly jumped up, ran into the bathroom and began "slicin' his wrist with a razor blade." Frightened, the friend fled. He had seen blood and believed that Russo was genuinely trying to harm himself but had no idea why. He also recalled that Russo once said "a psychiatrist had told him that he had a split personality."[37]

While Russo wasn't the boy-next-door, on meeting him the first time people frequently found him likeable and surprisingly open. He was unusually verbal, with a large vocabulary and a substantial knowledge of New Orleans history. The satisfaction some find through writing, Russo achieved through talking. Talking was what he did best. Unfortunately for everyone, including the country at large, over a brief five-day period in 1967 Russo talked himself into a dangerously vulnerable legal position and Clay Shaw into a felony charge.

The night he learned that Shaw had been arrested, Russo had a revealing reaction. "'Well,' I said to myself, 'what have I done now?'" Because, he observed, "I could have been wrong. In my statement. I could have been mistaken." "My God," Russo said to Sciambra, "don't tell me that they have arrested that man on what I said." "No, not at all," Sciambra replied, "we have [the case] locked up. It is a lead pipe cinch. You are just another witness and may not even be called [to testify]."[38] In fact, he represented the entire legal basis for the charge filed against Clay Shaw.

The day after he arrested Shaw, Garrison again benefited from the hand of fate. United States Attorney General Designate Ramsey Clark had a blundering encounter with the press in Washington and provided Garrison with another credibility boost. Emerging from a Senate confirmation hearing on his nomination, Clark answered questions about events in New Orleans by saying that Clay Shaw had been investigated by the FBI in 1963 and cleared. Clark's statement was a simple mistake. He should have said "Bertrand" had been investigated. Shaw at first took comfort in the report. Assuming he had been investigated because of Oswald's pamphleteering in front of the Trade Mart, Shaw told reporters he had not known about the FBI investigation but was delighted and pleased that he had been cleared by them. That same day, the bureaucratic snafu was compounded when a befuddled spokesman for the Department of Justice, pressed on the issue, said of Bertrand and Shaw, "We think it's the same guy."[39]

As the government paper trail now shows, this was a sensitive matter, an error of some magnitude by the brand new Attorney General of the United States.[40] The problem heated up when Shaw's attorney, Edward Wegmann, requested the information obtained by the FBI in its investigation of Shaw. Since there had been no investigation, both Clark and the FBI were now on the spot. As one exasperated Department of Justice employee told a friendly reporter who called asking for an explanation, "We can't very well say that Clark has wood in his head." Responding finally to Wegmann's request for a "public clarification," the Department of Justice explained that in 1963 "nothing arose indicating a need to investigate Mr. Shaw" and that Clark's statement had been in error.[41] This innocent explanation was never accepted by Garrison. Today, the incident is part of the lore of his case, one of those quirky events that fueled the possibility he might really be on to something.[42]

Not everything was going Garrison's way, though. When he arrested Clay Shaw, he did more than shock and divide the citizenry of New Orleans. He brought to a head the conflict at Life magazine over the Garrison issue that had been put on a back burner earlier in the year. According to David Chandler, shortly after Louis Ivon clapped handcuffs onto Shaw, several members of Life's senior staff (including Managing Editor George Hunt) attended a dinner in a Miami restaurant. The main topic of conversation was Jim Garrison and the riveting events taking place in New Orleans; the talk quickly grew heated. The debate boiled down to whether Billings or Chandler was right about Garrison. At a crucial moment, a legendary former *Time* editor, Holland McCombs, who had known Clay Shaw fifteen years, scribbled a check (the amount is unclear) and slapped it down on the table. I'll bet any part of this, McCombs declared, that Chandler is right. He "got no takers," McCombs later told Chandler.[43]

McCombs, whose prestige was matched that night by the force of his conviction, swayed Managing Editor Hunt and precipitated the first stage of his withdrawal from the arrangement with Garrison. While the final break would occur months later, the Miami dinner marked the beginning of the end of *Life's* support.[44] According to Chandler, Hunt killed the big story slated for April publication that Billings was preparing to write. Garrison's picture would not be appearing on *Life's* cover. *Life* would not be presenting Jim Garrison's version of the assassination to the American people.

When Garrison learned of *Life's* decision, he moved at once to fill the void. From the flock of journalists perched in New Orleans, he selected the one from the magazine that had given him his first major publicity, *The Saturday Evening Post*.[45] It was a decision Garrison would live to regret. For writer James Phelan, a logical man with an eye for detail, would soon pen an article that exposed the gaping hole in the testimony of Perry Russo, the second near-fatal catastrophe to befall Jim Garrison's case.

CHAPTER SEVEN

JAMES PHELAN AND *THE SATURDAY EVENING POST*

[Phelan was] a gravel-throated
mick-faced journalist of the old
school. Lean and spare and in his
fifties, he would be at home in a
revival of *The Front Page*. I could
easily picture him in another era,
panning for gold up in the
Yukon.[1]

—James Kirkwood, 1970

When news of Garrison's investigation first broke, James Phelan was
unaware of what was happening in New Orleans. He was working on
another story and trapped five days in a Chicago airport by a snow
storm. By the time he returned to New York, David Ferrie was dead,
Garrison had proclaimed the case "solved," and the media had flood-
ed into New Orleans, but not the *Post*. Believing Phelan had an inside
track with Garrison, Chief Editor Don McKinney held the assignment
for him. McKinney and *Post* publisher, Otto Friedrich, were excited
about the events in New Orleans. "This could be one of the biggest stories of our times," McKinney told Phelan. "If Garrison has what he says
he has, he is going to rewrite history."[2]

Phelan was delighted to be handed this choice assignment, but worried about his late start ("everyone else was already there"). "Hoping
that [Garrison] had solved this thing," Phelan boarded a plane that night
and arrived in New Orleans the evening of February 27. Encountering
a madhouse at Tulane and Broad the next day, he left a note with a
Garrison aide saying, "I'm over at the Royal Orleans hotel—I've joined
the thundering herd—and if you ever get a minute give me a call."[3]

Sitting in the Press Club bar late the following afternoon, Phelan heard on television that Clay Shaw had been arrested. "Everybody," Phelan later recalled, "was just flabbergasted. All the people who knew him couldn't believe it." Phelan had never heard of him but was quickly filled in by other reporters. Clay Shaw, Phelan thought, "is one hell of a story."

The next day, Phelan got his first look at the accused. Shortly before 2:00 P.M. at the office of his attorney, Shaw read a prepared statement in a room jammed wall-to-wall with reporters, one of them Phelan. "I am shocked and dismayed at the charges which have been filed against me," Shaw said. "I am completely innocent." "I have not conspired with anyone at any time or at any place to murder our late and esteemed president," for whom he had "only the highest and utmost respect and admiration." He did not know Lee Harvey Oswald. He did not know David Ferrie. He had never been to Ferrie's apartment. He had never used the name "Clay Bertrand." Phelan found Shaw "impressive," "well-spoken" and "specific about having admired Kennedy," but then, Phelan said, no one expected Shaw to say, "Okay, guys, I did it."[4]

That same day, Garrison sprang another surprise when one of his assistants filed a motion for a preliminary hearing, an extraordinary step for a district attorney to take.[*] Defense attorneys favor preliminary hearings because the prosecution must reveal enough of its case to convince the court that the defendant should be held for trial. But ordinarily, prosecutors prefer to avoid showing their hand. Phelan was as baffled as everyone else. "We do not understand the motivation of Mr. Garrison," said one of Shaw's attorneys.[5] Even Judge Bernard J. Bagert, who granted the motion and set the hearing for March 14, termed it an "unusual" request for the state to make. The defense team decided that Garrison was planning to stage a performance. They moved to quash the hearing until Garrison filed a bill of particulars that identified the others allegedly involved,[†] the con-

---

[*] In order to proceed to trial Garrison needed only to file a bill of information on Shaw's arrest, which he had said he intended to do.

[†] Their names were available only in the application for the search warrant on Shaw's residence. (See note p. 7.) Shaw had not yet been charged formally—he was only booked; and while the information on his Arrest Register claimed he had conspired with "one or more other persons," they were not identified (*New Orleans Times-Picayune*, March 9, 1967; Clay L. Shaw, Arrest Register, No. 08051, March 1, 1967).

fidential informant, and the when, where, and what of the alleged conspiracy. Judge Bagert rejected their plea, granting only their request concerning the informant. "I disagree violently with this finding," William
Wegmann told the court. "We are entitled to cross-examine. We are entitled to be prepared and not come in here and shoot off the cuff. We don't
want to come in here Tuesday and have the state go wild and put on a big
show."[6] Bagert was unmoved. The big show was on its way.

But it was two weeks in the offing. Phelan began chasing down wild
stories that were sprouting everywhere and waiting to hear from
Garrison. On Friday, March 3, four days after Phelan arrived in New
Orleans, Garrison finally called. He apologized for the delay, said he had
"a proposal" for Phelan, and invited him to lunch. They met at the New
Orleans Athletic Club, but had little opportunity to talk because of the
people "coming up to the table and congratulating Garrison." Afterwards,
in the cab taking Garrison back to his office, he told Phelan he was going
to Las Vegas "to get away for some rest" and some sun, and he wanted
Phelan to join him. "I'll tell you the whole incredible story," Garrison
promised. To prevent the rest of the media from catching on, Garrison
suggested they travel separately, with Phelan leaving first and Garrison following the next day. Phelan agreed and caught a plane out that evening.[7]

Phelan thought he just had been handed an "incredible exclusive story," he
later wrote, "on a silver platter." It appeared that way. Phelan knew nothing
about Garrison's deal with *Life* and how it had "gone sour." He thought
Garrison had called him "because," he later joked, "of my irresistible
personality." As he winged his way west, the six-foot, fifty-four-year-
old Phelan knew only that he was about to hear from Garrison himself
the inside story of the New Orleans plot that had killed the president,
the story the whole world was waiting to hear.[8]

Phelan found Las Vegas an odd and distant locale for a New Orleans
district attorney to choose for a retreat, but he later learned it was a
favorite vacation spot for Garrison.[9] Phelan had written several articles
about that improbable gambling town, invented and operated by gangsters, and he, too, was familiar with it. He checked into the Dunes, where
he had stayed in the past. Garrison arrived on Saturday and Phelan picked
him up at the airport. At Garrison's instructions, Phelan drove him to the
Sands, where Garrison registered under the alias "W. O. Robinson,"

which was Garrison's maternal grandfather's name. Garrison said he needed some sleep, so they arranged to rendezvous on Sunday. To Phelan that meant another day wasted and he began to wonder why he was there. Unbeknownst to him, Garrison was not alone. Two companions had accompanied him. He may have wanted sleep that night or he may have wanted some entertainment. As Phelan said, "I was never part of Garrison's social life."[10]

In two lengthy meetings the next day, Garrison laid out his thinking and described his "evidence." He began their first session, which took place in the Sands Garden Room over brunch, by criticizing the Warren Report ("junk" gathered by "squirrels") and explained that he had solved the Dallas puzzle through "imagination and evaluation." He said they had "uncovered a whole series of odd connections" by examining "old street directories, [and] old telephone books" and "to understand the overall picture" Phelan had to keep in mind "that the Kennedy assassination was like Alice in Wonderland: *Nothing was what it seemed to be. Black was white, white was black.*" Soon he latched onto his favorite subject, "the trip that Ferrie made to Houston the day after Kennedy was killed." It was, Garrison told Phelan, as he had told others in the past few months and would continue to repeat, in one form or another, the rest of his life, "a most curious trip, by a curious man to a curious place at a curious time." That trip, Garrison said, was the initial "thread" that when he "tugged it" had "unraveled this whole case."[11]

By now, Garrison had assigned Ferrie a new role. His destination that day, the Winterland ice skating rink, was actually "the message center," Garrison said. And he insisted that Ferrie "never put on his skates,"* but had spent the afternoon hanging around the telephone. When Phelan asked what message Ferrie had received, who had called him, or whom Ferrie had called, Garrison admitted that he didn't know that "yet."† When Phelan pointed out the story's lack of substance (he repeatedly asked "where's the evidence?"), Garrison gave him a dossier on Ferrie prepared by a private investigative firm. It catalogued Ferrie's schooling, his tortured personal life, and his peripatetic employment record,

---

* Ferrie told the FBI he skated and Alvin Beaubouef recently confirmed that he did.
† Garrison never established that Ferrie did anything but spend some time at the telephone. According to Alvin Beaubouef, Ferrie was a telephone addict.

but contained nothing that linked him even remotely to the assassination. Phelan read it, told Garrison it was interesting but he couldn't see its relevance. Garrison responded with more of the same.[12]

Suddenly, Garrison ended the meeting. He said three men in a nearby booth were FBI agents, that the Bureau had him under surveillance, following him everywhere and in New Orleans tapping his phones. He asked Phelan to come that evening to his room at the Sands. Phelan headed back to the Dunes with his once-soaring expectations beginning to sag. That night he showed up at Garrison's room and found him in shirt-sleeve wearing a gun in a shoulder holster. Garrison removed the gun, emptied its shells into his hand, and showed Phelan one of them. It was, Garrison said, a "magnum load" that his gun couldn't handle and he couldn't figure out who had put it into his gun. If it were fired, he said, the weapon would explode. As Phelan watched, Garrison put all six shells back into the gun.[13]

Then Garrison returned to his narrative. He described the group of CIA-supported anti-Castro Cubans in New Orleans that Ferrie had joined. Oswald, too, was involved with them, but he hadn't fired "a shot at anyone," Garrison declared. (He defined Oswald's role in the president's murder as that of a "participant, decoy, and patsy.") David Ferrie, Garrison explained, had spun the group off from the original plan against Castro and created "an assassination team to kill the president."[14]

The motive? "It was a homosexual thrill-killing, plus the excitement of getting away with a perfect crime," Garrison stated, reciting the outlandish story Perry Russo had heard. Garrison compared it to the famous 1920s Loeb-Leopold murder of Bobby Franks in Chicago. "John Kennedy was everything that Dave Ferrie was not—a successful, handsome, popular, wealthy, virile man," Garrison said. "You can just picture the charge Ferrie got out of plotting his death." Garrison had deduced this, he said, because Ferrie, Ruby, Oswald, and Shaw were all homosexual. Phelan pointed out that Oswald was married and the father of two children. Oswald, Garrison replied, was "a switch-hitter who couldn't satisfy his wife." The thrill-killing notion coupled with the episode with the shells gave Phelan pause—it crossed his mind that Garrison might be unhinged.[15]

Phelan also was having difficulty piecing together a coherent picture.

He had heard nothing solid, he told Garrison, nothing that he could possibly write. He continued to press for *evidence*. "It doesn't hang together," Phelan insisted. Garrison replied that it did. He then retrieved a fat manila envelope covered with stamps from the dresser, tore into it, examined the documents inside, and handed two of them to Phelan. They contained the information that his witness would give at Shaw's preliminary hearing the following week, Garrison said, and only his key aides knew about it. This witness tied everything together, Garrison stated. "He's my case against Shaw." Garrison told Phelan to read the documents that evening and then he would see the whole picture. They would meet the next morning, Garrison said, and see if Phelan had changed his mind.[16]

Phelan left with his expectations climbing again. For the past two weeks people throughout the world had been wondering what it was that Garrison had discovered. And I had the answer, Phelan later said, in my pocket. As he walked back to the Dunes, Phelan considered the possibility that Garrison had been teasing him—feeding him peripheral information while deliberately withholding the central evidence. Then, at the end, delivering the goods. This wishful thinking would soon evaporate.[17]

The two documents Phelan took away from Garrison's hotel room that night described two interviews with Perry Russo. One was Andrew Sciambra's 3,500-word memorandum detailing his first conversation with Russo in Baton Rouge on February 25. The other was a thirteen-page transcript of Russo's March 1 interview conducted by Dr. Fatter while Russo was hypnotized. Phelan read the documents through once. Then, incredulous, he read them again. Finally, he read them a third time. He said later that after reading all the material (about 6,000 words) the first time, "I thought I must have missed something. I went back and read it again" and experienced "an epiphany." He was up all night. "I kept reading them and then going back and checking them, and reading, and checking, and reading." What he realized as he pored over those pages, he said, *"knocked me out of my chair."* What he realized was that the incriminating story Perry Russo told under hypnosis about hearing Ferrie, Oswald, and Shaw plotting the president's murder in Ferrie's apartment was entirely absent from Russo's first statement in Baton Rouge. And the omission could be no mere oversight, for the memorandum specifically stated that Russo had seen Clay Shaw *twice* and described those two occasions. The plotting session wasn't there.[18]

It was clear to Phelan, who was knowledgeable about hypnosis, its suggestibility and the neutral questioning it required, that the third Shaw sighting, the one at Ferrie's party, had been developed during Russo's hypnosis session by the leading questions posed by Dr. Fatter.* The hypnosis transcript, Phelan noted, "discredited Russo as a witness" and the Sciambra memorandum "directly impeached him."[19] It was inconceivable to Phelan that Garrison had arrested Clay Shaw on the basis of these statements by Russo. Yet Garrison had said it himself: "He's my case against Shaw." At that moment, Phelan was the first person outside Garrison's inner circle to learn the identity and story of Garrison's confidential informant. He also was the first person, inside or out, who recognized and could prove the enormous injustice underway in New Orleans.

Phelan arose the next morning with his mind "reeling," wondering what he should say to Garrison. "I'm there representing the *Post*," Phelan explained later, "and I got a hell of a story, but I know the story they want, and I ain't got it; I got something else." So he called his boss, Don McKinney, and told him he was in Las Vegas with Garrison and "yes it was wonderful but the story ain't what we thought." He then summarized the situation, explaining that he was due to meet with Garrison at ten o'clock. McKinney said he wanted to speak to Managing Editor Otto Friedrich and told Phelan to call back in thirty minutes. Friedrich, Phelan knew, "thought there was something wrong with the Warren Report" and wanted the other story.

The message from Otto Friedrich was not a happy one. "Otto was kind of pissed off at me," Phelan said later. When he called again, McKinney passed on the message: "Otto says, 'Tell Phelan to let Garrison make his own case.'" Keep quiet, in other words. Russo had told two different stories, McKinney said, and the question is: what will he say under oath? McKinney told Phelan not to confront Garrison—to wait and see what Russo said on the witness stand at the preliminary hearing. "Then we'll take it from there." Phelan had received his marching orders.[20]

When he handed the documents over, Garrison had put no restrictions on them. So Phelan arranged to have them copied at the Desert

* Later Phelan would learn about the sodium Pentothal interview and the initial bare-bones reference Russo made to the plot party while drugged.

Inn, which was just across the street.[21] By the time Phelan returned the documents to Garrison that day, he had figured out something to say. He told Garrison that Russo was "quite some witness" who "was carrying a hell of a case for a solitary witness." Garrison replied that arresting Shaw was his decision alone and that some of his aides had opposed it. "This is not the first time I've charged a person before I've made the case," he admitted. But Shaw was now in "the sweatbox," he said, and eventually he would "break down and tell me everything."[22]

"This was a Garrison I had never seen before," Phelan would write, "arrogant, prejudicial, blindly confident that whatever he suspected had happened had to have happened." Before he left, Phelan asked Garrison why Ferrie and Shaw, whom Garrison had portrayed as cunning and cautious, had run the risk of discussing their plans to assassinate the president in front of Russo. How did they know Russo wouldn't go to the FBI and reveal what he had heard? Garrison shook his head. That hadn't occurred to him. It was, he replied, "a *good* question."[23]

Phelan flew home for a few days' rest before returning to New Orleans for the preliminary hearing. Along with Garrison's documents, Phelan took with him a rock-solid certainty that Garrison's case against Shaw was a fraud. Phelan also assumed it would come to an immediate halt once Garrison knew what he knew and realized the truth about Russo's testimony.

Garrison stayed in Las Vegas a full week, departing March 11. While there he remained in control of operations in New Orleans. He ran up a phone bill of $125, *large* for those days, staying in close touch with his men who were busy preparing Perry Russo for his upcoming appearance at the preliminary hearing.[24] Before he took the stand, Russo would undergo an incomplete lie-detector test, a second hypnosis interview, a third hypnosis interview, and a rehearsal.

Roy Jacob, a Jefferson Parish Deputy Sheriff, administered the polygraph. When asked if he knew Clay Shaw and Lee Harvey Oswald, Russo's "yes" answers indicated, in the language of the trade, "deception-criteria," and his responses in general caused Jacob to suspect he was dealing with a troubled personality. Jacob conducted the test in the office of Leonard Gurvich, younger brother of William Gurvich and, like him, a dollar-a-year investigator for the district attorney's office. Leonard

Gurvich waited outside during the test. When Jacob came out, he said to Gurvich, "Lennie, we got problems." Russo had told Jacob that the story "wasn't true," that he was "just trying to help Mr. Garrison" because he believed in what Garrison was doing. Like Jacob, Gurvich was shocked. Jacob left to find Andrew Sciambra. Russo, alone momentarily with Gurvich, told him he was "confused" and "shook up" and didn't know what to do. "Tell the truth, Perry," Gurvich advised. "You can't get in trouble if you tell the truth." Jacob returned with Sciambra; the testing was over. Garrison's men took away Jacob's list of questions and instructed him not to tell anyone what had happened.[25]

The next day Garrison tried another tack. He turned to Dr. Fatter who again hypnotized Russo. Fatter gleaned only a single new piece of information and it echoed a story in the New Orleans newspapers the week before. The article had described Clay Shaw's presence at the San Francisco World Trade Center the day President Kennedy was assassinated. When hypnotized this time, Russo stated that at the assassination plot party "Clem Bertrand" had said that when the president was shot he would be "on the Coast."[26] Garrison ordered a third hypnosis three days later. Again, Fatter elicited only a single new item of interest. Russo explained why "Clem" planned to be on "the Coast" that day: Ferrie said they should be seen "in public" in order to "establish alibis." Ferrie stated that he "would be making a speech" at Southeastern College. "Leon," though, said nothing.[27] (No one in Garrison's camp seemed to notice that these "alibis" made no sense, that Shaw didn't need to travel 2,000 miles to be in the public eye, and Ferrie arrived at Southeastern College two days too late.)

The important part of this third hypnosis came at the end, in Dr. Fatter's final instructions to Russo. He told him that "anytime" he wanted to, he could become "calm, cool, and collected" and do the "task" he had come there to do. That his memory would become "acute"; "things will seem to pop into" his mind and he could "permit these [stories] to come into" his mind "exactly" as he "had seen them."[28] This posthypnotic suggestion would serve Russo well when he testified two days later.

The night before the preliminary hearing, Garrison arranged for Russo to be taken to the Ramada Inn on Tulane Avenue for a final briefing by Lynn Loisel, Al Oser, James Alcock, Louis Ivon, and Andrew Sciambra.

Russo said later that he was asked "to repeat things over and over and over. Rat-a-tat, rat-a-tat . . . non-stop." Garrison's men were all "wearing their guns." Sciambra at one point "had his out" and was "wavin' it around and saying what this was going to do to Shaw and how it was going to force the government to admit it had lied to America about Kennedy's death." Until then, Russo said, he liked Sciambra but his behavior that night gave Russo "a funny feeling."[29] It was Sciambra, Russo said, "all excited like he was playing Dick Tracy," who gave Russo the transcript of his hypnosis sessions to read. "He would ask me the questions like Dr. Fatter asked me." "It was like a script to play," Russo said. "In other words, you play Hamlet and I'll play Horatio. And you say your lines and I'll say mine."[30] The grilling continued until Alcock decided Russo had had enough.

Garrison was leaving nothing to chance.

CHAPTER EIGHT

THE PRELIMINARY HEARING

When the mind is numbed with
horror, the heart frozen with
apprehension, where does one
find words to describe that
which is almost indescribable?[1]
—Clay Shaw (journal entry), March 1967

Let this gentleman walk out of
here without this stigma.
—William Wegmann (to the Court),
March 17, 1967

They say the atmosphere was festive the day Clay Shaw's preliminary
hearing began before Judges Bernard J. Bagert, Matthew S. Braniff, and
Malcolm V. O'Hara. The media frenzy resembled that at the O. J.
Simpson trial in Los Angeles three decades later. Television cameramen
and photographers, banned inside the Criminal District Court building, set up shop on the steps outside. Everyone entering or exiting confronted the swarming press gauntlet. Hundreds of spectators appeared,
hoping for a glimpse of the principals. Thousands sought the few available seats in the courtroom. Seventy-four were reserved for the press,
one for James Phelan.

Security measures were unusually tight. When Shaw arrived with his
attorneys about 10:00 A.M., the Orleans Parish criminal sheriff asked
Shaw to enter the building through a side door. Shaw's attorney
refused. His client had done nothing wrong, Edward Wegmann said.
"We will go through the main entrance." But when a gun was found
hidden near where Clay Shaw had parked his car, Wegmann changed
his mind. Thereafter, Shaw was allowed to drive inside the prison

grounds, park next to the courthouse, and use the Sheriff's entrance.[2] Media representatives were photographed and issued passes that were checked at the door. Following a threatening telephone call, all spectators were frisked. Deputy sheriffs posted along the walls of the courtroom kept a close watch on the audience.

Sunburned from Las Vegas, Jim Garrison showed up with two investigators, five assistants,[*] and security on his mind too. He had been saying Shaw was going to commit suicide and it would be good if he did. But now Garrison feared Shaw might try to harm him instead. So he asked William Gurvich to sit between them in the courtroom. It was foolish, awkward for Gurvich, and he objected, but he did it.[3]

The first three witnesses testified to technical matters.[†] Then the state called Perry Russo and everyone learned what Phelan already knew, the identity of Garrison's mystery witness. Garrison conducted the examination. Russo—"calm, cool and collected"—told the story from his first hypnosis interview, plus Shaw and Ferrie being "in the public eye" the day of the assassination to establish alibis. Phelan listened "with fascination," he would later write, as "Russo related his marvelously detailed hypnotic vision—the story that differed so greatly from the one 'Moo' Sciambra had originally reported."[4] Phelan noted how neatly finished the narrative was. Russo attended the party, heard the plotting, and after Ferrie's death told Andrew Sciambra about it. Russo gave no hint of its metamorphosis.

Like a Perry Mason movie where the key witness at a trial points a finger at the defendant and says "he did it," Garrison's show had its theatrical moment. But in staging it, Garrison had devised something more devastating than mere finger pointing. At Garrison's instructions, Russo stepped down from the witness chair, walked across the room to "the rear of Shaw's chair" and there "placed his outstretched arm over Shaw's head," identifying him as the alleged conspirator "Clem Bertrand." Shaw sat staring straight ahead.[5] Russo thus delivered the big show's big bang. Garrison timed it perfectly—court was then recessed for lunch.

---

[*] The assistant district attorneys of record were: Alvin V. Oser, James L. Alcock and Michael L. Karmazin.

[†] A New Orleans police detective said that on August 9, 1963, he arrested Lee Harvey Oswald and three "Spanish individuals" who were engaged in "an altercation" on Canal Street; a police forensic specialist and the coroner's photographer testified about David Ferrie's death.

Shaw and his attorneys were completely surprised by Russo's testimony. Having been denied discovery, and officially informed of Russo's name only that morning, they had no time to investigate him. During the lunch break, they gathered what information they could, with Salvatore Panzeca and a colleague "doing most of the leg work." Also during lunch, Shaw told one of his attorneys that Russo's face "looked, somehow, familiar." The mystery was resolved that afternoon when Garrison resumed his direct examination of Russo and he described knocking on Shaw's door to identify him, under the pretense of selling insurance.[6]

When Garrison was finished, the defense postponed its questioning of Russo, and court was abruptly recessed at 3:30 that afternoon. That allowed Shaw's attorneys a few hours to do their best to devise a strategy for their cross-examination. Meanwhile, the local newspapers shouted his name in front-page headlines: HEARD SHAW, OSWALD, FERRIE PLOT JFK KILLING, SAYS RUSSO.

The following day Russo again took the stand. "Do you believe in God?" asked F. Irvin Dymond, the defense team's fifty-three-year-old lead trial attorney—a tall, attractive man with a resonant voice, a stately air, and a commanding courtroom presence. The defense had heard Russo was an atheist and was trying to undermine his credibility by showing that the oath he had just sworn was meaningless. "It would depend on the definition," Russo replied. He then demonstrated an uncanny ability to dissemble. Dymond pressed Russo about his academic and employment records, as well as two audio recordings, trying to prove he had made false or contradictory statements. But Russo's verbal slipperiness continued to serve him well. "Russo has been extremely well coached," Clay Shaw noted in his journal that day. "It is going to be difficult to shake his testimony, except for the obvious logical fact that such a meeting as he describes could not have occurred among sensible and reasonable people."[7]

Shaw was correct. Over the next day and a half, the defense was unable to shake Russo's basic story, though Dymond did elicit some damaging admissions. Yes, Russo said, he had undergone psychiatric treatment from October 1959 until sometime in 1961. He had last visited a psychiatrist around October or September of 1965 and he had perhaps talked to a psychiatrist "on the phone" in 1966. He denied ever trying to commit suicide. Regarding his interview with a Baton Rouge television reporter, in which Russo stated he "had never heard of Oswald" until after the assassination, Russo explained that he did not know Lee Harvey Oswald, that he knew "Leon" Oswald (who was whiskered, dirty and had rumpled hair);* Russo had said earlier that the similarity between "Leon" and "Lee" never occurred to him. When Dymond pointed out that in the same interview Russo had stated that David Ferrie's remarks about assassinating the president had been made "in a joking way," Russo admitted that Ferrie did say it "jokingly" during the summer, but later, in September, "things" changed a bit.[8]

When Dymond noted that Oswald left New Orleans permanently on September 25 but Russo claimed he saw Oswald in October, Russo stuck to the later date.† When Dymond wondered why Russo had failed to come forward sooner, Russo offered several explanations. He wasn't one to push himself onto people; Ferrie and the others "did not say anything about Dallas"; "Ferrie was never implicated," and everyone said Oswald acting alone had committed the crime. Anyway, he didn't really think the plotting was meant seriously—he had heard many similar remarks from "people on the street" angry about integration. When Dymond suggested Russo had seized upon Ferrie's death to get himself "a little publicity," Russo claimed that, until Ferrie died, he didn't realize the man under investigation was the Ferrie he knew.[9]

Toward the end of Russo's cross-examination, Dymond addressed the nature of the plotting session. "Was it understood," he asked, "that these three men [Oswald, Ferrie, and Shaw] would actively participate in the assassination?" "I did not get that impression," Russo replied. Dymond directed his final questions to Russo's encounter with the defendant on Shaw's own doorstep shortly before his arrest. Russo admitted that knocking on Shaw's door had been "a risky thing" to do.

---

* An audio recording of this February 24, 1967, interview was played in open court. A New Orleans television station also broadcast the interview the night before Dymond began his cross-examination, providing Russo and the prosecution time to devise answers to Dymond's inevitable questions about it.

† To establish the date of Oswald's departure, Dymond attempted to introduce the Warren Report as evidence, but the court, referring to the Report as "hearsay evidence," forcefully denied the motion: "You are not serious, are you?" asked Judge Bagert (preliminary hearing transcript, p. 198).

He was "sure" Shaw recognized him, Russo said, and insisted he had "absolutely" no trouble identifying Shaw.[10] That ended it. Dymond had taken a toll, but Russo had survived.

The next two witnesses, Drs. Nicholas Chetta and Esmond Fatter, over strenuous defense objections, vouched for the credibility of Russo's story and his mental health. Dr. Fatter described hypnotizing Russo and declared that the hypnoses refreshed Russo's memory. Cross-examining him, William Wegmann asked if Russo was under the doctor's post-hypnotic suggestion while on the witness stand. "He could have [been] if he accepted the suggestion," Fatter replied, giving no indication that his actions might have been inappropriate. Dr. Chetta stated flatly that Russo fulfilled "all the requirements of legal sanity." Chetta, too, recounted the three hypnosis sessions and, as oblivious as ever, declared that repeated hypnotic trances induce "better recall." As for sodium Pentothal, he explained that it produces "a drug-induced state of hypnosis." While admitting that a subject "can lie" while under its influence, he claimed that if the administering physician was experienced in using it that he could "pick up the fallacies."[11]

A leading expert in the use of sodium Pentothal, psychiatrist Edwin A. Weinstein, was so troubled by Dr. Chetta's testimony that he answered him in a piece in the *Washington Post*. Chetta, he wrote, was "grossly distorting the medical facts" about both hypnosis and sodium Pentothal. Under their influence, "subjects may give highly fictional accounts of past events and describe incidents that never happened." The action of the drug on recall, he explained, "is profoundly influenced by the stress of the situation in which it is administered and the relationship between the subject and his questioners."[12] * But the court didn't hear Dr. Weinstein. The court heard Dr. Chetta.

His reassuring testimony took place Thursday afternoon. That same day, at Orleans Parish Prison, a brand new eleventh-hour witness was about to emerge. Inmate Vernon Bundy, a twenty-nine-year-old nar-

---

* Dr. Weinstein recently recalled an instance where a soldier under the drug "told a dramatic story" about "searching for his brother among the dead and wounded [on a WWII battlefield]." They discovered this soldier "did indeed have a brother" but he had "never left the States" (Edwin A. Weinstein, M.D., letter to author, March 13, 1995). Dr. Weinstein's experiences "are recorded in the official U.S. Army medical history of the war."

cotics addict, had written a letter to the court saying he had information. He was interviewed in prison that evening by William Gurvich and two other Garrison aides.[13] The next day Bundy told his story again, this time in the D.A.'s office to Garrison himself. Afterwards, Garrison ordered a curious sort of lie-detector test.

Asst. D.A. Charles Ward arrived at the polygraph office with Bundy in tow about noon. Ward told examiner James Kruebbe that Bundy might testify in court that very day and then he gave Kruebbe what Kruebbe later termed "peculiar" instructions. Ward told him to find out if Bundy was acting on instructions from anyone,* and if "certain information" that Ward refused to divulge, which Bundy had given Garrison about Clay Shaw and Lee Harvey Oswald, was true. Withholding the central information from the examiner was unusual, but Kruebbe administered the test anyway. Immediately afterwards, he went upstairs to the district attorney's office and in the presence of Charles Ward and James Alcock told Garrison that Bundy "wasn't telling the truth." But, Kruebbe said, "no one put him up to it," that Bundy "was doing it of his own accord," and he was "looking for something." (That something, Kruebbe later said, was "out of prison.") Kruebbe listened as Garrison and his two aides argued. I told you so, is how Ward and Alcock reacted. They insisted that Bundy "wasn't necessary" to establish "probable cause" and shouldn't be used as a witness in any event. Garrison disagreed strenuously, and he had the final word. "We didn't tell him what to say," Garrison declared, "let the jury decide whether or not he's telling the truth."[14]

A short time later, Garrison entered the crowded courtroom for Friday's afternoon session. His sunburn was beginning to peel and he was looking fit. It was his first appearance since Wednesday morning. His presence brought an excited buzz from the audience, which realized that his arrival signaled "another major happening." Vernon Bundy's name was called and a stocky black man in a plaid shirt walked quickly to the stand, raised his hand, and swore to tell the truth.[15]

As Garrison led him through it, Bundy told the following story. One Monday morning in June or July 1963, he was near the seawall at the Pontchartrain lakefront about 9:15, preparing to give himself a heroin

* Garrison and his men were worried about the defense planting stories to embarrass them.

fix, when a black four-door sedan pulled up and parked. A tall white man with grey hair wearing a suit and tie emerged. "It's a hot day" he said, as he passed behind Bundy. The man then walked away from Bundy a distance of some twenty or twenty-five feet. About "five or seven minutes" later he was joined by a "young fellow" who arrived "on foot." The young man needed a shave and haircut and Bundy referred to him as a "beatnik." Bundy watched the two men talk and heard the young one in an "outburst" say, "What am I going to tell her?" The older man replied, "Don't worry about it. I told you I'm going to take care of it." Bundy claimed he then saw the older man hand the other one what looked like "a roll of money." The young man stuck the money in his pants pocket and Bundy noted that in the same pocket the man was carrying what looked like "pamphlets." After a while, the two men left, going their separate ways, and Bundy injected his heroin. Afterwards, looking for something to wrap his equipment in, he retrieved a yellow paper from the ground with "something about Cuba written on it."[16]

Garrison showed Bundy photographs of Lee Harvey Oswald, whom Bundy identified as the younger man, and Clay Shaw, who Bundy said was the other one.* Then, following the same instructions that Garrison had given Russo, Bundy stepped down from the witness stand, crossed to the defense table, and placed his hand above Clay Shaw's head, identifying him as the man he saw with Oswald.

On cross by Dymond, Bundy admitted that he sometimes stole to support his drug habit, that he was presently serving time in the parish prison, and that he was uncertain about the month and the time of day that he witnessed the encounter at Lake Pontchartrain. But, like Russo, Bundy stuck to his basic story.

A series of exhibits were entered into the record. Then Asst. D.A. Alvin Oser rested Garrison's case against Clay Shaw.

Irvin Dymond attempted (for the second time) to introduce the Warren Report into the record, but the court, by a two-to-one vote (Judge O'Hara dissented), rebuffed him. Dymond then rested for the defense.

* In the statement he gave in prison, Bundy said he heard Shaw call the other man "Pete" (Vernon Bundy, Jr., interview at Orleans Parish Prison, with William Gurvich, Charlie Jonau, and Cliency Navarre, March 16, 1967). On the witness stand this obviously incorrect feature had vanished.

William Wegmann, in what the local newspaper would describe as "an impassioned summation," attacked the case the prosecution had presented, declaring it failed to justify holding Shaw for trial. "At best it's evidence that might warrant further investigation, but it was not sufficient to say to this man, 'You are one of the people who might have killed the president of the United States.'" And if the court did so, it would be subjecting Shaw "to all kinds of ridicule and risk."* Summarizing for the prosecution, Asst. D.A. James Alcock said the state was basing its case on the testimony of its two key witnesses, Perry Russo and Vernon Bundy.[17]

James Kruebbe, learning from a newspaper account what Bundy's "certain information" was, found it ridiculous and was shocked that Garrison had actually put him on the witness stand. His doing so exemplifies much.

The three-judge panel deliberated thirty-four minutes. Shaw smoked, drank water, and walked aimlessly around the defense table, the strain of the past few days etched in his grim expression and the circles beneath his eyes. In his courtroom demeanor, he had followed the instructions of his lawyers, but had found it "very difficult" to sit listening to the accusations made against him "without showing any emotion." Shaw realized that those who knew him would reject Russo's testimony, knowing "that I would have better sense than to plot with two nuts like that in the presence of a twenty-two-year-old boy I'd never seen before." Bundy's testimony struck Shaw as so improbable that Garrison's introducing it seemed to him "almost a contemptuous gesture toward the judges." Shaw still "hoped against hope" that the case would end here.[18]

When the panel returned, Shaw stared straight ahead as the presiding judge read the unanimous verdict. *Probable cause had been established; further legal steps were justified.*† Clay Shaw would stand trial for having conspired with David Ferrie, Lee Harvey Oswald, and others to kill

---

* Shaw's attorneys thought "it quite likely" his home "might be bombed or burned" (his insurance company thought so, too—they canceled his homeowners policy); this is one reason Shaw stayed away from his home the entire month of March (Shaw Narrative, p. 3).
† Reportedly, Judge O'Hara initially was "not inclined" to hold Shaw for trial, but was persuaded to go along with the other two judges (Shaw Journal, p. 68).

President John F. Kennedy.* It was Clay Shaw's fifty-fourth birthday.† He was admitted to Southern Baptist Hospital the following day for rest and treatment of chronic back trouble. His calm outward appearance masked a fierce internal turmoil. "It was like living a nightmare," he later told a friend, "like the end of the world."[19]

In the hallway outside the courtroom, Garrison was asked for his reaction. "The judges have made the statement," he said. "Is there anything else to say?" Garrison had won a substantial victory. The ruling, as one writer observed, "made him a national media celebrity" and "gave an aura of substance to his conspiracy solution." This moment was the high point of his career. Yet Garrison had presented the court with no substantive evidence of conspiracy and none whatever of an overt act in furtherance of it, a requirement under Louisiana law. Many found Bundy's testimony, as Shaw had, almost laughably improbable.‡ The three judges were well aware of the shortcomings of Garrison's evidence. One of them, Malcolm O'Hara, in a conversation with a Life representative four days after the verdict "continuously referred to the hearing as: 'that shit last week.'"§ Judge Bagert defended their ruling, claiming if they had cut Shaw loose, "the nation and the world would have charged a fix." Irvin Dymond believed nothing could have prevented the outcome, that it was "a done deal" from the beginning. It probably was. "The decision is cut and dried," Perry Russo later said he was told beforehand, "unless he fell absolutely to pieces on the witness stand."[20]

James Phelan now had the answer to the question his editor posed when Phelan called him from Las Vegas. He knew what Russo would say under oath. Phelan's next step was to confront Garrison and "get an

---

* Five days later Garrison would take Russo before the grand jury and obtain an indictment against Shaw, which specified that the plotting occurred between September 1 and October 10, 1963. Neither this hearing nor the grand jury indictment were necessary to take Shaw to trial.
† When Judge Bagert, an old high school friend of Shaw, had entered the courtroom that morning, he had "very merrily wished [Shaw] a happy birthday." Bagert apparently had learned of it from a news account (Shaw Journal, p. 67).
‡ Bundy was paroled "within a month" (Shaw Narrative, p. 10).
§ Garrison's evidence was "water thin" and his case "a joke," Judge O'Hara told this writer. The panel voted as it did, he said, "because the defense didn't put on any defense" (telephone interview, Nov. 20, 1993). But it was the court that denied Shaw's team the information it needed to mount a more effective defense.

explanation." He called Garrison at home, said he was bothered by something, and Garrison invited him over. Phelan found Garrison spending the evening with his wife and children. Almost immediately, William Gurvich and his wife showed up. Phelan explained that Sciambra's first report "contained nothing about a party, a plot or a Bertrand." Garrison's "jaw dropped." "It doesn't?" he said. "That's when I *knew* he hadn't read it," Phelan later said. "I thought, oh man, what are you doing? You've arrested the man. They're going to hold him to trial and Garrison never even read the basic document. I said, 'No, it doesn't.' He said, 'Well, I'll have to get Sciambra out here to explain it.'"[21]

Garrison telephoned and Sciambra arrived straight away. The women were shooed out of the study and Garrison said to Phelan, "Tell him what the problem is." Phelan did. "You don't know what the shit you're talking about!" Sciambra said. "Yes, I do," Phelan replied. "I got a copy of your memorandum. It's down in the hotel safe. I've read that memo so many times I can almost recite it verbatim for you. And I'll make a bet with you. If there's anything about a plot to kill Kennedy in [it], I will resign from the *Post*. If it isn't there, you resign from the D.A.'s office."[22]

Sciambra backed off right away. He had been busy with a lot of other things and maybe, he said, "I forgot to put it in. But, Jim, you remember when I came down from Baton Rouge, I said, 'Boy, when I tell you what I got you're gonna kiss me.' That's what Sciambra said. And Garrison didn't back him up. Garrison didn't say anything," Phelan recalled. "He just sat there and listened to the whole thing." Sciambra and Phelan continued to argue with escalating ferocity until the meeting broke up. When Phelan departed, the hostility was unresolved, and so was the issue that had brought him to Garrison's home.[23]

Phelan had taken a cab out, so Gurvich drove him back to his hotel. Gurvich had sat silently in the corner of Garrison's den listening and saying nothing. But on the drive into town, he revealed how terribly upset he was. "Russo's the whole case," he told Phelan. "And you just shot him out of the water. I sat there and listened to [Sciambra] telling you he had so many things to do. That memo was the most important thing [he did]. He wrote it, rewrote it, polished it. For him to say that he forgot to put the plot to kill Kennedy in it just won't wash . . . I've had some doubts about this case but it's over [for me] now."[24]

Garrison himself had said little that night and his reaction to Phelan's bombshell was unclear. The next day he clarified it. He called Phelan, invited him to lunch at Broussard's, and spent the time trying to convince Phelan that Russo was "okay." But Phelan knew what he knew. "You've got a suggestible witness," he said. "Well, that's no problem," Garrison said. "We don't make suggestions to witnesses."[25]

Phelan was determined to cover all bases. So after lunch he hunted down Sciambra at Tulane and Broad and asked to see his original notes from the first interview. If the notes contained the information missing from his memorandum, then, Phelan said, he would agree that Sciambra had merely forgotten to include it. Sciambra said that, after typing his report, he had "burned" them. Phelan then asked to talk to Russo. Sciambra arranged it. Phelan drove straight to Baton Rouge, taking with him photographer Matt Herron.

At Russo's apartment, after some conversation, Phelan handed Russo Sciambra's memorandum and told him what it was. Then he said, "I'm gonna use it in the *Post*. Tell me if there's anything wrong [with it]." Russo read it through, made four minor corrections and said nothing about anything being omitted. "Then you first related the assassination plot when?" Phelan asked. "Down in New Orleans," Russo replied. After they left, Phelan said to Herron, "Did you hear that?" "Yeah," Herron said. "Burn it in your head, kid," Phelan told him, because someday "I'm going to have to tell this story and you're my witness."[26]

Phelan flew back to New York on March 23, taking with him the full documentary record of Russo's interrogations prior to the preliminary hearing.* He told his story to Don McKinney and Otto Friedrich, showing them copies of the documents, and related it to others in a series of meetings with staffers and lawyers. It was not the story they wanted but there was never any doubt about their publishing it. "Rush to Judgment in New Orleans" was featured on the May 6, 1967, cover of the magazine, with the caption, "A PLOT TO KILL KENNEDY? The story behind the New Orleans investigation." Garrison finally had his national cover story, though it was a far cry from what he had in mind.

---

* In addition to what Garrison gave him in Las Vegas, Phelan had obtained the third hypnosis transcript and Sciambra's report on the sodium Pentothal interview.

The article recapped Phelan's experiences with Garrison in New Orleans and Las Vegas, detailed the peculiar course of Garrison's probe and the odd assortment of characters involved, and noted the fertile field Garrison was working. In the latest poll only 36 percent of the public believed that Oswald acted alone. But the centerpiece was Perry Russo's evolving testimony, Moo Moo Sciambra's memorandum, and the conspiracy party he "forgot" to include. Using Garrison's own material, Phelan had exposed the empty foundation of Garrison's case against Clay Shaw. Garrison made no public comment about the article, but expressed his outrage in private. "Garrison said Phelan fucked him," Russo later stated. "He was real pissed about [Phelan] turning on him." Garrison said they had been friends for years and Phelan was now complaining about "technical points."[27] Ever Garrison's point man, Andrew Sciambra blasted Phelan in a televised statement that was published in the newspapers. Calling the article "incomplete and distorted," Sciambra challenged Phelan to repeat his charges in front of the New Orleans grand jury.

Phelan's article should have felled Garrison's case but it didn't. "I knew that if Garrison were honest and responsible, that he'd have to withdraw the case, he'd have to kill it," Phelan said.[28] It was reasonable to think so. It seems unlikely that any district attorney in any other major city in the United States would have gone forward under the circumstances. If nothing else, public opinion, the local news media, or prevailing political forces would have intervened. But in New Orleans, where the two newspapers spoke in unison, where Garrison's power surpassed even the governor's, and where unethical, irrational behavior by elected officials was rooted in the region's historical DNA, the hole Phelan had exposed was first denied and then ignored. No editorials demanded an explanation. The citizenry didn't complain. No civic leaders called for an investigation. Many simply believed Garrison could do no wrong. For those who knew better, his past victories over the judges and others had demonstrated what could happen to those who criticized him. No one wanted to lose their job.

As for his supporters outside New Orleans, some were disillusioned but probably not many. For Garrison's appeal had never been to logic but to the passions vested in the assassination of President Kennedy. That was the source of his strength and the reason he was, and still is, held to a lower standard. It is also why many were willing to give him the benefit of the doubt where Russo was concerned, *to wait and see* what additional evidence he presented at the trial. Garrison had tapped into a national wellspring of emotion that protected him like a Teflon shield.

Garrison himself reacted to Phelan's article the way he had to Phelan's visit after the preliminary hearing. It was another problem to be *dealt with*. Garrison kept his head down, sent Sciambra out to dissemble, and pretended nothing had happened. It worked.

Garrison survived disaster again.

But this was not the last threat to his investigation that would have to be *dealt with*.

CHAPTER NINE

HOW GARRISON NEUTRALIZED THE OPPOSITION

> . . . [Garrison] is a dangerous man. And I keep asking myself how many other Garrisons can there be. If it can happen here, it can happen anywhere else in the country.[1]
>
> —Clay Shaw, 1969

About ten o'clock in the evening on March 9, 1967, twenty-one-year-old Alvin Beaubouef, at home with his wife and child, answered a knock at his front door. He found two of Garrison's police investigators standing there. Lynn Loisel and Louis Ivon asked Beaubouef to step outside and he did. In the conversation that followed, Garrison's men offered Beaubouef a substantial sum of money, reportedly as much as $15,000, a job with an airline (Beaubouef's dream), and a hero's role in the case. In return they wanted him to fill in "the missing links" in David Ferrie's story.

Garrison sent his men to make this offer because he knew David Ferrie was involved in the assassination. Alvin Beaubouef had accompanied Ferrie on his trip to Houston the night of the assassination; therefore, he must know something. Ivon and Loisel said just that that night: we know you know something. The D.A.'s office had already interviewed Beaubouef twice. Both times he denied knowing anything about the assassination or Ferrie's alleged involvement. The last time, Beaubouef had said he was willing to take a polygraph test.[2] Still, here they were back again. Beaubouef later said he thought they wanted information about Ferrie's private life. He told them he would do anything he could to help but he wanted to speak to his wife and attorney about it first. That was fine. Loisel said they would put the offer in writing in any form Beaubouef wished.

The next day Beaubouef called his attorney, Hugh Exnicios, and described what had occurred, saying he knew nothing about the assassination. Exnicios represented David Ferrie's estate and felt strongly that Ferrie was an intelligent, moral person, who would not have been involved in such a crime.[3] To him it sounded as though Garrison's men were trying to purchase false information. Exnicios called the district attorney's office and arranged for Loisel to come to his office that afternoon for a meeting that would include Beaubouef. Then Exnicios set up a concealed tape recorder that he activated (exactly when is unclear) after Loisel entered the office.[4]

In the secretly recorded conversation that followed, Loisel repeated the offer made the night before, with one revision. The airline job and the hero's role were the same but the amount of money was now $3,000. Loisel said he was only interested in information about the assassination and he wanted only the truth. He also said Jim Garrison had authorized the three items offered. Loisel assured them that Beaubouef did not have to worry about being an accessory for withholding until now the information he supplied. "There's ninety-nine thousand ways we could skin that cat," Loisel said. Nor would there be any danger of Beaubouef incriminating himself because they could "change the story around," Loisel explained, to eliminate him from "any type of conspiracy or what have you."[5]

Exnicios asked what would happen if it turned out Beaubouef didn't know anything. The deal was only good, Loisel said, if Beaubouef could provide "the missing links." Otherwise, the deal was off. Loisel then left the room so Beaubouef and Exnicios could confer in private. Beaubouef repeated that he knew nothing about the assassination. Exnicios warned him that saying no to Loisel would result in a subpoena. They decided Beaubouef would agree to take the three tests that Loisel had said might be required—truth serum, hypnosis and a polygraph.* Loisel left that day with the understanding that Beaubouef would be available that weekend, but the tests were never administered.

Thirty-four-year-old Exnicios believed the tape recording he now

---

* When Loisel mentioned these tests is unclear; it may have been the previous evening or before the recorder was activated.

possessed was evidence that Loisel, acting on Garrison's express authority, had tried to bribe Beaubouef (who was out of work and needed money) to supply false testimony. In the period that followed, Exnicios offered the tape for $5,000 to the news media, without success, and to Shaw's defense team. Irvin Dymond and William Wegmann listened to the recording in Exnicios's office. "There is no question that a bribe was offered," Wegmann said recently. "But there was no way my brother [Edward Wegmann] was going to buy that tape."[6] Wegmann and Dymond did arrange to have it transcribed.

Exnicios distributed the transcript to various agencies.[*] He also played the tape for Frank Langridge, the district attorney of Jefferson Parish, where Exnicios's office was located and the jurisdiction of the alleged bribe. He was hoping Langridge would file criminal charges against Garrison, Ivon and Loisel. Langridge took no official action. He did, however, contact his friend Jim Garrison and tell him about the tape.[7] Garrison informed his men.

On the evening of April 11, Ivon and Loisel again visited Beaubouef at his home. He would later tell a police investigator that they had threatened to circulate embarrassing pictures of him (confiscated in 1963 from Ferrie's apartment), and threatened him with physical harm. "I don't want to get into any shit," Beaubouef claimed Loisel said, "and before I do I'll put a hot load of lead up your ass."[8] Both men, Beaubouef recently recalled, had their hands on him. "One of them's got one hand wound in my clothing holding me and his other hand has his gun in my face and he shoved it in my mouth."[†] While he no longer recalls the exact words that were spoken, Beaubouef does remember the message. "They were saying, 'If you don't retract this, we're going to kill you.'" Beaubouef believed them. He appeared the next day at Tulane and Broad and signed a sworn statement saying that no one in the district attorney's office offered him a bribe.

But that was not the end of it. Beaubouef was soon telling media representatives about the offer and the threats. Newsweek published a lengthy

---

[*] The U.S. Attorney in New Orleans, the Louisiana State Attorney General, and the Bar Association's Ethics Committee.
[†] Louis Ivon recently said the claim that they laid hands on him is "completely untrue" (telephone conversation with author, June 28, 1996).

account by Hugh Aynesworth of the episode. Both local newspapers ran articles about it and the story was picked up by other newspapers nationwide. Beaubouef's new attorney* took the matter to the New Orleans Police Department, which conducted a month-long investigation. Ivon and Loisel admitted making the offer but insisted they were only after the truth and denied threatening Beaubouef.[9] The police investigator concluded that Loisel and Ivon had not violated any of the rules of the department's Code of Conduct.†

That let everyone off the hook without resolving the basic controversy. But because the police report on its investigation was withheld from the public until recently, the matter simply faded away at the time. Yet it has remained a hotly contested issue over the years. Although Beaubouef was willing, neither Garrison nor anyone in the police department challenged him with a polygraph test. A media representative working on a story about Garrison's investigation did. Beaubouef passed.[10]

Unlike most who did battle with Garrison in this period, Alvin Beaubouef survived relatively unscathed. James Phelan was another. His second New Orleans experience began the latter part of May with a telephone call from the renowned producer, Fred Freed. Freed was preparing a documentary for NBC, a White Paper on Garrison to be broadcast in June, and he hired Phelan to assist in the research. Despite advice from two attorneys to stay out of Garrison's reach, Phelan was soon on his way. His assignment was to persuade the mercurial Perry Russo to go before a camera and tell the truth.

On his first day back in town, through an intermediary, Phelan let Garrison know he was there and did not intend to hide. He then waited for the grand jury subpoena he assumed would be forthcoming. He was wrong. Garrison passed word to Phelan that he would not be subpoenaed unless he publicly embarrassed the district attorney's office. As Phelan later said, he had sense enough to avoid doing that. So despite Andrew Sciambra's bluster about putting Phelan together with the

---

* To avoid a conflict of interest, Hugh Exnicios had told Beaubouef to obtain new counsel.
† Yet according to writer-attorney Milton Brener, under Louisiana Statutes public bribery need not involve false information, only something of value offered to a potential witness with the intent to influence his conduct as a witness (Brener, *The Garrison Case*, p. 176).

grand jury, when the opportunity arose, Garrison didn't want Phelan telling those twelve men his story.

Over the next six days, Phelan met six times with Perry Russo at his New Orleans apartment. Russo was friendly and quite willing to talk but Phelan quickly realized that the record player Russo was always turning on and off was a bugging device. The red light stayed on even when the machine was off.[11] So their real conversations took place elsewhere. Phelan talked "about justice, the truth," and "what [Russo] was doing to Shaw, if his story was phony." Russo was coy; he wouldn't say yes or no to appearing on the NBC program. He was stringing Phelan along. But he also confided in him. He let Phelan know that he was afraid he had identified the wrong man, and that he was angry about being the primary witness when he had been told he was just helping to support an airtight case. Russo readily admitted he no longer knew "the difference between reality and fantasy" and repeatedly expressed his concern that Garrison would retaliate against him if he should back away from his story.[12] * Phelan left New Orleans uncertain whether or not Russo was going to appear on the program.

Back in New York, Phelan soon learned that Garrison was scheduled to address a convention of New York district attorneys at the Laurel Country Club in the Catskills. Still hopeful that Garrison would see the light if he just had the facts about Russo, Phelan decided to attend the convention and confront Garrison with Russo's latest statements. The night of Garrison's appearance, Phelan approached him as he entered the banquet room. Both men were friendly and they arranged to meet after dinner.[13]

They spent about ninety minutes talking in a little bar at the Club. Garrison finally had an answer for the question Phelan had asked him in Las Vegas—why did the masterminds of this plot discuss their plans in front of Russo, a casual bystander? "He's in the plot, too," Garrison said. Phelan found this absurd and stomped on it so hard Garrison dropped it. Garrison also recalled Sciambra's claim that he had briefed him orally

---

* At their last meeting Russo told Phelan he recalled two quite different parties at Ferrie's apartment. One, where Ferrie was playing the piano, appeared like vivid images on a color television screen; the other, which Russo described in court, was "dull and faint" like a bad black and white picture. Phelan believed the vivid piano-playing party really happened, and the other was a product of Dr. Fatter's leading questions and Russo's suggestibility (Phelan Interview).

FALSE WITNESS

about the plot party. "I don't really know what I actually remember," Garrison said, "and what I 'remember' because Sciambra wants me to remember." Phelan then described Russo's latest statements to him. Russo, Garrison said, "was talking out of both sides of his mouth."[14]

Garrison seemed swayed by what Phelan told him. He suggested a meeting with Russo, Phelan, and himself, where Phelan would confront Russo with his statements. "If he cops out to half of it," Garrison said, "I'll drop the case against Clay Shaw." Phelan was enormously pleased and relieved. Garrison at last was going to do the right thing. The meeting, Garrison said, would take place within the next ten days. Phelan agreed to fly to New Orleans on a moment's notice. But the meeting never occurred. Phelan waited for weeks. He called Garrison and wrote him two letters. Garrison replied in a letter dated July 12, confirming the agreement but accusing Phelan of "pecking away at a peripheral point." At last Phelan realized that Garrison had conned him. "He was so convincing [that night in the Catskills]," Phelan later recalled. "He said, 'I don't want to go in a ditch by charging the wrong man.'"[15] But that was just part of the con. Phelan had posed a new threat that night and Garrison was handling it.

Another threat surfaced on May 23. The Garrison camp was electrified by the news that NBC's Walter Sheridan had sniffed out lie detector technician Roy Jacob and learned about Russo's disastrous polygraph. Faced with the prospect of an "expert" saying on network television that Russo had "failed" a lie-detector test, Garrison reluctantly ordered Russo to take another one.[16] It was administered on June 19 by New Orleans Police Department polygraph technician Edward O'Donnell. But he was no more successful than Roy Jacob had been. After only three irrelevant questions, such as "Were you born in New Orleans?" Russo's "erratic pneumograph tracing"* and "physical movements" caused O'Donnell to shut the machine off and remove the attachments. Russo then began talking and startled O'Donnell with a succession of disclosures, the most damaging being that Clay Shaw had not been at Ferrie's assassination plot party.[17]

---

* This "could be caused," O'Donnell wrote, "by general nervous tension or by the fact that the person intended to lie during the test" (Edward O'Donnell, Report to Jim Garrison, regarding Perry Russo Interview, June 20, 1967 [Appendix B in this book]).

·114·

After Russo left, O'Donnell made a beeline to Garrison's office and in the presence of James Alcock told Garrison what had occurred. Garrison, O'Donnell later recounted, "went into a rage." "Jesus Christ!" Garrison shouted, "that son of a bitch has sold out to the CIA! He has sold out to NBC!"

Later that day, Lynn Loisel and Louis Ivon showed up at O'Donnell's office. "They told me it would be better for everyone if I forgot what happened." Garrison wanted O'Donnell to keep his mouth shut and he certainly wanted no official report. As soon as the two left, O'Donnell began dictating one. The next day he sent copies to several officials, including the superintendent of police. The original he personally delivered to Garrison.

Some weeks later, Garrison called O'Donnell into a meeting in his office. Also there were Alcock, Sciambra, and Russo. Garrison handed O'Donnell's report to Russo. Did you say this? Garrison asked. Russo "began to hem and haw" but when O'Donnell implied that their session had been recorded, Russo admitted the report was accurate. "After Russo recanted," O'Donnell later remarked, "I said *no way is there going to be a trial*. How can you go to court when your star witness says 'what I've told you isn't true'?" Garrison tried, unsuccessfully, to have O'Donnell fired.[18]

Meanwhile, the bad news continued to filter into Garrison's office about the NBC investigation. On May 17 Garrison became so angry at what he was hearing that he ordered two members of Fred Freed's team, Richard Townley and Walter Sheridan, *arrested* and, Garrison said, he wanted them *handcuffed and beaten*. A worried William Gurvich went to James Alcock who interceded. Arrested for what? Alcock asked Garrison. "What do you mean, *for what*—just arrest [them]," he replied. When Alcock protested that there were "no grounds," Garrison admonished him for being "so legalistic"; but neither Gurvich or Alcock carried out his order.[19]

NBC's much-anticipated White Paper, "The J.F.K. Conspiracy: The Case of Jim Garrison" aired on June 19. It leveled the most serious public charges to date against Garrison and his aides. They knew what was coming because William Gurvich attended a 2:00 A.M. screening in New York. In the morning Gurvich called and described it to Asst. D.A. Charles Ward. That afternoon Gurvich told Garrison about it. The show began with James Phelan explaining that the assassination plot party was missing from Russo's first interview. Phelan was not producer Freed's first choice to open the show. Freed wanted Russo, but he had finally turned them down. "The hell with truth," Russo had said to Sheridan. "The hell with justice. You're asking me to sacrifice myself for Shaw [by telling the truth] and I won't do it."[20] Freed's second choice had been Garrison's main investigator, but Gurvich, too, had refused.

As Garrison feared, Freed spotlighted the results of Russo's first poly-graph.[21] But that wasn't all. Freed also showcased Vernon Bundy's lie-detector test. It "indicated," said Narrator Frank McGee, "that Bundy was lying." The program reported as well the effort of Charles Ward to prevent Garrison from putting Bundy on the stand. And two burglars, Miguel Torres and John Cancler, prison-mates of Bundy, stated that he told them he had lied in order to get "cut loose" from Angola.[22] McGee pointed out that Garrison, fully aware of the test results, put both Russo and Bundy on the stand and won his victory at the preliminary hearing based on their testimony.[23]

Miguel Torres and John Cancler had more to say. Torres charged that Garrison aides had tried to persuade him to identify Clay Shaw as Clay Bertrand and to testify that he had participated in "sex orgies" with Shaw at his home. Cancler, a "high-class" burglar known as John the Baptist, claimed that a Garrison investigator had urged him to enter Shaw's home and plant evidence.*The program's most far-reaching dis-closure came from Dean Andrews. Clay Shaw was not Clay Bertrand. "I wouldn't know Clay Shaw if I fell over him on the street dead," Andrews was quoted as saying.[24]

Garrison was infuriated by the broadcast and immediately went on the offensive. He accused NBC of "trying to torpedo" his case. He said the network's objective was "to bring an end to the investigation into the facts of the assassination"; and he accused Walter Sheridan of mak-ing improper offers to Perry Russo.[25] In an ironic mirror image of the Beaubouef affair, Garrison soon charged both Sheridan and Townley

---

* This break-in story was not an NBC fabrication, as has been charged. It sur-faced *before* NBC's representatives heard it. William Gurvich learned about it in January from the Garrison aide who had been given the break-in assignment (*Los Angeles Times*, June 29, 1967; Gurvich Conference, tape #2, pp. 6–7); and John Cancler told his attorney, Milton Brener, about it probably in March (Brener, *The Garrison Case*, pp. 189–190).

with bribery for allegedly offering Perry Russo a job and a place to live in California. Garrison's counterattack gave his supporters hope by making it appear that his accusations against NBC had some merit.

The NBC broadcast marked the beginning of a grim two-week period for Garrison. Aaron Kohn, managing director of the Metropolitan Crime Commission (a private watchdog organization), demanded that State Attorney General Jack Gremillion investigate Garrison's activities. Gremillion demurred, claiming he lacked the authority. But the biggest blow to Garrison came from his own camp with the defection of investigator William Gurvich.[26] That turned into a riveting public drama. The fuse was lit when Gurvich met secretly with Robert Kennedy and briefed him on Garrison's investigation.[*] That ninety-minute session on June 8 began at Kennedy's Virginia home, continued in a cab, and ended at the airport with the two men sitting on the edge of a luggage conveyor.[27]

Gurvich was trying to work behind the scenes but someone leaked news of the meeting to a Long Island daily published by Robert Kennedy's friend and former Lyndon Johnson aide Bill Moyers. Gurvich, choosing his words carefully, spoke to a reporter for the newspaper on June 22. That story ran the next day. Gurvich told the reporter that Garrison was "sincere" in what he was doing but "broadly hinted" that the case was without substance. That evening NBC News reported that Gurvich had told RFK there was "no basis in fact and no material evidence in Garrison's case for an assassination plot" against President Kennedy.[28]

Deeply stung, Garrison attacked Gurvich with a vengeance. He first put out word that Gurvich hadn't been involved in the case for the last couple of months. Then he released a statement belittling Gurvich as the operator of a "night-watchman service" and "little more than a chauffeur and photographer" for the district attorney's office, all grossly untrue.[†]

---

[*] Walter Sheridan (who had been a special assistant to Robert Kennedy when he was attorney general) arranged the meeting at Kennedy's request. Gurvich agreed, he later said, because he feared Kennedy would think "there actually was something in New Orleans and might be overly optimistic and hopeful" about solving his brother's murder (Gurvich, interview, WWL-TV, June 27, 1967).

[†] Gurvich was one of the select six who received copies of the "master file"; he had "a full set of keys" to the district attorney's office; he used Garrison's car; "shared" Garrison's desk; was praised by Garrison at his big February Fontainebleau press conference; and the weekend after the RFK story broke Gurvich was in New York interviewing a witness in the case.

Garrison also pointed a finger as usual at the federal government. "A tremendous amount of federal power is being brought to bear on anyone connected with our investigation," he said; "the official Washington attitude is that our inquiry must be stopped at all cost."[29]

Nothing hurt Garrison more than the defection of Gurvich, a key member of his original group. The owner and executive vice-president of a large, well-known security service and detective agency founded by his father (a former FBI agent), Gurvich was highly respected nationally and internationally for his investigatory skills. He and his brother, Leonard Gurvich, had worked for Garrison since he first took office and requested their assistance. Tall and trim at forty-two, he was described by one writer as "handsome though graying" and "a casting director's idea" of a private investigator.[30] Gurvich began working on the case in December 1966 and he played an important and conspicuous role.

His first reaction to Garrison's personal attack on him was low key. He told a reporter for the New York Times that he had "grave misgivings" about Garrison's inquiry and intended to urge Garrison to rethink the case.[31] He arrived back in New Orleans that same day, a Sunday, and wired Garrison, requesting a 10:30 appointment Monday morning. But when he arrived on Monday, Garrison saw to it that he was humiliated. Louis Ivon stopped him from entering the inner area by blocking his way. Gurvich tried to reach Garrison using the telephone at the reception desk, without success. James Alcock then appeared and escorted him inside. About fifteen minutes later, he left, telling reporters that he had waited long enough. Shortly afterwards, he called the district attorney's office and officially resigned his dollar-a-year post. The gloves were now off.

Gurvich told the press that Garrison was "irrational" and that some of his witnesses should be charged with perjury. He said on local television that Garrison employed methods that were "illegal and unethical."[32] He also made it clear that he was going to try to convince the grand jury that Clay Shaw should not have been indicted in the first place, and that Garrison's investigation should be stopped.[33] Gurvich had declared war on Jim Garrison. But by appealing to the grand jury, he had placed himself directly in the sights of Garrison's heaviest artillery. Worst of all, it was a hopeless move. Gurvich thought these grand jurors still had jurisdiction over Shaw's indictment, but it was out of their hands. Yet even if they could have undone it, as Gurvich hoped, they would not have. They were under Garrison's spell as well as his thumb.

This jury functioned as Garrison's personal tool. As its legal advisor, the district attorney controlled it under ordinary circumstances. That was especially true in this instance. Seven members of this jury (known as the LaBiche grand jury after its foreman, Albert V. LaBiche) were Legionnaires and, like Garrison, members of the New Orleans Athletic Club, which Garrison used as an alternate office. Some of them reportedly contributed money to his cause.[34] * Moreover, the entire jury had been indoctrinated by Garrison. He brought in Warren Report critics Mark Lane, Harold Weisberg, William Turner, and others to lecture them about the Dallas shooting, using photographs, drawings, and charts.

At the beginning Garrison had assured these jurors that he knew who "the real assassins were and would haul them to justice." They believed him. In an extraordinary March session, he made it clear that he didn't just expect their "cooperation"; he was demanding it. If they didn't toe the line, Garrison said he would shut the investigation down.[35] Gurvich underestimated Garrison's iron grip on this body. He believed he, too, had friends there and could make them see the light.

The day after Gurvich resigned, he received a grand jury subpoena for the next day. It arrived at ten o'clock that night. The late-hour notification was a typical Garrison move. It allowed Gurvich no time to collect files or assemble affidavits and witnesses to support his claims, as he had planned to do. The following morning he arrived alone and empty-handed at the grand jury room, defiantly sporting an "Even Paranoids Have Enemies" button. In another routine tactic Garrison kept him waiting while a small army of witnesses entered the room ahead of him.[36] He was finally admitted, exhausted and ill (from a bleeding ulcer), eight hours later. Inside, Gurvich faced the twelve jurors, Jim Garrison, and five assistant district attorneys. He testified about an hour in a testy, contentious exchange and left with the understanding that he would be recalled at a later date.[37]

At 10:00 P.M., after more than twelve hours in session, Foreman LaBiche appeared and to the waiting news representatives read a

---

* Responding to motions filed by Shaw's attorneys, the foreman denied that he or any of the other grand jurors contributed to Garrison's fund (*New Orleans States-Item*, May 18, 1967).

sweeping statement that exonerated Jim Garrison of any wrongdoing. "No new evidence has been produced," LaBiche stated, "to confirm any of the allegations that have been made to date by critics of Mr. Garrison's case."[38] Garrison had won the day. He had bounced back from the NBC program and he had defused the Gurvich challenge. Eventually, he charged Gurvich with stealing the Shaw case master file. It wasn't much of a charge, but at least it was something.

He was more successful with Dean Andrews.

Questioned on March 16 by Garrison's men in front of the grand jury, Andrews had abided by his deal with Garrison. He said that he couldn't say whether or not Shaw was Bertrand. The grand jury returned a perjury indictment against him. The "three-thousand-pound canary" had pounced. Andrews pleaded not guilty and was granted a jury trial. He was then suspended from his position as assistant district attorney in Jefferson Parish. About a month later, a new five-count perjury indictment was handed down.[39] Shortly afterward, Garrison—"flushed with victory"— told writer Epstein that, like everyone else, he liked Andrews, "but I have to show him I mean business." "Andrews," Garrison said, "was protecting Shaw."[40]

Andrews now understood the situation. He would either reverse his course and give Garrison the testimony he wanted against Clay Shaw or face serious prosecution. The comic figure was faced with a tragic choice. Throw Clay Shaw to the wolves or be devoured himself. There is no inkling that Andrews ever considered lying about Shaw to save himself. When the chips were down, Andrews acted out of conscience and did the honorable thing.[41]

On June 28 Andrews appeared unsummoned outside the grand jury room, determined to be heard. While the jurors inside were listening to the parade of witnesses assembled by Garrison to refute Gurvich and the NBC charges, Andrews addressed the reporters outside. He revealed that "Clay Bertrand" was actually his old friend, bar owner Eugene Davis. But Davis, he said, knew nothing whatever about the assassination. The grand jurors issued a subpoena instanter for Andrews and he was soon talking inside. "If this case is based on the fact that Clay L. Shaw is Clay Bertrand," he told them, "it's a joke." The name Clay Bertrand originated at a "fag wedding" reception years before, he said. A woman named Helen Girt, also known as "Big Jo" or "Butch" introduced Gene Davis to Andrews as "Clay Bertrand." Andrews had known Davis for years and the introduction was merely banter.[42] He said he had repeatedly told Garrison that Clay Shaw was not Bertrand. He now declared the same to the grand jurors: "Clay Shaw is not Clay Bertrand," he stated. "Indict me if you want to." He also described the deal he had cut with Garrison prior to Shaw's arrest and how he had abided by it. "I kept my deal with the giant. I said I can't say he is and I can't say he ain't and I got indicted for it."[43]

When asked by a reporter why he had not revealed Bertrand's identity sooner, Andrews said he wanted to protect Davis, an innocent bystander. Eugene Davis immediately denied he ever used the name Bertrand, and signed a sworn statement to that effect. He also said he never called Andrews "in reference to representation of Lee Harvey Oswald."* On both points, Andrews unequivocally agreed.

On July 5, the same day his fourth child was born, Andrews resigned his job with the Jefferson Parish district attorney's office to avoid being fired. He had one last card to play before his trial and he did it as conspicuously as possible—in a press conference at the New Orleans Press Club. In a dramatic and categorical *mea culpa* he publicly acknowledged his wrongdoing. "Clay Shaw," he said emphatically, "ain't Clay Bertrand. Amen." Clay Bertrand, Andrews said, "never existed." In claiming he did, Andrews admitted, he had been motivated by the desire to jump on the publicity train and ride it to glory. He should have named his fictitious caller Leroy Bertrand, he said. The next day Garrison lodged additional perjury charges against Andrews for his statements to the grand jury identifying Gene Davis as Bertrand.

Andrews entered the courtroom for his trial in August with eleven counts of perjury against him. After five days of testimony, the jury convicted him on three of them, all for failing to identify Clay Shaw as Clay Bertrand. The trial was a sad affair. One reporter noted that Andrews, alone for a moment during a recess, "wept briefly." The verdict was not a popular one. "I almost cried," William Gurvich said.

---

* But Davis did call Andrews while he was in the hospital. Early in the Garrison probe Davis confirmed that to Asst. D.A. James Alcock. This led Alcock to suggest "that Dean might have just made up the name Bertrand" (Bethell Diary, pp. 1, 2, 10).

"That same sympathy for Andrews," the *Los Angeles Times* reporter wrote, "was frequently expressed throughout the Criminal Courts Building." A medical report ordered by the court described Andrews as suffering from edema, septicemic shock, and cardiac decomposition. Judge Frank J. Shea nevertheless sentenced him to eighteen months in jail. Perjury, Shea said, in remarks laden with unintended irony, undermines the entire judicial system and "must not be condoned. If not suppressed, it will make meaningless the truth and will encourage willful and irresponsible falsehoods among those who now fear the consequences of such a lie." It is "all the more reprehensible in the words of an attorney since it can only lead to contempt for the law and courts."[44] In a case founded on lies, Dean Andrews was convicted because he refused to tell one.

In his triumph over Andrews, Garrison had finally delivered on his promise, made six months earlier at his first Kennedy investigation press conference, that there would be convictions. Garrison believed no one noticed or cared what convictions were for, as long as they were convictions. That is why he pressed so many inconsequential suits. Eventually, he would charge twelve individuals in cases only peripherally related to the Shaw investigation, three of them against reporters. To his supporters these were meant to show he was delivering on his promises. To his opponents they were a message: criticizing the district attorney was a risky business. Many of those indicted, like Dean Andrews, were uncooperative witnesses whom Garrison was either punishing, coercing, or both. While these lawsuits had neither merit nor substantive impact on the case, for some of those charged, they were the source of long-term difficulties.

Garrison admitted to those close to him that he was engaging in "intimidation," bringing charges "to make" people give him the information he wanted.[45] Members of his staff worried about his tactics and he met with frequent resistance from some. One assistant district attorney removed himself from the investigation, telling Edward O'Donnell, "I'm not getting involved in this and anyone who does is crazy."[46] Others wanted out but remained, presumably for financial or professional reasons. (Reportedly, some of Garrison's top aides stayed because he promised them judgeships.) Various sources attest to the opposition within Garrison's own camp.* In the early days of the case, Leonard Gurvich was speaking on the telephone to a senior assistant district attorney who began to cry. "Garrison," the assistant said, "is ruining the office and everybody in it."[47] Yet none of these men raised a hand to help William Gurvich when he tried to put a stop to what Garrison was doing.

For Garrison to save face and salvage his credibility, he had to overcome the Gurvich threat, but that bestowed little glory. His victory over Andrews, a figure mentioned in the Warren Report, did. It restored some of his luster, tarnished by the NBC show and Gurvich's public condemnation. Ironically, Garrison actually benefited from the media criticism. Many saw him as a besieged and unfairly maligned figure. Garrison also garnered a more concrete bonus. He complained to the Federal Communications Commission about the NBC program, demanded equal time, and was granted thirty minutes in which to respond.

In his nationwide broadcast, Garrison achieved the exposure *Life* and the *Post* had failed to deliver. He exploited that fully over the next six months, accepting speaking engagements, appearing on radio and television programs, addressing forums coast to coast and granting interviews to friendly reporters. (A sampling of his constantly shifting theories on the who, how, and why of the assassination is found on pages 181–182.) *Playboy*, one of the nation's most popular magazines, ran a lengthy, sympathetic profile. Capping off this media blitz, comedian Mort Sahl arranged for Garrison to appear on Johnny Carson's *Tonight Show*. (Clay Shaw's attorneys telegrammed their protest.) Inspired by all the attention, Garrison expanded his conspiracy ideas to a galactic scale. During a speech in Los Angeles, he named LBJ. Sounding like Marc Antony praising Caesar, Garrison denied he was saying President Johnson was involved, but noted that he had profited more than anyone else from Jack Kennedy's death. Then he asked rhetorically, wouldn't it be nice to know Johnson wasn't involved instead of just assuming?[48] † On that same trip Garrison identified another "conspirator," an employee of the International Council of Christian Churches who resided in North

---

* This opposition was chronicled in the Gurvich tapes and, more extensively, in the Bethell Diary.
† "They think him a liberal," Shaw wrote, when the *Los Angeles Free Press* devoted five pages to Garrison's speech. "He is the very face of fascism" (Shaw Notes, Dec. 19, 1967, p. 22).

Hollywood, one Edgar Eugene Bradley.

Garrison charged Bradley, like Shaw, with conspiracy to murder the president and claimed that Bradley for years had been working for the U.S. intelligence apparatus. "I shot *who?*" Bradley blurted on hearing the news. The charge against Bradley (which was prompted by a letter from a man in Van Nuys, California, who claimed that Bradley had tried to have JFK killed when he was a senator) was perhaps Garrison's most obviously bogus move.* At the time he had no evidence Bradley was ever in New Orleans or Dallas, much less that he conspired to assassinate the president. Nor was Bradley connected to Shaw, Oswald, or Ferrie, and Garrison's charge against Bradley didn't claim that he was.† James Alcock, indignant over the entire affair, told a staff member that he would refuse to prosecute Bradley. "Let's keep our fingers crossed," he said, in the hope that Bradley wouldn't be extradited.[49] Alcock got his wish when California's Governor Reagan rejected the request.

If the Bradley charge was Garrison's most transparent act, his attack on Robert Kennedy was the sorriest. Kennedy incurred Garrison's wrath by releasing a statement defending his friend Walter Sheridan. Garrison retaliated, claiming Kennedy was impeding his investigation. Kennedy didn't want the "real assassins" caught, Garrison said, because it "would interfere with his political career."[50]

Though most of the media were already disillusioned with Garrison, much of the public was undecided and a large segment, still convinced "he must have something," was waiting for that *something* to be revealed at Clay Shaw's trial. Back in March, Shaw had expected that trial to take place within three to six months, which he considered "a long time to live under the conditions in which [he] was living." By October, Shaw was referring to those conditions as a "maelstrom." He feared that Garrison's ongoing public statements had created an inflammatory

---

* William Turner, the *Ramparts* [magazine] staff writer and Garrison volunteer who unearthed the letter in Garrison's files and sparked the Bradley investigation, reportedly admitted to Tom Bethell that Garrison didn't believe Bradley was guilty and that charging him was a ploy in the publicity war Garrison was waging (Bethell Diary, pp. 19 and 29).

† Soon, however, two incriminating statements suddenly appeared in Garrison's Bradley file. One placed Bradley at Dealey Plaza on November 22, 1963, and was signed by former Dallas Deputy Sheriff Roger Craig; the other linked Bradley to David Ferrie, and was signed by Perry Russo (Bethell Diary, p. 28).

atmosphere that jeopardized the prospects for a fair trial. As long as Garrison continued to "[shoot] off his big fat mouth," as Shaw put it, he wanted his attorneys to delay the trial. His attorneys were more concerned about laying the groundwork for an appeal in the event Shaw was convicted; they accomplished that by filing various motions on a variety of issues. They also had no choice but to investigate all of Garrison's new "leads" in the case. As Shaw's financial reserves hemorrhaged, three to six months stretched into two years. He spent the time studying the Warren Report and the writings of its critics, tracking developments and Garrison's every word, and searching for a way "to take the offensive."[51]

In public Garrison was unwavering during this hiatus, but in private was hoping the government would block the case or that something would happen to Shaw. With great conviction, he assured his staff that the trial would never occur. James Alcock told a colleague that he wanted to believe Garrison was right but doubted that he was.[52] Alcock had reason to worry. Garrison had delegated the principal trial function to him. Garrison would deliver opening and closing remarks and he would interview a couple of witnesses, but Alcock would be the one in court every day, ostensibly in charge. Yet it was Garrison's game plan. He was running the show. He was calling the shots. A win would have been an enormous achievement for Garrison and, by appearing to hand the reins to his assistant, he had someone to blame if anything went wrong.

Keeping his staff in the dark about the overall picture allowed Garrison to imply he had evidence they didn't know about that buttressed what they did. Reportedly, as the trial date approached, Alcock went to Garrison and asked to be informed about the rest of his case. "You've got it," Garrison replied to his stunned assistant, "there isn't anything else." I asked Alcock if that story was true. "I'm not getting into that," he replied sharply.[53] According to an impeccable source close to the case, the night before the trial began Alcock "broke down" at the home of another assistant district attorney and said he didn't know what to do. That he was being "forced" to prosecute an innocent man.

CHAPTER TEN

THE TRIAL, PART ONE: CLAY SHAW

> Criminal conspiracy is the agree-
> ment or combination of two or
> more persons for the specific
> purpose of committing any
> crime; provided that . . . one or
> more of such parties does an act
> in furtherance of the object of
> the agreement. . . .
>
> —*Criminal Code of Louisiana*

> Listen, kid, all of that bullshit
> doesn't mean a thing. Who's right
> or who's wrong—this is New
> Orleans![1]
>
> —*Pershing Gervais (to James Kirkwood), 1969*

For a city that looks to its politics for entertainment, Clay Shaw's trial was the equivalent of Armstrong stepping onto the moon. After two years of anticipation, jury selection was scheduled to begin January 21, 1969. But on the seventeenth, James Alcock requested an indefinite continuance, citing a report just released by Attorney General Ramsey Clark regarding President Kennedy's autopsy. The report, Alcock said, was prejudicial to the state's case.[2] Some believed Garrison had been looking for a way out and on battle eve had found it. That Friday it suddenly looked as though Clay Shaw would never stand trial. Over the weekend, however, Garrison either reconsidered or was grandstanding to begin with because on Monday Alcock withdrew the motion. The state, he said, was "ready to go to trial tomorrow."

The Big Event was going to happen after all. Even the upcoming

Mardi Gras celebration paled by comparison. The wife of a former assistant district attorney, herself a law student at the time, said recently that the trial was more exciting than any movie could convey. The international press corps had already swamped the city and the world's attention was once more riveted on Tulane and Broad, this time the second-floor courtroom of Judge Edward A. Haggerty, Jr., a silver-haired, craggy-faced Irishman, known to have a drinking problem. All the security measures at the preliminary hearing were again in place, plus two closed circuit television cameras.

At the prosecution's table that first day were Asst. D.A.s Andrew Sciambra, Alvin Oser, William Alford, Numa Bertel, and the diminutive, thirty-six-year-old team leader, James Alcock, somber and smart, with thick black hair and square black-rimmed glasses. Representing Clay Shaw were the same four men who had handled his case from the outset: veteran trial lawyer F. Irvin Dymond,* Edward F. Wegmann, William J. Wegmann,† and Salvatore Panzeca. Incredibly, the first prospective juror called was named John Kennedy; he was immediately excused after admitting he already had formed a fixed opinion.

Fourteen plodding days later, from the 1,200 prospects who appeared, the two sides finally settled on an all-male panel with two alternates. Nine of the twelve and both alternates were white, three black, five under thirty and three in their fifties. The lineup was solidly working class and its breadth of interest and intellectual reach failed to impress the media representatives who witnessed the process. If the reporters felt well-disposed toward any of them, it was a black thirty-one-year-old high school teacher. Clay Shaw and his attorneys concurred, believing he might be pro-defense and a leader in the jury room. That was ironic in light of what occurred during deliberations.

---

* Just before the trial began Dymond received a telephone call from a man identifying himself as Perry Russo who said he wanted to meet with him at the lakefront late that night. Dymond, uncertain what to expect, borrowed a gun from his next-door neighbor and drove to the location specified, but no one showed up (Dymond, interview with author, Nov. 2, 1995).

† Like Garrison, Shaw, and Dymond, the Wegmann brothers were veterans of WWII. As the skipper of an LST, Navy Lieutenant (j.g.) Edward Wegmann had seen action in the Pacific campaign. So had Army Corporal (later Second Lieutenant) William Wegmann, also serving on an LST, who was creased on the head by a bullet while standing on the beach at Saipan.

The following day, Jim Garrison, looking "fresh and fit" in front of a stand-up microphone, read his fifteen-page opening statement, which he called "a blueprint of what the State intends to prove." Any doubt that he planned to put the Warren Report on trial was resolved when he finished forty-two minutes later. Evidence about the events at Dealey Plaza was necessary, Garrison said, "because it confirms the existence of a conspiracy and because it confirms the significance and relevance of the planning which occurred in New Orleans." The state would present the Zapruder film of the shooting and testimony "corroborating" what it showed, "that the president's fatal shot was received from the front." Garrison named five overt acts the state would prove: the plotting session in Ferrie's apartment; the discussion of rifles, escape routes and alibis; the trip to the West Coast by Shaw the day of the assassination; the trip to Houston by Ferrie that same day; and Oswald's carrying a rifle into the Texas School Book Depository. Garrison delivered two surprises. He referred to *another party* that he said took place in June 1963 "in an apartment in the French Quarter," where Shaw and Ferrie discussed their assassination plans. And he unveiled a new group of witnesses from Clinton and Jackson, Louisiana, the hill country north of Baton Rouge. They would testify, he said, that in the latter part of August or the early part of September 1963, Oswald had visited that region with Clay Shaw and David Ferrie. (These eight witnesses—six men and two women—would have a long and prominent "shelf life.")[3]

Defense attorney Dymond in his opening remarks pinpointed the "core of the State's case"—the "alleged conspiratorial meeting" at Ferrie's apartment. He said the defense would prove that Shaw never "laid eyes on either" Ferrie or Oswald and that Perry Russo was "a notoriety-seeking liar." He cautioned against "the pageantry" of the Dealey Plaza evidence obscuring "the actual issues in this case." "We are not here to defend the findings of the Warren Commission," he declared. "We are not trying the Warren Report in this courtroom."[4] But that's what happened. The defense was forced to ignore the evidence challenging the Warren Report or try to refute it. They finally decided to do the latter.

The state's lead-off witness,[5] Edwin Lea McGehee, a soft-spoken, bespectacled barber, was the first of the so-called Clinton witnesses. On a "cool" afternoon when the air conditioner was off and the door was open, he saw a dark-colored, battered car resembling "a Kaiser or a Frazer or an old Nash" drive up and park in front of his one-chair barber shop. Then a man he later realized was Lee Harvey Oswald entered. Oswald was there about fifteen minutes while McGehee cut his hair and as they talked McGehee noticed a women in the front seat of the car and in the back "a bassinet." Oswald wanted to know how to go about obtaining a job at nearby East Louisiana State Hospital. McGehee suggested that the local State Representative, Reeves Morgan, might be able to help and gave Oswald instructions to Morgan's home about three miles out of town. Morgan took the stand next and said Oswald arrived on an evening when he was burning trash in his fireplace and that "it felt good sitting there by it." Morgan told Oswald, who was there about twenty-five minutes, that he couldn't help him get a job at the hospital but suggested that "it wouldn't hurt if he was a registered voter." Morgan claimed that after the assassination he told the FBI about Oswald's visit but "they already knew it." (The FBI has no record of a call from Morgan.)

Town Marshal John Manchester, lean and cowboy-handsome, was one of four witnesses who picked up the story from there. They said they saw Oswald, Ferrie, and Shaw in a black '61 or '62 Cadillac parked outside the registrar of voters office in the town of Clinton (population then—1,569). Not all of them saw Ferrie and Oswald. But all four saw the car and the driver and, from the witness stand, pointed to Clay Shaw as the man behind the wheel. Manchester claimed he spoke to the driver, who said he was "a representative of the International Trade Mart in New Orleans." Manchester described him as "big" with gray hair and a ruddy complexion. The other three witnesses also referred to his size and "gray hair." One said he was wearing a light-colored hat.

Following Manchester was the Registrar of Voters, Henry Earl Palmer. He testified that the black Cadillac, with the two men inside, was parked near his office from 10:30 in the morning to 3:30 that afternoon and he saw it a total of six times as he went in and out. The passenger had "heavy" eyebrows and "messed-up hair," Palmer said, like that in the picture he was shown of David Ferrie. On Dymond's cross-examination, Palmer admitted that his identification of the men in the car was based on seeing only the back of the driver's head and shoulders and only "one" of the passenger's "bushy eyebrows." Palmer first saw Lee Harvey Oswald that morning, standing in the slow-moving line, mostly blacks, waiting to register. It was mid-afternoon before Oswald finally entered his office. He showed Palmer his Navy I.D. card, bearing "a New Orleans address," and said he wanted "a job at the hospital in Jackson." Palmer told him "he did not have to be a registered voter" to get a job there. Oswald (who didn't meet registration requirements anyway) thanked him and left.

The other two who testified about this incident were both black men. Corrie Collins, head of the local chapter of the Congress of Racial Equality (CORE), was assisting in the voter registration drive that day. He said he saw the black Cadillac, with three men—two in front, one in back—drive up and park near the registrar's office about ten that morning. Only Collins claimed he saw all three inside the car. The one in the rear Collins identified as Oswald. Collins saw him exit the car and enter the registrar's office. Collins said the passenger was David Ferrie and he, too, remarked on Ferrie's hair and eyebrows, saying they "didn't seem real." William Dunn was another CORE worker. Dunn was unsure about any passengers in the car, but he identified a picture of Oswald as the "young white boy" he saw standing in line waiting to register.

Rounding out this scenario were two women. A receptionist at East Louisiana State Hospital, Bobbie Dedon, said she remembered directing Oswald to the personnel office. A clerk in that department, Maxine Kemp, said she saw an application in the files with the name, "Oswald, Harvey."

There was little the defense could do with these witnesses. Dymond, arguing hearsay, did prevent most of Oswald's alleged statements from being repeated, which stripped the testimony of some of its impact. He also effectively ridiculed the identifications of Shaw and Ferrie made five years after the fact and based only on fleeting glimpses of the two men. But Manchester and Palmer did more than that. They provided powerful evidence—Shaw had named his place of business to Manchester, and Oswald had produced a military identification card for Palmer. The defense believed all these people were lying but had no way to prove it.

Though these witnesses had no direct bearing on the conspiracy charge, they made Perry Russo's story seem more likely. They also cast a cloud over Shaw's credibility since he said he never met either Oswald or Ferrie, and Dymond had just repeated that in his opening statement. This was no small matter in light of the legal dictum voiced by the judge during jury selection that if the jurors believed a witness "lied in one instance" about a "material fact," they had "the right to disregard" the witness's "entire testimony."

The racially mixed Clinton witnesses, with their nicely interlaced stories and folksy civic leaders, were a strong opening for the state. It would be twenty-five years before the truth about their testimony was discovered by this writer (as described in chapter 13).

On the trial's second day, the black heroin addict, Vernon Bundy, took the stand and repeated what he said at the preliminary hearing. To illustrate why he was certain it was Shaw he saw passing money to Oswald that day at the lakefront, Bundy staged a "demonstration." At his direction, Shaw went to the back of the courtroom and with Bundy watching, walked forward. As he passed, Bundy looked down at Shaw's feet. Bundy asked Shaw to repeat this exercise, which he did. "I watched his foot the way it twisted," Bundy testified, after resuming the witness stand. He was referring to the slightly splayed way Shaw sometimes walked because of his bad back. "The twisting of his foot had frightened me that day on the seawall when I was about to cook my drugs." He said he saw it again at the preliminary hearing when Shaw entered the courtroom.*

Bundy's demonstration was devastatingly effective and reminiscent of the touch at the preliminary hearing when Garrison had Russo and Bundy walk to Shaw's chair and place their hands over Shaw's head. Garrison had devised a new choreography. Dymond did what he could to recoup, pointing out the absurdity of an addict leaving the safety of his home to shoot drugs in a public place. That did not, however, erase the impact of Bundy's performance.

The state's next witness was a surprise in a variety of ways. Charles I. Spiesel, an accountant who had lived in New Orleans in 1963 but presently resided in New York City, was a nicely dressed, professional-looking man who spoke well and made quite a positive impression as Alcock led him though his story. On an evening in June 1963, at a bar in the French Quarter, Spiesel met David Ferrie, who was with two

---

* Recently a former assistant district attorney under Garrison (who had no involvement in the Shaw case), said it wasn't unknown for the D.A.'s men to file charges and then go out and "gather" evidence to make the charges work. What Bundy did, picking out a particular characteristic and identifying it as the basis for an identification, he said, is *how it's done.*

women and another man. Spiesel accompanied the group to a party at an apartment near "Dauphine and Esplanade." This was Clay Shaw's neighborhood, and Shaw was one of the ten or eleven men at the party. Spiesel was introduced to all but he remembered only Shaw by name. The women left, as well as the other man in Ferrie's original group. Those who remained ended up sitting around a large table criticizing President Kennedy. At one point someone said, "Somebody ought to kill the son of a b!" The conversation, Spiesel said, seemed to amuse Shaw. Another man, "about five feet nine inches tall" with "a beard and dirty blonde hair and one finger in a splint" asked how it could be accomplished. The others concluded that "it had to be done with a high-powered rifle [with a] telescopic lens and about a mile away." According to Spiesel, who "was quite alarmed by the tone of the conversation," Shaw and Ferrie discussed how the killer could make his getaway, with Ferrie agreeing that it could be done by airplane.[6]

People present in the courtroom that day speak about the hush that fell over the room as Spiesel spoke. "You could literally hear a pin drop," a woman said recently. Spiesel told "a tidy story," one reporter wrote. And he told it well. Shaw and his attorneys and supporters were stunned and grim. First the Clinton eight, followed by Bundy's demonstration, and now this. About then, Salvatore Panzeca was being pestered by one of the court deputies. "I keep getting messages," Panzeca recently recalled, "that my next door neighbor, Bill Storm, is calling me." Panzeca was annoyed. Didn't Storm know this trial was important? Finally he gave in, left the courtroom, and called Storm back. "He says, 'Sal, I hear on the radio that Mr. Spiesel is testifying against your client. Let me tell you a little bit about him. I worked with him for many months in a CPA firm. And,' he says, 'I'm telling you the guy is a nut. He hears voices. He thinks the world is tape recording his life. He had his daughter, before she went away to college, fingerprinted.' And he's giving me all this in a real hurried way and I'm saying, 'Bill, are you sure?' 'Oh, yes, Sal, I know the guy is kooky. He sued the City of New York.' He's telling me all this and I can't write it down fast enough. I said, 'Bill, stay by this number.' I go inside and I start telling Bill Wegmann, I said, 'When Irvin gets to cross-examine ask [Spiesel] these things about voices, tape recordings, people suing him for being too short,' and Bill Wegmann thinks I'm crazy!"[7]

The questions were passed to Dymond and when his turn came he coaxed some devastating admissions from Spiesel. In 1965 he had filed a $16 million law suit against a psychiatrist, a detective agency, a horse-racing association and others charging that they had, among other things, interfered with his sex life. The defendants had conspired to convince people that he and his family were Communists, Spiesel said, and during 1962, 1963, and 1964 had put him under a "hypnotic spell." In 1964 he sued the City of New York for subjecting him to "hypnosis and mental torture." Dymond also forced him to concede that he had tried to sell his conspiracy party story to CBS for $2,000. The defense arranged for a copy of the pleading in Spiesel's multi-million-dollar lawsuit to be flown to New Orleans overnight. Dymond had it in hand when he resumed his cross-examination on Saturday morning and used it to glean more damaging details from the hapless Spiesel.[8]

The grilling was winding down when Dymond requested that the witness point out the apartment in the French Quarter where the alleged plotting party occurred. Over the objections of the prosecution, Judge Haggerty agreed, ordering that the jurors and principals be transported to the French Quarter. "Carnival came a little early," read one news account of the circuslike scene near Dauphine and Esplanade as the media hordes arrived, creating a monumental traffic jam. Back in the courtroom afterwards, Spiesel returned to the stand and confirmed that he had been unable to find the apartment in question.[9]

Everyone agreed that Dymond's questioning of Spiesel was a turning point. "The sky fell in," Alcock said.[10] Until then, it seemed as though the Garrison juggernaut was about to flatten Clay Shaw. News accounts described Garrison's men appearing "shocked" at Spiesel's admissions. They weren't. Before the trial began, Garrison sent two assistant district attorneys to New York to interview Spiesel. When they returned, one of them said, "Well, he'd make a great witness, but he's crazy." How crazy was he? "He fingerprints his children in the morning to make sure that the federal government hasn't substituted dead ringers in the middle of the night." That should have been crazy enough to keep him off the stand.*

* When I pointed out to James Alcock that Garrison in his memoir blamed him for putting Spiesel on the stand, Alcock stared down at his desk and replied tightly, "He was the district attorney. I was an assistant district attorney" (James Alcock, interview with author, Dec. 3, 1993).

But as one of Garrison's staff members later wrote, Spiesel's variety of madness seemed unlikely to be exposed. His "demeanor was normal." He had "a good job." He did "professional work." And what defense attorney "would think to ask a surprise witness, *Do you fingerprint your children?*"[11]

Perry Russo took the stand Monday morning and testified two full days. "He was the star of the show," author James Kirkwood wrote. "The state knew it, the defense and the defendant, the judge and the jury knew it—and Perry Raymond Russo knew it." Kirkwood thought Russo appeared terrified at first. He had cause. He knew the defense was going to confront him with his statements to Edward O'Donnell and James Phelan. He knew that the gap in the Sciambra memorandum had to be closed. He could only wonder what else the defense had in store for him.

Like Bundy, Russo recited basically the same story he had told at the preliminary hearing, though this time Russo didn't mention his two friends* being at Ferrie's apartment the night the plotting occurred. But he pointed to Clay Shaw as the big, "wide-shouldered, distinguished-looking" man he had seen there. In a preemptive move, Alcock launched into the major weakness of his own case, Sciambra's memorandum, asking Russo the question. What did he tell Sciambra at that first interview in Baton Rouge? In a seemingly reluctant response, Russo referred to seeing Shaw at the Kennedy rally and the service station and then said he had told Sciambra about seeing Shaw "up at Ferrie's apartment." He meant the assassination plotting party, which Alcock now called a "meeting." And did he tell Sciambra "essentially" what he had told the jury about that meeting? "Not in as great detail," Russo said, "but in essence, yes." Alcock later asked the same question again and Russo's answer was virtually incomprehensible. That Russo did such a feeble job fixing the Sciambra memorandum may suggest the depth of his own personal struggle.[12]

All 3,500 meandering words of that document were heard in the courtroom that day, after Dymond demanded it and the judge agreed. It was read by James Alcock with author Sciambra sitting at his side. Then Alcock guided Russo as he corrected some twenty-six errors in it. The most significant was the number of times Russo had seen Shaw—at least three, not two, as Sciambra had written. With that, Russo plugged the seepage around the larger hole.

* Niles Peterson and Sandra Moffett.

The defense now had its turn with Russo. This time, unlike the preliminary hearing, Dymond was quiet and non-aggressive in his questioning. Russo relaxed. And an odd bonding occurred, followed by a curiously sympathetic exchange. On both days Russo responded with helpful equivocations. He admitted that the conversation in Ferrie's apartment had all the characteristics of an inconsequential bull session. He objected to Dymond's description of Shaw, Oswald, and Ferrie as conspirators. "I don't call them conspirators," Russo said. "I have never used that word." He conceded to the soft-talking Dymond that he never heard Oswald or Shaw agree to kill the president. Only Ferrie had said, as he had many times in the past, "We will kill him." Since conspiracy requires agreement from two or more persons, this was a blow to the state's case.[13] The *States-Item*, on the street while Russo was still on the stand, bannered the news in its headline: DIDN'T HEAR SHAW, OSWALD AGREE TO KILL, RUSSO SAYS.

Russo had made damaging statements at the preliminary hearing and afterwards to various individuals, primarily James Phelan and Edward O'Donnell. Dymond now relentlessly pursued them. Russo hedged. He denied. He explained. He rambled. He performed a mind-numbing verbal tap dance. Yes, he had claimed that his two friends were at the conspiracy party, but only because Dymond had *badgered* him into it. Why had he told Edward O'Donnell that he didn't know whether or not Shaw was at Ferrie's party? Because the newspeople had made it "hard" for him to know one way or the other. Yes, he told O'Donnell that he identified Shaw at the preliminary hearing only because Dymond's "God question" "turned [him] on." But, after all, Dymond had "gone for the jugular." Yes, he probably did tell Phelan he would like to sit down with Shaw to resolve doubts about his identification of him. But that was because he wanted to be 1,000 percent sure instead of just 100 percent. Yes, he had said to Phelan, "if Garrison knew what I told my priest in Baton Rouge after the Shaw hearing he would go through the ceiling." But he had an explanation for that too. Bafflingly, it included the sort of "vague memories" one might have from a "basketball game."[14]

As Russo's marathon appearance concluded, he handed the defense another gift. Dymond asked about the "conspiratorial meeting" Russo had sat in on. "I never said anything about a conspiracy," Russo declared. "I didn't sit in on any conspiracies." Dymond finished by inquiring about Russo's failure to tell reporter Bill Bankston about the plotting session during his first interview in Baton Rouge. Russo again dodged and weaved. But his final response indirectly acknowledged his testimony's transformation. The story he told Bankston, he admitted, was "that I knew David Ferrie." That ended Russo's star turn. His personal saga would lumber on into the next decade and beyond. But his fifteen minutes of celebrity were over.[15]

He had taken the stand the day before, facing an impossible task of his own making. He knew he had to stick to his story or Garrison would charge him with perjury or worse. Yet some part of him wanted to tell the seductive Dymond the truth. He tried to do both, and ended up sounding almost delusional. Reading the three-inch-thick transcript is like being immersed in a dark and tangled mental terrain.

Appropriately, Russo's sanity was the next subject. Alcock requested that the court allow the preliminary hearing testimony of the deceased coroner, who vouched for Russo's mental health, to be entered into the record. The next morning William Wegmann argued energetically against its admission. "The question," Wegmann said, "is not whether Russo was sane in 1967. The question is whether he is sane in 1969!" The prosecution won but it was no great victory. As the sixty-seven-page transcript was read, "three jurors slept," a wire service reported, "Shaw napped and the judge's eyelids drooped." Those who could, fled.[16]

Andrew Sciambra took the stand afterwards and brought the room to life again. Attractive and pugnacious, he was there to salvage the state's case by trashing his own document. "That memorandum was hastily done," he said, "it was incomplete, it was inaccurate, there were omissions in it, and it does not reflect what Perry Russo told me during my first interview." Despite that acknowledgment and the twenty-six errors catalogued by Russo the previous day, Sciambra insisted that he had captured correctly the "essence" in all instances. He even admitted including his own "interpretations" and "assumptions" rather than always reporting what Russo had actually said. This impressionistic approach to evidence gathering was a damaging confession. It suggested that he had behaved more like a writer molding a story than an attorney seeking information.[17]

As for the absence of the conspiracy party, Sciambra provided a three-pronged explanation: the distracting atmosphere of Russo's apartment; his oral briefing of Garrison; and his being less "concerned" with the memorandum's content because the sodium-Pentothal report (which he claimed he wrote first) covered the same ground. William Wegmann, handling the cross-examination, suggested that as a "practicing criminal attorney," Sciambra should have known that the memorandum on the first interview would be admissible in court, but the sodium-Pentothal report would not be. Unfazed, Sciambra replied that he "didn't think about it." Wegmann's cross-examination grew progressively more heated and culminated with Sciambra calling James Phelan an out-of-state "journalistic prostitute," unable to "objectively report what he should." Invited by Wegmann to characterize Edward O'Donnell as a prostitute, Sciambra declined. When Wegmann asked if Sciambra believed he had "objectively reported" what Russo said to him in Baton Rouge, Sciambra admitted he might be "a sloppy memorandum writer" but that didn't make him "a prostitute."[18]

In his irrational attack on Phelan, Sciambra was expressing more than anger about his own embarrassing situation. He was giving voice to the loss of reason in the district attorney's office over the past two years toward newsmen who reported negatively about Garrison's investigation. Though Garrison exploited the national and historical import of the Kennedy assassination to the hilt, Sciambra's "out-of-state" comment is a glimpse of the parochial attitude that prevailed then and still lingers today among some of Garrison's former staff. Phelan was seen as an outsider meddling in a local matter.

The next witness was R. C. Rolland, president of the Winterland Skating Rink in Houston. He testified that on November 23, 1963, when Ferrie and his friends visited the rink, Ferrie had deliberately called attention to himself, implying that Ferrie wanted to be remembered. Ferrie made several telephone calls, Rolland said, and he didn't skate.* Whether or not Ferrie put on skates was irrelevant except to

---

* Rolland wasn't at the rink when Ferrie arrived. Since Ferrie skated only a little, he was probably off the ice before Rolland arrived (Rolland, interview with Andrew Sciambra, May 21, 1968; Ferrie, FBI interview, Nov. 25, 1963; Beaubouef Interview).

Garrison, who had incorporated Rolland's information into his sinister view of Ferrie's trip.[19] That Garrison believed it would advance his case against Shaw for the jury to hear about Ferrie, the day after the assassination, making himself conspicuous (which he often did), skating or not skating, and using the telephone, tells us nothing about Ferrie but speaks volumes about Garrison.

A black postman, James Hardiman, then took the stand. During the summer of 1966, while Shaw was on vacation, Hardiman said he delivered mail addressed to "Clem Bertrand" to the home of Clay Shaw's longtime friend, Jeff Biddison. On cross Hardiman "recognized" a fictitious name—Cliff Boudreaux—that Dymond had just made up. Hardiman said he had delivered mail to Biddison's home addressed to Boudreaux as well. As James Kirkwood pointed out, it may be pertinent that nine months earlier Hardiman's twenty-year-old-son had been arrested for theft, and two years later no action "appeared to have been taken by the district attorney's office."[20]

After the postman the thrust of the evidence shifted dramatically. For six and a half days, the focus had been on the New Orleans conspiracy. But now Garrison and his men commenced their attack on the conclusions of the Warren Report. In the period that followed, Clay Shaw went unmentioned for days. He became, literally, the forgotten man.

CHAPTER ELEVEN

THE TRIAL, PART TWO:
THE WARREN REPORT

> I only wish the press would allow
> our case to stand or fall on its
> merits in court.[1]
>
> —Jim Garrison, 1967

The prosecution began this phase of Garrison's case by calling Abraham Zapruder, the dress manufacturer famous for his home movie of the assassination. Garrison had subpoenaed the film, which was then owned by *Life* magazine. Zapruder's testimony paved the way for the trial's most sensational event, the showing of his movie in the courtroom. The other Dealey Plaza witnesses were a mixed lot, some impressive, some not. Ironically, a defense rebuttal witness, Kennedy autopsy pathologist Dr. Pierre Finck, gave the most significant medical testimony. None of this evidence had any bearing on the charge against Clay Shaw.

Dymond made that point when he objected to the entire Dallas line of inquiry. The events there, he said, were irrelevant "as to what happened here." Despite past rulings to the contrary and as expected, Judge Haggerty sided with the prosecution and the trial of the Warren Report was officially sanctioned.* Props were quickly unveiled: a mockup of Dealey Plaza, an aerial photograph, and a survey plat for topography. Jim Garrison made his third appearance in the courtroom for the occasion, remaining about thirty minutes. Handling this segment of the prosecution's case were Asst. D.A.'s Alvin Oser, with a crew cut and ringing delivery, and large, baby-faced William Alford.

Abraham Zapruder, balding, wearing glasses, and displaying a gentle

---

* At the preliminary hearing, when Shaw's attorneys attempted to introduce the Warren Report to support its case, the three-judge panel ridiculed the Report and denied the motion.

manner, told of standing on a concrete abutment next to the grassy knoll filming the motorcade as the presidential limousine approached. Zapruder heard a shot. The president "grabbed himself with his hands towards his chest or throat and leaned towards Jackie," Zapruder said. Then he heard another shot. "I saw the head practically open up," Zapruder stated (showing his emotion), "and blood and many more things, whatever it was, brains, just came out of his head." He stopped his camera, began walking around and crying out, "They killed him! They killed him!"[2]

This harrowing testimony was nothing compared to the film. Today most everyone has seen it; many possess their own copies, but in 1969, except for the Warren Commission, its staff, and a few others, only a handful of journalists and researchers had viewed the print at the National Archives in Washington, D.C. In terms of long-range influence, other than the jury's verdict, this public screening was the most important moment of the proceedings.[3]

Clay Shaw now became a spectator at his own trial. He, the attorneys, the press, and the audience all shifted to the jury side of the room, lining the walls in order to view the screen. In the darkened courtroom "the only sound was the subdued clatter of the projector," one reporter wrote. The film, he noted, clearly showed "Kennedy slumping forward and clutching his throat after he was hit for the first time. Seconds later, his head appears to snap backward as the bullet's impact causes it to virtually explode in a spray of blood and tissue . . . the intent audience gasped as the fatal shot destroyed the president's head."[4] The prosecution ran the film four more times that afternoon.* Before the trial concluded, it was shown nine more, always over Dymond's objection. For the defense, the film was more than grisly and unforgettable. They feared its impact would move the jury to exact retribution from the only target available, the defendant. Irvin Dymond labeled that Thursday afternoon their darkest hour.[5]

Over the next five days, the prosecution called two FBI agents, a photographic lab supervisor, a pathologist, as well as a batch of people pre-

---

* Garrison told one reporter that showing the film might cause a revolution; "they might even make me Vice-President!" Garrison said, grinning (Art Kevin, "Jolly Green Giant," Kennedy Assassination Chronicles, Summer 1997, p. 17).

sent at Dealey Plaza when the shots were fired. Dymond, laying the groundwork for an appeal, objected to the testimony of each on the grounds of irrelevancy to the issues in this case and, overruled each time, reserved a bill of exception, a litany also repeated for each of the many exhibits the state introduced.

The co-worker who drove Oswald to work the day of the assassination said Oswald carried a package into the building that morning, assumed to be the dismantled Mannlicher-Carcano rifle. Oswald told him the package contained "curtain rods." FBI photographic expert Lyndal Shaneyfelt took the stand and the film was shown four times outside the presence of the jury and again after the jurors came back. On cross-examination Dymond posed the question the prosecution had avoided. "My impression," Shaneyfelt replied (referring to the bullet that struck the president in the head), "is the shot came from the rear." The brain matter, he noted, was "going in a forward motion." And he indicated he had found no evidence that either of the shots that hit the president came from any direction other than the rear. The headline in that day's States-Item blared the news: JFK SHOT FROM REAR, FBI EXPERT TESTIFIES.[6] The prosecution immediately scrapped its plans to call Shaneyfelt's colleague, Robert Frazier, and the defense added him to its witness list.

Wilma Bond, Philip Willis, and Mary Moorman took the stand to tell about the photographs they took that showed the grassy knoll and the reaction of the crowd. Some ran toward it. A former railroad company employee on the triple overpass described seeing "a puff of smoke" coming from under the trees on the knoll. Later, on the rail behind the picket fence, he noticed "muddy footprints."* William Eugene Newman, Jr., one of several witnesses who thought the shots came from the knoll, was standing at the curb to the president's right. He saw President Kennedy's "ear flying off."† A Dallas motorcycle policeman riding behind the presidential limousine said he and his motorcycle

---

* As one of the local newspapers reported, when this witness (Richard Simmons) was interviewed four months after the assassination by the FBI, he referred to what he saw as "exhaust fumes of smoke" near the embankment, and seemed to associate it with a police motorcycle. In that interview, Simmons made no reference to the footprints (WC Vol. 22, p. 833).
† In photographs, Newman and his wife, who were directly in front of the knoll, can be seen on the ground covering their two children with their own bodies.

were splattered with "red splotches" and "grey matter" (consistent with human blood and tissue). A former Dallas deputy sheriff claimed that after the shooting he saw Oswald jump into a "light green Rambler station wagon" and later heard Oswald say the car belonged to Mrs. Paine.* A construction worker said he saw three men leaving the Texas School Book Depository and two of them entered a Rambler Station Wagon; the FBI, he claimed, warned him to keep his mouth shut.† A woman standing on Houston near Elm observed two men in another Dealey Plaza building and one of them, she said, was "holding a gun."[7]

Reporter David Snyder sat in the courtroom day after day listening to this testimony and "wondering what the hell it had to do with Clay Shaw." The defendant wondered, too. Shaw found it "fascinating" but couldn't see where he "fit in." He didn't. That was one of the fundamental flaws in Garrison's case.

Dr. John Nichols, an assistant professor of pathology at the University of Kansas, who had studied the Zapruder film, took the stand and prompted another showing of it. Nichols testified that the president and Governor Connally appeared to be reacting to a separate "stimulus."‡ Nichols also found the Zapruder film "compatible" with the gunshot wound to the head coming "from the front." (After a one-day recess for the Mardi Gras Rex Parade, court reconvened with Dr. Nichols still on the stand.) If the president had been struck in the rear of the head, Nichols said, his movement would have been forward.§ On cross, Dymond pointed out that Nichols's testimony was more about photography than forensic pathology. By asking Nichols to describe the steps in an autopsy, Dymond emphasized that this testimony was based solely on the Zapruder film.[8]

---

* This was Roger Craig, who, in Dec. 1967, moved to New Orleans and went to work for Willard E. Robertson, one of the founding members of Truth and Consequences.
† This witness, Richard Carr, in a 1964 FBI interview mentioned only one man at the building. He also said nothing to the FBI about the shot that hit the ground and "knocked a bunch of grass up," which he described in court.
‡ The Warren Commission concluded that a single bullet had passed through the president's throat and gone on to strike Governor Connally.
§ The President's head did move forward slightly, though it wasn't visible when viewing the film in motion, only when examined frame-by-frame (David Lifton, *Best Evidence* [New York: MacMillan, 1981], p. 49).

The prosecution returned to its New Orleans scenario in the person of Mrs. Jessie Parker, a black former hostess in the Eastern Airlines VIP room at New Orleans International Airport. She claimed that on December 14, 1966, she saw Clay Shaw sign the name "Clay Bertrand" in the guest book. The prosecution offered no theory to explain why Shaw, if he had conspired to murder the president using this alias, would have continued to use it afterwards. The signature appeared on the last line of a page, where it could have been added at any time by anyone.[9]

On the heels of the VIP lounge book signature, a plus for the prosecution, Alcock concluded his case with a spectacular defeat from Judge Haggerty. It involved the strange episode of Police Officer Aloysius J. Habighorst and Shaw's fingerprint card. Habighorst fingerprinted Shaw the night of his arrest and filled out the card. He claimed Shaw had admitted using the alias, "Clay Bertrand." It was then typed on the card, and Shaw signed it. Shaw said he had signed a blank card, which meant the alias was filled in afterwards. The state naturally wanted to present the card and Habighorst's testimony to the jury. But because Garrison had allowed the matter to be widely publicized six months earlier,* admissibility was now in question. The matter was argued outside the presence of the jury.[10]

Officer Habighorst testified that he obtained the information directly from Shaw. But three other police officers gave testimony inconsistent with Habighorst's. The sergeant assigned to guard Shaw was one of them. He was within a few feet of Shaw and heard no question about aliases asked. Two of Shaw's attorneys—Edward Wegmann and Salvatore Panzeca—then Shaw himself took the stand and hotly refuted Habighorst's story.[11] †

After asking some questions of his own, Judge Haggerty rejected the fingerprint card evidence. Shaw's constitutional rights, he said, had been violated twice.‡ But Haggerty had heard enough to be moved to express himself further. "So even if Officer Habighorst is telling the

---

* Habighorst was interviewed on television and the States-Item published a photograph of the card, along with his version of what occurred, all authorized by Jim Garrison and in violation of the court's pretrial guidelines. (See note 10.)
† Louis Ivon also testified regarding this issue; his memory was remarkably spotty.
‡ When his attorney was excluded from the Bureau of Identification room and when he was supposedly asked the question about aliases without being warned of his right to remain silent.

truth," Haggerty said, "and I doubt it very seriously . . ." Alcock leaped to his feet. "Are you passing on the credibility of the state's witnesses," he demanded, his voice trembling with outrage, "in front of the press and the world?" "The jury is not hearing it," Haggerty replied, "That is the main thing. The whole world can hear it. I do not believe Officer Habighorst." Then he said it again. "I do not believe him."[12]

STATE IS STUNNED BY JUDGE'S RULING, read the headline in a local newspaper. The *state* was not alone. Everyone was stunned, not by the ruling but the remark. Alcock immediately moved for a mistrial, which Haggerty immediately denied. Alcock said he would appeal to the Louisiana Supreme Court. That was fine with Haggerty, who adjourned court to await the Supreme Court's decision. He announced it the next morning. Denied. And Haggerty refused to reconsider his own decision. "I will not change my mind," he told Alcock.

The jury was brought in. Haggerty instructed the prosecution to call its next witness. Alcock "dramatically," by one account, "intoned the words, 'The state rests.'"

No one expected it. Everyone was waiting for the big disclosure that Garrison had to have up his sleeve. He had, after all, *solved* the case. For many who had believed in him, reality began seeping in. Yet the faithful still flocked to his side and the general sentiment among the media covering the trial who were sympathetic to Shaw remained extremely pessimistic. This was, after all, New Orleans.

Dymond quickly asked for a directed verdict of acquittal, claiming the state had failed to prove a prima facie case. Alcock objected and Judge Haggerty adjourned court to read Perry Russo's transcript before ruling. The courtroom was packed in the morning when Haggerty, without explanation, denied the motion, triggering applause and a few soft "yeas" from the spectators. One reporter attributed the outburst to people who didn't want the entertainment to end. Jim Garrison received the news in the judge's chambers and left immediately afterwards, saying, "I have no reaction. I have no nervous system anymore." "I am still confident I will be vindicated," Shaw told reporters.[13]

After a five-minute recess, the jury was brought in and the defense began its presentation.

The first witness was Marina Oswald Porter, the pretty, blue-eyed

Russian wife of the accused assassin who provided something for both sides. She and her friend Ruth Paine both testified that Lee Harvey Oswald was beardless and always neat and clean. He was nothing like the dirty, unkempt "Leon Oswald" Russo described. Both women also said that Ruth Paine's station wagon was parked outside her house in a Dallas suburb (where Marina was living) when the president was shot. As for the Clinton witnesses, Marina said neither she nor Oswald could drive a car. She had never been to Clinton, nor had he to her knowledge and she had never known him to use the name "Harvey Oswald." Until the trial she had never heard of Clay Shaw, Clay or Clem Bertrand, or Perry Russo. She didn't recognize the photographs of David Ferrie, and had never seen Clay Shaw until today.

On cross-examination she acknowledged that Oswald told her he had fired at General Edwin Walker, though she could not remember when it happened.* For awhile after Oswald lost his job at the Reily Coffee Company in New Orleans, he pretended he still was going to work and she admitted she had no idea where he went instead. But he was away from home only one night, she said, when he was in jail after his arrest in the leaflet-scuffling incident.

A business colleague of Clay Shaw and Shaw's secretary described his unusually heavy work load during the time he was allegedly seen in Clinton. Shaw was away from the office only one day, visiting his parents. Both said Shaw never wore a hat, as claimed by one of the Clinton witnesses, nor tight pants, as described by Perry Russo. Both also indicated his trip to the West Coast (prior to the assassination) was to fulfill a speaking engagement in Oregon.

The last challenge to the Clinton story came from a meteorologist. Two of the Clinton witnesses had tied their recollections to the cool weather they were experiencing at the time. But the meteorologist testified that during "late August or early September" 1963, the temperature in the Clinton–Jackson area was always in the high- to mid-nineties.[14]

The other half of the FBI team, ballistics expert Robert A. Frazier, now took the stand. He had examined, among other items, the president's clothing, the limousine, the bullet found at Parkland Hospital, and the fragments found in the president's car, as well as the Zapruder film and

* The incident occurred at Gen. Walker's Dallas home on April 10, 1963.

slides. The shots, he said, came from above and to the rear.[15]

Col. Pierre A. Finck, the chief forensic pathologist at President Kennedy's autopsy, was the first witness the next day. Though called by the defense, his testimony appeared to help the prosecution, as he spotlighted existing conflicts in the medical evidence and added new ones. A slender man, wearing large black-rimmed glasses, Finck testified a day and a half, longer than any other defense witness. His direct examination by Dymond went well. In discussing the back wound (which he described as "on the right side in the back of the neck") and the head wound, Finck stated unequivocally that "both bullets struck in the back, one in the back of the neck and the other in the back of the head." And he described the characteristics of each that led to that conclusion. For the defense, in its effort to support the Warren Report, so far so good.[16]

But on cross-examination by Oser, Finck admitted that the wound he saw in the president's back was "higher" than shown on the autopsy drawing. And Finck could not say why, when he examined the tracheotomy (performed at Parkland Hospital), he failed to see the bullet exit wound there. He admitted that the doctors at Parkland Hospital should have been consulted during the autopsy and could not explain why they were not. But, he said, "I was not in charge." Who then *was* in charge? Finck said that when Dr. Humes asked that question, an Army general replied, "I am." The general's name Finck could not remember. Why didn't the doctors dissect the neck wound? "I was told not to," Finck said, "but I don't recall by whom." He said the same about why he failed to remove the neck organs. Pressed by Oser, Finck said he was able to "probe" the back wound only a fraction of an inch because the muscles had contracted. Finck also stated that the X-rays showed the bullet (which he said exited at the approximate level of the president's neck tie knot) passed through the body without striking "major bones." Again pressed by Oser, Finck acknowledged that "there was no evidence of bone injury." As for the report on the autopsy by the panel of four doctors recently released by Attorney General Ramsey Clark (which almost derailed the trial), Finck had no recollection of the small "rectangular structure" in the brain, nor the metallic fragments in the throat wound described by the panel. And Finck insisted that the panel had placed the head entrance wound three inches too high.[17]*

The defense had called Dr. Finck to establish that the autopsy supported the findings of the Warren Report.[18] In his conclusions, Finck did that. The devil was in the details. Speaking to a writer afterwards, Irvin Dymond attributed Finck's difficulties to his unfamiliarity with the cross-examination process. While his performance was dispiriting to the defense, Shaw and his attorneys understood that any anomalies in the medical record had no bearing on the New Orleans scenario or the guilt or innocence of Clay Shaw. The worry was whether or not the jury understood that.

"First father" of the case, Dean A. Andrews, Jr., sporting his usual dark glasses and cocky air, took the stand a convicted perjurer free on bail with, as James Alcock informed the court, "another perjury case" pending. If Garrison thought this *other case* would encourage Andrews to cooperate that day, he misunderstood Andrews's determination to purge himself. Since Andrews's conviction was on appeal, the court ruled it could not be mentioned, but the subject matter, meaning "Clay Bertrand," could be. Dymond went straight to the call Andrews received while in the hospital the weekend of the assassination. Was that call from the defendant? He had never received a telephone call from Clay Shaw, Andrews replied. He did not know Clay Shaw and had never even seen his picture until it appeared in the newspaper in connection with Garrison's investigation.[19]

He told of his telephone calls from his hospital bed and his encounters with FBI Agent Regis Kennedy.† Andrews spoke about his condition that weekend, his "double pneumonia" and his sedation. Dymond tried repeatedly to elicit information about the "fictitious name" he used to identify the person who called him. Andrews, though, took the fifth (to protect himself from further perjury charges) and was sustained. Then, inexplicably, he answered one of Dymond's questions about Clay Bertrand. "No," Andrews said, Clay Shaw was not the Clay Bertrand to whom he had referred in his conversations with Agent Kennedy.

---

* This discrepancy, Finck claimed, was due to the panel's measurements having been made on X-rays, which "[do] not give a scale reproduction of the subject" (trial testimony, Feb. 25, 1969, pp. 22–24).
† Agent Kennedy had been called earlier by the state and testified about interviewing Andrews. Kennedy said he spent twenty hours unsuccessfully trying to locate "Clay Bertrand" (trial transcript, Feb. 17, 1969, pp. 6, 9).

Andrews could have pleaded the fifth again but he chose instead to clear Clay Shaw.[20]

On cross-examination Alcock dwelt at length on the alleged Oswald visits to Andrews's office in the Summer of 1963, and Andrews spun out one final time the details about the "swishes" and the "Mex," unable at this low point in his life to relinquish this last bit of face-saving fantasy. Because he had answered some questions about "Bertrand," Andrews was now forced to respond to all inquiries from Alcock about the Bertrand telephone call. But Andrews *telling all* didn't help the prosecution. The jury had already heard about the 1950s "fag wedding reception" at the Rendezvous bar where "Big Jo," aka Helen Girt, introduced Andrews to one "Clay Bertrand." Now Alcock forced Andrews to name "Gene Davis" as the person who had telephoned him in the hospital the Saturday after the assassination. Andrews explained, as he had two years earlier to the press gathered outside the grand jury room and then inside to the jurors themselves, that he had used the name "Clay Bertrand as a cover name" to protect Gene Davis, who was a completely innocent party.[21]

Andrews insisted he "didn't deliberately lie" to the Warren Commission. "I might have overloaded my mouth with the importance of being a witness in front of [it]," he said, "I call it huffing and puffing." But he termed that testimony, "page after page of bull." In the hospital "under sedation I elected a course that I have never been able to get away from. I either get indicted or I get charged," he said, "I started it and it has been whiplashing ever since, I can't stop it." When Gene Davis telephoned him that Saturday, he was calling about the sale of an automobile, not about Oswald, he explained. "I don't know whether I suggested—man I would be famous if I could go to Dallas and defend Lee Harvey Oswald, whoever gets that job is going to be a famous lawyer" or if the idea just came about in the course of the conversation.[22]

Alcock then nailed it down. "Are you now telling this Court," Alcock said, "under oath that no one called you on behalf of the representation of Lee Harvey Oswald in Dallas?" "Per se," Andrews replied, "my answer is yes, no one called me to say that." Why then did he call Monk Zelden? "Don't forget I am in the hospital sick, I might have believed it myself or thought after a while I was retained there, so I called Monk. I would like to be famous, too, other than as a perjurer." This brought laughter in the courtroom but, as one writer noted, Clay Shaw didn't join in. "Nobody," Andrews said, meaning the FBI and Secret Service, would tell him what he had said in the beginning, which is why his later statements were so contradictory. "I elected in my judgment not to involve a person who has absolutely nothing to do with Kennedy, in no way, shape or form, and I got hooked with it. I elected to stick with it, and here I sit."[23]

Judge Haggerty, the implications of this testimony taking hold, asked Andrews where he got the name Clay Bertrand. Andrews described searching for something to use as a cover for Gene Davis and remembering the "fag" reception and the introduction. "I got there in the middle of the thing and Big Jo says, 'Meet Clay Bertrand.'" Everybody, Andrews said, "burst out laughing" because it was Gene Davis. "I have been introduced as Algonquin J. Calhoun but people know me as Dean Andrews, know it is not my name." Alcock had little success probing Andrews for answers. Yes, he made conflicting statements, he said, but "Clay Bertrand is a figment of my imagination." Andrews said he had told "the DA's office" that Shaw wasn't Bertrand. He had told the grand jury. Nobody believed him. "If I had my life to live over again," he declared, "I would say his name was John Jones."[24]

Toward the end of Andrews's testimony, Judge Haggerty requested a five-minute conference in his chambers with the attorneys for both sides. Officially what transpired there is unknown but writer James Kirkwood was told that Judge Haggerty, "shaken" by Andrews's revelations, raised the possibility that the state might want "to make a reassessment of their position in this case." Reportedly, the prosecution said it lacked the "authority" to do that.[25]

It had been over two years since Garrison first revealed his mad notion to Andrews that "Bertrand" was Clay Shaw. Nothing Andrews had been able to say had moved Garrison from that position. As Bertrand was his invention, Andrews bore some responsibility for Shaw's plight. Guilt ridden, as any person with a conscience would have been, and at no small risk to himself, that day Andrews had done everything he could to rectify that wrong.

Another witness worried about a miscarriage of justice occurring was Charles A. Appel, Jr., a graphologist in charge of FBI handwriting analysis for twenty-four years and nationally known for breaking the

Lindbergh kidnaping case. He waived his fee when told the defendant couldn't afford it. Appel had studied Clay Shaw's handwriting and the "Clay Bertrand" signature in the airport VIP lounge book. "Shaw did not write the entry in the book," Appel testified. The entry in the book "was made by some other writer entirely."[26]

Clay Shaw's friend of twenty-three years, Jeff Biddison, described by one writer as "a good-looking man in his forties," testified that in all that time he had never seen Shaw dressed in tight pants or wearing a hat. While Shaw was in Europe, Biddison had received Shaw's mail at his office, not his home, and had never received any mail addressed to "Clay Bertrand" nor to "Clifford Boudreaux," one of the names Dymond made up, which the mailman claimed to recognize.

James Phelan took the stand worried that the hearsay rule might prevent him from telling everything that needed to be told. His concern was unnecessary. Led by Dymond through his experiences with Jim Garrison, Andrew Sciambra, and Perry Russo, Phelan managed to tell the jury absolutely all of it.

He wasn't the only volunteer witness for the defense. For two years the police technician who administered Russo's second polygraph test, Lt. Edward Mark O'Donnell (Homicide Division's new Assistant Commanding Officer), had believed the case would never go to trial. Realizing he was wrong, about two weeks before it began, he called Irvin Dymond. "I couldn't sit idly by," he told this writer, "and see an innocent man persecuted."* Described by one reporter as "tall, handsome, and poised," O'Donnell was allowed to testify only in a limited way about his encounter with Perry Russo but managed to put into the record that Russo had said Shaw wasn't present at the plotting session. He also described writing his report and the confrontation it ignited in Garrison's office.[27]

Clay Shaw finally took the stand in his own defense that same morning. His direct examination was a chorus of denials. He had never met Lee Harvey Oswald, David Ferrie, or, until this case began, Perry Raymond Russo. He had never been to Ferrie's apartment. Never visited Clinton. Did

---

* By testifying, O'Donnell was breaking law enforcement's code of silence, alienating many of his colleagues, and defying Garrison, the most powerful man in the state.

not own a black Cadillac (nor did the Trade Mart).* He had never worn a hat. Had never seen Vernon Bundy prior to the preliminary hearing. Never met with anyone at the lakefront seawall. Nor given Oswald money. He had never seen Charles Spiesel. He had never been in the Eastern Airlines VIP room at the airport (and had been unaware the room existed). The signature in the guest book was not his. The only "alias" he had ever used was "Allen White" (his grandmothers' maiden names) on a play he wrote. He was never known as "Clay Bertrand" or "Clem Bertrand." He *was* present when Kennedy spoke at the Nashville Street wharf. In fact, he was part of the city's Reception Committee but he was wearing a conservative business suit. He had never worn tight pants.[28]

The summer of 1963 was one of the busiest times in his career due to the proposed construction of the thirty-three-story International Trade Mart building.† "I have never worked harder in my life," he said. During that period, he was absent from work only one day, in late September, to visit his father in Hammond, and while he was there his secretary called him about a business matter. His trip to the West Coast was initiated in September by a telephone call from a representative of a world development conference in Portland, Oregon, inviting him to speak there on November 26 and offering to pay his expenses. "Was this trip a cover up for any assassination plot?" asked Dymond. "No, certainly not," Shaw replied. Garrison had blasted the CIA for two years, but neither he nor any of his assistants mentioned that agency in the course of the trial. It was Dymond who asked, "have you ever worked for the Central Intelligence Agency?"‡ "No, I have not," Shaw said. He denied even jokingly or casually talking about killing a president of the United States. When asked if he had conspired with David Ferrie and Lee Harvey Oswald to murder John Kennedy, Shaw replied, "No I did not!" In his final question, Dymond inquired if Shaw at any time had wanted "President Kennedy to die?" "Certainly not," Shaw said.[29]

---

* He had borrowed his friend's only once, in 1966 to visit his ailing father in Hammond.
† Leases totalling $1,425,000 a year were needed for the project to succeed and his job was to obtain them during the ninety-day period from July 8 to October 8. If he had failed there would have been no new building.
‡ Clay Shaw and the CIA are discussed further in chapter 14.

On cross Alcock didn't lay a glove on Shaw. He didn't seem to try.* He elicited more details about Shaw's trip to the Coast and his presence, the day of the assassination, in San Francisco where Shaw was scheduled to address a luncheon at the World Trade Center. Alcock introduced a letter showing that the Director of International Relations for the city of New Orleans, Mario Bermúdez, had solicited the speaking engagement on Shaw's behalf. It was Shaw's recollection that the Executive Director of San Francisco's World Trade Center, Monroe Sullivan, had invited him in early November. Bermúdez might have made the overture, Shaw said, but he had neither knowledge nor memory of it.[30]

Shaw acknowledged that in his March 2, 1967, press conference, he made the mistake of referring to Lee Harvey Oswald as Harvey Lee Oswald (which corresponded with the name "Harvey Oswald" supposedly on the job application at the hospital near Clinton).† Shaw said he had never met any of the Clinton witnesses. Nor Dean Andrews. Alcock established that Shaw and David Ferrie had one mutual friend, Layton Martens. After a final inconsequential question referring to a drawing made by Charles Spiesel, Alcock was finished. So was Dymond. "At this time," he said, "the defense rests."[31]

Alcock's soft cross-examination surprised Shaw supporters, as well as Shaw himself. To one writer who spoke to him immediately afterwards, Shaw appeared somewhat stunned that it had gone so well and that there had been no surprises. Alcock had asked some seemingly trivial questions and never challenged Shaw on the two big ones: the CIA and the crime with which he was charged. Shaw would have held his ground on both, but it seems strange that the prosecution didn't force him to do so. Though considering the reports of Alcock's dismay at prosecuting Shaw, perhaps it isn't strange at all.

After lunch the prosecution led off its rebuttal with Oswald's foreman in the summer of 1963, and established that he had fired Oswald

---

* Alcock dwelt on Spiesel's French Quarter tour and the building Spiesel selected at 906 Esplanade that Shaw owned in the 1950s. Shaw also once owned the building next door.
† Alcock was suggesting that this "error" with Oswald's name showed a link between Shaw and Oswald. But in the earliest reference to the application, an official at the hospital said the name allegedly on it was "L. Harvey Oswald" (Guy Broyles, interview with Andrew Sciambra, Jan. 23, 1968).

more than a month before Marina Oswald knew about it.

Bar and grill operator Eugene Davis took the stand and denied calling Dean Andrews in the hospital shortly after the assassination.* He denied being introduced as Clay Bertrand and he denied being Clay Bertrand. On cross by Dymond, Davis acknowledged sending Andrews clients and was forced to admit that the Rendezvous Room had been "predominantly frequented by homosexuals." When Dymond inquired if perhaps Big Jo had made the Clay Bertrand introduction without Davis hearing or being aware of it, Davis replied, "I would say I wouldn't hear a word she said without she asked me for a drink."[32]

The defense was on a roll, but not for long.

The next two witnesses, a husband and wife who had contacted the prosecution that morning, were a blow to Shaw and his supporters. Nicholas M. Tadin took the stand first, followed by his wife Matilda, who repeated the basics of her husband's story. She said on the witness stand she only came forward because her husband told her she had a duty to do so and, later, in his summation, Dymond noted that she appeared "scared to death." The Tadins claimed that, in the summer of 1964, they saw David Ferrie at the airport emerge from a hangar door with Shaw a few feet behind him. Shaw walked to his car, while Ferrie approached Tadin who said, "Dave, what you got, a new student here?" and Ferrie responded, "No, [he] is a friend of mine, Mr. Clay Shaw. He is in charge of the International Trade Mart." Dymond would say about the Tadins in his closing argument that they were either lying or mistaken. On cross he confronted Tadin with his two-year delay in coming forward. Tadin said he "didn't want to get involved." When asked why he was willing to get involved this morning but not at the preliminary hearing, Tadin claimed he was prompted by hearing on television that Shaw said he didn't know Ferrie. The defense was deeply disturbed by this testimony and its timing—coming near the end of the trial. Like the Clinton story at the beginning, if believed, it reflected on Shaw's credibility.[33]

The last day of testimony, Friday, February 28, began with Dr. Nichols again taking the stand for the prosecution. This time he was

---

* As noted earlier, Eugene Davis admitted to James Alcock in a 1967 telephone call that he had called Andrews while he was in the hospital (Bethell Diary, pp. 1, 10).

there to counter the testimony of Dr. Finck and FBI ballistics expert, Robert Frazier. For the bullet that struck the president in the back to have passed through his body without hitting bone, as Finck said it did, the angle of fire had to be from the side, Nichols testified, specifically a lateral angle of "twenty-eight degrees." Otherwise "the cervical vertebra" would have been "fractured." Moreover, for a bullet fired at that angle to go on to strike Gov. Connally, Nichols stated, the governor had to be seated approximately eighteen inches to the president's left. (Connally was sitting almost directly in front of the president.) Nichols was not allowed to state whether the twenty-eight-degree angle was possible from the alleged sniper's nest in the Texas School Book Depository, but presumably it wasn't.[34]

A photographer for the Orleans Parish Coroner's office, Peter Schuster, described enlarging and analyzing a photograph which captured the grassy knoll area as the shots were being fired. Schuster submitted blow-ups of the picture's "right top corner" where he claimed to see "a man" who appeared "to be holding something." An incredulous Irvin Dymond ridiculed this claim and forced Schuster to admit he couldn't say the something was a gun.

The trial's final witness was described by one writer as "a fading blond beauty in her sixties." Elizabeth McCarthy was Garrison's rebuttal to the defense's FBI handwriting expert, Charles Appel. Garrison had retained her "yesterday." The credentials she described and her experience were embarrassingly modest.* In her "opinion," she said, it was "highly probable" that Clay Shaw signed the name "Clay Bertrand" in the airport VIP lounge book. Dymond concluded his cross by asking if she was "being paid to testify." "Well, I hope so," she replied. "It is my business."[35]

After lunch Dymond filed a second motion for a directed verdict, adding to the previous arguments "the unrefuted testimony of Dean Andrews," which showed "that the name 'Clay Bertrand' had a completely fictitious origin, consequently rendering the case itself a fictitious one." To the surprise of no one, Judge Haggerty denied it.

The proceedings were galloping to a conclusion. In the next eight and a half hours, including a dinner recess, Alcock and Oser delivered argu-

---

* None of her degrees had included handwriting analysis classes; she studied the subject under what she termed an "authority" in the field, and a chemist.

ments for the state. Dymond presented the closing statement for the defense. Oser, then Alcock rebutted it. And Jim Garrison delivered the state's concluding statement, the trial's final speech. Alcock began about three o'clock that afternoon. He said the defense promise to show that Shaw didn't know David Ferrie or Lee Harvey Oswald "lay shattered, broken, and forever irretrievable in the dust of Clinton, Louisiana." He predicted Dymond would say "that the state's case rises or falls upon the testimony of Perry Russo." Alcock agreed with that. What Russo heard planned, Alcock said, was corroborated by later events—David Ferrie's journey to Houston, Clay Shaw's trip to the West Coast, and Oswald's presence at Dealey Plaza the day the president was shot.

A lengthy recess followed. All the props originally used with the Dealey Plaza witnesses were again set up. Then Alvin Oser delivered his refutation of the Warren Report, by one account a bit theatrically. He managed to run the crucial Zapruder frames one last time. Jim Garrison entered the courtroom while Oser was speaking. But Garrison didn't return from the dinner break that followed. That's when Irvin Dymond made his final appeal to the jury—beginning about 7:40 P.M.

In a low-key, conversational tone, Dymond asked the jurors to set Clay Shaw free and told them why they should. Clay Shaw, Dymond said, was on trial for one reason only, "to create a forum for the presentation of this attack upon the Warren Commission." Dymond rejected the state's suggestion that the Warren Commission and U.S. government were guilty of "one giant fraud." He emphasized, however, that "a verdict of acquittal" did not "constitute your stamp of approval" on the Warren Report. The validity of the Commission's conclusions was an issue separate and distinct from the charge against Clay Shaw. What happened in Dallas did not bear on what had occurred in New Orleans. "It doesn't matter whether there was one man" at Dealey Plaza "or ten," Dymond said, "no case of conspiracy has been made out against this Defendant."

Most of Dymond's statement was devoted to the New Orleans scenario and Perry Russo. Alcock was "dead right," Dymond said, the case "stands or falls" on Russo's testimony. He reviewed the "seven facets" of the state's case: the Clinton witnesses, coming forward more than five years after the alleged sightings; Vernon Bundy, leaving the safety of his home to shoot up on drugs in public. Spiesel, "this poor little paranoid bookkeeper," who thought he was being followed and hypnotized against his will. Hardiman, the mailman who remembered delivering mail to Dymond's fictitious "Cliff Boudreaux." Shaw's trip to the West Coast—why would a man in New Orleans travel to the West Coast to establish "an alibi for a crime that is being committed in Dallas?" The VIP lounge book signature, disproved by one of the "foremost" handwriting experts in the country, as well as common sense. And the plot party in Ferrie's apartment, testified to by Russo, "a liar." Even if all "seven facets" were true, Dymond said, they were not sufficient to "make this Defendant guilty of conspiracy."

"I hate to beat a dead dog," Dymond said, referring to Sciambra's memorandum and its missing plot party, which drew some chuckles. "This," he said, "is like a man going lion hunting and killing a lion and a rabbit, coming back and writing a story about the trip and forgetting to mention the lion." He reminded the jurors of the testimony of Jim Phelan, "labeled by Mr. Sciambra a 'journalistic prostitute'" but "back-stopped" by one of their own, Lt. O'Donnell. For Russo to become so angry at being asked if he believed in God that he lied under oath, was not a normal reaction, Dymond said. And "Perry Raymond Russo is not a normal individual."

In closing, Dymond returned to the source. "It all came from the mind of Dean Andrews." Dymond admitted Andrews had "lied before" but now, risking further charges, with nothing to gain, took the stand "and shamelessly belittled himself'" in order to tell the truth. Dymond told the jurors the "entire world was waiting to find out" if they would "convict a man on this Alice-in-Wonderland situation." He repeated his charge that the trial was a forum for an attack on the Warren Report and that Shaw was a patsy "picked" to provide that forum. Again he asked the jurors to separate the two. "Don't let the horror of this awful deed that was committed in Dallas cause you to convict an innocent man just to try to balance the scales." His final statement was, "I ask you to vote your conscience, follow the law, and don't make a mistake."

After another recess, a brief rebuttal by Alvin Oser, and a longer one by James Alcock, shortly before 11:00 P.M., an impeccably dressed Jim Garrison strode into the courtroom and was soon addressing the jury with his harmonious voice and quiet assurance. He spoke only twenty-five minutes and referred five times to the Zapruder film, waving the

"Dallas flag," as Dymond had warned he would. He mentioned only those who testified about the assassination: Dr. Finck, FBI Agent Frazier, and four Dealey Plaza witnesses.* Reaching for the gold ring that evening, Garrison said not one word about Perry Russo, Vernon Bundy, Charles Spiesel, the mailman, the VIP room hostess, or any of the others.

He spoke of abstract and lofty matters. "Power" thwarting "justice." Men, he said, had to make justice "occur," which often meant fighting power. He called the government's investigation of the president's assassination "the greatest fraud in the history of our country," adding that "it was probably the greatest fraud ever perpetrated in the history of humankind." He referred repeatedly to the function of "juries," and the message was unmistakable. The remedy to the "greatest fraud" in humankind's history was this jury and its verdict. Tonight the work of those "important and powerful and politically astute men" on the Warren Commission could be undone by this "jury of citizens." Amazingly, he ended his remarks by appropriating Jack Kennedy's most famous line. "I suggest that you 'ask not what your country can do for you but what you can do for your country.'" Which was? They could "cause justice to happen for the first time in this matter." They could show "that this is still a government of the people." If they did that, as long as they lived nothing would ever be "more important than that."[36]

When Garrison finished, James Kirkwood wrote, some of his supporters obviously wanted to applaud. A short pause in the proceedings followed, and when court resumed Garrison's wife remained but he was gone. The jury had opted to begin deliberations despite the late hour. Haggerty read the panel their instructions and the twelve men filed out to begin their deliberations. Haggerty dismissed the two alternates. Then he announced that court was in recess awaiting the verdict. It was 12:10 A.M. Most members of the press, even Shaw's most ardent supporters, believed the jury would vote to convict. Not because the evidence was there; it wasn't. But because this was New Orleans where conventional rules didn't apply, and because Garrison's persona and his remarkable power of speech enthralled so many. It wasn't just the press that thought so. Nina Sulzer, the Sheriff's administrative assistant (who helped with security in the courtroom), and a devoted friend of Shaw,

* Richard Randolph Carr, Mr. and Mrs. Newman, and Roger Craig.

was convinced of it, and Judge Haggerty's minute clerk had been betting lunches on it for days. Pershing Gervais had influenced the thinking of some, including James Phelan who also thought the worst was on its way. Garrison had the last word and Gervais claimed that was all "the boobs in the jury box" would remember.[37]

While they waited for the verdict, many milled about in the hallway (the doors to the building had been locked), but Clay Shaw remained in the courtroom, chain smoking and humming tunelessly, as he awaited his fate. It wasn't long coming. The jury was gone a scant fifty-four minutes and some members of the audience and press had to scurry to regain their seats. As the twelve filed in, none were smiling, none looked at Shaw, both said to be bad signs for a defendant. The time was 1:04 A.M.

"Gentlemen of the jury, have you reached a verdict?" Foreman Sidney J. Hebert, Jr., a fifty-five-year-old retired fire captain, nodded affirmatively. Judge Haggerty asked to see it. Hebert handed the long sheet of paper to the minute clerk. He passed it to the judge, who examined it and returned it to the clerk. "Stand up, Mr. Shaw," Haggerty said. Shaw stood up. "Mr. Clerk, you may read it, sir," Haggerty said. "We, the jury," the clerk read, "find the defendant, Clay L. Shaw, not guilty."

Shouting, shrieking, sobbing, and general pandemonium erupted in the courtroom. Some women spectators cried out, No! No!, but mostly it was a whoop of joy. Shaw grasped the hand of his long-time attorney, Edward Wegmann. "Thank you," Shaw said. Alcock, looking exhausted and shaking his head, sat slumped in his chair at the prosecution table. He declined to poll the jury. Reportedly, Mark Lane left the courtroom looking gloomy. Shaw, smiling broadly, moved to the jury box and shook the hands of the twelve men as they departed. Then he was ushered out a side door by Sheriff Louis Hyde and a phalanx of deputies. A few minutes later, sitting by himself in the back of a sheriff's car, siren wailing, Shaw was driven out of the Parish Prison and away from Tulane and Broad to the cheers of his supporters. It was like an "up" Hollywood ending—a noisy, satisfying spectacle.

His defense team adjourned to a "sailor's lounge" called The Spotlight run by a friend of Irvin Dymond, one Brother Savoy, who immediately ousted his other patrons, brought out "the good stuff," and turned his establishment over to the victory party. They celebrated into the dawn, along with many of the news representatives who had covered the trial. One member of the defense later greeted the day with no recollection of where he had parked his car the night before.

Jim Garrison's whereabouts when the curtain fell are unclear. He later claimed he was home and learned of the verdict by way of a telephone call. The other, more likely report said he was in his office when aides brought word of his defeat. He let loose with a roaring tirade. The verdict, he said, meant that the people of this country didn't want the truth about the assassination, a view that doesn't jibe with what the jurors said. They blamed him. Juror Larry Morgan, a twenty-four-year-old aircraft mechanic, was shocked by how weak the state's case was. He said the quality of Garrison's witnesses didn't fit the "seriousness" of the charge. Charles Ordes, a thirty-nine-year-old Continental Can supervisor, believed the state failed to present a case. He didn't think Garrison had enough to go to trial in the first place and that the grand jury should have stopped him. "I couldn't convict a man on that evidence," he said. "Garrison has a right to his opinion about the government and the Warren Commission," said twenty-eight-year-old David I. Powe, a credit manager, "but I just don't feel his opinion is enough to convict a man." Others agreed.[38]

Editorials appeared in a number of the nation's major newspapers applauding the verdict, condemning Garrison's abuse of power, and demanding action against him. Saturday, after two years of silence, the *New Orleans States-Item* ran a scathing front page commentary, calling for Garrison's resignation. Sunday, the equally remiss *Times-Picayune* followed suit. The American Bar Association announced that it would request a "probe" of the New Orleans D.A. and ask the Louisiana Bar Association to consider disciplinary action. And Garrison's old protagonist, Aaron Kohn of the New Orleans Metropolitan Crime Commission, referring to "various crimes" committed by "Garrison and members of his staff" during their Kennedy investigation, said his organization would be considering possible steps as well.

On Saturday, at a press conference held at the home of Edward Wegmann, a relaxed and smiling Clay Shaw, surrounded by his attorneys, called the past two years "a horrifying nightmare-like experience." He spoke of the financial drain, which meant he would be going back to work, and of his plans to write a couple of plays. He said he endorsed what Garrison said about the danger of power and authority preventing justice from happening but that Garrison had miscast himself as St. George and the federal government as the dragon. In reality, Garrison was the source of the "oppression" in New Orleans and Shaw and his attorneys represented "justice and humanity." Shaw refused to analyze Garrison but blasted the group of wealthy private citizens who had provided him money.* No D.A. should ever accept money from anyone, Shaw said, otherwise the rich could pay him to investigate anyone they chose. Shaw made it clear he was planning a lawsuit.† The verdict, he said, was "by no means the end of the matter." Pressed to provide details, both Shaw and Wegmann declined, preferring, Wegmann said, to wait until they were ready "to take definitive action."[39]

Garrison at last had been defeated. The forces of light finally had triumphed. Clay Shaw breathed the air of freedom for the first time in two years.

It lasted forty-eight hours.

Monday afternoon Garrison had Shaw rearrested and charged with two counts of perjury. The basis of the action was Shaw's statements on the witness stand that he had never met Lee Harvey Oswald or David Ferrie.

The nightmare resumed.

Shaw posted a $1,000 bond and again told reporters, "I never knew Oswald or Ferrie."

The posse after Garrison turned tail and ran. The local newspapers were suddenly neutral again. And nothing came of the bold declarations by the bar association or Aaron Kohn. Outside New Orleans some indignant media voices objected to Garrison's latest maneuver but they quickly lost interest. Those who had mistakenly touted the acquittal as a vindication of the Warren Report (the jurors made clear it was not) also fell silent.

Shortly after his dramatic rebound, Garrison was interviewed on television. Rejecting any idea of resigning, Garrison announced that he

---

* Shaw was outraged and wounded that the business community he had served for nineteen years financed Garrison's case against him.
† Shaw believed Garrison always feared he would be sued, which is why he used the extraordinary three-step trial procedure—bill of information, preliminary hearing, and grand jury indictment. He did it so he could argue, Shaw wrote, "that he was only doing his duty in trying me" (Shaw Narrative, p. 2).

was thinking of running again. He blamed losing the case on the rules of evidence that he said made it virtually impossible to present what was essentially a charge of "domestic espionage." He said the jurors had been concerned about the absence of a motive. (Their statements contradict this. They were concerned about the absence of *evidence*.) Garrison also said it was a mistake deciding not to use some witnesses who had "been in trouble," that he should have used them all. (Whom Garrison passed over and why is unclear, since Russo had an arrest record and Bundy was in prison and Garrison didn't hesitate to use them.)* Asked what started him after Shaw originally, Garrison turned once again to his favorite suspect, David Ferrie, and began describing his trip to Texas the day of the assassination.[40] †

The new charges lodged against Shaw carried a twenty-year jail sentence, and the risk of his being convicted was far greater this time. For one thing, the acquittal had not been as dead bang as first believed. The two alternate jurors, excused before deliberations, had both marked their ballots "guilty," and the first vote wasn't unanimous as widely reported. The black high school teacher, confused about the Clinton story, had voted to convict. His confusion was quickly cleared up and on the next ballot the verdict *was* unanimous. Yet several jurors, impressed by the Clinton witnesses, had acknowledged to the press that they believed Shaw had been acquainted with Oswald and Ferrie. At the perjury trial the key Clinton witnesses could be expected to testify again. Garrison's own attitude, later revealed by Perry Russo, was that a perjury conviction would have the same "effect" as convicting Shaw of

---

* Garrison most likely was referring to Reverend Clyde Johnson, known as "Slidin' Clyde," due to his slipperiness, a part-time backwoods preacher well known to law enforcement in several states. Johnson's bizarre story of meeting with Shaw and Jack Ruby in a Baton Rouge hotel where money changed hands was actually mentioned by James Alcock when he described, to the first panel of prospective jurors, the six overt acts the state would prove. But it was never mentioned again.

† For the first time, Garrison referred to Ferrie saying that on this trip he planned "to go duck hunting," which Oliver Stone would later showcase in his film. Ferrie never mentioned this duck-hunting notion (which is unequivocally disputed by Alvin Beaubouef, one of Ferrie's companions that weekend) during his multiple interviews in 1963. It first surfaced in 1966, when Ferrie was interviewed by Asst. D.A. John Volz; Ferrie also mentioned it, the night he died, to George Lardner. Why Ferrie invented this duck story is unclear. Perhaps he thought "hunting" sounded more manly than "ice skating."

conspiracy, that afterwards people would "forget" the other trial.

Garrison had found another angle to work. Once again, he was back in the driver's seat.

He would remain there another two years. In that time he was reelected; sued in a five-million-dollar damage suit filed by Clay Shaw's attorneys; compelled to answer their interrogatories and submit to a deposition. He published his first book, *Heritage of Stone*, a catalog of his theories about the assassination, emphasizing the role of the CIA. And he was named in Jack Anderson's column as the target of a New Orleans grand jury investigation on charges that he had "fondled" a thirteen-year-old boy at the New Orleans Athletic Club.[*] Garrison made no public statement about the allegation, nothing came of the matter, and it had no discernible effect on his life. Garrison, it seemed, was still in control of the situation. But that would soon change.

Since October 1967 Shaw had urged his attorneys to take action against Garrison in federal court. They had tried repeatedly and been rebuffed. But on the day Shaw's perjury trial was scheduled to begin, they filed a desperate plea in federal court and this time they succeeded. Shaw's wish was about to become reality, and Garrison's protracted and fraudulent prosecution of him was about to be brought to a screeching halt.

---

[*] This charge is discussed in chapter 16.

CHAPTER TWELVE

SHAW VS. GARRISON:
THE CHRISTENBERRY DECISION

> To characterize these facts as
> unique and bizarre is no exag-
> geration.*
> —Judge Herbert W. Christenberry (on Jim
> Garrison's prosecution of Clay Shaw), 1971

On January 26, 1971, Clay Shaw's attorneys finally turned the tables on Jim Garrison, casting him as the defendant in a bold new lawsuit they had filed eight days earlier in the U.S. District Court in New Orleans. They had asked the court to invoke its equity powers and stop Garrison from prosecuting the perjury charges. The court was holding a hearing on their motion. Over the past four years, Garrison had wielded the most feared legal power in Louisiana. But now he was forced to take the witness stand and explain his actions. As one observer noted, the hunter had become the hunted. Ten witnesses had already testified. It was the morning of the second day when Garrison's name was called in the federal courtroom of Judge Herbert W. Christenberry.

Garrison had been hospitalized with a back ailment and one reporter described him as appearing "drawn and stooped," with the back brace he was wearing visibly pushing against the fabric of his coat. But most striking was what appeared to be the disordered condition of Garrison's mind. Questioned by William Wegmann for more than two hours, Garrison made statements that were glaringly erroneous. Others were self-serving. Most were both. To Wegmann's more sensitive questions Garrison stated he didn't recall, or he simply refused to answer, claiming privileged information under Louisiana's Public Records Act.

---

* *Clay L. Shaw v. Jim Garrison*, Civil Action No. 71-135, May 27, 1971, 328 F.Supp. 390, p. 392.

Asked when Shaw first became a suspect, Garrison said Shaw was questioned three times and it was after the second that he fell under suspicion. "There was something about his answers which did not completely correspond and did not completely fit," Garrison said, "and it was after that that he became a suspect, and he was never again called for questioning without a lawyer." None of that was true.*

Garrison testified that Perry Russo was hypnotized only once. (He was hypnotized at least three times.)[1] When Edward O'Donnell's report on Russo came up, Garrison said he doubted the accuracy of polygraphs. (He used them widely.) He declared that press releases and press conferences were rare for him. (He engaged in both frequently.) He claimed he had recommended against putting the troubled bookkeeper, Charles Spiesel, on the witness stand, but "always let the assistants handle the trial."[2] (Using Spiesel was Garrison's decision.)† He acknowledged accusing the CIA of taking part in Kennedy's assassination but he denied claiming that the FBI, the Justice Department, the Dallas Police, or "oil-rich Texas millionaires" had been involved. (He accused the first two of covering up and the others of outright participation.)

The strangest assertion Garrison made concerned David Ferrie, whose death triggered the events that prompted Shaw's arrest six days later. Garrison claimed that Ferrie was still alive when Shaw was indicted. "David Ferrie was alive," repeated an incredulous William Wegmann, "when Shaw was indicted?" "Yes," Garrison said. "As a matter of fact, he was not only alive, but we were considering indicting him shortly before his death, and this followed Shaw, so he would have been alive."[3] So demonstrably untrue is this that the natural assumption is that Garrison was merely mistaken. But something more complex seems to have been going on here. Garrison's mind appeared to be rearranging reality to suit his needs at any given moment. As William Wegmann bored in, Garrison's recollections seemed designed to avoid

---

* Prior to his arrest Shaw was interviewed only once about the assassination, and Garrison did not find that session incriminating at the time (see Appendix A, item 29). The day Shaw was arrested he was questioned for an hour or more with no attorney present and without being advised of his rights (trial transcript, Feb. 19, 1969, pp. 14–15; Christenberry transcript, pp. 369, 372 [Louis Ivon], pp. 459, 473–475 [Clay Shaw]).

† See note p. 134. Also, Garrison testified that "no witness could have been used [at Shaw's trial] without my passing on it" (Christenberry transcript, p. 246).

any and all embarrassing admissions. The remarkable number and nature of Garrison's mistakes that day give rise to thoughts about neurological disorders or deep-seated psychological pathology.

When asked what witnesses he had against Shaw prior to arresting him, Garrison refused to answer, saying it was a policy decision and to answer would be violating his oath of office. Judge Christenberry rejected that but said he would not force Garrison to respond. James Alcock had testified the day before that there had been only one witness, Perry Russo. In the absence of contrary information from Garrison, Christenberry said, Alcock's answer would stand. One witness only. Finally the basis of Shaw's arrest was unequivocally and publicly established.

Garrison's repeated claims of privilege eventually provoked a sharp rebuke from the judge. It came after Wegmann inquired about the Vernon Bundy conference held in Garrison's office during the preliminary hearing. Had not Garrison said, "'We did not tell [Bundy] to lie; put him on the stand' or words to that effect?" Wegmann asked. In his reply Garrison said, "I have an obligation to the people of New Orleans to protect my office from fishing expeditions. I refuse to answer the question." Judge Christenberry was not pleased. "You may think it is a fishing expedition," he said, "but this hearing was ordered by a panel of Judges of the Fifth Circuit Court, and I am carrying out their order in holding this hearing. That applies to the entire hearing, regardless of who the witness is. If you don't want to answer, I am not going to insist, but there are other witnesses from whose testimony I will be able to make a judgment in this case."[4] *

Christenberry later asked Garrison if anything came out of the investigation and the money that was spent "except the prosecution of Mr. Shaw." Garrison said it had but didn't elaborate. Christenberry persisted, inquiring if "any report [had] been made or any book been written detailing the investigation." Garrison replied that it was "in the making." The information gathered was "so voluminous" that the project "still lies ahead," but "in due course," he said, a "public report" would be made "to the citizens of New Orleans."[5] (It was never forthcoming.)

Wegmann turned to the editorials that appeared in the two New

---

* One of those "other witnesses" was New Orleans Police Lt. Edward O'Donnell, who was present during the Bundy conference (see chapter 14).

Orleans newspapers on March 1 and 2, 1969, following Shaw's acquittal, which called for Garrison to resign. Garrison denied that the editorials influenced his decision to file the perjury charges on March 3. He didn't leave it at that, though. He said he had "a warm feeling for those people over at the *States-Item* and the *Times-Picayune*." If they disagreed with him "in one particular case or another," that was "just one of those things that happens to a man in politics." But the Shaw trial wasn't just "another" case, and "those people" at the newspapers weren't just *disagreeing*. They were trying to run him out of office and he was infuriated by it. Garrison's pretense of sentiment toward Clay Shaw was even more implausible. "I cannot emphasize too strongly that no one would be happier than I to see Clay Shaw acquitted," Garrison said, "if that is the way the evidence develops at the trial."[6] No one was fooled by any of this, least of all the judge.

Herbert W. Christenberry, who would turn out to be Garrison's judicial Waterloo and Shaw's savior, was tall and heavyset, with a florid Irish face and prominent chin. He possessed a booming voice and hearty laugh, frequently heard, and was no stranger to idiosyncratic politics. His brother had served as Huey Long's secretary.* Appointed to the federal bench in 1947 by Harry Truman and like Truman in time transcending machine politics, Christenberry was a tough and forthright no-nonsense jurist, with a reputation, as Cynthia Wegmann, Edward Wegmann's daughter, recently said, for "smelling a liar." A local reporter described him as "liberal, out of step, with a good sense for the little guy." Over the years, Christenberry handed down a number of important, and regionally unpopular, civil rights decisions, beginning in 1948 when he ruled it was unconstitutional to pay black teachers less than white teachers.†

---

* In an infamous 1935 incident at the Desoto Hotel in New Orleans, Herbert Christenberry was the "shorthand expert" who jotted down the surreptitiously gleaned conversation that Huey Long later described on the floor of the U.S. Senate as a plot to murder him. Long's supporters had used a Dictagraph on the end of a pole extended between two windows to overhear the discussion by anti-Longites in the adjoining room (T. Harry Williams, *Huey Long* [New York: Vintage Books, 1981], p. 840).

† In the 1960s he issued an injunction ordering the Ku Klux Klansmen to cease all "acts of terror"; decreed unconstitutional a series of laws passed by the state legislature to prevent integration of Louisiana's school system; and ordered school desegregation in Plaquemines Parish, a particularly pro-segregation region.

Given his background and character, Christenberry seems, in retrospect, the perfect jurist for the job he was handed.

That job began the day Shaw's attorneys made their last-ditch plea to federal court and it landed on Christenberry's docket. Their request was unusual, for federal courts rarely intervene in ongoing state cases, and are barred from doing so by federal statute, except in certain "special circumstances." Edward Wegmann, the only attorney on Shaw's team whose practice was limited to civil law, conceived this creative strategy. He also penned the twenty-four-page complaint.

That document, infused with Edward Wegmann's indignation, smoldering since Shaw's arrest, asserted in part that Garrison, acting in "bad faith," had misused and abused his powers, particularly "in the prosecution of innocent citizens," including Shaw. That he had conspired with members of Truth and Consequences "to accomplish his illegal purposes" and "harassed and intimidated" Shaw and others who incurred "his wrath." That he had engaged in an "illegal and useless" investigation of the assassination for "his own personal aggrandizement." Used the criminal courts of New Orleans "as a forum for his activities and as a shield" against those who disagreed. Unlawfully prosecuted Shaw for no "legitimate purposes." Published a book that gave him "a financial interest" in Shaw's continued prosecution. "Created an atmosphere of fear and terror in the community." And violated Shaw's rights to free speech, due process, and equal protection under the constitution. The longstanding allegations of wrongdoing by Garrison at long last had been expressed in a court of law.

But Judge Christenberry first rejected the plea, partly because the perjury trial was so imminent. Shaw's attorneys then appealed and won. That set the stage for the defining moment of this case, Judge Christenberry and his hearing, when all the chickens came home to roost. For some reason, this remarkable three-day proceeding has been virtually overlooked. Students of the case often have never heard of it. Even the transcript at first seemed to be unavailable. I traced it to a branch of the National Archives in Fort Worth, Texas, and in 1995 obtained a copy.

Shaw's attorneys called seventeen witnesses. Garrison's representatives, Asst. D.A.s John Volz, William Alford, Andrew Sciambra, and Numa Bertel, called none, claiming they felt no need. Irvin Dymond explained to this writer why he thought Garrison mounted no defense. "They couldn't find anyone who wasn't afraid to lie," Dymond said. "They were afraid that Christenberry would examine any witness very closely and cause them to be charged with perjury."[7] No longer on Garrison's turf, the rules of engagement had shifted dramatically. In the one-sided contest that ensued, in addition to Garrison himself, three of his closest aides and the trio that founded Truth and Consequences underwent merciless interrogation by Shaw's team. Even Judge Malcolm O'Hara was compelled to defend his decision to go forward with the perjury case.

Emotions ran high from the outset. The tone was set during arguments on Garrison's motion to dismiss, which charged Shaw's attorneys with "trickery." Garrison's men exhibited an attitude of outraged victimization that persisted from then on. When Judge Christenberry remarked that their "trickery" charge was "unfortunate," William Alford fervently defended Garrison and charged that Shaw's attorneys had violated "the very things the [legal] profession stands for." "I suggest you control yourself, counsel," Christenberry said, "you don't have to yell." Alford continued, though, and Christenberry told him to "sit down." But he stayed on his feet. "Didn't you hear me?" Christenberry said, "have a seat."

From then on, the exchanges were peppered with Christenberry's sometimes stern reproaches for the overheated reactions of Garrison's men. They repeatedly objected to the testimony being heard[*] and Christenberry repeatedly overruled them. Fervor, it seems, was the only weapon at their disposal. Their frustration was genuine. But their emotional displays probably mirrored Garrison's own personal outrage at having the destiny of his case, which seemed so entwined with his own destiny, snatched from his control. He was good at transferring his feelings to others.

Christenberry dealt Garrison's men their first defeat almost immediately when he denied their motion to dismiss. Volz said he "vehemently" objected. "Just object," Christenberry replied, "You needn't make it vehement." His vehemence was sparked by Christenberry's blunt preamble to his denial. If Shaw's attorneys proved their allegations, injunctive relief might be justified, Christenberry said. "This may be such an

---

* Mostly the defense claimed the testimony was irrelevant because it didn't bear directly on the perjury charge.

unusual case, such an extraordinary case that it may be necessary to carve out another exception" to the anti-injunction statute.[8] Less than thirty minutes into the hearing, Christenberry had tipped his hand, and what Garrison's men heard distressed them. Their anxiety mounted as one witness after another took the stand. Nothing went their way.

The first ones testified about the formation of Truth and Consequences and the money, $99,488.97, which Garrison had spent on his Kennedy investigation. Of that, some $70,000 flowed to him from T & C. Founding member Willard E. Robertson had donated $30,000, which he had borrowed, with the understanding that Garrison would repay it "when the funds were available."[9] All these private contributions were disbursed at Garrison's sole discretion, with virtually no controls. Some was spent on security measures at Garrison's home. More than a year and a half after the T & C account became inactive, Robertson was still owed his $30,000. Garrison had made no accounting to Robertson or his organization. Neither he nor the other two founders, Cecil M. Shilstone and Joseph M. Rault, Jr., could say with any specificity how Garrison had spent the money.[10]

Judge Christenberry questioned the propriety of private citizens furnishing a public official funds to run his office with no accounting required of how he spent it. But these men saw nothing wrong in what they had done. The possibility that without oversight such money could be "misspent," as the judge expressed it, or used to "coerce or bribe" witnesses, as William Wegmann put it, never occurred to any of them. They trusted Garrison. Like others, they had been seduced by the patriotic frenzy of his rhetoric. The influence flowed both directions. The encouragement and especially the financial aid they provided exerted pressure on Garrison to deliver.

Testimony of other witnesses revealed how far Garrison was prepared to go to do that. William Gurvich described some of Garrison's absurd assignments,* and some quite serious. He told of ignoring

* In March 1967 Garrison called late one night from Las Vegas and told Gurvich to fly out and "bring him six bullets and a green sports shirt," which Gurvich did. He also attended a show at the Las Vegas Thunderbird Hotel, called "Bottoms Up," whose star performer (Breck Wall) had been in Dallas the day of the assassination and was regarded by Garrison as a suspect. As James Phelan later described, a *Life* photographer with a hidden camera snapped pictures of that show while Gurvich recorded the audio on a hidden tape recorder (*Scandals*, pp. 154, 164).

Garrison's order to arrest, handcuff, and beat newsmen Walter Sheridan and Richard Townley. And he described Garrison's plan, never carried out, to retrieve tape recordings he believed the FBI had made of his telephone conversations by raiding the local FBI offices using "redpepper guns." John Volz characterized this as a Garrison "joke." Judge Christenberry was unconvinced. "It seems strange to me," Christenberry said, "that a district attorney would joke about raiding an FBI office, and even prescribe the kind of gun that is to be used." Gurvich said he resigned from the D.A.'s office because he believed what Garrison was doing "was a fraudulent, criminal act."[11]

Attorney Hugh Exnicios described how he secretly recorded Lynn Loisel's offer to Alvin Beaubouef of $3,000 and a job with an airline in return for certain testimony.* And New Orleans Police Lt. Edward O'Donnell again told about his conversation with Perry Russo, in which Russo withdrew his identification of Clay Shaw. O'Donnell also described Garrison's reaction when he heard the news.

Clay Shaw took the stand and one final time denied knowing Lee Harvey Oswald and David Ferrie. He said in another trial he would again waive his right to immunity and so testify. He recounted the nightmare he had endured for almost four years.† He had received death threats in the mail. Almost all his money had been drained. He had been unable to find a job. And he had experienced devastating humiliation. Once the recipient of endless invitations to speak at various affairs, he had become a social pariah. Shaw recalled the last city function he had been invited to attend, two months after the preliminary hearing. When a photographer tried to snap a picture of Shaw with the mayor, the horrified man ducked down behind his wife. It sounded amusing, Shaw said, "but it was not amusing to me." The period since his arrest had been "very agonizing." "When you are charged with having committed the most heinous crime I suppose that you could be charged with, your life habits suddenly

---

* A transcription of the recording, authenticated by the court reporter who typed it, was placed into evidence.
† Struggling to understand why Garrison targeted him, Shaw once told his cousin that he and Garrison had not been friends for years, and Shaw thought the animosity was caused by their disagreement over the French Quarter. Shaw wanted to preserve it, and Garrison wanted to develop it (telephone conversation with Willie Joe Yarbrough, Jr., July 16, 1996).

become a lot more restricted, you find yourself being, I guess you would say, hated, shunned, avoided, and just generally your life becomes a great deal more miserable as you try to live with something like that."[12]

The man responsible for Shaw's plight, Perry Russo, a potentially devastating witness against Garrison, was among those subpoenaed by Shaw's attorneys. He made a brief, dramatic appearance. But he told no tales, at least not on the witness stand. In a move that surprised everyone but the defense team, Russo pleaded the fifth. He did it to save himself from a perjury charge. More than once, Garrison had warned Russo he would be charged if he changed his story, and Russo had done precisely that. The day before he took the stand, finding himself seated in court next to a family member of one of Shaw's attorneys, Russo asked if Shaw's team would like to talk to him. I'm sure they would, was the reply. Russo said he was willing, and arrangements were made.[13]

He arrived at Irvin Dymond's office at seven that evening, took a seat, and categorically recanted his story. The man in Ferrie's apartment was "absolutely not" Clay Shaw, Russo said, and he blamed Andrew Sciambra for persuading him to make the identification in the first place. Over the next three months, in three additional lengthy sessions with Shaw's team (which were tape recorded), Russo expanded on this. He corroborated Edward O'Donnell's testimony about the lie-detector test. He denied ever hearing the name "Clay Bertrand" until Sciambra mentioned it to him. Described how a photograph he knew to be Oswald was converted into a *sketch* of Ferrie's roommate, "Leon." Recalled his horrific reaction to the sodium-Pentothal interview. Detailed how Sciambra had brainwashed him, and how he was coached like an actor in a play for his appearance at the preliminary hearing. Recounted favors extended by Garrison and his staff, at least one of them significantly illegal.* He told of money Garrison gave him and promises of more. He also recalled being warned that if he backed away from his story, "the courthouse [would be] planted on top of me." That threat guaranteed he would never tell the truth from the witness stand.[14]

More recently, during two interviews with me, Russo stated unequivocally that "[Shaw] was in fact innocent"; that "he did not conspire to kill the president"; that "there was no conspiracy." Russo

* This is described in chapter 16.

remarked, too, that he agreed with Dymond that Garrison didn't have enough information to convict Shaw of anything, and, he added, "in retrospect I don't think they should have prosecuted him." "I always thought that what happened was a tragedy just immeasurable against Shaw's psyche," Russo said, "and whatever happened to me was minuscule in comparison to what happened to him . . . and as I look back I say Garrison never should have done it."[15]

While none of this was heard in Christenberry's courtroom, Russo taking the fifth was statement enough.* Garrison's key witness, who provided the sole legal basis for the conspiracy charge against Clay Shaw, had removed himself from the case.

At the conclusion of the hearing, Judge Christenberry issued a preliminary injunction, temporarily halting Garrison's prosecution of Shaw on the perjury charges. Though it would be four months before he handed down his final decision, Christenberry had said enough to make it clear that he found Shaw's case persuasive. Nevertheless, when he issued his opinion on May 27, it was a stunning victory for Shaw. Christenberry criticized Garrison in the most unrestrained language possible. He called attention to the genesis issue, the fact that Garrison had provided no evidentiary basis to explain Shaw's initial December 1966 interrogation. Christenberry concluded there had never been any "factual basis for questioning Shaw about the assassination" in the first place.† But he leveled his harshest remarks at Garrison's reliance on the testimony of Perry Russo. Garrison "resorted to the use of drugs and hypnosis on Russo," Christenberry wrote, "purportedly to 'corroborate' but more likely to concoct his story."

Citing Garrison's claim that the $70,000 provided by Truth and Consequences had "nothing to do" with the case against Shaw, Christenberry wrote that "the incongruity of this statement is apparent

---

* Judge Christenberry, responding to an objection from Asst. D.A. William Alford, inquired why, if Garrison's representatives wanted Russo to testify, they didn't grant him immunity from prosecution. "We can't do that," Alford replied (Christenberry transcript, p. 484).

† What would this crusty judge have said, I wonder, had Garrison's "silly syllogism" been recited in his courtroom and the truth been revealed—that Garrison's suspicions about Shaw were based on casual marginalia jotted by Asst. D.A. Frank Klein in a paperback copy of the Warren Report (see note p. 47).

and appalling." He noted that only Shaw's arrest had given Garrison the "jurisdictional ground" to justify his investigation of the assassination. "Without Shaw," Christenberry observed, "there could be no probe." He also pointed out that "when Shaw was arrested the money came in; when he was acquitted, it stopped." He noted that Garrison's financial backers expected results and that "the perjury charge" was one of Garrison's efforts "to produce" those "results." It was brought in "bad faith," represented "selective law enforcement," and, Christenberry said, referring to Garrison's recently published book, Heritage of Stone, was motivated in part by Garrison's "desire for financial gain."

Nothing agitated Christenberry more than the circumstances of Shaw's arrest after he had voluntarily presented himself to the D.A.'s office for questioning. "During this time," Christenberry noted, "a representative of Life Magazine photographed Shaw through a two-way mirror unbeknownst to him."* Christenberry called the manner in which Shaw's arrest was accomplished "outrageous and inexcusable." While Shaw could have been taken downstairs in the private elevator in Garrison's office, instead he was led "handcuffed into the hallway" where cameramen and reporters had mysteriously materialized and "was shoved and pushed through the crowd," all of which appeared on television. The private elevator had not been used, Christenberry concluded, because it "would not have afforded the publicity Garrison was obviously seeking." Characterizing this as "a case of continuing harassment and multiple prosecutions," with the likelihood that both would "continue in the future" without "direct federal court intervention," Christenberry granted the request for a permanent injunction.† With it, he did more than free Clay Shaw. He convicted Jim Garrison.[16]

The Jolly Green Giant finally had met his match.

Garrison appealed to the District Court and lost. He appealed to the U.S. Supreme Court and lost there as well. He did not take defeat quietly. After the Supreme Court refused to hear the case, he issued a nine-page press release asserting that the decision "puts the final nail in John Kennedy's coffin." He again charged that Oswald had been a scapegoat

---

* One of those pictures is today in the National Archives.
† Christenberry's decision broke new ground in the area of equitable estoppel and is today taught in law schools.

and that the CIA assassinated the president. But what Garrison did or said no longer mattered. The judiciary had finally dropped the curtain on his act. Shaw's attorneys had saved him from another trumped up prosecution and the likelihood, based on the Clinton witnesses alone, of a conviction and a twenty-year jail term.

Justice long delayed at last had prevailed.

But Garrison had extracted a high price from those trapped in his web.

David Ferrie "wasn't a perfect person," journalist David Snyder said recently, "but he was doing okay until Garrison went after him." Ferrie's friends speak bitterly about Garrison's persecution of him and those in his circle. One of them recently attributed his success (he's a prosperous businessman with a flourishing family) to the academic tutoring and general encouragement that Ferrie provided him (and others) during troubled times in earlier years. Ferrie's funeral services (a Low Requiem Mass at St. Matthias Church and interment in St. Bernard Memorial Cemetery, arranged by a local law firm contacted by his brother),\ were virtually unobserved. Only two people attended, an unidentified man and woman. The pallbearers were hired.

Dean Andrews appealed his 1967 perjury conviction and *seven* years later the charges were dismissed on what was reportedly a trumped-up technicality.[17] No one wanted Dean to go to jail, a New Orleans attorney said recently. That was small solace for him. The indictment alone had ruined his private practice and cost him his job. As the father of four, eventually five, Andrews felt the financial squeeze. At one point, he was reduced to sleeping on a cot in the back of the Criminal District Court Library. He worked for a time at Mahogany Hall, a traditional jazz house in the French Quarter, serving as master of ceremonies and playing the bass fiddle. Later, he did a stint as a barker at a joint on Bourbon Street earning twelve dollars a night. Later still, he worked as a clerk at the Criminal District Court building. An out-of-town reporter who ran into him there said recently he was shocked by the change in Andrews. All the life had gone out of him. When he died in April 1981, no obituary was published.

Perry Russo was already on a downward slide, even before the Christenberry hearing. It began after Shaw's acquittal in 1969. He lost his job with the insurance company and had difficulty finding another. He tried to join the New Orleans Police Department and was again administered a polygraph by Edward O'Donnell. During it, Russo admitted to buying "stolen property." He also said "that he had engaged in homosexual acts approximately one hundred times," first at the age of thirteen and the last time about six weeks prior.[18] Russo had no difficulty completing the polygraph and all his answers were judged to be "truthful." But the New Orleans Police Department declined to hire him. In 1974 he was arrested and charged with possession of barbiturates, amphetamines, and heroin, and of contributing to the delinquency of a juvenile. He finally hit rock bottom and was sleeping in the park. After that, he began driving a taxi.* When he was last seen by this writer, his taxi needed body work, new upholstery and a wash. He, too, overweight and unkempt, appeared in need of attention. The trim, well-groomed, confidential informant who had first appeared in public at the preliminary hearing twenty-seven years earlier was unrecognizable.

A year later, Russo suffered a fatal heart attack. He was fifty-two. Dave Snyder, reflecting on Russo's life, was asked if he didn't feel a bit sorry for him. "Yeah," he replied, "I know what you mean. But I remember when Russo was on top of things and back then he was a blustery, bragging, swaggering jerk."[19] Remember—one should. Anyone trying to understand this case must grapple with the enigma of this man's motivations. His desire for celebrity and financial reward, and his psychological problems (whatever they were), surely affected his actions. But central to what occurred was his relationship with Moo Moo Sciambra. At their first meeting in Baton Rouge, if Russo had been less pliable, less eager to tell Sciambra what he wanted to hear, the entire prosecution might have been avoided. But Russo *was* pliable, *was* eager, then and in the days immediately following. The sense I had after studying the record and speaking at length with Russo is that, more than anything else, he was caught up in the emotional tide Garrison generated and passed on to those around him. Russo felt the full force of it in Sciambra, his chief contact.

Three years after the hearing that freed him, Clay Shaw, a robust man whose only previous medical problem had been with his back, died of cancer at the age of sixty-one. Many believe the stress of his legal ordeal

---

* Over the years, whenever it suited his purpose, Russo reverted to his fabricated story. He was able "to get away with it" because only a handful of people knew about his wide-ranging admissions to the defense team in 1971.

contributed to his death. He died without fulfilling his plans for further travel, without completing the plays he intended to write, living in reduced circumstances in a modest house, with two friends and a hired medical student caring for him. Though he experienced many long dark nights of the soul, Shaw never surrendered to bitterness. He did resort to alcohol, though. The journal he kept, which in 1996 a friend of Shaw permitted Dave Snyder to examine, reveals that. "The psychic pain was so intense," Shaw wrote four days after his arrest, "that I found myself drinking a martini at six A.M." Previously a light social drinker, he turned to it for solace as his life disintegrated, his mind "numbed with horror," his heart "frozen with apprehension."[20]

He once thought of suicide as an option but decided he would endure. "Tomorrow," he wrote as April approached, "I take up the burden of the second month in supporting the insupportable, tolerating the intolerable, and bearing the unbearable." He tried but was unable to hate Garrison. "The big, shambling behemoth," Shaw called him, "driven as he is by the lust for power and attention." "But try as I would," he wrote, "I could only feel that this poor son-of-a-bitch needs help far worse than I do."[21] Shaw kept going, helped by some close friends, his religious faith, the counsel of Jesuit priests, and prayer. Throughout those terrible years, he was awesomely dignified and stoic, almost saintly.

He behaved so splendidly that it was difficult to connect with him. Had he openly displayed just a bit of anger, or the anguish he poured into his journal, he would have seemed less distant and opaque. William Wegmann, a bespectacled, quick, and sardonic legal eagle, was asked recently if he would have done anything differently in retrospect. "No," he said thoughtfully. Then wryly but with feeling, he added, "I'm sorry I didn't take a poke at Garrison." That, everyone can relate to. It is the type of reaction that makes Dean Andrews, who cried in public, and David Ferrie, who vented his rage to anyone who would listen, understandable. For almost three decades, until Snyder published the journal excerpts, Clay Shaw has seemed a tragic but remote figure frozen in time. We now know how difficult it was for him to go day after day "without showing any emotion." Perhaps the control that enabled him to do that helped him through those grim final months. His ordeal ended shortly after midnight on August 15, 1974.

He was buried with an unmarked tombstone.

Later, Edward Wegmann arranged for a memorial plaque to be installed at the Spanish Stables, one of the buildings Shaw had restored in the French Quarter. The brief message on the plaque mentions Shaw's restoration work and his conception of the International Trade Mart. The final sentence reads: "Clay Shaw was a patron of the humanities and an invaluable citizen, respected, admired and loved by many."*

When he died, a glitch in the Louisiana law terminated his multi-million-dollar damage suit against Garrison, the founding members of Truth and Consequences, Dr. Fatter and Perry Russo, which was close to being settled out of court in the "six-figure range." But Garrison and his financial backers knew they had been in a fight and had escaped serious monetary loss by the skin of their teeth. Garrison was beset by other problems as well. In 1973 he was acquitted of taking bribes to protect illegal pinball operations. In his bid for reelection three months later, he lost to a boyishly attractive opponent, Harry F. Connick, who accused Garrison of abusing the powers of his office. Garrison twice ran unsuccessfully for a seat on the State Supreme Court. But in 1978 he won a spot on Louisiana's Fourth Circuit Court of Appeals and slipped quietly into obscurity.

That should have been the end of it.

Then in 1979, the Committee established by the U.S. House of Representatives to investigate the assassinations of President Kennedy and Martin Luther King reviewed the events in New Orleans. The Committee concluded "that the Clinton witnesses were credible and significant." While admitting that "points" existed that could challenge their credibility, the Committee decided the Clinton witnesses were "telling the truth as they knew it." The Committee thereby applied its imprimatur to a corner of Garrison's investigation. The Committee's Chief Counsel, G. Robert Blakey, later called Garrison's case "a fraud." But the damage was done. The first official government statement issued on the assassination since the Warren Report had extended respectability, however narrowly, to Jim Garrison's mad charade.[22]

Garrison's phenomenal comeback was underway.

Yet even some in Garrison's own camp have questioned the reliabil-

---

* In 1994 Perry Russo took me to see this plaque. Sitting behind the wheel of his taxi, he recited the inscription from memory.

ity of the Clinton witnesses,* and rightly so. For I discovered a previously unknown Garrison investigator who, unwittingly, has cast serious doubt on the credibility of the Clinton scenario. This investigator, whose participation in the Clinton area Garrison concealed over the years, supplied new evidence that supports what many have long suspected—that the Clinton story was a complete fabrication.

---

* Louis Ivon, when asked if he had ever stated that the Clinton witnesses weren't credible, replied that he would never make such a statement about anybody, "whether I believed them or not." Asked directly if he believed the Clinton witnesses, Ivon replied, "That's a difficult question for me to answer. I don't know if I believe them. I just don't know" (telephone conversation with author, June 28, 1996). When the subject of the Clinton witnesses arose during an interview with James Alcock, he insisted that he had nothing whatsoever to do with the Clinton investigation, that it was entirely the responsibility of Andrew Sciambra (Alcock Interview). Ivon made a similar statement.

GARRISON EXPOUNDS ON THE ASSASSINATION: A SAMPLING OF HIS 1967 THEORIES

In late February, Garrison confided to various reporters that the plotters first planned to assassinate Fidel Castro, with Lee Harvey Oswald as the shooter. But when Oswald was denied entry to Cuba, they switched to President Kennedy.[1]

In March, Garrison said the assassination was the work of "one master planner, a few idiots, and the passive involvement of many others." The "mafia" was not involved.[2]

That same month, he explained that besides anti-Castro Cuban refugees and homosexuals, masochists (who would do anything for a thrill) were a part of the plot. "If you placed a masochist in a room along with a button that would blow up the White House," Garrison said, "he probably would press that button for the thrill of it."[3]

By May, Garrison was claiming that "it was not that hard to find out what happened and how President Kennedy was killed. . . . We have even located photographs in which we have found the men behind the grassy knoll and stone wall before they dropped completely out of sight. . . . Although they are not distinct enough [that] you can make an identification from the faces."[4]

Also in May, he said there were "at least two pairs of men in the front— apparently two men behind the stone wall and two behind the picket fence." The job "of the second man in each case was to pick up the actual cartridges, taken on the bounce so to speak, so that the cartridges could be disposed of as quickly as the guns. . . ." And there was "at least one man in the back who was shooting, [but not from] the sixth floor of the book depository."[5]

In his television broadcast in July, Garrison stated that there were at least three assassins in Dallas at Dealey Plaza, two firing from the rear and one from the right front.[6]

In a letter written in August, he told Bertrand Russell that at the higher levels of the plot were conspirators with "Neo-Nazi" political views, and among them was Clay Shaw.[7]

"There are elements of the Dallas establishment that are deeply involved [in the assassination]," he said in September, "and some of the members of the White Russian community are part of it. Now, they had total control of Marina [Oswald]." Also deeply involved were "elements of the Dallas police," a Minutemen controlled element, and some members of the John Birch Society. Sponsoring the operation was a group of "insanely patriotic oil millionaires." The "corroborating evidence" to support these charges, Garrison said, "is in our files."[8]

He concluded the year with descriptions of the events at Dealey Plaza. "Just a little bit in front of where the President was killed there is a sewer opening" that is accessible through a manhole, he said in early December. "The man who killed President Kennedy fired a .45 caliber pistol" from that manhole, then "fled" through the sewers "to another part of the city."[9]

At a press conference the day after Christmas, Garrison said there was "an infinitely larger number [of people involved in the conspiracy] than you would dream," and in Dealey Plaza alone, there could have been as many as fifteen, including lookouts, men operating radios, supervisors, and so on. "It was very large and very well organized," he said.[10]

Clay Shaw, the accused—
"I was inclined to tell
Garrison's men,
'Gentlemen, this is a very
bad joke.'"

Jim Garrison, the district
attorney—
"There is a certain tendency
to climb where opportunity
presents itself."

Jack Martin, the tipster—
Described himself as: "Author,
former newspaperman, professional soldier, adventurer, and
philosopher."

David Ferrie, the pilot, Garrison's favorite suspect—
"Martin has a special vendetta for me."

Dean Andrews,
the Runyonesque
attorney—
"I can't let Shaw get
convicted—the Giant
is trying to put the hat
on this poor bastard
because of me."

NEW ORLEANS, LA.
112 723
8   9   63

Lee Harvey Oswald, the
alleged assassin—
Charged with disturbing
the peace after a dispute
with anti-Castro Cubans.

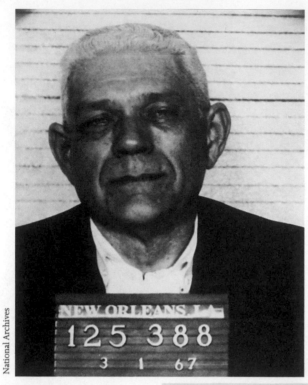

Clay Shaw—
"The feeling of being
a stunned animal,
which marked the
first part of the
month, seems to have
gone now."

James Phelan, the *Saturday
Evening Post* writer—
"Garrison was humorous,
witty, literate, articulate,
charismatic, affable, and
mean as a rattlesnake."

Clay Shaw and Edward F. Wegmann during the preliminary hearing.

Andrew Sciambra, Garrison's point man—
"I sat down on the chair and I put my brief case on top of my legs and I put the legal pad on top of the brief case, I wrote like that."

Perry Russo, Garrison's witness—
"Sciambra didn't take any notes."

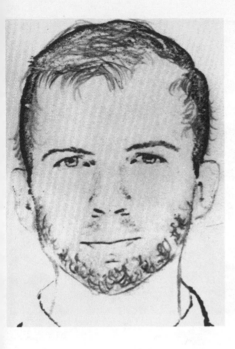

Sketch of "Leon" Oswald—
Created by drawing a beard on
Oswald's picture.

Vernon Bundy, the prisoner—
James Kruebbe: "His testimony was incredible from day
one."

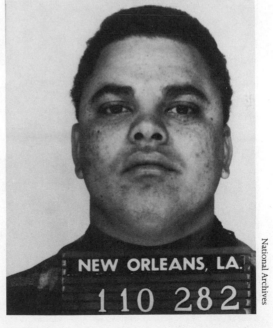

NEW ORLEANS, LA.

110 282

Edward O'Donnell, the polygraph technician— "I said, 'Perry, what the hell's wrong with you?'"

Jim Garrison— "People worry about the crime 'syndicate,' but the real danger is the political establishment, power massing against the individual."

James Alcock, Garrison's
lead prosecutor—
"I wasn't part of those
fancy lunches. I wasn't a
part of the inner circle."

Charles Spiesel, Garrison's
calculated risk—
Hypnotized by "fifty or
sixty" people.

FOR THE DEFENSE

Crown Portraits, Inc.

F. Irvin Dymond, Shaw's lead trial attorney— "I think Garrison was just totally unscrupulous. I don't think there's any limit to what he would have done to convict Clay Shaw."

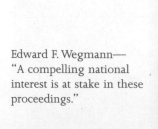

Greystone Photographers

Edward F. Wegmann— "A compelling national interest is at stake in these proceedings."

William J. Wegmann—
"You have to understand
that district attorneys in
this area for years con-
trolled the political system
at Tulane and Broad."

Salvatore Panzeca—
"I recognized Mr. Shaw's
name when he identified
himself. And I simply took
the position—well, I'll be
down there and we'll
straighten it out."

Courtesy Salvatore Panzeca

Judge Herbert W. Christenberry, Garrison's nemesis—
"Garrison makes several references to the Dreyfus case. When we consider Garrison's actions toward Shaw it is small wonder that in writing his book that classic example of injustice came to his mind."

Estus Morgan,
mystery man—
Unwitting "participant" in the
Clinton scenario.

Shaw (standing, back to wall) and Ferrie look-alike Robert Brannon (in overcoat).
This is the picture Stone claimed Garrison discovered after the 1969 trial, which
proved Shaw and Ferrie knew each other. But Garrison had the picture in 1967 and
he knew then that the man in the overcoat wasn't Ferrie.

Oliver Stone, the filmmaker— "Thomas Jefferson urged on us the notion that when truth can compete in a free marketplace of ideas, it will prevail."

Clay Shaw— "My moments of absolute black despair are increasingly rare. I am trying to take the whole matter stoically. . ."

PART TWO
FRAUD PERPETUATED

CHAPTER THIRTEEN

THE CLINTON SCENARIO AND THE
HOUSE SELECT COMMITTEE

Clinton, that's Klan country.[1]
—*William Wegmann*, 1993

Clinton had to be a complete fix![2]
—*Irvin Dymond*, 1993

I was told that we could discredit
these witnesses because Garrison's men "did it wrong." That
the witnesses were told what to
say and they said it.[3]
—*Salvatore Panzeca*, 1993

Three years before Jim Garrison died, a documentary filmmaker interviewed him about his Clinton witnesses. Explaining why his investigators
went to that area in the first place, Garrison spoke vaguely about his office
getting wind of Lee Harvey Oswald being there.[4] It was a typically obscure
answer. From the beginning, Garrison cloaked his Clinton investigation in
secrecy. Only his closest aides knew about it and its origins have never
been revealed. At the trial, none of the witnesses could say why Garrison's
men contacted them and Garrison himself avoided a direct answer. "We
picked up a lead," he wrote in his memoir, one he called "slim," and "a
whisper in the air," as though it wafted down from the hill country on a
gentle breeze. That was not the case but that was Garrison's story and he
stuck to it. Today, those eight witnesses from that rural hamlet (located
about 30 miles north of Baton Rouge and 120 miles north of New
Orleans) represent what remains of Garrison's credibility.

On the witness stand, each of them provided information that comple-
mented the testimony that preceded it, their story progressing like a well-

made play. Oswald arrived at Edwin Lea McGehee's barber shop near Clinton one day in late August or early September with a woman in an old beat-up car.[5] Seeking a job at nearby East Louisiana State Hospital, Oswald was sent by McGehee to the home of State Representative Reeves Morgan. Encouraged by Morgan to register to vote, Oswald next turned up in Clinton with Clay Shaw and David Ferrie in a black Cadillac. Town Marshall John Manchester, Registrar of Voters Henry Earl Palmer, and two black men working for the Congress of Racial Equality (CORE)—William Dunn and Corrie Collins—saw the car. All remembered Shaw, two remembered Ferrie and three remembered Oswald. After waiting in line more than five hours, Oswald finally spoke to Palmer who told him he didn't need to register to vote to work at the hospital. Oswald politely left. He then appeared at the hospital asking for directions to the personnel department. Later, a clerk in that department noticed his job application in the files.

Garrison launched his case with that seamless narrative because he believed it would deliver a knockout punch for the prosecution. "Just wait til the first day, it's gonna be all over the first day," Andrew Sciambra boasted to Perry Russo before the trial. Sciambra was talking about "the Clinton people," Russo explained. Sciambra also told Russo that afterwards "you won't be all that important."[6] Garrison was confident about these witnesses because of the remarkable cohesion of their stories and the seemingly rock-solid respectability of those holding public office. The three in positions of public trust strengthened the perceived integrity of them all, as did the group's racial mix.* But a recently released FBI report reveals that Town Marshal Manchester and Registrar of Voters Palmer were members of the Ku Klux Klan. In 1964 Palmer was the "Exalted Cyclops."[7]

These two Klansmen furnished the pivotal Clinton testimony: Manchester heard Shaw say he worked for the International Trade Mart and Palmer saw Oswald's military identification. So they provided the "unimpeachable" identification of both men. But as Klansmen, Manchester and Palmer have lost their unassailable credibility along

---

* In the summer of 1963, as the civil rights movement was just beginning to wrench the South, Clinton was targeted by CORE for a voter-registration drive. It was in the midst of that tumult that Oswald allegedly arrived and was observed and remembered by six people. Four of those in warring camps that summer (Manchester and Palmer on one side, Collins and Dunn the other) presented a strangely united front six years later, testifying for Garrison.

with their mantle of civic rectitude. Instead, they interject into the Clinton story an influential and violence-prone organization with a secret membership and private agenda. From the beginning, many suspected that the black witnesses were coerced. While that may or may not be the case, the specter of the Klan supports the idea. The full meaning of this Klan connection is unclear and may never be known. But anyone looking for a pool of witnesses to draw upon, and secrecy, would have found both in the Klan's membership rolls and its many friends.*

Skeptics of the Clinton testimony abounded from the outset. "Manchester was completely unreliable," former Clinton District Attorney Richard H. Kilbourne said recently. "You could easily plant something in his mind and he would say it as a fact." As for Reeves Morgan, "He would say anything," Kilbourne remarked. "I said from the time I first heard about it that I didn't think there was a thing on earth to it and I still feel that way. I never took it seriously. All these people were impressionable and they got to talking and pretty soon they talked themselves into it. Get a rumor started and the next thing someone is telling it as a fact. When you get to the bottom of it you find out there is nothing to it."[8] That was the benign explanation. Others thought something more calculated had occurred.

Some noticed the conspicuous repetition of phrasing, which called to mind actors reciting lines in a play. McGehee and Morgan both recalled the time of year as the latter part of August or the first part of September, which Sciambra repeated as he interviewed the others. Asked how they identified men they observed only a few brief minutes six years earlier, Manchester stated, "I don't forget faces." "I don't hardly forget [a] face," said William Dunn.[9] Those describing Ferrie referred only to his "hair" and "eyebrows," as though he consisted of nothing more. Four of them recalled Shaw's "grey" hair and his build, and two of them said he had a "ruddy complexion."[10] Explaining why they didn't notify the Warren Commission or any other

*Garrison's battles with Washington and his anti-U.S. government pronouncements earned him strong support in these quarters (see note 28). Ironically, blacks, too, were supportive of him because of their devotion to Jack Kennedy and their perception of Garrison as his champion. A political source in Baton Rouge back then told one reporter that Garrison's JFK investigation was part of a larger political scheme, involving Senator Long, and apparently spawned by the civil-rights struggle. Reportedly, the plan called for Garrison to run for the Vice-Presidency on a ticket with Alabama Governor George Wallace as the Presidential candidate (Fred Powledge, "Is Garrison Faking?" The New Republic, June 17, 1967).

authorities about Oswald being in Clinton, Manchester and Collins offered the same peculiar reason. "I figured if they wanted it they could come and get it," said Manchester. "I felt like if they wanted to know they would ask me," said Collins.[11] (Neither was able to say how the Commissioners could have asked when they weren't informed about it in the first place.)

Some critics noted the oddity of the Clinton story. Oswald seeking work in such a remote location made no sense, except to Garrison. He claimed to the end that those manipulating Oswald wanted him working at the hospital (a psychiatric facility) so they could switch his records from employee to patient to support a later charge that he was a mental case.[12] Garrison found nothing preposterous about that idea. He also found nothing strange about these three "conspirators" calling attention to themselves shortly before they participated in the crime of the century.

He wasn't bothered either by the timing of the story's appearance. No one heard about Oswald being in Clinton (or at the hospital) until *after* Garrison began his investigation.* Yet once the assassination rocked the country, the local citizenry should have been buzzing about Oswald's visit. In this small community, people know each other and talking is a way of life. Four years passed, though, before the word "got out."

For many, all this added up to a bogus tale. But it didn't prove much. Over the years professional and amateur sleuths alike had combed this trail and found little—a whiff of smoke here and there, but no smoking gun. I journeyed to Clinton in 1993 only because I needed to see it for myself. So low were my expectations that I scheduled only a twenty-four-hour stay. That seemed time enough until Aline Woodside, then the head of East Louisiana State Hospital's personnel department, made an offhand remark that opened an unexpected door.

She had just described that long-ago visit to the hospital by a Garrison investigator, State Policeman Francis Frugé, now deceased. At his direction, she and others had conducted an exhaustive, fruitless search for Oswald's job application. "No," she replied to my question, no one in personnel remembered seeing Oswald, giving him an application, or interviewing him. "We didn't think she saw it," Woodside said, refer-

---

* Several Clinton residents stated this, among them a doctor at the hospital, former Clinton District Attorney Richard Kilbourne, and former hospital personnel chief Aline Woodside.

ring to the clerk who claimed she spotted the application in the files. Woodside had hinted as much already; so I wasn't surprised. Moments later, I was gathering up my things to leave when she remembered something. "Frugé had an assistant with him," she said, "a lady."

That *was* a surprise. I had never seen or heard any reference to such a person.*

Woodside couldn't remember her name but she made a telephone call and seconds later had retrieved it, along with the name of the town where she was living in 1967. Locating her was almost as easy; I found her the following week. But by then, I was home in California and she refused to speak about the case on the telephone. Yes, she said, her voice soft and southern, she would talk to me about Clinton. Not this way though. Only in person. She was polite, kind, and unmovable. If you're supposed to use my information, she said, "it will happen." Clearly she thought her information was valuable and, instinctively, so did I. Two months later, I trekked back to Louisiana to meet and interview this mystery lady. I found an articulate, impeccably groomed, and attractive woman in her sixties, who remains today a Garrison loyalist. Her name is Anne Hundley Dischler.†

On February 4, 1994, at her home in Eunice, Louisiana, west of Baton Rouge, Dischler, now an ordained minister in the Full Gospel Church,‡ sat on a sofa intently examining the sheaf of papers on her lap. She was looking at the twenty-six-year-old notes she had recorded during the five-month period when she and Francis Frugé wheeled along the roads of the hill country north of Baton Rouge, chasing a lead on Oswald that never quite panned out, at least not for them.

---

* Almost two years later, I found traces of her in Garrison's old office files: a folder containing expense receipts, a 1968 newspaper clipping referring to her work for Garrison, and three documents that mention her.

† Prior to her assignment with Garrison's office, Dischler had worked for various state agencies, sometimes undercover. She was once temporarily commissioned a deputy sheriff for a narcotics investigation; another assignment involved state corruption. At one time she was the only undercover agent paid by the Louisiana State Department of Revenue. Later she was transferred to the Louisiana State Sovereignty Commission.

‡ She left investigative work not long after the Garrison assignment and served twelve years in a prison ministry, working some of the toughest institutions in the country—Angola for one. Married to Donald Dischler since she was in her teens, she has raised seven children and in 1994 had twenty-seven grandchildren. In addition to her ministry, she owns and operates a retail fabric store, is an expert seamstress, bakes her own bread, and can shoot with the best of them.

Assigned to the Garrison probe in late February, Frugé invited Dischler to assist him. They had worked together in the past and she readily agreed. For three months they followed dead-end "Oswald" leads; then a tip steered them to Clinton. In his book Garrison claimed the team there was Francis Frugé and Andrew Sciambra. It wasn't. The team in Clinton was Frugé and Dischler. They worked with Louis Ivon and his partner at the time, Frank Meloche, but their main contact in the district attorney's office, Dischler said, was Andrew Sciambra. They met with Sciambra periodically and fed him their information. Recalling that period as we studied her records, carefully preserved for over a quarter century, Dischler cleared up some of the mystery that has surrounded this testimony. She also, unintentionally, challenged the legitimacy of the entire Clinton scenario.

In Dischler's notes I discovered the date that their informant launched that scenario: May 18, 1967, three weeks after James Phelan's *Saturday Evening Post* article demolished the basis for Clay Shaw's arrest. The tipster maneuvered so quietly that until now, no one outside Garrison's innermost circle knew he was the source. Jack N. Rogers (Counsel for Louisiana's Joint Legislative Committee on Un-American Activities) delivered the message to the State Sovereignty Commission. From there, Fred Dent, Jr., passed it on to Francis Frugé and Anne Dischler. Dischler recorded it in her abbreviated handwritten field notes, creating the first documented reference to the Clinton story. The informant was Registrar of Voters and KKK Exalted Cyclops Henry Earl Palmer.[13]

As mentioned at the beginning of this chapter, Garrison called the Clinton lead "slim" and spoke of it poetically as a "whisper in the air." But its real genesis was neither slim nor poetic. A long-time Louisiana political reporter recently described the State Sovereignty Commission as "the Gestapo" of its day. "If they wanted to kick in your door," he said, "they kicked in your door." And Palmer outlined in his tip virtually the entire tale later recited in Judge Haggerty's courtroom: Lee Harvey Oswald, arriving in a Cadillac accompanied by Clay Shaw and David Ferrie, attempted to register to vote in Clinton; Oswald also sought employment at the hospital. Garrison had implied what one would expect if the Clinton story were authentic, that it grew one step at a time, as first one person then another recounted his or her recollections. It didn't. When Anne Dischler jotted that brief message from the Sovereignty Commission in her steno pad, she was inscribing the essential elements of the final story.[14]

Moreover, in identifying the source, she was also identifying the key Clinton player, Henry Earl Palmer, the interrogator of Oswald. And while someone else seems to have slipped Palmer's information into the bureaucratic maze, instigating Palmer's interview, I later learned otherwise. Jack Rogers, the original conduit,[15] was married to Palmer's former wife. So anyone mapping the real course of this tip would draw a short circular line beginning and ending with Palmer.

In her notes, dated and written in a rapid but lucid hand, Dischler chronicled a broad and intense search for information to corroborate Palmer's tip, recording a remarkable number and variety of names. The Congress of Racial Equality is mentioned, as is Ned Touchstone, publisher of the [White] Citizens Council newsletter, *The Councilor*. In addition to Jack Rogers, other prominent Louisiana political figures (such as Judge John Rarick) are there, and an occasional visitor from Washington, D.C. Governor McKeithen, Dischler said, sometimes made an appearance at their meetings. But most of them are ordinary people, contacted because they were somewhere when something occurred or knew someone who was. She entered long lists from Palmer's voting rolls, individuals to be questioned in the hope one would remember Oswald, his companions, or the Cadillac. Five other Clinton witnesses appear: Lea McGehee, Reeves Morgan, John Manchester, Corrie Collins, and Bobbie Dedon. Dischler said she recognized the name of another, Maxine Kemp, but recalled nothing about her. Only William Dunn, one of the two black CORE workers, was entirely new to her.[16] In all, Dischler filled three shorthand notebooks that she turned over to Garrison's office where they were copied and returned to her. Deeply committed to the work she and Frugé were doing, Dischler remembers it vividly.

During our two-day interview, she delivered four surprises, three of them shockers. Her description of what she and Frugé were seeking was the relatively minor one. "Garrison's office gave us the report," she said, "that these four men—Ferrie, Shaw, Oswald, and [Guy] Banister—had been [to Clinton] and we were supposed to dig up information as to what Oswald was up to there." Garrison's official version (and the trial testimony) placed only three men in Clinton, and

Banister wasn't one of them. Richard Billings did indicate in his notes that the number of men in the car was four, but no one in Garrison's office ever claimed that publicly, nor that the fourth man was Banister. That would fit with Garrison's thinking, however. He believed what occurred in Banister's office was the *key*. Dischler also said that when she and Frugé arrived in Clinton, some of the people they spoke to had already seen one of the pictures they were using.[17]

Dischler's first stunner was her description of that picture. It was a three-by-five, black-and-white photograph of the Cadillac supposedly taken while the car was parked across the street from the registrar's office. Inside were the four men. "Clay Shaw was in the driver's seat— it looked like him to me," she said. "I remember the white-haired man in the picture and the small face of Oswald. It seems like Oswald was on the passenger side of the front seat but I'm not sure. And it seems like I remember a darkened area in the back of the car where [Ferrie and Banister] were supposed to have been." This picture came from the district attorney's office, she said, perhaps from Sciambra. She recalls it being in a folder and Sciambra, she said, always had a folder, though it could have been one of Frugé's. The picture received special treatment. Dischler never had it in her possession, and Frugé had it and "showed" it but only at the beginning and only for a short while.[18]

No one ever claimed that any picture of the black Cadillac taken in Clinton existed, much less one with Shaw and Oswald inside.* But anyone with a composite such as that would have possessed a powerful brainwashing tool. And someone with that picture, Dischler said, had been there ahead of them. Who it was remains a mystery.

Dischler's second stunner was what their informant, Henry Earl Palmer, had to say. He told them Oswald actually registered to vote and signed the register. Palmer showed them where Oswald had written his name and the signature had been erased and another name written over it. But when they returned the next day to get a copy, Palmer told them the page was "missing." He showed them the book, which Dischler believes was bound in some way, and said, "You see this is all that's left." He couldn't or

---

* This suggests that the claims that Garrison used manufactured documents and photographs may have been true (Gurvich Conference, p. 16 [quoting Perry Russo]; Posner, *Case Closed*, p. 435 [quoting Gordon Novel]).

wouldn't tell them who he thought had erased the name in the first place, Dischler said, nor who he thought had removed the page.[19]

Startled by the dramatic conflict here with Palmer's courtroom testimony (and the implications), I pressed Dischler about this. "It looked like where Oswald had signed his name," she stated firmly. "You could make out part of the 'O' and, while I was looking at the signature, Henry Earl Palmer was saying to me that 'this is where Oswald signed.'" I told her that Palmer didn't testify to any of that in court. (He said Oswald couldn't meet the registration requirements.) "Someone else told me that too," she replied.[20]

Apparently, someone had second thoughts about the Oswald-signed-the-register story. Henry Earl Palmer is deceased and the register has not survived—the current registrar of voters, barber Edwin Lea McGehee, recently stated that his files contain no such book.*

The last jolt came straight from Dischler's notes and it, too, strikes at the heart of the Clinton story. At Shaw's trial, Corrie Collins described *one* man, Lee Harvey Oswald, stepping out of the black Cadillac. That isn't what he said to Frugé and Dischler. According to Dischler's notes, Collins told them that "two casually dressed men got out of [the black] car" and went to the registrar's office.[21] Collins believed they "got in line." One of them, he said, was possibly wearing "blue jeans," the other was "in white."

The question is: who were the two men—one in blue jeans, the other in white—Collins saw exit the car? And what was their role in the Clinton scenario?

Collins told Frugé and Dischler that he knew one of them, and his name may have been "Morgan." But Morgan's first name is unclear. In her notes Dischler mentioned both Estus Morgan, who died in a car accident in 1966, and "Zip" Morgan, a local resident who operated a hardware business; she also indicated that the man may not have been "a Morgan."[22]

---

* McGehee (who took office in 1979—long after the federal Voting Rights Act of 1965 drastically altered registration procedures) said that nowadays a registrant signs only an application and he believed the same was true in 1963. But three lifelong residents of the area, who registered before 1965, recently recalled signing such a book. One of them, Mildred Matthews, a retired black school teacher, even remembered Palmer saying to her, "You passed [the test], you can sign the book. I'll send your voting [authorization] card later." Palmer apparently used the register as a mailing list. (McGehee, interview with author, Dec. 6, 1993, and telephone conversation, June 21, 1996; Woodrow Wilson and Mrs. Wilson, and Mildred Matthews, telephone conversations with author, June 27, 1996.)

The man Collins described as wearing "white" Dischler managed to definitely identify. He was "Winslow Foster," an employee at the hospital.[23] Shortly after Dischler recorded that in her steno pad, Garrison took her and Frugé off the case, in effect burying the Foster–Morgan lead for twenty-seven years, until I began pursuing it in 1994. What I discovered indicates that the second man Corrie Collins saw exit the car was, indeed, Estus Morgan.

I began my search with Winslow Foster. From his employment records, I learned that Foster, a WWII veteran born in Eudora, Arkansas, was forty-eight years old in 1963; he worked at the hospital eleven years and left the area in 1969. Eventually, I located two people in the Clinton–Jackson region who knew Foster, and another (now residing in Mississippi) who linked him to Estus Morgan. One said Foster was living in Sondheimer, Louisiana, when he died sometime in the 1970s. He recalled Foster as a husky five feet eleven inches, 240 pounds, with a fair complexion and sandy hair. The other said Foster was unmarried and called him "a country boy" and "a good man." Both remarked on Foster's work at the hospital—he was an attendant in the alcoholic ward. I asked one of them what sort of clothes Foster wore and he said that because of Foster's job he "had to wear white."[24]

The individual who tied Foster to Estus Morgan was Morgan's second wife, Nellie Louise Morgan. She described her former husband as about six feet tall, 180 pounds, with a dark complexion, black hair turning grey, and a glass eye. Born in Monticello, Mississippi, in 1907, Morgan also joined the Army during WWII; in 1963 he would have been fifty-six years old. When asked how Morgan usually dressed, she replied, "most of the time he wore blue jeans." Before he and Nellie Louise Morgan were married, he, too, had worked at the hospital. One of his friends there, she said, was *Winslow Foster*.[25]

Foster's name was unknown to me until I encountered it in Dischler's notes. But Estus Morgan was linked to the Clinton tale from the first day of Shaw's trial. That's when Henry Earl Palmer took the witness stand and named Estus Morgan as one of two white men, the other being Oswald, who stood in the registration line in late August or early September 1963, and attempted to register. In light of the new information we now have, it seems virtually certain that those two white men waiting in line were actually Estus Morgan and Winslow Foster.

Their innocent trip to the registrar's office in 1963 apparently laid the foundation for the Clinton scenario. The unfamiliar black car that brought them to town, in particular, would be remembered. The recollection of it may have been the catalyst that led to the story's development in the first place—a black car was essential to the scenario because Clay Shaw was known to have access to one.* Who conceived this story is unknown, and precisely how they implemented it is unclear. What is known is that the neatly designed testimony recited at Shaw's trial was meant to be the only version of the events in Clinton that the public ever heard. The story's real roots, buried twenty-six years in Anne Dischler's notes, were never meant to be revealed.

Because of those notes, we know an unfamiliar black car really did appear in Clinton at the registrar's office the summer of 1963. Corrie Collins saw it.† Collins also saw Winslow Foster and his friend Estus Morgan exit that car and join the registration line. We know, too, that neither Foster nor Morgan came close to resembling Oswald and could not have been mistaken for him.‡ How, then, did Oswald enter the picture? The answer, I believe, involves Estus Morgan.

Since Henry Earl Palmer first mentioned him at Shaw's trial, Estus Morgan has been a mysterious presence in the Clinton saga. His official role, for instance, has changed dramatically over time. First he was Oswald's companion. Then he was demoted to bystander status.§ But

---

* Shaw's long-time friend Jeff Biddison owned a late-model black Cadillac, which Shaw, on one occasion in 1966, had borrowed to visit his father, who lived near Clinton.

† Andrew Sciambra would later report that Collins said he remembered the black car because it was "the only black strange car" he saw in Clinton that summer (Sciambra, Memorandum to Jim Garrison, Jan. 31, 1968, regarding Clinton, Louisiana).

‡ "Zip" Morgan (who was fortyish, short, with graying wavy hair and a full face) didn't resemble Oswald either.

§ Palmer testified that Morgan and Oswald were in the same registration line but were not together. Yet in his earliest (May 29, 1967) signed statement, Palmer said that Morgan and Oswald *were together*. Other early reports confirm that: An undated summary of the Clinton testimony, found in Garrison's old files, states that Oswald was in line "in company of white man Estus Morgan"; and on May 23, 1967, Richard Billings wrote in his notes that two men exited from the car, joined the line, and tried to register. One of them appeared to be Oswald; the other man was identified as Estus Morgan. That was the original pretrial story, and the reason Frugé and Dischler were showing people a picture of Estus Morgan.

the strangest aspect of Estus Morgan's actual situation was the unlikely way it paralleled Oswald's story: Morgan, too, wanted a job at the hospital;* he, too, was trying to register to enhance that possibility; he, too, was told to see Representative Reeves Morgan, and he showed up at the registrar's office at the same time Oswald did.[26] These remarkable similarities suggest that whoever was shaping the Clinton scenario simply appropriated the entire "profile" of Estus Morgan, who really did appear at the registrar's office in 1963, and attributed it to Lee Harvey Oswald, who never appeared there at all.

For what is most important about Corrie Collins's first statement to Frugé and Dischler is what Collins didn't say. He didn't say he saw Lee Harvey Oswald exit the car that day. He didn't mention Oswald.

When Corrie Collins later testified on the witness stand, one of the items he retained from his statement to Frugé and Dischler was the hat he said the driver of the car was wearing.[†] Since Shaw never wore one, Collins's insistence that the driver did has always seemed odd. Why he kept the hat is unclear.[‡] But it is one of the few details in his testimony supported by Dischler's notes.

Frugé and Dischler interviewed Corrie Collins on October 3, 1967, and Dischler identified Winslow Foster as the man in white that same day. On October 9, Dischler made her last working entry in her steno pads when she recorded additional information about Winslow Foster. Four days later, she wrote her final note: "To New Orleans" it reads, "to turn in last report to Louis Ivon." Without explanation, Garrison had abruptly removed Frugé and Dischler from the case. One of their contacts in the D.A.'s office told Dischler the investigation had to be "shut down" because of threats against Garrison's family. But Garrison didn't shut it down. He turned it over to Andrew Sciambra.

Shortly before Garrison dismissed Frugé and Dischler, who had conducted an energetic and honest effort, James Alcock told Tom Bethell

---

* Morgan was successful in being rehired at the hospital and was working there when he was killed in 1966 (Eleanore Morgan, interview with Andrew Sciambra, Jan. 3, 1968; regarding Morgan's death, see *Hammond Daily Star*, Sept. 19, 1966, and the *Ponchatoula Enterprise*, Sept. 23, 1966).
† Collins told Fruge and Dischler that the driver was a large man wearing a hat and tie (Dischler Notes, Oct. 3, 1967).
‡ Efforts to locate and interview Collins for this book were unsuccessful.

that "the Clinton angle 'wasn't working out.'"[27] Perhaps Garrison jettisoned Frugé and Dischler because they had failed to find the witnesses he needed. But more likely, it was because of their unwitting pursuit of unwanted information about the real occupants of the black car. For while Estus Morgan was conveniently dead, Winslow Foster was alive and still working at the hospital. The next step for Frugé and Dischler was to interview him. By shutting down their investigation, Garrison prevented that interview from ever taking place.

Over the next fifteen months preceding the trial, under Andrew Sciambra's supervision, Henry Earl Palmer finalized his story.[28] John Manchester overcame his hesitancy (his first statement contained fourteen I *don't recalls*). William Dunn stepped forward for the prosecution.* And Corrie Collins overhauled his recollections:[29] He identified the driver of the black car as Clay Shaw. Recalled David Ferrie sitting next to him. And replaced the two men he saw exiting the car with one, and identified him as Lee Harvey Oswald.[30]

Who was really driving the black car (which may or may not have been a Cadillac) is unknown. But the possibility that it was Clay Shaw ranges from zero to somewhere deep in the minus column. The same applies to the presence of Ferrie and Oswald.†

The House Select Committee conducted a lengthy inquiry into the Clinton matter. It even had an investigator living there for a while. Why its staff failed to locate and interview Anne Dischler is unclear.[31] But as a result, the committee experienced an information gap that allowed it to embrace the Clinton witnesses. They, it turns out, did some heavy carrying for the committee in its report. By tying Ferrie to Oswald, they bolstered the theory that the assassination was committed by members of organized crime and anti-Castro Cubans. Since Ferrie was associated with both, linking him to Oswald linked those groups to Oswald as well, and thereby to the assassination itself. To create this connection, though,

---

* In his first interview, William Dunn identified one of the men sitting in the front seat of the Cadillac as "Thomas Edward Beckham," a David Ferrie associate who does not appear in Dunn's trial testimony, or anyone else's (Frank Ruiz and Kent Simms, Memorandum to Louis Ivon, dated Jan. 31, 1968, re Interview of William Dunn, Jan. 17, 1968).
† Oswald's alleged appearance at East Louisiana State Hospital is equally suspect (see note 30).

the committee relied on a nebulous and suspect linkage, much like those favored by Jim Garrison. But that was the best the committee could do.

Yet by embracing Garrison's case even limitedly, the committee put itself in a bind. For it wanted only the Ferrie–Oswald piece of the Clinton pie, not Clay Shaw, and even made a half-hearted assertion in Shaw's defense aimed at sparing him, which only called attention to its quandary. The committee was "inclined to believe," it stated in its Report, that Oswald was in Clinton "in the company of David Ferrie, if not Clay Shaw."* But since Shaw supposedly told the town marshal he was with the International Trade Mart in New Orleans, Shaw's identification was stronger than Ferrie's. The committee could not subdivide the Clinton tale. They were all there, or none were. If the pie were poisoned, the toxins run throughout. The committee knew better, and regretted what it meant to Clay Shaw, but couldn't resist devouring the pie. Why is clear enough.

Without Clinton, the committee had next to nothing tying Ferrie to Oswald. The two may have crossed paths in the Civil Air Patrol when Oswald was fifteen. David Ferrie didn't remember it, but he never denied the possibility. There was also the 544 Camp Street address Oswald stamped on some of his literature, which Garrison and later Stone made much of. It supposedly linked Oswald to Ferrie's associate, Guy Banister, because his office was in the same building. Yet many find the 544 Camp Street address unconvincing as an Oswald–Ferrie link. For one thing, Oswald worked near the building and would have been familiar with it if he were looking for a phony business address to use on his leaflets.†
For another, there was no access to Banister's office from the Camp Street side. One had to exit the building, walk around the corner and enter through the door on Lafayette.[32] So while a person inside 544 Camp was technically in the same structure as Banister's office, for all practical purposes, he was in a separate building. As the committee noted, Oswald never rented that office and no one ever identified him as being there. Nor did any credible testimony ever place him in Banister's.

Anyway, in 1963 Banister didn't have the resources of a big-time intelligence operation. He couldn't even pay his rent. The owner of the building let him stay only because no one else wanted the space.[33]

---

* Select Committee Report, p. 145 (emphasis added).
† For additional discussion of Oswald and Camp Street, see Appendix A, item 10.

Banister did keep a file on Oswald but maintaining files on people is what Banister did. He was a rabid anti-communist who conducted political monitoring of various individuals and groups. If he had not had a file on Oswald, it would have been strange. According to two people who saw it, the file contained the sort of material (clippings) that Banister would collect on someone he was watching, not the sort he would have on an operative he was running.

The committee's other evidence of a Ferrie–Oswald connection amounted to even less—the tall tale that Oswald, when he was arrested, had in his possession David Ferrie's library card. Jack Martin invented that story during his alcoholic telephoning rampage the weekend of the assassination. He admitted that to the FBI. But in its Report, the House Select Committee inexplicably repeated the story without mentioning Martin's role.[34] The committee's overall treatment of Martin, who was interviewed after he contacted the committee, was odd. Omitting his mental problems and criminal past, it presented him as less than reliable but motivated by "sincere concerns and some legitimate suspicions."[35] But Martin was simply doing with this committee what he had done the weekend of the assassination and during Garrison's investigation—spinning tall tales and manipulating people. That worked to this committee's advantage. For in its sympathetic interpretation of Martin, as with the Clinton witnesses, the committee was promoting its view of David Ferrie, a view remarkably similar to Jim Garrison's. In some of its supporting volumes, the language even echoes the flimsy linkages Garrison used. All this leaves the impression that parts of the committee's report were somehow Garrisonized.*

The committee's senior staff writer was Richard Billings, formerly with *Life*, who arranged that magazine's "secret deal" with Garrison. According to David Chandler, Billings continued to support Garrison after management at *Life* began "to pull the plug." In 1968 he tried to reestablish a relationship with Garrison. In a letter that said he believed in Garrison's efforts regarding the assassination, Billings asked Garrison for a meeting. But Garrison, unhappy about some articles Billings had written, harshly rejected him. Nevertheless, in 1969 Billings refused a request from Shaw's attorney to testify at the trial.[36]

---

* Garrison himself had helped his cause along by turning over material to the committee, granting interviews, and winning converts among its staff.

The report Billings helped Chief Counsel G. Robert Blakey construct gave a qualified and reluctant nod of approval to Garrison's wild romp across the nation's consciousness a decade earlier.* But most of us who were following the case paid scant attention to the committee's half-hearted embrace of Jim Garrison. We were focused on the bigger picture—the committee's televised hearings and Blakey's momentous pronouncement that the assassination was probably the "result of a conspiracy."† Yet the country gained little practical benefit from all that, for the Justice Department declined to investigate. The media, the government and the nation moved on to other matters.

In the long run, the committee bequeathed a mixed legacy. Worst of all, it bestowed some credibility on Garrison's investigation. By endorsing his discredited ideas about Oswald and Ferrie, the committee breathed life into him. No one could have realized that all those years ago or foreseen the consequences. But today, it's clear that when the committee endorsed the Clinton witnesses, it set the stage for Jim Garrison's fourth resurrection, the most amazing of all.

The phoenix was again in motion.

In more ways than one. For he had turned into an author. Few noticed, however, until 1988, when Sheridan Square Press published what may be the strangest memoir in all of American letters, Garrison's rendition of his case against Clay Shaw.

---

* Of course, the committee's focus on organized crime differed drastically from Garrison's position—the Mafia being the only group he ever specifically absolved of involvement in the assassination. As Rosemary James wrote, "Garrison always refused to investigate any leads that pointed in [the direction of the Mafia]. Reporters who made such suggestions were threatened personally with grand jury inquisition and indictment. It makes you wonder what Garrison and his acolytes then and now really are about. Creating smoke screens, perhaps?" (James, "Letters," the New Orleans Times Picayune, June 20, 1991.)

† The Committee endorsed the Warren Commission's single-bullet theory and concluded that Oswald fired three shots: the first missed, the second passed through the president's throat and went on to wound Governor Connally, and the third struck the president in the head. But based on acoustical evidence indicating a missed shot was fired from the front, the committee also concluded that a second gun was involved.

CHAPTER FOURTEEN

ON THE TRAIL OF THE ASSASSINS

> Every word she writes is a lie,
> including "a" and "the."
> —Mary McCarthy (concerning
> Lillian Hellman)

Having lived through The Jim Garrison Era, I felt no urge to read *On the Trail of the Assassins: My Investigation and Prosecution of the Murder of President Kennedy*, his book about it,* until I began researching the case in 1993. When I finally sat down with it, I was expecting a biased account, but was unprepared for what I found. Wherever reality failed to suit his needs, Garrison simply changed it.

He handled Perry Russo's lie-detector tests in a typical fashion. Early in his investigation, Garrison twice ordered Perry Russo to undergo polygraph examinations, which he failed to pass. One was administered by Jefferson Parish Deputy Sheriff Roy Jacob, the other by New Orleans Police Department polygraph technician Edward O'Donnell.[1] Both set off fireworks in Garrison's office. So it was surprising to find Garrison saying in his memoir that he had considered using a lie-detector test on Russo but "rejected the idea."[2] Twenty-one years earlier, in *Playboy* magazine, Garrison said Russo *passed* his polygraph.[3] Perhaps Garrison thought denying the tests occurred might discourage researchers from probing the subject. Experts might debate the meaning of Russo's two unsuccessful lie-detector tests. But the record is unequivocal that they took place.†

---

* *A Heritage of Stone*, Garrison's first book, published in 1970, reportedly provided the basis for this memoir, which was the last of three books Garrison wrote. (*The Star Spangled Contract*, a novel concerning a presidential assassination, published in 1976, was the second.)

† In addition to Edward O'Donnell's report (Appendix B), he later testified under oath in two courtrooms (at Clay Shaw's trial and the Christenberry hearing) and those transcripts have been preserved.

Garrison was just as misleading about Vernon Bundy, the drug addict who failed his test an hour or so before he testified at the preliminary hearing. In that same *Playboy* article, Garrison said Bundy, too, had *passed* his polygraph.[4] In his book, however, Garrison didn't mention the test. He claimed that Bundy was interrogated until they were convinced of his truthfulness.[5] Actually, Garrison barely had time to hear Bundy's story and have him tested before he took the witness stand, and no one thought he was telling the truth, including Garrison. Quite the contrary. But in his memoir, he told a different story.

Erasing history is not that easy though. James Kruebbe still remembers the polygraph and the discussion afterwards between Garrison and his assistants, and described both to me. Kruebbe's two-page Work Report about the incident still exists. Edward O'Donnell, who also was present during the quarrel in Garrison's office, testified at the Christenberry hearing and put into the record his personal recollection of Garrison's statement: "I don't care if [Bundy] is lying or not. We are not telling him to lie. We are going to use him." When Garrison took the witness stand in that same courtroom and was asked under oath if he had said that, he didn't deny it. He refused to answer.[6]

Garrison also dissembled in his book about the Beaubouef bribery tape. This was the secretly recorded conversation in which a Garrison investigator, with Garrison's authorization, offered Alvin Beaubouef $3,000 and a job with an airline in return for incriminating testimony against David Ferrie. Beaubouef, his attorneys, Garrison's aides, a member of the New Orleans Police Department, and others created a vast paper trail that tracked this episode. The court reporter who typed a transcript of the recording* verified it in federal court. Garrison's two investigators admitted to a deputy superintendent of police that they offered Beaubouef the money. And that same deputy superintendent *listened to the recording* and mentioned that in his official report.[7]

Yet Garrison said in his book that Beaubouef admitted the bribe was never offered, and Garrison declared flatly that the recording never

---

* In 1997, after unsuccessful efforts under the Freedom of Information Act, I appealed to the head of the Justice Department's Criminal Division (the agency withholding the document at the National Archives) and finally obtained a copy of this transcript.

existed. As Garrison well knew, both occurred, and he also knew the Police Department's investigation confirmed that. The conversation did take place, the offer *was* made, and it *was* recorded. Again, the evidence is unequivocal.[8]

The evidence is also unequivocal about the events of February 18, 1967. That was the day the Times-Picayune printed David Ferrie's candid interview on its front page and an unflattering editorial about Garrison in the back. Writing about that Saturday in his book, Garrison described himself in the presence of two aides reading the editorial. Though outraged by it, he spoke not a word. Instead, he vented his anger by bending a pen from his desk set "into a perfect 'U.'" Then, he wrote, he told his secretary to send the clamoring press away. He would not be seeing them today. He was going home to work. After stuffing his briefcase with books, he exited by way of his private elevator, thus avoiding the reporters entirely.[9]

That's what Garrison should have done. But it isn't what he did. Late that day he held a press conference and issued the first of his public declarations about his Kennedy investigation. (Described in chapter 5.) In that first encounter with the press, Garrison forged his future course. Afterwards, there was no way he could retreat, no way he could withdraw what he had said. But more than two decades later in this memoir, he rid himself of those impulsive statements by deleting the troublesome press conference from his story. In its place he created the office scene and a more fitting self-portrait: the beleaguered D.A. victimized by an irresponsible press, a stoic bender-of-pens who withdrew to the sanctuary of his home with his books to work. Unfortunately for Garrison, the reporters present that Saturday wrote about the press conference in the stories they filed.[10]

As in life, Clay Shaw bears the brunt of this revisionist history. Garrison never had a substantive case against Shaw supported by legitimate evidence. That's why the jury acquitted him in fifty-four minutes. Shaw himself described the case well when he referred to it as "strange and obscure" and "Jerry built." Garrison camouflaged all that in his book by invoking the CIA like a mantra. He portrayed Shaw as a major player in high-level CIA circles, but never acknowledged the disreputable nature of the source of his information for that claim. It came from an Italian Communist Party newspaper well-known for its anti-American, pro-Soviet bloc articles that were often entirely false. In this instance, the writers apparently were prompted by the publicity attending Clay Shaw's arrest and the opportunity it afforded. A later article in the same newspaper claimed Shaw was responsible for organizing President Kennedy's trip to Texas. That was too outrageous even for Garrison to embrace.[11]

Clay Shaw at one time did provide routine information to the CIA's Domestic Contact Service, as did thousands of Americans traveling abroad in those Cold War years.[12] One of Garrison's own financial backers and a founding member of Truth and Consequences, Cecil Maxwell Shilstone, was named in a CIA report as possibly being such a contact.[13] If the CIA had not approached Shaw for help, it would have been unusual, given his position with the International Trade Mart. That did not make him, as Garrison claimed, "an employee" of that agency, big time or otherwise, nor did it make him a conspirator, any more than it did the thousands of other loyal Americans who aided it. But even if Shaw were a CIA employee, he would have assisted that agency out of the same patriotic feelings most Americans share. Garrison never allowed for that possibility.

Shaw could have cleared this matter up at his trial and it is regrettable that he didn't. When his attorney asked if he had ever worked for the CIA, if Shaw had simply replied, "No, but I have provided that agency with information from time to time," the subject would today be a dead issue. But reportedly, the decision-makers at the CIA wanted Shaw's association with it kept secret, fearing Garrison would misinterpret it. A late-sixties CIA report states flatly, "We have never renumerated [Shaw]."[14]

Still, the full extent of his association with the agency is for now unclear. Clouding the issue is a CIA project from the 1960s known as QK/ENCHANT. The CIA apparently approved Shaw (perhaps without his knowledge) for this project,* which, by one unofficial account, was nothing more than a program for routine debriefing of individuals involved in international trade. At this point, what QK/ENCHANT actu-

---

* Shaw's name and a number appear in a CIA document, along with the name and number of J. Monroe Sullivan, former Executive Director of the San Francisco World Trade Center, who had been granted "a covert security approval" for Project QK/ENCHANT (Raymond G. Rocca, CIA memorandum, April 26, 1967, "Enclosure 21," item 11, p. 4). Sullivan recently denied ever working for the CIA or having any knowledge of any such project (telephone conversation with author, Oct. 12, 1997). See also handwritten notes by HSCA staffer reviewing [Shaw] CIA documents, describing Sullivan's "covert security approval" as for "unwitting" use (National Archives record number 180-10143-10220).

ally was, whether or not it ever came to fruition, and what, if anything, Shaw knew about it, also remain unknown. But Shaw's work for the CIA, whatever it was, is irrelevant. Since Garrison never connected him to the assassination, linking him to the CIA meant nothing thirty years ago, and it means nothing today.

Shaw isn't the only one Garrison maligned in his book. Based solely on memory, he reported dialogue, more than two decades old, which supposedly laid the bedrock for his investigation. In the most important of these reconstructed conversations, Garrison described Dean Andrews implicitly admitting to him that Shaw was Bertrand.[15] Yet if Andrews had, Garrison would have used that against him at the time with the press, the grand jury, and in the courtroom. He would not have waited twenty-one years to reveal Andrews's confession in his book. Garrison waited because until Andrews's death in 1981 he couldn't put those words into Andrews's mouth without being publicly contradicted by him.

Garrison explained that conversations with some witnesses lacked substantiation because the original documents were "stolen." The reader is supposed to take Garrison's word that he is remembering them correctly. Yet even when he refers to a written statement, he presents nothing to support its allegations except his faith. One witness told of secret plane trips with Clay Shaw. Another claimed pre-assassination knowledge of the crime. One Edward Whalen told the most serious story, were it true. He said that Ferrie, Shaw, and Andrews tried to hire Garrison's murder. Whalen disclosed this plot to kill Garrison to James Alcock. Alcock dutifully recorded it, and Garrison cited the Alcock interview in his memoir. But in 1994, when I asked Alcock about Whalen, Alcock didn't even recall the name. To jog his memory, I had to remind him of the murder plot. At that point, his eyes wandered and he had nothing to say. Yet Garrison not only treated these tales as credible, he vouched for the men telling them. After studying one for some three hours, Garrison wrote, he was convinced that "weaving a fabricated tale was not in this man's makeup,"[16] a testimonial as empty as a moonscape, but convincing perhaps to unwary readers who trust their narrator.

The strangest anecdote Garrison related in his book is an encounter he had at Los Angeles International Airport and it doesn't yield to research in any ordinary sense. When waiting for his luggage, it was his habit, he explained, to spend the time sitting on a toilet in the men's room reading a magazine. He chose that spot because there were no chairs in the baggage collection area. On this particular occasion, he purchased a copy of *Time* magazine, entered the men's room, selected the first booth, sat down, and commenced to read. Then he heard someone enter the booth next to him and was immediately concerned. When he heard "whispering," he at once rushed out of the stall and confronted two airport policemen; he quickly exited from the men's room and encountered several others, one of whom yelled at him, asking how long he had been inside. Garrison informed the reader that his stay had been no more than two or three minutes maximum but he yelled back at the officer, telling him, basically, to mind his own business, and walked on out. Garrison claimed to believe that he had foiled a plan by the CIA to set him up for a sex charge to discredit him and his investigation. He offered an elaborate explanation of how it would have been done, involving his telephone records and an earlier phone call received from a former homosexual client.[17] As related, this incident reeks of paranoia and perhaps something more complex, to be discussed further in chapter 16.

Garrison's propinquity theory (the idea that proximity to a person or thing implies a connection), though he never used that term in the book, rears its head from time to time.* Garrison applied this odd notion to almost any situation. He assumed a person was connected to an intelligence agency because he maintained a residence or an office near it. He imagined individuals were cohorts who rented post office boxes in the same building. He divined a connection when a woman hailing from Chicago crossed paths with a man from that same city. And while he didn't say so in the book, he was automatically suspicious of anyone living next door to any of his suspects. Garrison didn't believe coincidences happened. The two vagabonds arrested in the Oklahoma City Federal Building bombing because their itineraries paralleled sus-

---

* Garrison wrote a two-part memorandum dated February 10 and April 7, 1967, entitled, "Time and Propinquity: Factors In Phase One." This, Tom Bethell wrote, was "predicated on the supposition that if people live anywhere near one another, they are therefore to be suspected of being associated in some way." "I need hardly say," Bethell remarked, "that nobody in the office takes the 'propinquity factor' seriously except for Garrison himself." Bethell also quoted Garrison as saying, while he thumbed through the city directory: "'Sooner or later, because people are lazy, you catch them out on propinquity'" (Bethell Diary, p. 23).

pect Timothy McVeigh's would have faced criminal charges if Garrison had been running that investigation.

But perhaps the most bewildering statement Garrison made in his memoir concerns the *innocence* of Lee Harvey Oswald. Garrison wrote that a jury convinced of Oswald's innocence would be forced to consider conspiracy and, therefore, would be more likely to convict Clay Shaw. Yet Garrison himself named Oswald a co-conspirator, using him to link Shaw to the crime, and also to establish the requisite overt act. Garrison's own men tried to establish Oswald's guilt at Shaw's trial in order to prove their case. If Oswald were innocent, Garrison's charge against Shaw was demolished.[18]

Garrison so misrepresented his New Orleans evidence in these pages that it's tempting to assume his Dealey Plaza evidence must be better. It isn't. He wrote that President Kennedy was in essence *hijacked* on November 22, that the route of the motorcade was changed *that morning* from its original course, causing the cars to travel down Houston and Elm where the shooters were waiting. This last-minute switch, he claimed, was more evidence of high-level complicity.[19] But no last-minute switch occurred. Both the *Dallas Times-Herald* and *Morning News* published the motorcade's precise route through Dealey Plaza (and onto the Stemmons Freeway via Houston and Elm) a full three days before the assassination.[20]

Anyone who wants to know if any particular claim Garrison made has any validity at all must trace it back to its roots. Nothing he wrote can be trusted. Not even *a* and *the*. The ordinary reader, of course, has no way of knowing that. I, too, was lulled into complacency by the book's easy prose.

Reading it was for me like seeing someone I knew reflected in a funhouse mirror—the story was recognizable but grossly misshaped. I didn't identify the problem at first. It took a second, slower read to spot the first "error," and the next, then another, and another, and another, until finally the light went on: *It's all wrong.*

The reviewer for the *Times-Picayune* unwittingly hit the nail on the head when she said the book "reads like a novel."[21] It should. Most of Garrison's engaging story is fiction. He treated all events, however verifiable, as mutable and subject to his revision.* An oversight or two I

---

* In a 1967 Foreword to Harold Weisberg's *Oswald in New Orleans*, Garrison wrote that "those in control of the government machinery sometimes find it necessary to re-write history....The truth becomes not what occurred but what they announce has occurred." That is an accurate description of his own memoir.

might attribute to poor memory, especially if the incidents were unimportant. But they weren't, and Garrison laced his narrative with them. (See Appendix A.) When I realized that, I was astonished, first by the fact of it, then the audacity. I found it baffling and scary—baffling that Garrison imagined he could get away with it, scary that so far he has succeeded spectacularly. He accomplished with his typewriter what he had failed to do in a court of law. He convicted Clay Shaw.

The publisher who nurtured his effort to completion, Ellen Ray and her Sheridan Square Press,* apparently did little or no fact-checking. Perhaps that's understandable. Her author, after all, was a former district attorney and a sitting judge. Today, her publishing house, it seems, has ceased to exist. Its one big success, though, was a far-reaching "triumph," and its influence continues even now. Seven years after it was published, the paperback version is in its twentieth printing.† Until I assembled the facts in this book, no one had demonstrated the stunning falsity of Garrison's account.

Throughout his life and in these "recollections," Garrison created the illusion that his investigation had substance by framing it in the rhetoric of American foreign policy and a high-level government conspiracy. He had no evidence for that except his empty case against Clay Shaw. In the closing passage of his book, Garrison assailed the Department of Justice for still refusing to conduct an "honest investigation." Yet no investigation could have been more dishonest then his own. Oliver Stone had no way of knowing that to begin with and once Garrison became his mentor, the likelihood of his realizing it was slim.

In 1990 Garrison put Stone in touch with L. Fletcher Prouty, a retired Air Force colonel, who had read Garrison's manuscript and corresponded with him about it. Prouty, who espouses a sweeping conspiratorial view of history, was associated with, among others, the far-right Liberty Lobby.[22] Stone now had a second mentor. He hired Prouty as an advisor and he became a significant player in the events surround-

---

* A subsidiary of the Institute for Media Analysis, a small, old-fashioned leftist organization best known for the regularity of its attacks on the *New York Times.*
† The hardback edition was barely reviewed but the Warner Books soft cover (published after the film was released) was thirteen weeks on the *New York Times* Paperback Best Sellers list.

ing the making of the film.

After he optioned the movie rights to Garrison's book, Stone met in early 1989 with representatives from Warner Bros. Over dinner at a Beverly Hills restaurant, Stone pitched his idea, he later told an interviewer, in fifteen or twenty minutes. The studio's president, Terry Semel,* told that same writer "it took [me] two minutes to be totally ensconced in the whole idea."[23] Bankrolled by Warner Bros., Stone proceeded with plans to create a $20 million film. That figure soon doubled and ultimately would reach at least $60 million. By then the prospects for Stone's enlightenment about Garrison dropped to virtually nil.

Various factors contributed to Jim Garrison's final resurrection on the silver screen. But mostly, Garrison brought it about himself through his endless drive for self-justification. David Ferrie died, spelling the end at the very beginning. But Garrison parlayed that into his biggest boost. James Phelan exposed Perry Russo's testimony as a fraud. But Garrison sought new witnesses to support Russo's story. Shaw was acquitted. But Garrison launched a new offensive. Judge Christenberry ended the game and convicted Garrison. But Garrison turned to his typewriter and reinterpreted his fall. Examining the real record of Jim Garrison's investigation is like viewing up close the mangled wreckage of a high-speed car crash. In his book, Garrison reshaped that wreckage into a brand new vehicle, the latest model, irresistible, gleaming on the showroom floor.

Oliver Stone climbed inside and drove it home.

---

* Also present were Bob Daly, Chairman of the Board and Chief Executive Officer, and Bill Gerber, a production executive.

CHAPTER FIFTEEN

JFK: THE FILM

> Oliver Stone can't change history.
> But he can take an innocent dead
> man and yank him out of his
> grave and make him look guilty.
> He can make this crazy prosecutor
> look like a matinee idol. But that
> isn't going to work because the
> truth is mighty and will prevail.[1]
>
> —James Phelan, 1993

Shortly before Oliver Stone began shooting his movie, Jim Garrison told a local reporter he couldn't talk about the film because his contract with Stone prohibited it. Garrison did have something to say about the choice of Kevin Costner to portray him—"a first-class selection." About the script—"a beautiful job." And about Stone—"it's like having a Eugene O'Neill write it." Stone himself would soon be drawing parallels between his efforts and Shakespeare's. Though, as he put it, he wasn't saying he was "as good as Shakespeare."[2]

Born in New York City to wealth and privilege, Oliver Stone was sixteen, in a prestigious boarding school on the Ivy League track when his parents divorced, a seismic event in his life. The following summer, Stone took a trip alone to New Orleans. It was 1963, and later he would remark on the coincidence of the timing. He was walking the streets of The City That Care Forgot when Lee Harvey Oswald was there, only a few months before the assassination. Two other family traumas marked Stone's teenage years. His father lost all his money on the stock market and Stone broke with his parents. He left Yale (after one year) and headed off on his own. After a stint in Vietnam teaching English, and a period in the merchant marine, he returned home, lived awhile in Mexico, then returned briefly to Yale. In 1966 he completed a long, autobiographical novel that was rejected by publishers.* Stone reacted by joining the Army, which returned him to Vietnam, where he later said he expected to die and welcomed the idea. Stone spent fifteen months (in 1967 and 1968) there. He did acid and smoked pot. Injured twice in combat, he was awarded a Purple Heart and Bronze Star. He returned home altered by his experiences, filled with rage, ready, he said, to grab a gun and go after President Nixon. He was back from the war only ten days when he was arrested for marijuana possession. That same year, using the G.I. Bill, he entered film school at New York University, where he studied under Martin Scorsese. Ten years later, after a move to Hollywood, he wrote the screenplay for Midnight Express and won his first Academy Award. But it was the enormous financial success of Platoon (it cost $5 million and grossed $250 million) in 1986 that transformed Stone into a major force on the Hollywood scene. The film also made him an icon for those (including this writer) who had opposed the Vietnam war. Two years later, he encountered Ellen Ray in that elevator, read Garrison's book, and had the epiphany that started him down the path that led to JFK.[3]

Stone would make a film that dealt with large historical issues, but it was a deeply personal expression. He once said about his cinematic technique that he believed in "unleashing the pure wash of emotion across the mind to let you see the inner myth, the spirit of the thing." Asked later where reason came in, he said "reason counts for something" but could become "negative energy" and that "the deeper truths" come from one's "gut."[†] In that same interview, Stone defended Leni Riefenstahl, the brilliant German filmmaker who glorified the Third Reich, on the grounds that "she was a believer in Hitler" at the time. Riefenstahl "followed her emotions" as an artist. "This," Stone said, "is what I do."[4]

To help him glorify Jim Garrison, Stone hired Garrison's editor, Zachary Sklar, to co-write the screenplay.[‡] For research, he brought on board a recent Yale graduate, Jane Rusconi. To play the role of Big Jim,

---

* In September 1997, A Child's Night Dream, Stone's revised novel, was published by St. Martin's Press.

† This point of view overlooks the tendency of serious glitches to take up residence in one's "gut," making it a risky guide to truth seeking.

‡ Stone also optioned another book, Jim Marrs's Crossfire, an encyclopedia of assassination theories, which enabled Stone to draw on a wealth of information without spending more money on rights to other books.

Stone first approached Harrison Ford, but Ford was unavailable. Stone had an unsuccessful luncheon discussion with Mel Gibson, but denies offering Gibson the part. Kevin Costner, Stone claims, was always his preference. (By one account, it was Costner's wife who read Garrison's book and urged Costner to make the film.) Costner lacked Garrison's dominating six-foot-seven-inch physical stature, melodious voice, and impulsive, volatile nature. He seemed to many an odd, even wimpy selection. Yet Costner fit perfectly the Capraesque All American Nice Guy and Defender of Democracy that Garrison had created in his book.

Tommy Lee Jones as Clay Shaw was almost as unlikely, entirely devoid of the modesty and kindness that people who knew Shaw talk about. But, of course, Stone wasn't interested in those qualities. Supposedly, he wanted the sense of *menace* that Jones projects. The role of Lee Harvey Oswald went to an English actor, Gary Oldman, who re-created the look and sound of that most enigmatic of men with amazing accuracy. For several small but important parts, Stone cannily selected a group of old-timers (Jack Lemmon, Walter Matthau, Ed Asner, and Joe Pesci) whose familiar and trusted faces brought to the film all the positive feelings and credibility that had accrued to them over the years. Jim Garrison, himself, in a cameo performance, played Chief Justice Earl Warren. The thankless role of Garrison's nagging wife was believably played by Sissy Spacek. Stone's characterization of her was misleading though. Elizabeth Garrison had a better understanding of the situation than her husband's Hollywood disciple.

Stone made some revealing comments in a series of interviews shortly before filming began: he referred to JFK as a "history lesson," described himself as "a cinematic historian," and admitted, "I'm trying to reshape the world through movies." Reflecting on his earlier films, and how he would be remembered, Stone said he hoped his legacy would be "that I was a good historian as well as a good dramatist."[5] Yet he didn't go about his investigation of President Kennedy's assassination like a historian seeking truth but like a director looking for a good story, one that lent itself to a cinematic format and possessed maximum dramatic impact. He listened to some quite improbable people hawking their wares and incorporated some of them into his script.[6] While Garrison had been somewhat restrained in his fabrications, Stone knew no bounds. He dramatized "events" that were uncorroborated or unreliably reported, and he invented people and scenes that directly contradicted the facts. Whatever the story line needed that wasn't available, Stone concocted.

Yet he invested great effort in achieving the look of authenticity. In Dallas he paid $50,000 for the right to film on the sixth floor of the Texas School Book Depository, site of the so-called sniper's nest. He had part of the building that had been removed rebuilt. Ordered replicas created of 3,000 book cartons, window frames painted, trees trimmed, and railroad tracks replaced behind the grassy knoll. That authentic look was very important, Stone explained to an interviewer. But outside Stone's circle, many were worried about the distinction between the look and the reality of Jim Garrison. A goodly number of those concerned resided in Garrison's hometown. Stone spoke to some of them, going through the motions of hearing the other side of the story.

One of those he visited in New Orleans was F. Irvin Dymond, an impressive, charismatic man, who later recalled their conversation. It lasted about ten minutes, with Stone asking questions. No, Dymond had said, he did not believe Garrison acted in good faith. Nor had Asst. D.A. James Alcock. Alcock was too smart not to realize that they had no case. Dymond told Stone "his idea of the whole thing was just completely contrary to the actual facts," which Stone seemed "shocked to hear." Not that he didn't believe it, Dymond added, but he was shocked that Dymond would say it. When Stone left his office, Dymond recalled, Stone was not a happy man. Stone also visited the current district attorney, Harry Connick, who told him Garrison's prosecution of Clay Shaw "was the grossest miscarriage of justice" Connick knew about.[7]

To this and the ongoing public criticism of his project, Stone reacted for the most part as though it were coming from some monolithic hostile force. That mirrored Garrison's reaction in the sixties when he accused anyone who spoke against him of working for the federal government. Yet not all the negative signals coming Stone's way were from the opposition. Some came from Garrison's own camp. James Alcock for instance. He met on one occasion with Stone, Costner, and Garrison, but the session did not go well. "Jim was still going on with some of the theories that were totally contrary to what we were trying to prove in the case," Alcock recalled recently. "I guess they could sense I wasn't going to be part of that."[8] They never got back to him. What Alcock had to say didn't fit with Garrison's theories (now Stone's) or his revisionist version of his investigation.

That's what Stone wanted. That's what he filmed—Garrison discovering *the plot that killed the president.* Stone added some newer information, and now and then accurately portrayed a real event. His centerpiece and rationale is presented by a conspiratorial *deep throat* known only as "X." His sixteen-minute virtual monologue would have buried any ordinary movie. This one survives it mostly because movies work emotionally, not rationally. The splendid actor helped, too. Donald Sutherland makes even the absurdities sound believable. Stone concluded his story with a wildly inaccurate rendition of Shaw's trial. Costner-Garrison delivers a rousing flag-and-country closing statement to the jury that bears little resemblance to what Garrison actually said, except for the final sentence. Reportedly as a joke, Stone filmed an alternate ending in which the jury voted to convict Shaw.

Stone opened his film with a lengthy montage of rapid-fire black and white newsreel-like footage, beginning with President Eisenhower's famous warning about the danger of the military-industrial complex. This sequence sets up Stone's overarching political statement, the film's realistic this-is-history look and sound, and breathtaking pace. The latter, constructed in the editing room after the film was shot, is the principal reason the information-burdened story works. Stone launched his Garrison plot line with the Raymond Chandler-type incident that had originally captured his imagination in Garrison's book—the pistol-whipping of Jack Martin on the evening of the assassination.[9]

Martin is played by Jack Lemmon as a vulnerable puppy-dog-like-drunk savagely brutalized by tanklike Attila-the-Hun Ed Asner as Guy Banister.* Something like this incident did happen, of course. But Martin's explanation that night to the New Orleans police that the quarrel was over some long-distance telephone calls was recast by Stone in a far more sinister light. Stone also exaggerated the viciousness of the beating; Martin received only minor medical treatment. Stone shaped the role of Martin, like all the real people in the film, to fit his story's needs. That is to say, he created a fictional person.

---

* As Garrison had done in his book, Stone used this episode to introduce the anti-Castro activities of Banister and his alleged confederates, Lee Harvey Oswald and Clay Shaw.

He did the same with David Ferrie. The first reporter to interview Ferrie after news of Garrison's investigation broke, recently said he couldn't stand to watch the movie because it was *all* wrong, but David Ferrie was *so* wrong it was pathetic. Stone committed many excesses in achieving his vision and two of the more extravagant involve Ferrie. Stone has him virtually confessing to the crime.* In reality, Ferrie repeatedly denied any involvement in it, and he repeatedly denied knowing Oswald. He even volunteered to take a lie-detector test and sodium Pentothal.[10]

He wasn't murdered by intruders in the night either. Stone's lurid version of Ferrie's death generated more reaction than any other individual scene. James Alcock was one of those complaining. The evening Ferrie died, according to Alcock, he and Louis Ivon were across the street keeping Ferrie's apartment under surveillance, all night long. "I didn't see any *murder*," Alcock said recently, with an air of exasperation. He knew where the idea came from though. In the meeting he had with Garrison, Stone, and Costner, Costner referred to Ferrie's death as "the murder." "I knew immediately," Alcock said, that Costner "had been talking to Garrison." The scene in the movie "where people were pouring stuff down Ferrie's throat and killing him—that just *didn't happen*," Alcock stated.[11] He was right, of course, about the source of this idea. As Garrison's old friend, Orleans Parish Coroner Frank Minyard explained to an interviewer, Garrison believed "that someone had passed a tube down through [Ferrie's] mouth" through "his esophagus into his stomach and pumped in a large quantity of [the thyroid medication] Proloid."[12] Stone took that macabre notion and gave it cinematic life.

He did the same with Garrison's account of Dean Andrews, played by the deceased John Candy. In a restaurant scene with Garrison, a sweaty, repulsively obese, and sinister-looking Andrews stuffs his face† while flashbacks establish unequivocally that Clay Shaw was Clay Bertrand. Stone reinforced this falsehood in other scenes. At one point, Andrews blurts out

---

* Stone's basis for this scene was Louis Ivon's recollections of the evening he spent with Ferrie at the Fontainebleau Motel ("Oliver Stone Talks Back," *Premiere*, Jan. 1992, pp. 69-70). But what Ferrie actually said that night is, to say the least, unclear (as discussed in note 10).

† No one seeing this film would guess that this easy-to-hate villain created by Stone was actually a funny and fun-loving (if flawed) human being, liked by virtually everyone. Or that aside from Clay Shaw he is probably the most sympathetic of Garrison's victims.

to Garrison that he's afraid of being murdered by the feds if he gives up Bertrand's real name. He thereby acknowledged there *was* a "Bertrand." The real Andrews insisted to the end of his days that Bertrand never existed. He specifically said that Bertrand was not Clay Shaw. He repeatedly told Garrison that. He told Garrison's aides, the grand jury, writers Edward Epstein and Milton Brener, and various reporters. Weeping, he told Shaw attorney Salvatore Panzeca. He told the judge and jury at Shaw's trial, and in interviews in later years he continued to say it. Garrison never proved otherwise. Yet Stone makes it appear as though half of New Orleans not only knew Bertrand existed but knew he was Shaw.

He also injected life into one of Garrison's oldest canards, the so-called tramps, the three arrested in the railroad yards after the shooting. Garrison said they were too clean and well-dressed to be real tramps. Stone repeated that in the film and, by blending their real pictures with actors re-creating them, made them appear involved in the killing. Echoing Garrison, Stone indignantly cited the "negligence" of "Dallas law enforcement [officials]" for failing to take their names. After the film was released, reporters discovered long-suppressed documents revealing that the Dallas Police *did* take their names and they were just what they seemed to be, tramps. The night before the assassination, they had bathed, shaved and received clean clothes at a shelter, which explained their "suspicious" appearance.[13] *

"Bill Boxley" didn't fare any better than the tramps in Stone's hands. Boxley supposedly spied on Garrison's investigation for the government. Stone offers him up as one of the alibis meant to explain Shaw's acquittal. His real name was William C. Wood and he once worked for the CIA.† Dubbed *Boxley* by Garrison, who gladly hired him hoping to gain insight into that agency, he is shown in the film being pressured and strong-armed by an FBI agent. Boxley finally abandons Garrison. "[Now] they have everything, Chief," moans a Garrison aide. He means

---

* Over the years the tramps have been the subject of endless commentary and research. Their pictures are like a conspiratorial Rorschach test. People see in them whatever they are inclined to see, usually Watergate burglars E. Howard Hunt, Frank Sturgis and convicted hitman Charles Harrelson (the actor Woody Harrelson's father). In some quarters the effort to unravel the assassination by 'identifying' the tramps continues today.
† Alcoholism ended Wood's CIA career.

that Boxley has revealed Garrison's case to the other side. What really happened, as journalist George Lardner pointed out, was that Boxley's devotion to Garrison drove him to come up with evidence Garrison needed to make his case, a not uncommon reaction. But when Garrison, encouraged by information from Boxley, almost indicted a dead man (construction worker Robert L. Perrin) for assassinating the president, Garrison saved face by firing Boxley and announcing he was a CIA plant.[14] The joke at the heart of the Boxley affair is that he could have given "everything" to the other side and it wouldn't have mattered since Garrison's case never amounted to anything but wild fantasies and vague linkages, anchored in the conjured testimony of Perry Russo.*

Stone excluded Russo from his film. That is comparable to telling the story of the Oklahoma City Federal Building disaster and leaving out the bomb. As the witness who triggered Shaw's arrest and furnished the entire legal basis for the trial, Russo's absence from the film is conspicuous.† But Stone made a sly move deleting him. Among other things, he avoided scenes of Russo being drugged and hypnotized and his repeated recantations. Stone wriggled around The Russo Problem by creating an (admittedly) fictional surrogate for him in the homosexual prison inmate, Willie O'Keefe, amusingly played by Kevin Bacon.[15] In one scene, O'Keefe, supposedly Shaw's hired lover, is shown dining at Shaw's home. Each man is seated at one end of a long table, sumptuously appointed, being served by a uniformed waiter. Stone took this dinner scene straight from Garrison's book. Garrison had based it on unsubstantiated information from David Logan, one of those witnesses whose statement Garrison claimed was stolen.[16]

Stone's Clay Shaw is no more true-to-life than Willie O'Keefe. Stone depicted Shaw as an arrogant, elitist sybarite, a butch homosexual with a taste for elegance, younger men, and conspiracy, plotting to murder the president. In one of Stone's most offensive sequences, he dressed Shaw in drag and shows him cavorting with David Ferrie at a homo-

---

* William Gurvich and Tom Bethell, who did defect and turn material over to Shaw's defense team, were not infiltrators; they simply came to realize an innocent man was being railroaded.
† Russo was on the set. Stone gave him a small part in the film and, according to Russo, hired him as a technical advisor for the homosexual scenes, particularly those involving sadomasochism.

sexual party.* In defense of this scene, Stone claimed that "after the trial ended, Garrison came across two photos of Shaw and Ferrie together at a party—proof positive that they knew each other." Stone insisted that he had merely restaged the photos and their "situations."[17] But Stone's restaging was a gross distortion of these innocuous photographs, the racier of which shows Shaw and Jeff Biddison dressed in business suits with "mop-strand" wigs on their heads. Moreover, all of Stone's information concerning the pictures was incorrect. They did not surface *after* the trial; they were published by a Garrison supporter in a widely read newsletter almost two years *before* the trial. And even prior to their publication, a Garrison aide showed one of them to Biddison. Garrison didn't use them at the trial because he knew (and he knew Shaw's attorneys knew) the "David Ferrie" in the pictures wasn't Ferrie at all but a former radio announcer who resembled him named Robert Brannon.[18] †Two decades later, Garrison revised the history of the pictures for Oliver Stone's benefit. Stone, having swallowed Garrison whole, gave the pictures cinematic life and passed on Garrison's version of them to the press. In real life, Garrison never linked Clay Shaw to David Ferrie except by way of the Clinton witnesses, and the obviously suspect trial appearances of the Tadins.

He never tied Shaw to Dallas either and, except theoretically, Garrison never connected his case to Washington. Stone did both. He did it by creating the man X, a retired military officer, "one of those secret guys in the Pentagon," as he calls himself. X provides the information about the link between the low-level New Orleans operation and the shadowy plotters in Washington, D.C. In a meeting wholly invented by Stone, Garrison and X rendezvous on the steps of the Lincoln Memorial. There, in that amazingly protracted sixteen-minute discourse, Donald

---

* Perry Russo said that in one of those party scenes (which didn't make it into the movie) Joe Pesci (Ferrie) was beating Tommy Lee Jones (Shaw) with a chain and Stone pushed Pesci to the point where he finally complained that if he didn't stop he was going to end up hurting Jones (Russo, interview with author, Feb. 7, 1994).

† In a print of the original picture, Brannon's "eyebrows" were "not quite as prominent" as they were in the published version (report on "Citizens' Council Newspaper The [Councilor]," regarding investigation conducted May 18, 19, and 23, 1967, on behalf of Shaw's attorneys). This suggests that the picture was touched up to make the Ferrie resemblance more pronounced.

Sutherland proceeds to tell all about the president's murder.

Just before the assassination, X was sent out of the country on a phony assignment to prevent him from providing "additional security in Texas," one of his routine duties. He recites a series of other supposedly suspicious occurrences that weekend, none of which were really suspicious at all. He claims the telephone system in Washington was shut down for a full hour "to keep the wrong story from spreading." Telephone service was slow after the assassination because of the volume of calls, but it was never shut down.* He says the New Zealand newspapers published biographical data about Oswald too quickly, meaning the plotters were putting out a "black ops" cover story. Also wrong. When Oswald defected to Russia, the media had created files on him that were immediately available the day of the assassination.

X assures Garrison he is closer than he thinks to the truth, and explains the why of the assassination—Kennedy's military decisions, primarily his plan to withdraw American troops from Vietnam, alienated powerful people. He tells Garrison to consider who benefited† rather than pursuing who did it and how, which he calls "just scenery for the public." X explains that "the organizing principle of any society is for war," that "the authority of the state over its people resides in its war powers." A hundred billion dollars in defense contracts were at stake and Kennedy was refusing to wage war. That led to the decision "by the people in the loop" to assassinate him.

Stone learned about this war principle from his technical advisor, Garrison's friend, and the real-life model for X, Fletcher Prouty.‡ Prouty first revealed its origins in a 1989 Liberty Lobby radio broadcast—it originated in a secret report assembled by a coterie of power brokers working in an underground bunker called Iron Mountain. After

---

* Among others, ABC television newscaster Sam Donaldson challenged Stone on this. "I made a dozen calls during that time from the Capitol to the White House and elsewhere in Washington," he said. "The telephone system wasn't out." "I'll have to look into that," Stone replied (Sam Donaldson, interview with Oliver Stone, "Prime Time," Jan. 1992).

† Innocent people often benefit from crimes they didn't commit. If one follows Stone's paradigm, Aristotle Onassis would be a legitimate suspect.

‡ As writer Edward Epstein pointed out, while Prouty had worked in the Pentagon's Office of Special Operations (which supplied hardware for covert actions), unlike his fictional counterpart, Prouty did not provide security, additional or otherwise, for the president (Epstein, "The Second Coming of Jim Garrison," The Atlantic Monthly, March 1993).

studying the consequences of a permanent peace, they concluded that war was essential for America's survival. Prouty, however, had missed the point. "The Report from Iron Mountain on the Possibility and Desirability of Peace" that he and Stone took so seriously, and which ended up in Stone's movie, was written in 1967 as a parody of think tanks by satirist Leonard Lewin.[19] The book was a joke.*

X finishes his speech and rejects Garrison's request to testify at Shaw's trial. He would be arrested, institutionalized, "maybe worse," he says. He wishes Garrison luck and departs, leaving Garrison and the audience with the knowledge that the plot Garrison has unearthed in New Orleans was born in the corridors of power in Washington. Stone thereby created another false impression about Shaw's trial—that if only this political insider had told his story on the witness stand, Clay Shaw might have been convicted and Garrison triumphant. In fact, if some real-life equivalent of X *had* related his "evidence" in a courtroom, Shaw's attorneys would have turned him into a laughingstock. But in the film, his information stands unchallenged. And by verifying Garrison's ideas, X gives Stone's story a huge credibility boost.

X also propels the action forward by telling Garrison what he must do next. "Make arrests," he instructs. "Stir the shitstorm. Hope to reach a point of critical mass that will start a chain reaction of people coming forward. Then the government will crack." This advice, which sounds perfectly reasonable because it's in a movie, is Oliver Stone's explanation for *why* Garrison did what he did, even though, as Costner-Garrison said, he didn't have "much of a case." Inspired by it, Garrison arrests Clay Shaw. Once more, Stone had found a way around the real cause of Shaw's arrest, Perry Russo's false testimony.

Stone also found a way around the defense's case. He omitted it. Dean Andrews, Charles Appel, Edward O'Donnell, James Phelan (to name a few) never take the stand in the film. What Stone did show, he misrepresented. Shaw's attorneys, for instance, are unattractive connivers. He has Irvin Dymond discredit Willie O'Keefe in front of the jury by call-

---

* Apparently still unaware it was a hoax, Stone later described the "fabled" Iron Mountain report as "based on a study commissioned by Defense Secretary Robert McNamara in August 1963 to justify the big, planned changes in defense spending contemplated by Kennedy" (Oliver Stone, "Introduction," to Prouty's *JFK: The CIA, Vietnam and the Plot to Assassinate John F. Kennedy*, pp. x, xi).

ing him "a confessed homosexual convicted of solicitation [and] pandering." Thus Stone tells the audience that Shaw was acquitted in part because his attorney hypocritically exposed Willie O'Keefe's sexual behavior. But the real Willie O'Keefe, Perry Russo, destroyed himself by what he said on and off the witness stand. Dymond never took the low road. Garrison was the one who did that. Stone finished the job. He *shows us* Shaw was homosexual and guilty of conspiracy as well.

In one particularly irksome scene, repeated at the trial, Stone has Shaw at the police station telling the booking officer that his alias is "Clay Bertrand." The real testimony was so overwhelming that Shaw never uttered those words that the trial judge (who usually ruled in favor of the prosecution) refused to allow the testimony.* In the film, when the judge rules against him, Garrison exclaims, But that's our case! It was not their case and at the time no one claimed it was. Here again, Stone used a ploy to avoid dramatizing Garrison's real courtroom debacle, Perry Russo's testimony, which sank like a rock and Garrison's case with it.

Stone turned Garrison's closing argument into a soapbox for his view of Washington as a bed of snakes run by war-mongering business interests. He also used it to conclude his film and spike its emotional high point: "President Kennedy was killed by a conspiracy that was planned in advance at the highest levels of our government," Garrison tells the jurors, "and it was carried out by fanatical and disciplined cold warriors in the Pentagon and CIA's covert apparatus, among them Clay Shaw here before you. It was a public execution. And it was covered up by like-minded individuals in the Dallas Police Department, the Secret Service, the FBI, and the White House, all the way up, including J. Edgar Hoover and Lyndon Johnson, whom I consider accomplices after the fact."

Garrison didn't say anything like that at the real trial. He didn't mention the Dallas Police Department, the Secret Service, the FBI or the White House. He didn't invoke the name of *any* government agency, or Hoover, or Johnson. He didn't mention the CIA. Shaw's attorney, Irvin Dymond, was the only one who brought up the CIA. He did it when he asked Shaw, "Have you ever worked for the Central Intelligence Agency?"[20] Garrison,

---

*This is the fingerprint card episode, involving Officer Habighorst, described in chapter 11.

in his closing statement, made only an obscure reference to "domestic espionage." Only once, in a general allusion, did he utter Clay Shaw's name.

In the movie, Stone not only had Costner identify Shaw as a CIA conspirator to the jurors, he crafted Shaw's final appearance to make him look like a perfumed parlor snake. Surrounded by reporters after his acquittal, Shaw handles a cigarette in a long black holder. Smugly victorious, he makes a limp-wristed comment about the fancy culinary dish he is going to whip up when he gets home. The real Clay Shaw, a relieved and grateful man, made no statements that night. He thanked his attorneys. He thanked the jurors. Then a circle of deputies whisked him out of the courtroom through a back door.

Stone also invented the final scene with Garrison. But, unlike the one with Shaw, Stone rendered it with pathos. We see Garrison in a long shot after the verdict leaving the Criminal District Court building with his wife and son.* He has lost the battle but not the war, rehabilitated now in the minds of fifty million-plus moviegoers. By ending at that point, Stone sidestepped the last act of Garrison's real-life drama, the Christenberry hearing two years later that named Garrison the guilty party. Stone wasn't interested in that. He needed a hero to sell his complex bill of goods— a conspiracy so immense that virtually no one is beyond suspicion.

But it is not the purpose of this book to object to Stone's film for saying that President Johnson did it; that elements of the CIA, anti-Castro Cubans, war profiteers, military, and Dallas police did it; and that some elements of the FBI, Secret Service, and the rest of the government not directly involved beforehand helped to cover it up afterwards, with a boost from major media representatives. I have no personal knowledge that would exonerate any of those named, any more than Jim Garrison and Oliver Stone had personal knowledge of their complicity. The purpose of this book *is* to object to the film saying that Clay Shaw did it, and depicting Jim Garrison as a splendid fellow, a hero for our times.

Stone said the Garrison in his film was a metaphor for all those writers and researchers who disagree with the Warren Report. But Garrison is too particularized, too hopelessly who he is to stand for anything more. Costner theorizing about various Dealey Plaza scenarios didn't humanize

---

* The real Garrison wasn't in the courtroom when the verdict came down and wasn't seen publicly in the building afterward.

Garrison's actions or enlarge his person. Garrison set himself apart from most of those who have labored in this field by his unyielding godlike certitude.* Near the end of his life, he did acknowledge that he had "made some mistakes" but he never said what they were and he maintained that he was right to try Clay Shaw. "If it was an error," Garrison said, with a typical rhetorical ring, "then it was an error that I was obliged to make."[21]

The *error Garrison was obliged to make* caught up with Oliver Stone while he was filming his movie. In April he was in Dallas "having a ball," he told an interviewer. "I like the people. The extras have been great. The crew has been good. People have been very generous and open." But when he shifted to New Orleans, he encountered the ghost of Clay Shaw. People who had known him and Garrison protested in articles, on the news, and in letters to the editor. "I know for a fact that Garrison deliberately proceeded with a fraudulent case against Clay Shaw," wrote Rosemary James, one of those who broke the original story about Garrison's investigation. "He knew he had nothing, his key assistants— Jim Alcock, Al Oser, and John Volz—knew he had nothing and yet [Garrison] proceeded in the most Machiavellian fashion to abuse the power entrusted to him." Stone she called a "gullible from La-La Land with a $60 million budget who wants to regurgitate all of that garbage."[22] In a later interview, James went further: "There are any number of theories as to why Garrison singled Clay out, but I don't pretend to know what goes on in the mind of someone who I think needs psychiatric help." She did have a suggestion though. "It was widely known that Clay was homosexual. He didn't flaunt it; he was very discreet in his personal life. At the same time, he led a very active social life. Some people felt that Garrison was actually jealous of Clay's success and the fact that he lived as a homosexual without any repercussions."[23]

Stone seemed surprised by the intensity of the reaction to "the Clay Shaw business," as he called it. But he dismissed it as "local" and "personal," like concerns in Dallas about its image. He, on the other hand, was grappling with a more important problem, one whose import was

---

* Most researchers have their theories but they also have their doubts. This case is too thick with contradictions and ambiguity for any honest truth seeker to be without them. And the majority of Americans who reject the Warren Report reflect that. There is neither consensus nor certainty among them either, except perhaps for the true believers created by Stone's film.

"universal." "I'm not that concerned," Stone said, "about whether [Shaw] was innocent or guilty. I don't think [he] was a particularly important figure in this thing."[24] Neither knowing nor caring if Shaw were innocent or guilty, Stone presented him to the world as a conspirator who plotted President Kennedy's murder. In real life, Garrison's entire case depended on Shaw's guilt. So does Stone's film. And it leaves the clear-cut understanding that, though acquitted, Shaw was guilty as sin. This is the necessary premise on which Garrison's story and Stone's deep inner truth are constructed.

When asked by film critic Roger Ebert if he thought he knew the "names of the guilty," Stone said he thought he did but declined to reveal them because "that's a very heavy thing to lay on somebody—to accuse them of killing the president."[25] But not where Shaw was concerned. Earlier, Stone drew a chilling comparison when he was again discussing Shaw, the issue that wouldn't go away, with another journalist. "Garrison was trying to force a break in the case," Stone said. "If he could do that, it was worth the sacrifice of one man. When they went onto the shores of Omaha Beach, they said, 'We're going to lose five, ten, fifteen thousand people to reach our objective.' I think Jim was in that kind of situation."[26] By this interpretation—in a maneuver that shoots the American justice system in the heart—Garrison selected Clay Shaw to serve as his legal cannon fodder. Stone saw nothing wrong with that.

Stone did admit that his hero had his faults. "[Garrison] had hubris, he had arrogance," Stone said, "he was blind like King Lear was blind, and he trusted too many people."[27] (In reality, it was those who trusted Garrison who came up empty-handed, or worse.) Stone was saying that Garrison was flawed the way everybody is. But Garrison's flaws weren't like everybody's. They were stranger. After the film was released, writer David Ehrenstein focused on one of Garrison's more disquieting secrets, which has long been common knowledge to many in New Orleans and to students of the case but went virtually unmentioned in the debate that raged over the film.

It was the "fondling charge" first reported by Jack Anderson on February 23, 1970, in a column that was published nationally but not in New Orleans. Probing the why of that, Ehrenstein questioned reporter David Snyder. "The boy came from a very prominent family,"

Snyder said, "and they never came forward." Snyder recently added that "no one wanted to drag the boy's family through the mud." Rosemary James told Ehrenstein that "there was an effort made to protect the child, which was why nothing came of it." Garrison has had "a very stormy personal life," James said, and "used to slap his wife around in public all the time." James also commented on the gap between the real Garrison and the film hero. "To cast someone like Kevin Costner to play him as Mr. Untouchable Robin Hood and to have scenes with him as this big family man sitting around the dinner table—it's just a big sick joke."[28]

Yet for most of the worldwide moviegoing public, Garrison has been more than resurrected; he has been transformed. In that magical way that movies work, Kevin Costner and Jim Garrison are now one.

CHAPTER SIXTEEN

GARRISON WAS NO KEVIN COSTNER

> Kevin was the perfect choice for
> Jim Garrison because he reminds
> me of those Gary Cooper, Jimmy
> Stewart qualities—a moral sim-
> plicity and a quiet understate-
> ment. . . . I will never regret hav-
> ing visited Jim Garrison's soul; it
> made me a better man.[1]
>
> —Oliver Stone, 1991

> The minds of most humans are a
> labyrinth and Garrison's mind is
> more labyrinthine than most.[2]
>
> —Clay Shaw, 1969

Oliver Stone has stamped his vision of Jim Garrison indelibly on the col-
lective consciousness of the moviegoing world. For the millions who have
seen the film JFK, and all those in the future who will, Jim Garrison is as
Kevin Costner portrayed him: an ordinary, decent and caring, mild-man-
nered family man and truth-seeking district attorney. Using logic, dogged
determination, and customary investigatory techniques, with a small
band of loyal aides, he battled the federal government, the biased media,
and a variety of sinister forces that conspired to prevent him from bringing the killers of President Kennedy to justice. He had but a single flaw.
He neglected his wife and children, an unfortunate but understandable
consequence of his all-consuming commitment to the Kennedy investigation. Garrison is also infused with the qualities and general star glow of
Kevin Costner's past performances. The quiet courage and incorruptibili-
ty of Eliot Ness, the spiritual true-heartedness of Dances with Wolves, the

selflessness of Robin Hood. Garrison now embodies all that, too. Reinvented by Hollywood, he shines like a new penny.

In what follows, I have tried to suggest the chasm that separates the real man from Stone's invention.

The real-life Garrison didn't behave like a reasonable person's idea of a district attorney. He wasn't sensible, responsible and just. He didn't exercise care in his public statements or actions, and his thinking was decidedly odd. In strikingly similar language, several observers have remarked on Garrison's peculiar attitude toward evidence. Former First Asst. D.A. Charles Ward described it best. "Most of the time you marshal the facts, then deduce your theories," said Ward, in a 1983 interview. "But Garrison deduced a theory, then he marshaled his facts. And if the facts didn't fit he'd say they had been altered by the CIA."[3] Years later, Garrison's old friend and former chief investigator, Pershing Gervais, made an almost identical comment. "Garrison inverted the criminal investigatory process," wrote Gervais in a letter to the Times-Picayune. "You should begin by assembling the facts and from the facts you may deduce a theory of the crime. Pure deductive reasoning. Garrison did the opposite. He started with a theory and then assembled some facts to support it. Those facts that fit the theory, he accepted. Those that did not, he either ignored or rejected as CIA misinformation."

Garrison himself cast some light on his method of investigating in a July 18, 1977, letter he wrote to a Select Committee staffer. In the letter, Garrison explained that the typical investigatory methods employed by law enforcement were a waste of time when applied to the mysteries of the assassination. Conventional techniques wouldn't work there, he said, because ordinary evidence (he mentions confessions, footprints, and fingerprints) was unavailable due to the hidden nature of the crime. A different tactic was required, and Garrison had devised one. His alternative was something he called "the application of models."[4]

Basically, this meant Garrison matched his suspects against a batch of categories he found suspicious: unconventional religions, military service, aerospace work, post office boxes, to name a few. Garrison tried on evidence the way he tried on clothes, and somewhere he was bound to find something that fit. He said just that in another memo that spoke of applying one model after another until the one that fit was located.[5]

To find a guilty party, Garrison only needed to select a suspect; he was sure to hit upon the incriminating evidentiary pattern eventually. Assuming that no real evidence existed, Garrison had invented a system to generate presumed evidence to serve in its stead.

Using a variation of it, Garrison deciphered certain numbers that he claimed were encoded. He did this by finding through trial and error a mathematical sequence that would convert the number into another. An example is the entry he found in Shaw's address book: "Lee Odom, P.O. Box 19106, Dallas, Texas." The number 19106 coincided with one found in Lee Harvey Oswald's notebook, but Oswald's was preceded by two Russian letters. Garrison insisted the entries were identical and were actually a coded form of Jack Ruby's unlisted telephone number, though his brother said Ruby's telephone number had never been unlisted. Nevertheless, Garrison converted the post office box number, 19106, into the allegedly unlisted telephone number, WH-1-5601, through the following entirely arbitrary steps. First, he rearranged the numbers (anything is allowed in this procedure), subtracted 1300, matched the two letters (PO) to numbers on the telephone dial, added those two numbers together and fudged a bit.[6] Unimpressed, Shaw's attorneys noted the obvious, that this system—in which the beginning number and the ending number are both known and the only mystery is how to move numerically from one to the other—could be used to convert any number into any other number. Garrison found that beside the point. If he could do it, it meant something.

Lee Odom, the man to whom the post office box belonged, was quickly located and interviewed. He described his one-and-only business meeting with Clay Shaw in 1966, when Odom was attempting to promote a bull fight in New Orleans. Neither Odom nor his mailing address had any connection to Ruby, Ruby's telephone number, or to Oswald. The similarity to his notebook entry was a coincidence. But, of course, in Garrison's world, unlike the real one, coincidences didn't exist.

Garrison arrived at many of his empty ideas through his application of models. To Garrison's way of thinking, the very absence of "traditional evidence" supported his suspicions.

Understandably, many found the nebulousness of Garrison's "facts" a cause for concern. One writer referred to them as "a mélange of coincidences and circumstances which have some kind of wispy relationship." Max Lerner called them "unlikely details" woven into "a hair-raising pattern of concern." Journalist James Phelan was more blunt about it. "I realized Garrison was a fraud, an ignoramus, or a crazy man," he said, describing his reaction after Garrison laid out his case in Las Vegas. "The legal charge for the things he had dug up on Ferrie," Phelan quipped, "is moping and gawking with intent to maneuver."[7]

Yet Garrison seemed convinced by what he found, which prompts the question that continually arises. What was wrong with the man? By one account, he was "a frustrated writer" of short stories that were repeatedly rejected by various magazines, which left him feeling "disappointed."[*] Apparently, his chosen profession didn't bring him contentment either. He talked about that one day to his aides and staffer Tom Bethell recorded what he said in his diary. Garrison explained that in law school he learned any case could be argued either way, depending on the precedents one selects. Determining the truth, therefore, had practically no bearing on the law. Once he saw that, Garrison said, the law no longer interested him.[8]

This indifference to the law Garrison expressed repeatedly in his actions during his Kennedy investigation. He put Vernon Bundy and Charles Spiesel on the witness stand knowing one was a liar and the other unbalanced. Garrison welcomed whatever might help that came his way. Jack Martin was an alcoholic with a criminal past and psychological problems severe enough to land him in a mental ward at least once. He was well-known for inventing information. One Garrison aide said Martin was "absolutely crazy." Another referred to him as a "sack of roaches." Richard Billings didn't trust him. And Garrison, himself, admitted that Martin often lied.[9] Yet, for at least a year, Martin had Garrison's ear, was part of his team, and Garrison gave him "expense" money—because Martin's stories were useful.[10][†] Pershing Gervais said that Garrison was never inter-

---

* In a 1952 letter returning some of Garrison's stories, a New York literary agent (A. L. Fierst) encouraged him to revise two of them, one of which concerned an assassin who murdered a politician (Garrison Papers, Box 6).

† Garrison just ignored Martin's more absurd charges. For instance, Martin claimed that Ferrie had done away with his own mother because she knew about his intimate relationship with Oswald. Martin also said that he had met Oswald in Ferrie's apartment (Martin Fontainebleau Interview).

ested in what was right or wrong—he was only interested in what worked.

Sometimes that meant breaking the law. Garrison's ordering William Gurvich to arrest and beat up two troublesome newsmen is a minor example. To keep his star witness Perry Russo happy, Garrison had a false criminal charge lodged against one of Russo's friends so the young man could evade the draft. Later the charge was dropped.[11] In one telling moment, Garrison even claimed that Judge Haggerty's order prohibiting public statements on the case didn't apply to him. "The district attorney," Garrison said, "can make any statements he wishes."[12]

If the law didn't interest Garrison, politics did. He told Pershing Gervais his Kennedy investigation would put him in the White House. To others he spoke of a seat in the U.S. Senate or the governor's mansion. Though he pretended to be a reluctant celebrity, shortly after his Kennedy investigation became a news story, above the door leading into the district attorney's office, he had his name installed in three-inch-high gold letters.[13] Kevin Costner's Garrison would never have done that. He wanted only to catch the president's killers and keep his family together.

Stone created a Garrison household in which the wife is the heavy. She nags him for neglecting her and the children, criticizes his obsession with the Kennedy assassination, suggesting it's beyond his jurisdiction. She even has a kind word for Clay Shaw and his contribution to the city. Finally, she threatens to leave. Stone began most of the home scenes at the dining table. At one point, he shows Costner engagingly feeding the family dog food from his own plate off his own spoon. Costner clearly loves and worries about his wife and children, to say nothing of the dog. Stone conjured up a cotton candy Hollywood image that is picture perfect.

In reality, Garrison's mistreatment of his wife was no secret. Two public incidents occurred at Brennan's restaurant. In the better known of these, Garrison grew progressively more drunk and abusive as the evening wore on and eventually threw a glass of wine in her face, then stormed out. As he was leaving, he passed Clay Shaw, seated at an adjacent table, and a witness to the incident.[*] Reportedly, this was not an isolated episode; Garrison's mistreatment of her was said to involve bodily injury, and was serious.[14] We cannot imagine Costner's Garrison

---

[*] Clay Shaw told friends he thought his having seen this might have influenced Garrison in his later prosecution of him.

behaving that way. But in real life, spousal abuse was only part of it.

When he was at the pinnacle of his popularity and notoriety, Garrison remarked on the forces out to sabotage his investigation. The next charge he expected from them, he said, was that he engaged in "child molesting."[15] Garrison probably was launching a preemptive strike with that remark. He undoubtedly had reason to fear that such a charge might occur. The wall of secrecy that shielded the dark side of Garrison's personal life cracked in 1969 in the aftermath of just such an act involving a thirteen-year-old boy. The boy's family wanted to file charges but were warned that Garrison was unpredictable and would be an extremely dangerous adversary. Aaron Kohn urged the family to prosecute. But concern about the boy's welfare and even his safety outweighed all else, and they took no action. Kohn then gave the information to the grand jury and someone leaked the story to columnist Jack Anderson. The grand jury foreman, William J. Krummel, Sr., confirmed off the record to Anderson that they were looking into it. But, Krummel said, "I'm afraid that if I say so [in public], they'll want to throw me in jail."[16] Krummel declined to be interviewed for this book; so what occurred in the grand jury's investigation is unknown. The family wisely decided to protect the boy and the grand jury could have done little without their assistance.

Jack Anderson personally spoke to the boy's father, described in the column Anderson wrote as "a prominent member of the New Orleans 'establishment.'" Anderson also spoke to two other family members, one of whom Anderson said "is one of the most respected men in the South." Anderson's column, long the most infamous unexplored landmark in Garrison's background, gave only a bare-bones account of what occurred. The grand jury was investigating a charge, Anderson reported, that "on a Sunday in June, 1969," Garrison had "fondled" a thirteen-year-old boy in the New Orleans Athletic Club.[17] * But Anderson wrote nothing more about it, and Garrison supporters have long claimed that the story was merely an effort to smear him. Yet some in New Orleans who know the family involved have insisted over the years that the episode occurred. An author of a recent book on the case verified the story with a family member. Until now, however, no one has heard from the victim.

* Anderson remarked on the irony, noting that Garrison had emphasized Clay Shaw's "alleged homosexuality," leaving him marked with "the sexual stigma."

GARRISON WAS NO KEVIN COSTNER

In September 1993 I contacted one of his relatives and he confirmed the incident. But he discouraged the idea of an interview with either the victim or his older brother who had been present when it happened. Eventually, though, after a pledge of anonymity, both men agreed to be interviewed. I first spoke by telephone to the victim, then a thirty-seven-year-old professional man. Two days later I met with his older brother in his office. Both told the same story from different perspectives.

"It was a family ritual," the older brother said, explaining why the two boys and their father were at the New Orleans Athletic Club that day. They were not members but a relative was and he had been inviting them on Sundays since their early childhood. Occasionally, a friend would accompany them, but on this particular Sunday it was only the father and two of his sons. The three were alone in the swimming pool area when Garrison approached them.* The father was lying on a leather-covered bed and the two boys were in the shallow end of the marble pool. "I remember Garrison walking into the pool area and there was no one else there but us," the older brother recalled. "He proceeded to lie down next to my father." The younger brother also recalled Garrison and his father, whom he described as "very social," talking and how "nice and polite" the conversation was.

Then "after a while," the older brother said, "my dad came to me and said 'Jim Garrison has invited us up to the Slumber Room to take a nap.' I thought that was like torture because I don't sleep in the day." His younger brother had a similar reaction. "I don't want to go up there," he recalled, "I'm thirteen years old. I don't want to take a nap, you know, it's Sunday morning." But the father said, "No, we ought to go, he's talking about the Kennedy assassination and we might find out something."

So they accompanied Garrison to the Slumber Room. "There was a strict protocol in this club," the older brother said. "And we were now Garrison's guests. Garrison was now running the show. He was in control. We had never been privy to this area before. Here's this big star and now we were going into the secret place in the club." The room resembled a "dormitory bunk room," he said. It was rectangular with an aisle

---

* They were swimming nude, which the club required to reduce contamination from bathing suits because the salt water in the marble pool could not be chlorinated.

down the middle and along the wall on either side a row of beds. On each were two sheets. Both men spoke about how dark it was. "You shut the door," the older brother stated, "and it was black." The younger brother remembered, "It was very very dark because it has no windows." He also recalled the air conditioner was on and "it was freezing cold." Standing at the door, Garrison said, "Everybody get into bed and I'm going to turn off the light." They all got into a bed. "I don't know where everyone was," the older brother said, "except that I was closest to the door and everyone else was deeper into the room." The younger brother remembered taking "a cot way to the back." Garrison took the one next to him. The father and older brother were on the other side of the room. The younger brother described what occurred.

> I don't know if Garrison set it up that way or not. Because all he had to do was sit on the edge of his bed, reach across, which he did you know, and lift the blanket. When Garrison first did it—my eyes were not adjusted to the dark and I saw, I could just make out the image of somebody. And it was. . . when somebody just lifts up a blanket and sticks their hand under there—and he didn't really grab. He just fondled a bit and then he sat back down and I jumped up and I went over to my brother and said, "[name deleted], are you playing a joke on me?" You know—a brother. I mean, I didn't know what was going on. I was oblivious anyway. And [his brother] said, "[name deleted], go back to bed. Daddy's going to be really mad at you if you cause any trouble in here." So I went back. He thought I was just being a little kid, you know. So then when [Garrison] did it again and I could tell who it was . . . then I went back to my brother and told him and he said, "Get the hell out of here."

The older brother went to his father and told him that they had "to leave right now." His father, unaware of anything out of the ordinary, objected at first but when his son again urged him to leave he realized something was wrong. The older brother then left the room and got dressed, which the younger brother had done already. A few minutes later, their father came out. "I told him what happened," the older brother recalled, "and he was visibly shaken." The father's clothes were in a different location and he left to get dressed. While the father was gone, Garrison came out. The older brother described his reaction.

> I walked up to him and I said, "You son of a bitch, you pervert, you queer." I was livid. I couldn't believe this guy tried to molest my little brother. I was really into Garrison's face. I was really threatening him. I was enraged. I may have put my hands on him. I know I scared him because he said, "You're assaulting me and I'm going to have to defend myself." And he went back toward his locker and I remember I could see in his locker there was a gun hanging in there—like a 38 snub nose revolver—hanging in a shoulder holster on a hook in his locker. At that point I became very concerned that Garrison was going to shoot me and I remember seeing, to my surprise, that there was another man who witnessed this. A man in his sixties, by the lavatories. I remember thinking, oh good, there's a witness to this, but he left the area because he didn't want to get involved. By this time my father had gotten dressed and sort of caught me at the tail end of this altercation. He was five-feet-ten-inches and I vividly remember him walking up to Garrison and he took his finger and he started poking him in the stomach and he said, "You fooled with the wrong people this time. You're not going to get away with this." Garrison said, "You're crazy. I don't know what you're talking about." And he said something to the effect that "I'm going to have your son arrested for assaulting me." At that time we left. We went home.

The phone began "ringing off the hook" as soon as they arrived home. The word already had spread. "It was a Sunday and Sundays were a festive time in our home," the older brother said. "My mother cooked dinner and we had friends over and we'd all go to church. I remember this electrical atmosphere in the house that Sunday because of this stuff going on." The first caller was Aaron Kohn, who had heard about what had happened. "You have to pursue this," Kohn said. "Your son must testify. This man has got to be stopped." The father called a relative, a local attorney, who advised against taking any action. He thought "terrible harm" would come to the boy and that the family "would never prove anything." A great deal of discussion ensued. The family was "warned" about the boy's safety. And the possibility of his being "kidnapped from school." Everyone, the brothers were told, "had to keep an eye on him until this thing calmed down."

As I sat in the pleasant suburban office listening to this twenty-seven-year-old story, the barely concealed outrage of this obviously compassionate and successful man was apparent. But it wasn't until he described what they next heard that I glimpsed the depth of the fear this family had suffered. "*They are going to bury the ax, and they are going to bury it last,* someone had warned them, *and it is going to be in [my brother's] back.* I remember my father telling us this," the older brother said, "and that is why we would have to be very careful." The younger brother remembers the precautions that were taken. He had to be "at a certain spot" at the end of the school day, where he was picked up. "They thought something was going to happen to me," he said. "I went to see the Kevin Costner movie—which made me sick, to glorify him like that. I saw Stone in the Napoleon House [cafe] one day—I wanted to tell him about this. But it's so awkward."[18]

What Garrison did in the Slumber Room that day may have been the tip of the iceberg. David Chandler, speaking from what he twice described as "firsthand knowledge," said Garrison was "basically a pedophile." That didn't necessarily mean he avoided older partners but, according to Chandler, Garrison preferred very young ones. His "overt preference," was adolescent girls, "around sixteen and younger," Chandler said. While he had no firsthand knowledge of "the boys," Chandler stated that he believed Garrison was "indifferent" to gender, that he didn't care "whether it was a boy or a girl." He wanted them "inexperienced and compliant" so he could be "the teacher." Garrison, Chandler said, had to be "in control."[19] Why Garrison would make such a move with other family members present in the same room is an unresolved question. Chandler thought Garrison might have been drunk when he did it. Nothing indicates that, however, and the victim rejected the idea. "I don't think it was alcohol," he said. "I think it was more like pills. That's just my opinion. I mean I was just a little bitty kid but [after they left the Slumber Room] he looked like somebody who was on drugs not alcohol.[20] He had that glazed kind of look on his eyes. I mean, he looked like a real lunatic."

A psychologist I spoke with (one of several mental health professionals consulted) suggested that the risk involved may have been part of the attraction. Or maybe Garrison simply felt safe in the dark. He was on extremely familiar turf at the New Orleans Athletic Club. He had made it his second office. He relaxed there. He held meetings there. He worked there. He ate there. He may have felt he could do anything he wished there. He was, after all, the district attorney, and Garrison clearly felt he was above the law. A well-known psychiatrist attributed it to that—Garrison's sense of his own power. He was accustomed to having his way and to being protected. If he had gotten away with something like this in the Slumber Room in the past and expected to get away with it again, he was right.

The older brother said that he is "still angry about what happened." Another family member, who wasn't at the Club that day but experienced the tumult that followed, as everyone in this family did, spoke with intensity about Garrison, calling him "a psychotic Darth Vader." Whether or not the boy actually was in physical danger, as the family believed he was, is a question no one can answer. But if the family had taken action, Garrison certainly would have gone on the offensive. Most likely he would have issued some outrageous countercharge. This family was in a no-win situation and the psychologists and psychiatrists I spoke to agreed that the family chose the correct course.* But the family members paid a price for permitting it to be swept under the rug. They seem a proud, close clan with considerable standing in the community. Yet they were forced to accept in silence this indignity. At the very least, that left behind feelings of powerlessness, especially for the men. By speaking out today, they are correcting in some small measure the wrong that was done to them. In setting that record straight, they also have exposed long-rumored and telling facets of Garrison's make-up.

For the Slumber Room episode means that Garrison had a homosexual side, as the psychiatrist mentioned earlier pointed out. Additional support for this comes from the State Attorney General's chief investigator, Frank W. Manning, who conducted a secret investigation of Garrison's office during his first term. Manning later told the FBI, in the words of the agent he spoke to, "[that] Garrison himself might be a sex deviate or at least he is a participant in some deviate activities

---

* One noted that since the abuse was relatively minor a court fight might have been more damaging than the incident itself.

with other homosexuals." Manning also said that Garrison and a couple of others had been "shaking down" the homosexual community. Hundreds were arrested, Manning said, and then released after making payoffs to have their cases cleared up.[21] These actions by Garrison against gays, the psychiatrist said, would have been part of his cover. That also applies to Garrison's description in his book of the odd incident that supposedly occurred in the men's room at LAX.

More important is what all this suggests about Garrison's underlying, perhaps unconscious, motivation—the possibility that he was driven to pursue Clay Shaw by his discomfort with his own sexuality. Perhaps the strangest example of Garrison's homophobia appeared in a 1986 letter he wrote reacting to Warren Report critic Paul Hoch's reference, in his newsletter, to Clay Shaw's sexual orientation. (Hoch's reference was part of a critical comment about Garrison, which Garrison ignored.) He recommended that Hoch immediately use soap to clean his mouth. He, himself, Garrison declared, had never publicly commented on the allegation that Shaw was homosexual, and, amazingly, Garrison dismissed that charge as a false rumor directed toward a dead man who could no longer speak for himself.[22] The pretense and denial there are glaring, since Garrison did everything in his power to exploit Shaw's homosexuality to the media, talking it up privately whenever he felt like it. Garrison's transparent pose in that letter suggests the depth of his fear of this subject: labeling Shaw a homosexual was for Garrison worse than accusing him of treason.*

Garrison's psychiatric state became an issue publicly as early as 1965 during the campaign for district attorney, when Garrison's opponent, Judge Malcolm O'Hara, released Garrison's 1951 military medical records to the press.† O'Hara tied Garrison's "anxiety reaction" (described in those records) to "the ugly force in him that drives him to destroy everyone who fails to bow to his will." It used to be called "a Napoleonic complex," O'Hara told reporters. Later, Clay Shaw made

* In Garrison's time, homosexuality was viewed as a sexual perversion, a threat to national security, "grounds for disbarment from federal employment," and political poison. (For a brief discussion of the forces at work on this issue in that period see Sidney Blumenthal, "The Cold War and the Closet," The New Yorker, May 17, 1997, p. 116.)
† Garrison's military medical diagnosis is discussed in chapter 2.

some interesting observations—he thought Garrison was "quite ill, mentally." He knew Garrison had seen several analysts, Shaw said, and that he was getting "worse all the time." Shaw believed there was "a division" in Garrison's mind. That with one half of it, he was "able to go out and fabricate evidence, and then by some osmosis, he [was] able to convince the other half that the fabrication is the truth. And then," Shaw said, "I think, he believes it implicitly."[23]

Aaron Kohn, who referred to Garrison's "tyrannical conduct," and the "fear" he instilled in people, believed he was "emotionally disturbed," and "compelled to act deceptively in order to preserve his own fundamental ego." William Wegmann, Pershing Gervais, William Gurvich, David Chandler, James Phelan, Edward O'Donnell, Rosemary James, and others unwilling to go on the record, expressed the belief that there was something seriously amiss with Garrison psychologically. In his book on this case, Milton Brener suggested that Garrison was "stark, raving mad."[24]

In my conversations with mental health professionals, two of them suggested that Garrison might have been a psychopath, not the homicidal variety, obviously, but the other end of the spectrum—the charming con artist. One referred me to some books on the subject, which I read with fascination, especially the work of Canadian psychiatrist Robert Hare. He studied the psychopathic personality for eighteen years and developed a detailed profile, along with a "psychopathy checklist" (widely used today as a diagnostic tool). In reading Dr. Hare's 1993 book, *Without Conscience*, I experienced an *aha* moment, a sense that I had found one of the answers I had been seeking. But I speak here with neither certainty nor the authority of a professional in this field, and with an awareness that the mind of man is truly a far country. Efforts to explain it are imperfect abstractions at best. I suggest only that anyone struggling, as I have been, to understand Garrison's inexplicable behavior should consider this a possibility. For Garrison seems to me to fit in almost every particular Dr. Hare's model of what he calls the white-collar subcriminal psychopath, also known as "successful psychopaths."

These are the ones who don't end up in prison. Instead, they "function reasonably well" as professionals of every possible stripe. They don't generally stray beyond the boundaries of the law. Or if they do, they usually aren't discovered. While just as destructive as the criminal variety, they manage to avoid exposure primarily because they are intelligent, socially adept, and often protected by their family background. They appear to be living a normal life, and go about obtaining their goals indifferent to the damage they do and without being held to account for it.[25]

What sets them apart is their *lack of a conscience*. That inner policeman for them doesn't exist. They abide by only those rules that suit their purposes. Their single motivation in life is to fulfill their own personal needs, whatever they happen to be, and at *any* cost to those around them. Yet because these individuals are appealing, sometimes even magnetic, most people are unable to recognize their real nature as masters of the con with a remarkable talent to deceive and manipulate. Often impulsive, they are usually quite verbal, witty, charming, likeable, and fun to be around.[26] New Orleans reporter Iris Kelso captured that side of Garrison in the obituary she wrote. She recalled his arrival one day in 1969 at an office where she and Rosemary James were waiting to interview him. Spotting them, Garrison "launched into a song," Kelso wrote. "'Everyday is ladies' day with me,' he sang in his big deep voice. He finished with a soft shoe routine, his head bowed and his arms spread at our feet."[27]

I found Jim Garrison striding across the pages of Dr. Hare's book, and never more so than when Hare writes about the ease with which such people lie. They lie as easily as they breathe. They do it even when they know the person they are lying to knows the truth.[28] Incapable of empathy, they feel no guilt or pain for those they injure. Rather, they paint themselves as the victim. Dr. Hare seems particularly on target when he discusses how psychopaths enjoy controlling others and the difficulty they experience when people express ideas that conflict with their own. Yet the charisma of the psychopath is often undeniable. Some people, Dr. Hare points out, even find them "electrifying."[29] This brings to mind Tom Bethell's reaction to a speech Garrison delivered in his office which held his aides transfixed. Bethell couldn't remember the words Garrison spoke, but after the first sentence, Bethell recalled, he and the others were simply mesmerized.[30]

Fortunately, such people have a tendency to shoot themselves in the foot, Dr. Hare tells us, which is what Garrison did when he arrested Clay Shaw with nothing up his evidentiary sleeve but Perry Russo. Rosemary James said Garrison "ruined his own career with a rather frivolous prosecution," that "he would have made a brilliant national politician but he cut off his own legs." Until the jury acquitted Clay Shaw, Garrison's political star definitely was ascending and Washington was within his reach. So if there is any solace in the wrenching injustice of this story, it is the possibility that the misery endured by Clay Shaw spared the country something worse.

Whatever it was that made Garrison tick, the spectacular ups and downs that he experienced in his public life must have taken a toll on him. So did Dealey Plaza. Psychologically, he never escaped the shadow of what occurred there. Perry Russo, who saw Garrison from time to time over the years, said he continued to talk about the assassination obsessively, often speaking of some new "lead" he was investigating, or wanted to investigate. Garrison's private life was unsettled as well. He and his wife finally divorced. A brief second marriage also ended in divorce. After that, he reportedly lived alone for a number of years, surrounded by his dogs and quietly fulfilling his judicial duties. Eventually, he remarried his first wife and, when he retired in November 1991, she nursed him during his final illness. After almost two decades of relative obscurity, his last few years must have felt triumphant. With his Hollywood-style resurrection and the simultaneous success of the paperback edition of his memoir, he once more basked in the spotlight. He also made a great deal of money. On October 21, 1992, Garrison died at the age of seventy of undisclosed "natural causes."*

Garrison's story is important for reasons beyond what occurred in New Orleans. The type of person he represents poses a perhaps universal quandary. For no one knows how to guard against people like him, and many (perhaps most) of us are susceptible to them. That unsettling reality may be the abiding lesson of this story. The belief most Americans share that what happened in Nazi Germany could never happen here seems to me less certain in light of Garrison. "The

---

* A spokesman for the coroner, who conducted an autopsy, stated that the "cause [of death] is confidential" and could not be released without the family's consent (telephone conversation with John Gagliano, Feb. 18, 1998).

importance of Garrison's case is not that he failed," Milton Brener wrote, "but that he could have succeeded."[31]

Even after he was stopped and the truth exposed in a federal courtroom, Garrison managed to reinvent himself through the awesome power of the arts. He crafted an engaging All-American Hero in his book that Oliver Stone enlarged and Kevin Costner enhanced, but it bore no resemblance to the real man or what actually happened. Yet it is that fictional phoenix that today soars in Hollywood's international sky.

It is a flight that has had its consequences. Unlike books that politicians leave behind, movies possess the power to set thousands marching, which is what Stone's did. For years, critics and others had been calling for the government to release its records on the assassination but Stone and his film made it happen. Adopting the suggestion of former House Select Committee staffer Kevin Walsh,[32] Stone added a written message about it at the end of the movie. Then he channeled the considerable passions the movie stirred to organize a Congressional lobbying effort to *free the files*, a message emblazoned on buttons and T-shirts.

This campaign was Stone's finest hour. It was also a shield he used to deflect criticism directed at him and his film. He donned that shield in Washington the morning of January 15, 1992, for one of his biggest moments, his speech (carried live on C-Span) to the National Press Club, with many of his critics in attendance. Stone used this singular moment to reproach the media for failing to investigate the assassination and to promote his own ideas about the case. He justified the film's broad conspiracy theory and defended Jim Garrison's prosecution of Clay Shaw.* In his concluding remarks Stone recited a list of government officials who were supporting his lobbying effort. Before the month was out, the sole surviving member of the Warren Commission, former

---

* Stone again repeated the false story about the bogus party picture of Shaw and "Ferrie." He noted that *three judges and the grand jury* "said go to trial," though the judges were afraid of Garrison and the grand jury was in his pocket. He referred to "three witnesses" (Oswald, Banister, and Ferrie) dying before Garrison went to trial, as though that were a handicap—it was Garrison's great enabler. Alive they could have defended themselves and given their lives an authentic shape. (Stone, speech at the National Press Club, Jan. 15, 1992, C-Span Transcript, pp. 12–13.)

President Gerald R. Ford, and thirteen former counsel and staff members had joined the ranks of those calling for the files to be released.* The momentum was just beginning and soon was irresistible.

On October 26, 1992, President George Bush signed the President John F. Kennedy Assassination Records Collection Act directing the National Archives to establish and make available to the public a collection of all assassination-related government records, requiring all government offices to transfer such records to the Archives, and establishing an independent review board to locate, declassify, and ensure disclosure of records being withheld. Stone had achieved what no one else had been able to do. Virtually single-handed, he had wrenched open the vaults of the nation's capital. In the process, he became the titular head of the reconstituted "movement" of researchers and writers on the case now dominated by pro-Garrison forces empowered by Stone and his film.

---

* Stone and Warner Bros. Chairman Robert A. Daly both expressed extravagant expectations about what these files would disclose. Stone hoped they would bring to the country "the full truth of the assassination." Daly said he was sure the files would confirm the film's statement that more than one assassin was involved. (Stone, speech at the National Press Club, Jan. 15, 1992, C-Span transcript, p. 7; Bernard Weinraub, "Valenti Calls J.F.K. 'Hoax' and 'Smear,'" *New York Times*, April 2, 1992.)

CHAPTER SEVENTEEN

THE MOVEMENT AND THE FILES

> The fact that many critics of the
> Warren Report have remained
> passionate advocates of the
> Garrison investigation . . . is a
> matter of regret and disappoint-
> ment. Nothing less than strict
> factual accuracy and absolute
> moral integrity must be deemed
> permissible, if justice is, indeed,
> to be served.*
>
> —*Sylvia Meagher, June 1967*

On a trip to Los Angeles in October 1967, Jim Garrison met with David S. Lifton, an early critic of the Warren Report. The purpose of their meeting was to discuss one Kerry Thornley, then a Los Angeles resident. He had known Lee Harvey Oswald in the Marines and was now an acquaintance of Lifton. Through information Lifton innocently supplied, Garrison would shortly indict Thornley for perjury (much to Lifton's horror), though that was not Garrison's original intention. Originally, Garrison was planning to use Thornley's testimony to indict another former Oswald Marine friend, John Rene Heindel.† When that didn't work out, Garrison simply converted Thornley, who at Lifton's urging had traveled to New Orleans to help Garrison, from a friendly witness into a suspect and indicted him instead.

An article Lifton wrote about his experience with Garrison contains

---

* Sylvia Meagher, *Accessories After the Fact* (New York: The Bobbs-Merrill Company, Inc., 1967), p. 457.
† Heindel was of interest because his nickname in the Marines was "Hidell" (an alias later used by Oswald), and he spoke Russian with Oswald. This was the information Lifton transmitted to Garrison.

a number of interesting threads. Garrison's paranoia and his "evidence" parallel James Phelan's experience in Las Vegas seven months earlier. "If a man walked by with a briefcase," Lifton wrote, "Garrison would point to him and whisper, 'That's an FBI agent.'" Garrison revealed to Lifton a telephone number that Garrison said was absolute proof of a link between Lee Harvey Oswald and Jack Ruby because it appeared in both Oswald's address book and on Ruby's telephone bill. Lifton hurried home, checked out Oswald's telephone book in the Warren Report's twenty-six volumes and discovered that the number (PE-8-1951) indeed was there. But it was a Fort Worth television station (KTVT, Channel 11). Oswald and Ruby were no more linked by this than they would have been by the gas company's telephone number. Anyone might have such a number in his address book; anyone might have called it and therefore have it appear on his telephone bill.

When Lifton pointed that out to Garrison the next day, he became "annoyed" and told Lifton to "stop arguing the defense." But Lifton persisted. He inquired what Garrison thought it meant. "Is there someone at the TV station who you can prove knew both men?" "It means," Garrison replied, "whatever the jury decides it means." "But what do you think, Jim?" Lifton demanded, "What is the truth of the matter?" At that, Garrison responded with a remark that fairly stunned Lifton: "After the fact," Garrison said, "there is no truth, there is only what the jury decides." (That is, there is only what works.) That admission explained "much of what has happened," Lifton wrote. "It is a convenient and accurate synopsis of Jim Garrison's approach to fact-finding, truth-finding, and justice."[1]

After his fifteen hours with the Jolly Green Giant and Kerry Thornley's indictment, Lifton was convinced that Garrison was "a reckless, irrational, even paranoid demagogue," as Lifton wrote, who, before he was finished, might "seriously hurt innocent people." Lifton was an early naysaying voice raised against Garrison from the ranks of the critics. Another was Sylvia Meagher, who excoriated her colleagues for failing to carry out a "disinterested evaluation of Garrison's evidence."* But most of the early critics jumped on Garrison's bandwagon and a number of them turned up in New Orleans volunteering their theories and some of them their

---

* Sylvia Meagher, letter, The New York Review of Books, September 3, 1967.

time. These Dealey Plaza Irregulars, as they were tagged, included Mark Lane, William Turner, Mary Ferrell, Harold Weisberg, Ray Marcus, Mort Sahl, and others. Garrison's thinking was deeply influenced by many of them, Lane and Weisberg in particular. But then, Garrison never encountered a conspiracy idea he didn't like. His constantly shifting public statements reflect that. Weisberg, who claimed he convinced Garrison of the Cubans' involvement and the CIA's, became disillusioned in time, as did others. The anti-Garrison camp grew after he revealed his evidence at Shaw's trial. Paul Hoch and many more joined it at that point. Today, Meagher is deceased and Lifton and Hoch are among the few visible members of the new movement willing to speak out against Garrison.

Oliver Stone and his organized effort to free the files created this new movement. Nothing like it existed before. The previous group of loose-knit researchers and writers, noted for their curious personalities and occasional stunning hostilities, squabbled among themselves, formed shifting alliances, and journeyed down decidedly independent paths. They agreed on little and rarely engaged in any unified action. Today's new movement nurtures consensus and organization, steered by Garrison-Stone disciples and their "Governing Boards," "Advisory Boards," "Executive Boards," and "Boards of Directors." They sponsor events, plan actions, publish newsletters, and rally the forces.

These Garrisonites are the public face of the movement but its larger "membership" is quite diverse, ranging from "Little Jims" who worship Garrison, to Lifton, the lone crusader against him. The large group occupying the middle ground "joined" for their own reasons and have little or no interest in Jim Garrison. They either don't know or care about him or they do know and, as Hoch says, they find "the Clay Shaw business embarrassing." The most vocal of the new movement, the "Little Jims," with their passionate belief in "Big Jim" and his case, have assumed his attitudes and investigatory techniques and appear determined to walk in his footsteps. They seem to believe, as he did, that all his critics were part of the government conspiracy out to stop him; that real evidence doesn't exist in this case and that his "application of models" is a legitimate way to find an alternative. They even seem to regard his propinquity theory as viable. But Garrison adopted these odd notions because they suited his nature, not because they were useful tools. Those embracing them today and creating their own *wispy connections* run the risk of appearing to be conspiratorial flat-earthers.[2]

Some are also attempting in a clumsy way to control what is written about Garrison. One, working at a private Washington archive, instructed me about what criticism was permissible. "You may say he abused his power" (presumably because Garrison himself admitted doing so), I was told. "You may go *that* far but no further." A favorite target of theirs is the media, having picked up Garrison's kill-the-messenger stance. Like him, they regard his negative press coverage as journalists in league with each other and with Washington to sabotage his case. Topping their enemies list are those whose work was the most influential: James Phelan, Hugh Aynesworth, George Lardner, Walter Sheridan, Rosemary James, and David Snyder. Yet all these individuals were assigned to cover the story and independently of each other concluded that Garrison was perpetuating a fraud.

For some reason, James Phelan has been singled out for special attention. After a forty-plus-year career in which he produced hundreds of magazine articles (only two about the Kennedy assassination) and completed his third book (his first was an international best seller),[3] Phelan died of lung cancer on September 8, 1997, at his home in Southern California. He was eighty-five. Anyone interested in this case should be grateful to him for his contribution to it. Instead, Garrison supporters have demonized him.[4] But if some government connection had sent Phelan to destroy Garrison's case, as the Garrisonites imply, he would have turned over the documents he obtained in Las Vegas to Shaw's attorneys. Irvin Dymond then would have made mincemeat of Perry Russo at the preliminary hearing, humiliated Garrison, and the whole charade would have collapsed right there. Phelan didn't turn the documents over because he was a reporter doing a job, not a sneak with a covert agenda.

The new movement wasn't the only unexpected consequence of Stone's film. It inspired a best-selling book from the opposition that challenged the conspiracy tenet—*Case Closed* by Gerald Posner. This 1993 examination of Oswald and the assassination was meant to restore confidence in the findings of the Warren Report and one of its major themes is that the critics of the report are the problem, not the evidence. But Posner ignored and misrepresented data,* and he didn't *close* anything. He did offer a sensible, objective-sounding voice that appealed to a wide audience, especially those put off by Stone's paranoia and his promotion of Jim Garrison. As Garrison himself had done more than two decades earlier, Oliver Stone produced a backlash and Posner reaped the benefit. But anyone who thinks Posner settled matters is overestimating his book and underestimating the legitimate arguments on the other side that over the years have created the grip the subject has on America's psyche. (Even George Lardner believes a missed shot was fired from the front.)[5] The one area where Posner might have closed a door—the Garrison–Stone New Orleans scenario—he left wide open. He dealt with Garrison in a single superficial chapter that necessarily omitted much of the story. Some of what is there is wrong.† Stone's movie Posner mentioned only in passing. He made his only substantive comments about it in a handful of footnotes.

To believe Posner closed the door on Garrison is to deny the power of film. After more than fifty million moviegoers saw JFK in theaters around the world,[6] Stone gave it a second life. In 1993 he released an inexpensive video version.‡ New viewers are now renting it and buying it with no end in sight. Every night, somewhere someone watches it. Jim Garrison today is playing on the small screen to a new generation and with no caveat. Those who saw the original movie were forewarned

---

*Two of Posner's more serious lapses: 1) Presenting the work of Failure Analysis Associates as definitive evidence that the shots originated from the sniper's nest in the Texas School Book Depository (Posner, *Case Closed*, pp. 334–335, 477–478). What Posner didn't reveal was that Failure Analysis Associates prepared the material he used for an ABA mock trial of Lee Harvey Oswald (in August 1992, as a promotional effort by the company) and that the company also prepared material for the other side that supported the *opposite* position. 2) Quoting the Warren Commission testimony of clinical psychologist Renatus Hartogs who testified that when he examined Lee Harvey Oswald (at age thirteen) he had recognized in Oswald a "dangerousness" and "potential for explosive, aggressive, assaultive acting out" (Posner, *Case Closed*, p. 12). Posner again omitted the core reality: that the Warren Commission attorney who questioned Hartogs exposed his testimony as self-serving, after-the-fact analysis, contradicted by the report Hartogs wrote at the time (WC vol. VIII, pp. 220–221).

† For example, Posner attacked the trial testimony of "Andrew Dunn" because it conflicted with Dunn's earlier statements (Posner, *Case Closed*, p. 146). The conflict, however, was Posner's own creation. Andrew Dunn, who made the earlier statements, died in 1968, the year before the trial. The man on the witness stand was William Dunn, Sr. (The two were not related.)

‡ Stone restored seventeen minutes cut from the feature release.

to some extent about Garrison by the media uproar. But all those shouting back then have fallen silent now. The video viewers today hear no
dissenting opinion. Garrison is the hero. Clay Shaw is the villain.

Some of those who support that vision squared off, after a fashion,
with some who don't at the public hearing held by the JFK Assassination
Records Review Board on June 28, 1995, in New Orleans. Steve Tyler, the
producer-director of an interesting 1992 documentary film on the
Garrison case, "He Must Have Something," was one of those who testified. Tyler described his conversion from a pro-Shaw position when he
was making the film, to anti-Shaw afterwards, from believing Shaw
innocent to thinking him probably guilty of something. It was Oliver
Stone who "planted the first seeds of disillusionment and doubt," Tyler
said, because despite having "access to all the available research on the
assassination," Stone felt "so strongly about Shaw's guilt."*

Also testifying that day was the lovely, petite, red-haired daughter of
Edward Wegmann, now deceased. Cynthia Wegmann—who became an
attorney because of the injustice she saw inflicted on Clay Shaw—spoke
movingly on Shaw's behalf and handed over her father's files to the
review board, saying she believed "that anyone who takes a look at these
records will realize how amorphous, how little evidence, if any, there
was [against Clay Shaw]."[7] It was her hope, she said, that once the public saw how "little there was" to Garrison's case that "they would allow
[Shaw] to remain at rest," a commendable, if unlikely, wish. But by
relinquishing her father's records to the National Archives, she established for Clay Shaw a small but significant beachhead.[†]

That was dramatically enlarged in the Spring of 1997 when a friend of
Shaw, at the urging of Dave Snyder, turned over to the review board seven
boxes of Shaw's personal papers, including the journal he kept shortly
after his arrest.[‡] In its pages, the voice of Clay Shaw may still be heard. It
is quietly desperate at times, unpretentious and humane, edged with a
writer's eye for detail. He recorded his daily life (meals, drinks, conver-

---

* Actually, Stone has stated that Shaw's guilt or innocence is of little concern to
  him.
† Previously, Edward Wegmann had offered to donate this material to Tulane
  University, but the offer was declined. (Cynthia Wegmann, telephone conver-
  sation with author, September 8, 1993.)
‡ This is the document that Snyder first revealed to the public in July 1996.

sations, kindnesses of friends and strangers),* his impressions, ideas, anger, his sometimes black depression, and his inward journey. The "shock" of his arrest made him "think about the great issues of God and eternity," he wrote, five days after that watershed day. "I can no longer avoid the fact that the time has come for some commitment to be made . . . and in a sense I am ashamed that it took such a catastrophe, that it took the iron of affliction to enter my soul, before making my decision. However, I begin to see now the path in which I must go."[8] His writings reveal an introspective man, intelligent and gifted, growing increasingly philosophical and spiritual as he coped with an impossible situation.

Above all, the voice in these pages is rational. That alone sets him apart from those who became his tormentors. Describing his interview at Garrison's office on Christmas Eve 1966, Shaw wrote, "like all the DA's assistants, and indeed the DA himself, [Andrew Sciambra] wore a pistol, which I found rather unnecessarily dramatic." It is impossible to imagine Jim Garrison entertaining such a thought.[9]

About that same interview, Shaw penned this passage:

> I explained to Sciambra that I had not at any time had an opportunity to see Oswald [when he was distributing leaflets at the Trade Mart], and had never met him under any other circumstances and added what turned out to be a very ironic remark—that it was perhaps unfortunate that I did not because then I might possibly have had a tiny footnote in history.[10]

When Sylvia Meagher wrote expressing her horror over his plight but objecting to the efforts of his attorneys to have the Warren Report made binding on the judiciary, Shaw made his position clear. In his four-page response, he said he found the Report's flaws understandable and its "central conclusions . . . absolutely correct and valid," and he laid out the logic of his thinking.[11]

---

* A cab driver named Marty picked Shaw up the day after the preliminary hearing, recognized him, and insisted on serving as his personal transportation service from then on, any hour, day or night, and he refused to accept payment. "Everybody knows what that big SOB is trying to do to you," he said. "You have enough problems on your mind." Over time Shaw tried repeatedly to give Marty money; he refused it (Shaw Journal, pp. 71–73).

Those who believe he was a master spy may be heartened to learn Shaw left his passports (his traveling dates and locations now may be checked); a file folder labeled *Permindex* (the alleged CIA organization), with a few letters in it and a brochure; and another file containing information about his activities during the months preceding the assassination. Others will find more enlightenment in correspondence such as that with Hale Boggs concerning Shaw's role on the Welcoming Committee for President Kennedy during his 1962 trip to New Orleans, and clippings about Shaw himself, which chronicle his early success as a playwright.[12]

"We now have [Shaw's] perspective on what happened to him," said Thomas Samoluk, the review board's deputy director, who traveled to New Orleans, reviewed the contents of Shaw's seven boxes, and brought them back to Washington, "and that is a very important addition to the historical record." Dave Snyder was more impassioned about it. "If you look at Shaw's letters to people he knew and at his journal," Snyder said, "you see Shaw was a very considerate, sensitive man, a very caring man. Most of the correspondence is ordinary, routine stuff—bread and butter [thank you] notes, for instance. But it shows Clay Shaw doing what Clay Shaw did, and doing it meticulously and well." In what he left behind, Shaw seems to be saying, "Look at this—for this is who I really was." In preserving this material, Shaw insured that his "footnote in history" will not be written entirely by others.

Shaw's documents, and those from Edward Wegmann's family, along with Tyler's film, are today part of the JFK Collection at the National Archives' handsome new building on grounds donated by the University of Maryland, a wooded setting adjoining the University's golf course in College Park, Maryland. The six-story glass and concrete state-of-the-art research facility is a 1.8 million square-foot structure with wide hallways and panoramic views, equipped with moveable shelving on tracks, a sophisticated computer setup, superb photographic equipment for researchers, environmental controls to protect the archival records, and cold storage vaults for photographs.

Among the articles being protected in those vaults is the Zapruder film, the collection's most famous item. The review board laid claim to the home movie by defining it as an "assassination record" under the terms of the 1992 Records Collection Act and it became part of the JFK

Collection officially on August 1, 1998.* At this writing, the Department of Justice and the Zapruder family have entered into arbitration to determine the price the government will pay for the film, with the ceiling set at $30 million. (The family, which under the arbitration agreement will retain ownership of the copyright, was asking for $18.5 million and the government was offering $3 million.)†

As required by law, the five-member review board (a panel of citizens made up of a judge from Minnesota and four academics with expertise in law, history and archives)‡ went out of business on September 30, 1998, simultaneously issuing its Final Report. In that 208-page document, the board noted that drawing conclusions concerning the assassination was not part of its mandate, and it drew none. It did acknowledge, however, that reaction to Oliver Stone's film prompted enactment of the "JFK Act." While the board discovered no "smoking gun" document, advocates of both sides found ammunition for their position in the report, which described the board's achievements, travails, and recommendations.

The report began by addressing the secrecy issue. "The problem was," the board members said in their opening chapter, "that 30 years of government secrecy" surrounding the assassination "led the American public to believe that the government had something to hide." They returned to this theme in their concluding section, charging that "[t]he federal government needlessly and wastefully classified and then withheld from public access countless important records that did not require such treatment."

During the board's four-year, $8 million effort, its members used their unprecedented powers boldly. They deposed witnesses, for instance, ordered the Zapruder film tested for authenticity and a bullet fragment from the presidential limousine tested for possible residue. They also obtained (over vigorous legal opposition from New Orleans District

---

* Researchers have been viewing the film at the National Archives since the 1960s, but the film was always privately owned. (Abraham Zapruder sold it to Time-Life, Inc., who sold it back to the Zapruder family in 1975.) In 1978 the Zapruder family placed the "camera original" in the Archives under a limited deposit agreement.

† The review board's plan to make low-priced digitized copies of the film available to the public through the Archives was preempted by the Zapruder family in July 1998, with the release of an inexpensive version (showcased in a forty-five-minute video), now in stores nationwide.

‡ Federal Judge John R. Tunheim, Chair; Columbia University historian Henry F. Graff; Ohio State University historian Kermit L. Hall; American University historian Anna K. Nelson; and Princeton University librarian William L. Joyce.

Attorney Harry Connick) Jim Garrison's old office files and grand jury transcripts. Yet, despite their aggressive endeavors, they feared that "critical records may have been withheld" by some government agencies. So they created a "compliance program," which required an officer from each agency "to warrant, under oath and penalty of perjury" that all relevant records had been turned over to the board.

Since taking office in April 1994, board members examined and released classified passages in more than 29,000 documents (the largest number from the CIA), processed the release of 33,000 more (the largest number from the FBI), and aided in the transmittal of many others, from various agencies and private citizens, to the JFK Collection at the National Archives.

Overall, some 4.5 million pages have poured into that collection since President Bush signed the Records Collection Act in 1992. Those documents—a virtual avalanche of paper—are today a magnet at College Park. According to Steven D. Tilley, the archivist in charge, many hundreds have examined some portion of the JFK Collection since the first big document release in August 1993. The number of schoolchildren doing projects on the assassination and making requests is increasing, Tilley noted, and the staff has twice done presentations of forensic (autopsy) material for a group from the Bronx High School of Science in New York. Researchers can access the collection's electronic reference system on the Internet, order documents by e-mail, and obtain some items through Westlaw and Lexis-Nexis.[13]

Because the largest contributions have come from sources that either monitored the New Orleans investigation or examined it afterwards,* a surprisingly large portion of the collection concerns Jim Garrison.

One Garrison document, in particular, that today resides among those millions of pages came to my attention a while back. It is a transcript of a statement Perry Russo made under hypnosis.† Garrison turned this document over to the House Select Committee in 1977

---

* The FBI, CIA, HSCA, and Church Committee.
† Jim Garrison, memorandum to Jonathan Blackmer, regarding "Statements of Perry Russo" made under hypnosis concerning "Clay Shaw, David Ferrie and other individuals" (hereinafter Garrison Memo), dated Aug. 16, 1977. Garrison implied there was only one hypnosis and this was it. There were at least three.

with a notation. Explaining why the pages were numbered oddly (one to seventeen and one to thirteen), Garrison wrote that the session was in two parts because Dr. Fatter had apparently "interposed" a "break" or "rest period" for Russo's benefit. He did not. Garrison's "document" is actually two documents, the transcript of the first hypnosis session and another, which took place eleven days later. Garrison combined them, reversing their chronology, and labeled them "A" and "B."[14] By so doing, he obliterated the damaging reality of both hypnosis interviews.[15] If the House Select Committee relied on this document in any way, it was misled.* No one should trust anything Garrison left behind.

The Garrison material, according to one unofficial guesstimate, may amount to as much as twenty percent of the overall collection. If so, of that 4.5 million, Garrison's portion amounts to some 900,000 pages.

The phoenix now has a substantial and permanent perch in America's official historical record.

---

* Garrison's cooperation with that committee was highly selective. He did not, for instance, turn over to it the early interviews with the Clinton witnesses. They were among the 15,000 pages his family donated to the Review Board.

CHAPTER EIGHTEEN

THE CONSEQUENCES

"Every man's rights are diminished when any man's rights are
threatened."[1]
— Clay Shaw (quoting President
John F. Kennedy), 1967

This is a story that speaks to the principal malaise of our times—the extraordinary decline in the trust Americans feel toward their government. Spanning three decades, the Garrison phenomenon both mirrored and influenced that downward spiral, which began at Dealey Plaza and accelerated after the publication of the Warren Report and the response it triggered from critics. While Garrison and his investigation were providing a base around which those forces for awhile coalesced, the country was awash in the escalating Vietnam war, the anti-war movement, the flower children rebellion, and a bitter, growing division in the land. In 1968 the back-to-back assassinations of Martin Luther King and Robert Kennedy further traumatized the nation and generated a new round of conspiracy theories. When it seemed nothing worse could happen, the Watergate debacle produced the first presidential resignation in America's history. Later, we learned that the CIA created revolutions and sometimes instigated murder; that the government funded radiation experiments on unsuspecting citizens; and more recently, the unanswered questions about the FBI shootout with the Weaver family in Idaho and the Branch Davidians in Waco, Texas.

At the bottom of that downward spiral stands the bombed-out shell of the Federal Building in Oklahoma City where 168 lives ended, some before they began. This mad act has spotlighted the rise of militias across the land, citizens armed to the teeth and convinced that Washington is Enemy Number One, that Armageddon is just around the corner, and that they are democracy's last best hope.*The anti-government sentiment espoused by the militia leaders has an oddly familiar ring. Their with-us or against-us stance, their apocalyptic scenarios, and their insistence that the government is the root of all evil sound amazingly like the rhetoric of Jim Garrison. Were he delivering his anti-Washington proclamations today, he would be virtually indistinguishable from them. And he too would have a following. It would be larger and more mainstream than the others. For, thanks to Oliver Stone, many believe (more or less) as Garrison did about the assassination. But those who do can no longer build their case, as Stone did, on Garrison's evidence. He had none.

What he did have was a good deal more in common with Branch Davidian cult leader David Koresh than anyone wants to admit. They were both magnetic personalities with a mesmerizing oratorical gift and a psychological kink, and both left innocent victims in their wake. David Ferrie died from a stroke likely precipitated by the pressure Garrison deliberately applied to his daily life. Edgar Eugene Bradley spent thirteen years fighting lawsuits to clear his name, which left him broke and at one point he almost lost his home.† Dean Andrews did not deserve what Garrison did to him. Nor did the others he charged: Walter Sheridan, David Chandler, Richard Townley, William Gurvich, Kerry Thornley, Layton Martens, John Cancler, Sergio Arcacha Smith, Morris Brownlee, and Gordon Novel. Clay Shaw endured a humiliating arrest, followed by a hellish four-year battle that ruined him financially and socially and sent him to an early grave. Yet he died having triumphed over Garrison. He also won a victory on the spiritual plane, though its nature is unknowable.

Garrison took a toll on the city of New Orleans that is less tangible, ongoing, and impossible to assess. Speaking to those affected by him, I repeatedly encountered the repressed anger still simmering there after all this time. They have never had closure in that city. After Shaw was acquitted in 1969, Garrison became irrelevant to the rest of the world

---

* A 1996 assessment of the militias concluded that the Oklahoma City bombing actually sparked a growth in membership (Richard A. Serrano, "Militias: The Ranks Are Swelling," Los Angeles Times, April 18, 1996).
† Garrison eventually dismissed the charges against Bradley, claiming he had been supplied "false information." In April 1991 Bradley met with Garrison, who told him they both had been "set up" (Bradley, telephone conversation with author, Aug. 13, 1993).

for the next twenty-two years, but not in New Orleans. Even after Judge Christenberry's ruling, Garrison continued to beat his own drum in his city, where the audience was captive. He also left behind a contingent of well-placed, powerful guardians of the Garrison flame, who continue to protect him and themselves by their silence, which is another way to bear false witness. Some of them seem to regard loyalty as a virtue superior even to truth and justice. Others don't want to go out on a limb in a city where Garrison still has influential friends. One former assistant district attorney who participated in the investigation at first agreed to speak to me, then changed his mind, remarking that he wanted "to see how this thing shakes down." Another declined, saying he never gave interviews on the subject as "a matter of principle." A former city official who played a brief but significant role spoke at length and with unconcealed fury about various Garrison outrages, but insisted the information was for background only. James Alcock was the exception, and he had very little to say. Of those who helped destroy Clay Shaw's life, the only one ever to express any remorse was Perry Russo.

One former Garrison aide who did agree to speak for the first time publicly was Leonard Gurvich, owner of the largest security guard service in New Orleans and the Gurvich Detective Agency.[2] In addition to being a dollar-a-year investigator for Garrison, Gurvich was also one of Garrison's drinking buddies, and they would sometimes go to the Playboy Club and play pool. He was one of the first to leave Garrison's investigation, quite awhile before his brother, William Gurvich. Yet few even noticed he was gone, Gurvich said, because of the way he did it. He went to First Asst. D.A. Charles Ward, a lifelong friend, and told him he was departing. That was it. Unlike his brother, who was trying to bring Garrison down, Leonard Gurvich made no public statements. "I would have preferred to just let the case and the public and history bring him down," Gurvich said. "Garrison was my friend, and you don't give up on your friends." In retrospect, though, he believes his brother was correct. "If right has to be served," Gurvich said, obviously moved by what he was saying, "then whatever way Billy decided to help it in the interest of justice, then Billy has to be right. I have to be wrong."

Even before the Russo polygraph fiasco,* Gurvich had heard from

* This is recounted in chapter 7.

Charles Ward that the case "was b.s. from the beginning." He also knew it from interviewing some of the witnesses involved. "There was no infallibility in any of us," he said, "but it was obvious after asking some simple questions that these people were crazy." As to how the crucial testimony of Perry Russo came about, Gurvich stated, "I know this— what Moo Moo [Sciambra] said wasn't true. You don't set out to solve the crime of the century, write that long memo and leave out the crime. That means that as an afterthought Russo comes in and now you begin to ask him other things and you begin to manufacture a case. I hate to say it but what else can you say?"

When his brother went public, it was difficult for the entire family because of the notoriety, Gurvich said. Some people "stayed away" from them, though no real friendships were lost and none of their clients left. "We became controversial," Gurvich said, and there was skepticism in some quarters until after Shaw's trial. "Billy was regarded by some in law enforcement, the ignorant, shall we say, as having ratted out. Billy hurt the gravy train. Billy broke the code of silence." Yet, as Gurvich pointed out at the time to "anybody who would listen," what his brother was speaking up about was not "a policeman who lost his temper and kicked some junkie." His brother blew the whistle because of the magnitude of the crime. First they "fabricated" the case against Shaw and then Garrison was giving "press releases to Russian newsmen and communist journalists around the world stating that our government knows who killed our president. You can't keep quiet about that," Gurvich said, his voice charged with indignation. "What happened to Shaw was the goddamnest thing I have ever seen in what we call the system of justice. They took a completely innocent man and set him up to save Garrison's own ass. That's it. Pure and simple. Garrison was not *that* stupid. He was not *that* crazy." Those on Garrison's staff who stuck with the case did it "for the reward," Gurvich said, and some of those who remained surprised him by staying. He believes the ones at the top who knew the score should have done what he did, maintain the code but *disappear*. "It's time," Gurvich said, "for all of them to tell the truth."

Oliver Stone eliminated that likelihood when he turned them all into Hollywood heroes. In the process, of course, he robbed Clay Shaw of his hard-won victory in the minds of millions. He also diminished whatever prospects remain for finding legitimate answers to the questions that remain in this case. For no one discovers truth by building on a lie. The immorality aside, it doesn't work in a practical sense: those moved to action are likely to follow the lie. To a large extent that is what they have done in this instance. The unwary will continue to emulate Jim Garrison and pursue his "leads" as long as he is perceived as a hero.

Genuine heroes saved the day in New Orleans, but their story Hollywood has yet to tell. They were the four men who defended Clay Shaw: F. Irvin Dymond, Edward F. Wegmann, William J. Wegmann, and Salvatore Panzeca.* When the most popular and powerful political figure in Louisiana set his sights on Clay Shaw, they were all that stood between him and twenty years behind bars. Unlike Shaw, whose fate was chosen for him, they stepped into the fray of their own volition, with nothing to gain and a great deal to lose. Charismatic, witty, and above all principled, they devoted four years to the struggle. For all their time and effort, they earned about $8,500 apiece.†

Clearly, they weren't driven by money. They saw a wrong about to happen and felt compelled to stop it. It is no coincidence that the newsmen who covered the trial tagged them "The Boy Scouts" for their dogged belief that justice would prevail because it should. William Wegmann recently remarked that the worst thing that happened to Garrison was Shaw's hiring them to defend him "because Garrison knew we could not be bought." Nor could they be intimidated. Had Shaw turned to others less talented, ethical or determined, his fate could have been quite different. Twice they came to his rescue. That is the real New Orleans story. It is an old-fashioned morality tale. The good guys versus the bad. Four Davids challenging Goliath, Big Jim, the Jolly Green Giant, and winning big, not once but twice.

---

* Shortly after his arrest, Shaw heard "through the grapevine that F. Lee Bailey would be very anxious to appear in the case and would charge, what was for him, a nominal fee." But Shaw decided to rely on the local "legal talent" (Shaw Journal, p. 47).
† Shaw's main expenses were investigatory, chasing down Garrison's endless charges. Overwhelmed with the awesome burden of defending the case, Shaw's attorneys at one point reached out to the federal government for help, but none was forthcoming. "I got the cold shoulder from Ramsey Clark," Irvin Dymond recalled, "and I got the cold shoulder from J. Edgar Hoover. He wouldn't even have us on his appointment book" (Dymond et al. Interview).

Edward Wegmann died November 20, 1989, of cancer, at the age of seventy-two. Cynthia Wegmann believes the prolonged burden of defending Clay Shaw shortened her father's life. "He was a great father, a great lawyer, and a good man," she wrote recently, "who had the quiet courage to do what was right." Irvin Dymond's distinguished career as a defense trial attorney ended January 17, 1998, when he succumbed to cancer. He was eighty-three. William Wegmann, who had resigned as an assistant district attorney in 1950, abandoned the criminal arena entirely after the Shaw case. Today, his firm is one of the most prestigious civil practices in the region. Salvatore Panzeca, a partner in the firm of Panzeca & D'Angelo, still practices general law and acts (as he has for the past sixteen years) as Judge Pro Tempore of the Orleans Parish Juvenile Court. William Gurvich died of a heart attack on February 7, 1991, at the age of sixty-five. After his courageous public battle with Garrison, Gurvich assisted Shaw's attorneys, and returned to the family business. He was still working as a private investigator at the time of his death. Edward O'Donnell continued to advance in the police department. When he retired in 1974, he was chief of homicide. Judge Herbert Christenberry's illustrious tenure on the federal bench came to a close, after almost three decades, on October 5, 1975, when he died of a heart attack. He was seventy-eight.

These are the men of New Orleans who deserve to be remembered and celebrated for what they did in the service of justice for Clay Shaw.

What Garrison did was far worse than anything I imagined over the years. Far worse than most can imagine, I suspect. A prosecutor in Oregon recently spent two years prying out of jail two people he put there. When he discovered someone else committed the crime, he didn't rest until they were freed. Most Americans still think their judicial system is like that. Flawed, yes, but in the hands of sensible men and women of good will, honest and responsible. Garrison behaved in a way that seems too alien to be true. And while it's almost too amazing and frightening to believe, as Milton Brener pointed out, all of it came from Garrison's "imagination"; he invented it all.[3]

So many were taken in by Garrison's evocative play on the anguish of Dealey Plaza. Certainly those who gave him money and moral support, the volunteers who flocked to his side from around the country, and those grand jurors who did his bidding were all mesmerized by the Kennedy standard he held aloft, the promise that he and he alone cared enough to go after the "destroyers of Camelot." Yet the twelve notably ordinary men who heard his evidence and sat in judgment on Clay Shaw were not taken in by him. The system worked. It worked in Garrison's hometown, in his backyard at Tulane and Broad, in a courtroom only a few marbled corridor feet from those tall double doors topped off by his name in three-inch high gold letters. Twelve men of good will, honest and responsible saw through his rhetoric and set Clay Shaw free. That is the glory of the real story. The demagogue didn't fool the man on the street. Oliver Stone did that.

He did it with an eye on history and a respectful salute to President Kennedy. But I wonder what President Kennedy, who loved this country's history and admired above all public figures who "stood fast for principle,"* would think about the destruction in his name of an innocent citizen and a movie that glorifies the politician responsible.

Clay Shaw's story is unique in our country's history. Perhaps nothing like it exists anywhere. The Dreyfus affair comes to mind. But for most of the world, Dreyfus remains vindicated, while Clay Shaw's good name has been blackened apparently irreparably. For as writer Brent Staples has said, "historical lies" given credibility by the movies are "nearly impossible to correct." The real Clay Shaw served his country honorably and well in World War II. He contributed to the cultural and financial well-being of his community, and he supported Jack Kennedy's presidency. Shaw also deserves to be recognized for the contribution he made to Oliver Stone's Congressional lobbying effort. Whatever the ultimate consequence of the Assassination Records Collection Act, Stone must share any credit for it with Clay Shaw, who paid for the release of the files with his life and reputation, not once but twice, and not willingly, since the dead cannot acquiesce. Or sue.

This one may have the last word though. For real historians love hard data and among the millions of pages that have flowed into the National Archives are many revealing ones from New Orleans, including the transcript of that final confrontation between Garrison and

---

* John F. Kennedy, *Profiles In Courage* (New York: Harper & Row, 1964), "Foreword To The Memorial Edition," by Robert F. Kennedy, p. 9.

Shaw in federal court, the Christenberry hearing.[4] Shaw's preliminary hearing and the Christenberry transcript are like two legal bookends, marking the beginning and the end of the real Jim Garrison–Clay Shaw story. In the power of that documentary record, now officially preserved in Washington, D.C., lies truth's best hope.

Reporter: What would you say your philosophy of life is?

Clay Shaw: The man who lives a successful
life is the man who develops his
potentials to their fullest . . . and
who makes it a policy to try not
to harm anybody else.[1]

—Press Conference, March 2, 1967

AFTERWORD

A GRAND JURY TRANSCRIPT SURFACES

On August 4, 1995, I received anonymously through the mail a six-page grand jury transcript.[*] It is a brief but dramatic interrogation of Perry Russo by Jim Garrison. The exchange on Garrison's part was hostile. He was angry because Russo had visited the office of Shaw's attorney, Edward F. Wegmann.[†] Moo Moo Sciambra, Russo's "babysitter," had seen him enter. Garrison was keeping a close watch on his star witness and was alarmed and threatened by Russo's hobnobbing with the enemy. Garrison reacted as he always did when he felt at risk. He attacked.

He hauled Russo in front of this body and made certain he didn't jump ship. He threatened Russo outright with a perjury charge if he changed his story and dropped a veiled threat of an "accessory" charge as well. Garrison also snapped his whip at his grand jurors that day. The secretary recording these minutes freeze-framed Garrison in his most revealing mode. We see him bullying—"I want that cooperation or I'll go to Judge Bagert and quietly shut this whole investigation down." We see him brainwashing—"I told you I knew who the real assassins were and would haul them to justice." It was Russo, though, who made this transcript invaluable by what he said that day. The others present made it so by what they knew and when they knew it.

Russo unwittingly exposed how he was manipulated: "Mr. Garrison told me he had four strong witnesses [a former Dallas police officer, a CIA guy and some others] that could place Ferrie, Clay Shaw and Oswald together after I heard them planning it," Russo said. (Garrison,

---

[*] In 1995 a former investigator in the New Orleans D.A.'s office leaked forty-four Garrison-era grand jury transcripts to the press. The transcript I received in the mail is not one of those.

[†] Many years later Perry Russo mentioned his visit to Wegmann's office to writer Hugh Aynesworth.

of course, had no one.) Russo said Mark Lane told him "that he uncovered information three days after the assassination that put Shaw and Ferrie in the midst of it." (Lane had nothing.) But Russo turned this session into a smoking gun when he revised his own testimony.

Two weeks earlier he testified under oath at the preliminary hearing that he saw Clay Shaw a total of *three* times, including *one* occasion at David Ferrie's home when the plotting occurred. Here, also under oath, he told the grand jury he saw Shaw at Ferrie's house "at least five . . . maybe six times."* Russo was either lying now or he was lying at the preliminary hearing. Prior to that hearing, Russo confessed to his first polygraph technician that his story was fiction from the outset. He also admitted it to his second polygraph operator and to Shaw's defense team. He lied at the preliminary hearing. He lied at his first grand jury appearance. He lied at this one. He lied at Shaw's trial. Today, thirty years later, we know that. But, if this transcript is legitimate (as I believe), it shows that *way back then* everyone in that grand jury room knew almost two years before the trial began that Perry Russo had lied at least once. Moreover, those who believed what he said this day knew he lied later at the trial when he repeated his preliminary hearing testimony. These grand jurors, Garrison, and his two key assistants—who handled that trial and were later appointed to the bench—all knew Garrison's pivotal witness was a perjurer.

The transcript I received in the mail is reproduced on the following pages.

---

* Why Russo increased the number of these phantom sightings may never be known with certainty. Most likely he was responding to pressure from Garrison to repair his story, badly damaged ten days earlier by the bomb James Phelan exploded in Garrison's den. Garrison knew this jury would soon be reading Phelan's article and Russo's "new" recollections probably were meant to nullify its impact. Russo was certainly trying to bolster his credibility in the eyes of these jurors who, to their credit, were skeptical even without Phelan's information.

AFTERWORD

ORLEANS PARISH GRAND JURY

PROCEEDINGS OF

MARCH 29, 1967

PRESENT: MESSRS. ALVIN V. OSER AND JAMES ALCOCK,
Assistant District Attorneys

JIM GARRISON
Orleans Parish District Attorney

MEMBERS OF THE ORLEANS PARISH GRAND JURY

WITNESS: PERRY RAYMOND RUSSO

*   *   *   *   *

Reported By:
Maureen B. Thiel,
Secretary
Orleans Parish Grand Jury

1.

PERRY RAYMOND RUSSO, being sworn in by the Foreman of the Orleans Parish Grand Jury, was questioned and answered as follows:

BY MR. JIM GARRISON:

Q.   You are the same Perry Raymond Russo who testified before this grand jury last week, are you not?

A.   Yes sir.

Q.   I believe you testified about seeing Clay Bertrand, whom we now have identified as Clay Shaw, several times at Dave Ferrie's house. Can you tell us again, how many times did you see him there?

A.   At least five...maybe six times, counting the times when they finally talked about it, the assassination, you know.

Q.   Did they, at any time, suggest that you do anything? Did they ask you to do anything? After all, you had heard so much of what they contemplated...

A.   No.

Q.   You were asked by one of the grand jury members here about what went through your mind after you heard the plan had been carried out. You said that you were too busy and, I take it, unconcerned, to tell anybody about it in 1963, 1964, 1965 or 1966. Why was that, Perry? I know the answer, but I want the gentlemen here to understand it too.

A.   I only saw him about five times in the days after...I mean, you know, in 1964. That was Ferrie. And he

never brought it up. I wasn't one to bring it up.
What would I have said, "How much did you get for
having the President killed?" Anybody who would do a
thing like that might kill anybody who asked about
it. And I was getting ready for law school and I just
wasn't interested in Ferrie anymore. Call it lack of
interest or whatever.

BY A GRAND JUROR:

Q.   Let me see if I understand here. You heard all this
and you know JFK was killed a few days later, just
the way you heard it planned. Yet, you were too busy
to get involved. Is that what you're saying, Mr.
Russo?

I mean I don't know how you could have slept at
night. Mr. Garrison has explained in great detail
that you are now making an almost supreme sacrifice
to come forward, to stand tall against some elements
in our government who have covered this whole horri-
ble thing up, but why didn't you say something?

A.   It isn't easy to tell a secret of such great scope.
And I didn't know for sure that they did it. I guess
Oswald was there, at least, but Ferrie was somewhere
else. Mr. Garrison told me he had four strong witnesses that could place Ferrie, Clay Shaw and Oswald
together after I heard them planning it, so maybe
what I saw and heard isn't all that important. I've

been assured that I was just the first one who got
involved with `em. Mr. Garrison has a former Dallas
police officer, a CIA guy and some others. Why don't
you ask them why they didn't come forward before
this too? Mark Lane, you know him, who was once a
senator, he told me that he uncovered information
three days after the assassination that put Shaw and
Ferrie in the midst of it. Why isn't anybody asking
him why he kept it secret for so long?

BY MR. GARRISON:

Q.   I don't think it's called for to jump on this witness, the one man who had guts enough to come here
and jump into all this mess. He has been hounded by
the go-along press, has been followed by private detectives, has been bribed by TIME magazine   to
change his story and has been ridiculed for the
truths he has told us. If you want to cast some
blame, I think maybe you'll have ample opportunity
when I get people like Walter Sheridan, Rick Townley,
James Phelan, Hue Aynesworth and Gordon Novel up
here...and I will. All of them will be subpoenaed.
And you haven't seen a criminal until you talk to
Regis Kennedy and William Gurvich. I've told you all
about Carlos Quiroga and Layten Martins. We have
evidence tying Quiroga to Dallas, Sheridan and Phelan
to taking bribe money from the CIA and a tape record-

ing of TIME trying to bribe this witness. And you
jump on him! If that's the way an honest grand jury
is going to handle the most important investigation
in U.S. history, I may not want to be a continuing
part of this whole show. When we began, I told you I
knew who the real assassins were and would haul them
to justice. You gave me your assurance you would keep
an open mind and work with me. So I want that cooperation or I'll go to Judge Bagert and quietly shut
this whole investigation down. Perry, I have a couple
other questions to ask, then if any more jurors want
answers, I'll open it up again, okay?

A. Okay. Shoot.

Q. Did you meet with Edward Wegmann, a lawyer for Clay
Shaw, at his office after you visited this grand jury
last week? I'll have to be honest with you. Mr.
Sciambra...Moo Moo...said he saw you on the same
floor as Wegmann's office. I know it's a free country, but with all the accusations flying around, I've
got to know what you've been doing.

A. The day after I left the grand jury, I got a call
from Mr. Wegmann. He was real polite, a gentleman to
me. He said he knew that me and C.G. Mitchell, an old
friend of mine, had got caught shoplifting at Schweg-
mann's and he said since I was in the public eye and
all, things might go bad for me when it hit the

5.

newspapers. He said he had a copy of the arrest report. He told me I'd better drop by to talk; that I might need a friendly lawyer. I told him I had already talked to Andy and that you had told him it wasn't nothin' important, that you would take care of it before it got to a grand jury. In return for what I've done for you in this case, you know. The only other thing he seemed interested in was about my truth serum stuff and the hypnosis. I told him I wasn't really under hypnosis anyway. He asked about Lefty Peterson and Al Landry and then I went home.

Q. You didn't relate what you discussed before the grand jury, did you?

A. No, not a bit. Mostly about the shoplifting. Andy told me that was taken care of, so I didn't see anything wrong with talking about it. He said they'd never been able to find that arrest record...that it was the least the D.A.'s office could do for the risks I'm taking. We was innocent anyway.

Q. Do you know the danger in talking to the defense lawyers? They're just out to destroy you and make this grand jury and me look like fools. Nobody can stop you from going where you want to or talking to whoever you want to, but the help my office has given you will certainly have to stop if we see a reoccurence of this type behavior. Do you understand me, Perry?

AFTERWORD

A.   Yes sir. Completely. I didn't mean...

Q.   One panel member asked last week if you might have some risk of being charged as an accessory after the fact. Mr. Alcock tried to explain the law to the questioner...and I hope we've straightened that out. There will be no such charges emanating from the Orleans Parish district attorney's office, so you don't have to be afraid -- if you don't change your story. In that case, the charge would not be accessory it would be perjury.

A.   I understand. I only know what I saw and heard...and I won't change that.

Q.   Since the grand jury has specifically asked that Dean Andrews be brought back this afternoon, I'm going to excuse you now, Perry. Thank you and keep your chin up.

A.   Okay. So long.

APPENDIX A

ON THE TRAIL OF THE ASSASSINS: MORE ANOMALIES

This appendix is not all-inclusive but an additional sampling only, a supplement to chapter 14, specifically, and the whole of *False Witness*, generally. The first page numbers refer to the Sheridan Square Press edition of Garrison's book, *On the Trail of the Assassins: My Investigation and Prosecution of the Murder of President Kennedy*; those in parentheses refer to the Warner Books paperback edition.

1. p. xi (xi)—Garrison's statement that prior to the trial he publicly linked Shaw to the CIA is probably true. But that admission is a stark contrast to Garrison's oft-repeated claim that he never made any negative public statements about Shaw before the trial (Kirkwood, *American Grotesque*, pp. 489, 574–575).

2. p. xii (xii)—Clay Shaw wasn't acquitted, as Garrison claims, because the jurors found no motivation, but because, as several jurors said at the time, Garrison had presented no *evidence* to support his case. (See chapter 11.)

3. p. 5 (3)—Guy Banister's pistol whipping of Jack Martin did not lead to Clay Shaw's prosecution. Perry Russo's assassination plot-party story did.

4. pp. 4–5 (3)—Garrison characterizes Guy Banister as an "occasional" drinker, a "highly composed individual" unlikely to engage in violence and excessive drinking, and describes his November 22, 1963, attack on Jack Martin as "unusual and explosive." But Banister was forced to retire from the New Orleans Police Department following an episode in which he reportedly "threatened a waiter with a pistol." Author Anthony Summers described Banister as "choleric" and "a heavy drinker." G. Robert Blakey and Richard Billings also described Banister as "a heavy drinker." According to them Banister had "a violent temper," and they referred to "reports that he shot a man during Mardi Gras festivities." (Anthony Summers, *Conspiracy* [New York: Paragon House, 1989], pp. 290–291; G. Robert Blakey and Richard N. Billings, *The Plot to Kill the President*, [New York: Times Books, 1981], pp. 165–166.)

5. p. 5 (3)—Contrary to Garrison's exciting narrative, the beating did not convert Jack Martin "into a bloody, battered mess," and he was not "carted off to Charity hospital" in a police car. Martin's wounds were relatively minor

("three small lacerations on the forehead and one laceration on the rear of the head"). And he went to Charity Hospital under his own steam. After he was treated he was well enough to take himself home. From his apartment he called the police, reported the incident, and a patrol car picked him up and took him to Baptist Hospital where he was examined and photographed. (New Orleans Police Department Report K-12634-63, Nov. 22, 1963, signed by Lt. Francis Martello.)

6. p. 5 (3)—Jack Martin did not share his ideas about David Ferrie with only one friend, as Garrison indicates. Martin passed on his fantasies to a good portion of the population of New Orleans. (See chapter 3.)

7. p. 6 (4)—Garrison claims that the weekend of the assassination his men discovered Oswald had been seen with Ferrie. That is not true. Neither his men, the New Orleans Police Department, the FBI, nor the Secret Service found any such evidence. That weekend the only information Garrison or anyone else had of an Oswald-Ferrie relationship came from Jack Martin's telephone rampage. (See chapter 3.)

8. p. 7 (5)—According to Garrison, Jack Martin's "thoroughly reliable" friend contacted Asst. D.A. Herman Kohlman and reported what Martin had told him, triggering Garrison's pursuit of Ferrie the weekend of the assassination. But Kohlman and the records of the Secret Service say otherwise. It was Martin, himself, who telephoned Kohlman at home (Secret Service Report, Nov. 24–29, 1963; Herman Kohlman, telephone conversation with author, July 29, 1996). By interjecting a supposedly "thoroughly reliable" friend into the picture (and also claiming, as described in the preceding item, that the D.A.'s office knew of other witnesses who saw Ferrie with Oswald), Garrison is trying to distance his initial "case" against Ferrie from its thoroughly unreliable instigator—Jack Martin. (Since several people who received telephone calls from Martin reported his claims to the Secret Service, it is entirely possible that someone also called the D.A.'s office about them. But, if so, the originating source, Martin, remained the same; and the record is unequivocal that Martin himself spoke to Kohlman directly.)

9. p. 7 (6)—David Ferrie did not leave New Orleans *one hour* after the assassination, as Garrison writes, but almost *six hours* afterwards. Proof of that is the telephone call (confirmed by the FBI) Ferrie placed, just before leaving, from Melvin Coffey's home to the Winterland Skating Rink in Houston. (See chapter 3.)

10. p. 24 (27)—There is no evidence that Banister or anyone else "stopped" Oswald from using the 544 Camp Street address on his literature. Reportedly, Oswald used the Camp Street address only on one occasion, Aug. 9, 1963, the day he deliberately caused a confrontation with the anti-Castro Cubans, which resulted in his arrest and a good deal of publicity. The publicity seems to have been what Oswald had in mind. Anticipating media scrutiny that day, it seems likely that he used the bogus office building address (instead of his home address) on his literature because it lent his Fair Play For Cuba "organization" (he was its only member) an air of legitimacy.

11. p. 39 (43)—Jack Martin's anonymity is one of the myths Garrison invented for his memoir. Garrison asserts that Martin demanded absolute secrecy, and refused to sign anything. In real life, Martin signed several documents. For instance: On Dec. 26, 1966, Martin signed a "Statement" in the district attorney's office, given to "Jim Garrison in the presence of Louis Ivon," which Ivon typed, and in which Martin claimed he saw David Ferrie in Guy Banister's office in the company of "three or four young men," one of them Oswald. On April 7, 1967, Martin signed a six-page version of his involvement in the case entitled, "General Statement & Affidavit Regarding Garrison Probe." On March 1, 1968, Martin (along with David Lewis) signed yet another, lengthier version of events, in two parts, this one entitled, "J.F.K. Assassination Investigation Report." These documents are today in the National Archives.

By claiming Martin insisted on anonymity, Garrison is providing an alibi to explain (1) why this pivotal witness never told his story to the grand jury; (2) why he never took the witness stand; and (3) why (back then) Garrison was telling the press he would never be foolish enough to listen to Martin. Garrison also is using Martin's alleged fear of exposure to heighten the drama of his narrative. But back in 1967 Jack Martin was enthusiastically promoting himself to the media (see, for example, Merriman Smith, "JFK Plot Quiz: Seamy Suspects," *Los Angeles Herald-Examiner*, March 5, 1967).

12. pp. 74–75 (85–86)—Garrison's claim that someone else posed for the backyard Oswald-with-rifle photographs and they were altered to appear to be Oswald is disputed by the testimony of Oswald's wife and his mother. Marina Oswald testified that she took the pictures of Oswald holding the rifle in the backyard of their Neely Street apartment in Dallas. Marguerite Oswald testified that after Oswald was arrested she saw such a photograph (inscribed "For my daughter June"), and that at the police station Marina had that picture "folded up in her shoe." Marina later tore the picture up, burned what she could of the pieces, and what was left Marguerite flushed down the toilet (WC Vol. 1, pp. 15–16, 117–118; 146, 152).

13. p. 80 (92)—In his first interview with the FBI, Dean Andrews did not describe Clay Bertrand as six feet two inches, as Garrison writes; Andrews said Bertrand was five feet seven inches (FBI interview, Nov. 25, 1963).

14. pp. 85–86 (98–99)—Contrary to Garrison's claim that his aides located several bartenders and bar owners in the French Quarter who knew Clay Shaw was Clay Bertrand, but they all refused to testify, Andrew Sciambra told Edward Epstein that he had "squeezed" the French Quarter and failed to find anyone who had ever heard of Clay Bertrand (Epstein, *Counterplot*, p. 50). Garrison told James Alcock and Tom Bethell the same thing (Bethell Diary, p.

11). If such witnesses had existed, Garrison would have hauled them before his grand jury and forced them to cooperate.

15. p. 87 (100)—Patience and "plodding footwork" had nothing to do with Garrison's notion that Shaw was Bertrand. Garrison arrived at that conclusion because of Shaw's first name and his homosexuality. William Gurvich, James Alcock and Tom Bethell confirmed that. (See chapter 4 and note p. 47.)

16. p. 152 (176)—Perry Russo *did not* make a positive identification of Clay Shaw in his first interview with Andrew Sciambra. Russo made only a vague, tentative identification, and two days later, when Russo arrived in New Orleans, he emphasized his uncertainty about it. Nor did Russo say initially that he knew Shaw as "Bertrand": even after the sodium Pentothal session, Russo said he didn't know anyone by that name. (See chapter 6.)

17. p. 106 (123)—Garrison makes it sound as though hordes of residents in Clinton remembered Oswald waiting in the registration line because he was the only white man there. But only *three* people, of the three hundred Garrison says were interviewed, testified that they remembered Oswald. Moreover, he was never the only white man in line. There was at least one other, Estus Morgan, by the testimony of Garrison's own witness, Henry Earl Palmer. (The number of whites probably was considerably higher than that, based on the lists of names—taken from the registrar's rolls, with race indicated—that Anne Dischler recorded in her notes.)

18. p. 106 (123)—Garrison's claim that "all" the Clinton witnesses gave definitive descriptions of David Ferrie, saying he was "wearing a crazy-looking wig and painted eyebrows," is false. None of them said that, or anything close. Only two Clinton witnesses even claimed they recalled Ferrie. Henry Earl Palmer said the man's hair and eyebrows "didn't seem real," and Corrie Collins said his hair was "messed up," his eyebrows "heavy" (trial transcript, Feb. 6, 1969, p. 84 [Palmer]; pp. 110–111 [Collins]).

19. p. 106 (124)—Contrary to Garrison's version of events, none of the four Clinton witnesses who claimed to recall the driver of the black car commented on his "manners," nor called him "distinguished." None of them said he "nodded politely"; no one claimed he "said hello." (See trial transcript, Henry Earl Palmer, John Manchester, and Corrie Collins on Feb. 6, 1969; and William Dunn, Sr. on Feb. 7, 1969.)

20. pp. 106-107 (124)—According to Garrison, the Clinton town marshal checked the black limousine's license plates with the State Police and found they were registered to the International Trade Mart. But that isn't what the marshal testified to at Shaw's trial. He said Shaw *told him* he worked at the International Trade Mart (John Manchester, trial transcript, Feb. 6, 1969, p. 60). If a check on the car actually had established the tie to the Trade Mart, Manchester would have said so on the witness stand and the documentary

evidence of that registration would have been entered into evidence.

21. p. 107 (125)—Garrison writes that Oswald showed "his Marine discharge card" to barber Edwin Lea McGehee, but nothing in the earliest statements and trial testimony supports that. According to that evidence, Oswald showed a military card to Registrar of Voters Henry Earl Palmer.

22. p. 108 (126)—Garrison's claim that Andrew Sciambra found a woman in personnel at East Louisiana State Hospital who interviewed Oswald isn't true. No evidence exists that Oswald was ever interviewed by anyone at the hospital. No one in personnel even remembered seeing him. The clerk who claimed she saw Oswald's application, Maxine Kemp, went to work at the hospital the year *after* the assassination. Oswald, of course, was dead by then. Moreover, Kemp told this writer she was never interviewed by Sciambra, only by Francis Frugé. (See chapter 13.)

23. p. 114 (132)—Richard Billings did not arrive in New Orleans in 1967; he arrived in December 1966. Moreover, Garrison himself prompted Billings's trip to Louisiana and the participation of *Life* magazine when Garrison contacted David Chandler, the unmentioned man in this memoir. By omitting Chandler from his story, Garrison creates the impression that the overture for the "secret deal" with *Life* was entirely the idea of *Life's* management. He also avoids the real reason *Life* withdrew from the arrangement: their loss of confidence in him following his arrest of Clay Shaw. (See chapter 6.)

24. p. 115 (133)—Garrison implies that $7,000—which James Alcock found David Ferrie had deposited in his bank account in 1963—was connected to the assassination plot. But the amount is hardly in keeping with the significance of the crime. What's more, Alcock indicated to Tom Bethell that he didn't believe Ferrie was involved in the assassination. In 1963, Ferrie's severance from Eastern Airlines was settled, and he received "a substantial sum of money" (Brener, *The Garrison Case*, p. 50).

25. pp. 119, 319 (138, 377)—Despite Garrison's claim that the "notes" of David Logan's statement were "stolen," the Logan transcript was among the material turned over to the National Archives by Garrison's family after his death. Garrison had at least two reasons to withhold this document: (1) it contradicts Garrison's claim that David Ferrie "introduced" Logan to Clay Shaw; and (2) its content rendered Logan noncredible.

26. p. 137 (159)—Contrary to Garrison's claim, the newspaper story on February 17, 1967, breaking the news of his Kennedy investigation, was neither "stunning" to Garrison, nor a "premature revelation." Garrison was shown the text of the article before it ran, and notified by the newspaper's publisher that it was going to appear. If he had wanted to, Garrison could have stopped it. (See chapter 5.)

27. p. 138 (161)—The media did not sniff out the information that David Ferrie was being targeted by Garrison's probe. Ferrie, himself, called reporter David Snyder at the *New Orleans States-Item*, offered to be interviewed, and identified himself as Garrison's chief suspect. Snyder's piece on Ferrie ran February 18, 1967. Until it appeared, no one in the media (or anywhere else outside Garrison's circle) had any idea that Ferrie was a suspect. Since Ferrie deliberately put himself on the front page of the newspaper, the media neither can be credited with, nor accused of sniffing him out. (See chapter 5.)

28. p. 142 (166)—Garrison's claim that Ferrie had no low metabolism problem, and, therefore, no reason to take the medication Proloid, isn't true. As a young man Ferrie had been diagnosed with a thyroid deficiency that was believed to be the cause of his alopecia (hair loss). (See three letters dated January 29, 1944, February 2, 1944, and February 4, 1944, from James Ferrie—David's father—to the administration at St. Charles Seminary, which David was attending.)

29. pp. 144–145 (168)—Garrison asserts that Shaw was interviewed *twice* before his interrogation and arrest on March 1, 1967, and that for the second interview Shaw was subpoenaed. During this second interview, in which Shaw was questioned "at great length," Garrison concluded Shaw was lying (about what Garrison doesn't say), and, consequently, Garrison decided to arrest Shaw "in the very near future."

This is entirely untrue. Prior to March 1, 1967, Shaw was questioned about the assassination only once, on December 24, 1966, and no subpoena was involved—only a telephone call to Shaw from a detective in Garrison's office. Shaw repeatedly and publicly described that first and only pre-arrest interview on Christmas Eve, and neither Garrison nor his aides ever challenged Shaw's statements, either with the media or at Shaw's trial. (Shaw Journal, pp. 1–5; Shaw NBC interview, pp. 1–10; Kirkwood, *American Grotesque*, pp. 19–20; Phelan–Shaw Interview.)

The first mention of this "second" interview surfaced four years after Shaw's arrest, at the Christenberry hearing, during Garrison's stunningly inaccurate testimony from the witness stand. Since he tied it to the Christmas season—as Shaw left the office, Garrison stated, Shaw said, "Merry Christmas"—it's clear that Garrison was referring to Shaw's 1966 Christmas Eve, non-subpoenaed, first and only pre-arrest interview. (As described earlier in this book, at the time, Garrison found that session exculpatory.) Garrison provided no evidence to support his claim of an incriminating, subpoenaed, second interview, none of his aides corroborated it, and when Shaw testified unequivocally under oath from the witness stand that he was interviewed "only once" prior to his arrest, none of Garrison's men disputed him. Moreover, grand jury testimony of William Gurvich, and concurrent statements by James Alcock, confirm that Perry Russo was the basis of Shaw's arrest—not any "second interview" with Shaw. It appears that Garrison invented this additional "incriminating" interview in an effort to obscure the fact that the sole basis for his arrest of Clay Shaw was Russo's unsubstantiated testimony. (Christenberry transcript, pp. 219

[Garrison], 456 [Shaw]; chapter 4, note 28; Gurvich, grand jury transcripts, June 28, 1967, pp. 18–20, and July 12, 1967, p. 62.)

30. p. 145 (168–169)—Garrison claims that he *selected* March 1 as arrest day. That he met with key members of his staff in his office at 5:30 P.M. and when everything was in order he obtained the necessary warrants from a judge who was expecting him. Then, he sent Louis Ivon out to arrest Shaw and also search his home; and Ivon and the others went out and brought Shaw back to the office.

None of this is true. As described in chapter 1, the subpoena for Shaw was issued in the morning. Hearing of it, Shaw voluntarily appeared at the D.A.'s office around noon and stayed there until his arrest several hours later. There is nothing to support the claim that Shaw's arrest was planned beforehand either. The evidence indicates it was a spur-of-the-moment decision, prompted by Shaw's refusal to submit to the testing Garrison requested. In addition to Shaw's unrefuted trial testimony and his testimony at the Christenberry hearing, Garrison's version of *arrest day* is also contradicted in part by Louis Ivon's testimony at both proceedings, and by the following: William Gurvich's statements to the defense team; Salvatore Panzeca and William Wegmann in interviews with the author; and by the local newspaper accounts describing the sequence of events that day at Tulane and Broad. (Shaw, trial transcript, Feb. 20, 1969, pp. 153, 154, Christenberry transcript, pp. 456–462; Ivon, trial transcript, Feb. 19, 1969, pp. 6–8, 13–15, Christenberry transcript, pp. 369–371; Gurvich Conference, p. 15; Dymond et al. Interview; *New Orleans States-Item*, March 1, 1967; *New Orleans Times-Picayune*, March 2, 1967.)

31. p. 145 (169)—Garrison's men did not telephone Salvatore Panzeca. Shaw himself placed the call. After he was told he would be arrested if he didn't take a lie-detector test, Shaw demanded that Garrison's men allow him to speak to his attorney. Shaw first tried to reach Edward F. Wegmann, then his brother William J. Wegmann, and finally he spoke to Salvatore Panzeca.

32. p. 162 (188–189)—Garrison's claim that he told James Phelan what Russo said *before* Russo was subjected to sodium Pentothal and hypnosis is contradicted by, among other things, the chronology of events. The sodium Pentothal was administered before Phelan even arrived in New Orleans. His plane landed the evening of February 27, 1967, and the Pentothal interview occurred earlier that day. The first hypnosis session took place on March 1 and Phelan's first meeting with Garrison was on March 3. Moreover, Garrison didn't "tell" Phelan anything about Russo initially—he *gave* Phelan the transcripts of Russo's interviews to read. That was in Las Vegas on March 5, six days *after* the "verification" process on Russo had begun. (See chapters 6 and 7.)

33. p. 162 (189)—The documentary record is equally clear about Garrison's false claim that Sciambra had obtained all relevant information from Russo before either the sodium Pentothal session or the first hypnosis took place.

Russo's plot that killed the president story was elicited in two basic steps: the sodium Pentothal interview on February 27, 1967, and the hypnosis sessions on March 1 and March 12. Prior to these "medical treatments" the assassination plot story did not exist.

34. pp. 162–163 (188–189)— The narrative on these pages implies that James Phelan was in the picture before management at Life withdrew its support. That is not the case. Garrison turned to Phelan only after he had begun to lose his support at Life, which followed the arrest of Clay Shaw. (See chapter 6.)

35. p. 170 (198)—Garrison dismisses the testimony of John Cancler and Miguel Torres on the grounds that they took the fifth before the grand jury. But Cancler and Torres were familiar with Garrison's MO: they took the fifth because they knew Garrison would charge them with perjury if they answered truthfully.

36. pp. 233–234 (272–273)—None of Shaw's attorneys ever heard of Richard Matthews, the man Garrison describes as part of Shaw's defense team, who supposedly engaged in whispered conversations with Shaw during the entire trial, and who Garrison speculates was Shaw's CIA liaison. William Wegmann, in a letter to the author, dated Dec. 18, 1995, responded to Garrison's charge as follows: "I have no idea who Richard Matthews may have been. . . . The scenario that is set forth is highly unlikely to ever have taken place for any number of reasons. Ed Haggerty ran a good courtroom. The deputy sheriffs assigned to his court would not have permitted the type of activity described because of the disruption it would have had on the trial."

But for Garrison, Matthews served an important literary function in this memoir by providing the otherwise missing link between Clay Shaw and the CIA. If Garrison had written his story as a screenplay, Matthews would be called a "plot point"—an indispensable factor.

37. pp. 236–237 (277)—Since Garrison was told beforehand by one of his assistant district attorneys that Charles Spiesel was "crazy" and Garrison chose to put Spiesel on the stand anyway, it is at best disingenuous of Garrison to accuse the opposing counsel of skulduggery for exposing Spiesel's madness.

38. p. 238 (278)—James Phelan's career was neither brief, nor was it based on Garrison or his key witness, Perry Russo. As a staff writer for The Saturday Evening Post, Phelan's career was flourishing before and after his encounter with Garrison. Nor did Phelan claim that Russo had identified Clay Shaw by mistake; Phelan wrote that Russo's initial interview by Andrew Sciambra didn't contain Russo's conspiracy story, which it did not.

39. p. 243 (284)—Garrison's description of Dean Andrews's testimony gives the impression that Andrews said he actually received a call requesting that he represent Oswald. But Andrews testified that he invented the entire story, that no one asked him to go to Dallas, that it was his own idea. (See chapter 11.)

40. note, p. 243 (284)—Garrison claims that out of concern for Dean Andrews's health, he saved Andrews from his jail sentence first by seeing to it that he was granted a new trial and then dismissing the case when it was returned to his office. But it was Judge Shea who dismissed the charges against Andrews (*New Orleans Times-Picayune*, Aug. 15, 1974). Garrison wasn't even in office at the time. (Harry Connick assumed the office on April 1, 1974).

41. pp. 249-250 (292)—No one was surprised when Clay Shaw testified at his own trial, least of all Garrison, despite what he writes in his memoir. There was never any question that Shaw would take the witness stand. He had been waiting two years to refute Garrison's charges and everyone knew it. Garrison's muddled notion that Shaw should have stayed off the witness stand in order to avoid being questioned about his alleged "relationship with David Ferrie" is nonsense. Shaw based his actions on what he knew to be the truth. If he *had* known Ferrie, Shaw would have been smart enough to admit it at the outset knowing that the D.A.'s office might find witnesses who would expose the relationship. The D.A.'s office never found any credible witnesses to such a relationship because it never existed. Moreover, the damaging cross-examination that Garrison speaks of didn't materialize. Quite the contrary. (See chapter 11.) Garrison here is trying to rewrite what occurred at the trial in order to justify the perjury charges he brought afterwards.

42. p. 250 (293)—The notion that Garrison felt no animosity toward Shaw, after his acquittal, because in plotting to murder President Kennedy Shaw was simply *doing his job*, and in bringing him to trial Garrison was simply *doing his*, is either silly or chilling, depending on whether or not Garrison actually believed what he wrote. Any normal person who believed Shaw was guilty of participating in the conspiracy that killed the president would have been outraged by his acquittal.

43. p. 251 (294)—There is no evidence that Shaw's connection with the Italian Centro Mondiale Commerciale and Permindex were part of a secret life as a high-level international intelligence agent. Shaw explained that his involve-ment with both entities came about when he agreed to serve on the board of directors, and the company then used his name. He said he was unaware of any of its political activities (Phelan–Shaw Interview). Shaw certainly made no effort to keep his association with the group a secret: in 1962 he listed it in the biographical information published in *Who's Who*. Had he been aware of the group's intelligence connection, it seems unlikely that he would have done that.

44. p. 276 (323)—Richard Helms and Victor Marchetti indicated that Shaw had been a *contact* of the CIA's Domestic Contact Service, not that he had been a CIA agent.

45. p. 252 (296)—Garrison lodged *two counts* of perjury against Shaw not one, as Garrison indicates here. He charged that Shaw had testified falsely when he

FALSE WITNESS

said he didn't know David Ferrie or Lee Harvey Oswald. Why Garrison erased
the Oswald half of the perjury charge in his book is unclear, but it is a significant falsification of the record.

46. p. 286 (335)—Garrison denies ever suggesting that oil billionaires from the
southwest financed the assassination. But he did say precisely that, more than
once. In a September 22, 1967, interview in Babylon, Long Island, on Station
WGLI, Garrison said "oil money helped finance" the assassination and he
specifically mentioned a "portion of the Dallas establishment of oil millionaires" (Brener, The Garrison Case, p. 213). On NBC four days later, Garrison stated that the assassination was sponsored by a group of "insanely patriotic oil
millionaires" (Garrison interview, "Mike Wallace at Large," transcript, Sept.
26, 1967). On November 1, 1967, he told a UPI reporter that the Dallas
shooting "was a Nazi operation whose sponsors include some of the oil-rich
millionaires in Texas." That same month, in a speech delivered in Los
Angeles, Garrison said one of the reasons Kennedy was killed was because
he was going after the oil depletion allowance (tax deduction) enjoyed by
the oil interests (Los Angeles Free Press, Nov. 17, 1967).

47. p. 274 (321)—Garrison claims Clay Shaw died under odd circumstances,
raising the possibility of foul play, and suggesting that his name belongs on
the list of mysterious deaths. This final appalling exploitation of Shaw even
in death is, like the rest of Garrison's allegations about Shaw, unsupported by
any evidence. The circumstances of Shaw's tragic death were in no way suspicious. Shaw had been suffering from terminal cancer for some time and,
along with medications, was receiving radiation treatments. Shaw was seen
regularly by his doctor, who visited him the day before he died and found
him in a near coma. The New Orleans Police Department conducted an
inquiry into Shaw's death and their ten-page report thoroughly detailed his
desperate physical condition, his medical appointments, and his physical
decline. It described the excruciating reality of his last days and the moment
he died, which was witnessed by the friend caring for him (Report of Dets.
John Dillmann, Fred Dantagnan and Lt. Robert Mutz, dated Aug. 28, 1974).

APPENDIX B

EDWARD O'DONNELL'S REPORT TO JIM GARRISON

Following is a word-for-word reproduction of Edward O'Donnell's report on the lie-detector test he administered to Perry Russo:

DETECTIVE BUREAU
June 20, 1967

To: Jim Garrison, District Attorney for Parish of Orleans
From: Sgt. Edward O'Donnell
Subject: Perry Russo Interview

Sgt. Edward O'Donnell would report that sometime in the beginning of June 1967 of being summoned to Mr. Andrew Sciambra's office. Upon meeting Mr. Sciambra, in the District Attorney's Office, he requested that I give a polygraph examination to one, Perry Russo. I told him I would be available anytime for this service. He informed me that Perry Russo would like to meet me prior to the taking of this test, as he has had a bad experience with Roy Jacob, who had given him a polygraph test sometime this past year. Mr. Sciambra went on to state that he felt Roy Jacob used improper polygraph technique and had antagonized Perry Russo in doing so.

   On Friday afternoon, at approximately 3:00 P.M., June 16, 1967, Mr. Sciambra brought Perry Russo to the Polygraph Room, located at Police Headquarters. I spoke with Perry Russo for approximately one hour at this time. During this interview, Perry Russo inquired about the nature of the polygraph examination. He wanted to know how it works. I explained the technique to him. He then suggested that I should ask him ten or twelve questions which he would submit to me and that he would purposely lie to some of them and see if I could determine which ones he lied to. I told Perry Russo that to demonstrate the polygraph technique for him to pick a number and write it down on a piece of paper and then put this paper in his pocket and not let me know what number he picked. During the test he was to answer no to all of the questions, forcing him to deliberately lie to the number which

·287·

he picked. This particular type of test is known as a Peak of Tension, type B. This test was concluded and I immediately told Perry Russo the question which he had lied to. Arrangements were then made with Mr. Sciambra and Mr. Perry Russo to have Perry Russo come back within the next few days to take a Standard Polygraph Examination relative to the case in point. It should be noted that while Perry Russo was in the polygraph room at this time, it was impossible to obtain a polygram which could be evaluated. This was because of the subject's erratic pneumograph tracing which could be caused by general nervous tension or by the fact that the person intended to lie during the test. Perry Russo explained that when the tubing was placed on his chest, it caused an uneasy feeling. Perry Russo and Mr. Sciambra then left this office stating that they would contact me within the next few days to conduct further tests.

On Monday, June 19, 1967, at about 1:45 PM, Mr. Sciambra brought Perry Russo to the Polygraph Room. Mr. Sciambra then stepped outside and waited in the Traffic Office. I conducted an interview with Perry Russo from 1:45 P.M. until 3:45 P.M. A great deal of this time was spent by Perry Russo talking about himself and his problems. I wrote out a list of questions which I intended to ask Perry Russo during the examination. These questions are as follows: 1— Were you born in New Orleans? 2—Are you 26 years of age? 3—Do you intend trying to lie to me during this test? 4—Have you told me the complete truth about this matter? 5—Do you smoke cigarettes? 6—Did you know David Ferrie? 7—Were you ever at David Ferrie's apartment on Louisiana Avenue? 8—Do you ever watch TV? 9—Did you ever see Clay Shaw at Ferrie's apartment? 10—while at Ferrie's apartment, did you ever meet a person named Leon Oswald? 11—Do you ever drink coffee? 12—While at Ferrie's apartment, did you hear these people discuss ways to assassinate Kennedy? 13—Did you take part in this discussion? 14—Did you hear Shaw mention the assassination of Kennedy?

The above questions were read to Perry Russo and he was asked if he understood them and if he could answer yes or no to these questions. He stated that he could, that the questions were perfectly clear to him. I then put the necessary attachments on Perry Russo and attempted to give him a Standard Polygraph Examination, using the above mentioned questions. After asking three questions, the test was stopped due to Perry Russo's erratic pneumograph tracing and his physical movements. Upon shutting off the instrument and taking the attachments from Perry Russo's body, the interview continued. Perry Russo expressed that he was under a great deal of pressure and wished that he had never gotten involved in this mess. I told him to forget about the pressures that I only wanted to obtain the truth from him relative to this case. It was explained to him that for his own peace of mind he should examine his conscience and determine what the truth is and once he does this he can stand on the truth now or ten years from now, and not have any misgivings about what he has done. I then told him, you know the questions that I intend to ask you during this test, is there anything you would wish to clarify with me. I then asked him was Clay Shaw at this party, he replied do you want to know the truth, I stated yes, he said I don't know if he was there or not. I told Perry that Shaw was the type of a man that if you were to see him, he would stand out in your mind and I asked him if he would give me a no or yes answer to this question. He stated that if he had to give a yes or no answer, he would have to say no. I then asked him why he went into court and positively identified Shaw as being at this party at David Ferrie's apartment. He stated that Dymond turned him on. The first question Dymond asked me was, do I believe in God. This is an area which I am highly sensitive about. He further stated that prior to going to the preliminary hearing, he was going to state that he did not know if Clay Shaw was at this party or not at this party. He was then asked if this conversation he heard at Dave Ferrie's apartment sounded like a legitimate plot to assassinate Kennedy. He stated, no it did not, it appeared to him like another bull session, like they were always having. He stated that quite frequently he and other people would sit around discussing such topics as the perfect murder or ways of defrauding insurance companies and getting away with it, but this doesn't mean that they would actually do such a thing. He was then asked to describe the conversation which he heard at David Ferrie's apartment and he stated that this was very vague in his mind and at this time he could not say who was saying what. He then expressed a desire to me to meet with Clay Shaw. I asked him what reason he would want such a meeting and he stated he would like to talk to Clay Shaw to size him up to determine if he was the kind of a person that would take part in such a plot. He then expressed a desire to me to know the contents of Mr. Garrison's complete case against Shaw. I asked him why he wanted to know this and he stated this would help him to come to a decision. I then told him that regardless of what Mr. Garrison has or does not have, he should make his own decisions after examining his conscience and determining what the truth is. He then asked me if he could leave and that he would call me later on in the week and he would come back by himself and I could go ahead with the test. I agreed to this and took him outside into the Traffic Office, where he met Mr. Sciambra. I then went upstairs to the District Attorney's Office, where I met Mr. Garrison and Assistant District Attorney Mr. Alcock and informed them of this interview and what I had learned while conducting this interview.

Respectfully Submitted,
Sgt. Edward O'Donnell

NOTES

Abbreviations:
WR: Warren Commission Report (U.S. Government Printing Office edition)
WC Vol.: The 26 volumes of Hearings and Exhibits accompanying the Warren
    Commission Report
CD: Warren Commission Document
HSCA: House Select Committee on Assassinations
HSCA Vol.: The 12 volumes of Hearings and Appendices accompanying the Report
    of the House Select Committee on Assassinations
AARC: Assassination Archives and Research Center

INTRODUCTION

1. L. Fletcher Prouty, *JFK: The CIA, Vietnam, and the Plot to Assassinate John F. Kennedy* (New York: Carol Publishing Group, 1992), "Introduction" by Oliver Stone, p. xiv.
2. Robert Scheer, "Oliver Stone Builds His Own Myths," *Los Angeles Times*, Calendar, Dec. 1991; Oliver Stone, interview with Larry King, March 23, 1996.
3. It may be that Harold Weisberg was not the only one maneuvering. Reportedly, in the fall of 1990, Stone was responsible for killing the movie based on Don DeLillo's book *Libra*, though Stone denies the charge. The script had been optioned by A&M Films; Phil Joanou had signed on to direct. According to writer Robert Sam Anson, the script was shorter and easier to shoot than Stone's, meaning that Joanou's project, if it proceeded, would probably beat Stone's to the marketplace. But it didn't proceed. Allegedly, people at Stone's agency (then headed by Mike Ovitz, said to be the most powerful man in Hollywood at the time) warned actors who had been interested "against questionable career moves," and they withdrew. Supposedly, Stone himself called the director, and he too backed away from the project. Stone has claimed the *Libra* script just wasn't good enough to make the grade and that no single person could kill a project in Hollywood (Robert Sam Anson, "The Shooting of JFK," *Esquire*, Nov. 1991, pp. 101, 102). Yet a movie project can fall apart for the slightest reason, and there was nothing slight about the forces arrayed against *Libra*.
4. David Baron, "Oliver's Story," *New Orleans Times-Picayune*, Lagniappe, May 24, 1991.
5. Brent Staples, "History by Default: The Blame Transcends Oliver Stone," *New York Times*, Dec. 25, 1991, in *JFK: The Book of the Film* (New York: Applause Books, 1992), pp. 311–312.
6. George F. Will, "Oliver Stone Gives Paranoia a Bad Name," *Los Angeles Times*, Dec. 24, 1991.

7. The four occasions: David Ferrie's death; Perry Russo's story exposed as a fraud by writer James Phelan; Clay Shaw's acquittal; the 1971 decision by federal Judge Herbert W. Christenberry.

CHAPTER ONE

1. James Phelan, "Clay Shaw," interview (hereinafter Phelan–Shaw Interview), *Penthouse*, Nov. 1969.
2. Clay Shaw, "Journal" (hereinafter Shaw Journal), p. 11; *New Orleans Times-Picayune*, March 2, 1967; Phelan–Shaw Interview.
3. Shaw Journal, pp. 12–14; Phelan–Shaw Interview; *New Orleans Times-Picayune*, March 2, 1967.
4. Shaw Journal, pp. 14–15; James Kirkwood, "Surviving," *Esquire*, Dec. 1968; Phelan–Shaw Interview. Shaw later recalled the test requested was a lie-detector test. But Salvatore Panzeca also said the first test Garrison mentioned to him was truth serum (F. Irvin Dymond, William J. Wegmann and Salvatore Panzeca, interview with author, Sept. 3, 1993 [hereinafter Dymond et al. Interview]).
5. Shaw Journal, pp. 15–16; Dymond et al. Interview.
6. Dymond et al. Interview.
7. Shaw Journal, pp. 14–16; Dymond et al. Interview.
8. Dymond et al. Interview; Shaw Journal, pp. 15–16; William Gurvich, grand jury testimony, June 28, 1967, pp. 18–20; Milton Brener, telephone conversation with author, Feb. 7, 1994. Regarding Garrison's decision to arrest Shaw, Brener said, "Shaw defied him," referring to Shaw's refusal to take the test Garrison requested.
9. Dymond et al. Interview; Shaw Journal, pp. 16–17; *New Orleans Times-Picayunee*, March 2, 1967.
10. Shaw Journal, p. 16; *New Orleans Times-Picayune*, March 2, 1967.
11. Cynthia Wegmann, interview with author, Nov. 3, 1993; Shaw Journal, p. 17.
12. Shaw Journal, p. 17; William J. Wegmann, telephone conversation with author, July 23, 1998; *New Orleans Times-Picayune*, March 2, 1967; Dymond et al. Interview.
13. Shaw Journal, pp. 17–19; Christenberry transcript, pp. 373 (Louis Ivon), 462 (Clay Shaw); *New Orleans Times-Picayune*, March 2, 1967.

CHAPTER TWO

1. Jim Garrison, *On the Trail of the Assassins: My Investigation and Prosecution of the Murder of President Kennedy* (New York: Sheridan Square Press, 1988), p 8.
2. FBI Memorandum, dated June 21, 1967, from W. A. Branigan to W. C. Sullivan. Earling R. Garrison's FBI Identification Division Record Number was 268658 (FBIHQ Main File 67-446884, James Carothers Garrison). See also "Records of Birth, Crawford County, Iowa," p. 86; *History of Crawford County Iowa*, Vol. 2, pp. 67–69 (in the archives of the State Historical Society of Iowa); "Earling Garrison Lodged in Jail Here Sunday," *Denison Review*, April 23, 1930; "Judge Peter S. Klinker Holds Court Here Sat.," *The Denison Bulletin*, April 30, 1930.

NOTES

3. Pershing Gervais, telephone conversation with author, March 15, 1994.
4. FBI Report by J. M. Lopez, regarding James Carothers Garrison, Bureau Applicant—Special Agent, Jan. 13, 1951. (FBIHQ Main File 67-446884, James Carothers Garrison.)
5. When Garrison was making headlines about the Kennedy assassination sixteen years later, an enterprising agent noticed that five years after leaving the FBI Garrison wrote about his father on a military form: "address 'unknown.'" This anomaly prompted a routine identification check that turned up Earling R. Garrison and his criminal record.
6. Judith Dorcas Garrison had been confined sometime prior to 1951 (see Jim Garrison's 1951 military medical history). One year later, after his background investigation had been completed and he had been accepted by the Bureau, Garrison listed his sister's name on one of his FBI appointment forms.
7. Jim Garrison, military medical history, 1951.
8. Dymond et al. Interview.
9. New Orleans Times-Picayune, Jan. 15, 1962; Milton E. Brener, The Garrison Case: A Study in the Abuse of Power (New York: Clarkson N. Potter, Inc., 1969), p. 5.
10. James Phelan, "The Vice Man Cometh," The Saturday Evening Post, June 1963.
11. Rosemary James and Jack Wardlaw, Plot or Politics?: The Garrison Case And Its Cast (New Orleans: Pelican Publishing House, 1967), p. 19.
12. Brener, The Garrison Case, p. 6. In the acrimonious run-off campaign that followed, both men leveled charges at each other. Garrison, in the first notable public display of his sensitivity to criticism, filed a libel suit against Dowling.
13. Garrison's victory in the general election was a foregone conclusion. As explained in the New Orleans Times-Picayune on March 5, 1962: "Winning the Democratic primary in New Orleans, has been tantamount to election since the Reconstruction era of the last century."
14. David Chandler, "The Devil's D.A.," New Orleans magazine, Nov. 1966, p. 31; Gene Roberts, "The Case of Jim Garrison and Lee Oswald," The New York Times Magazine, May 21, 1967, p. 33. One of Pershing Gervais's "infractions" was stealing Police Department graft money twice and blowing it on two heady first-class trips to New York City.
15. Chandler, "The Devil's D.A.," p. 32.
16. Roberts, "The Case of Jim Garrison and Lee Oswald," p. 33.
17. James and Wardlaw, Plot or Politics? p. 22; Brener, The Garrison Case, pp. 24, 25, 33.
18. Dymond et al. Interview.
19. David Chandler believed Garrison originally was a genuine reformer but that "something happened" during the summer of 1966 which changed him. Chandler insisted that the evidence of Garrison's organized crime connections, which were spelled out in a series of Life magazine articles published in the fall of 1967, was conclusive (David Chandler, telephone interview with author [hereinafter Chandler Interview], July 15, 1993).
20. Jack Wardlaw had previously published the first national article on Garrison in the National Observer (James and Wardlaw, Plot or Politics? p. 32).
21. Brener, The Garrison Case, pp. 2–3.

CHAPTER THREE

1. Jack Martin, Mercy Hospital records, December 27, 1956. Martin made the remark during his psychiatric confinement.
2. Dean Andrews, Clay Shaw trial testimony, Feb. 25, 1969, p. 142.
3. W. Guy Banister, "Biographical Sketch," HSCA Vol. 10, pp. 126–127.
4. This account is based solely on Jack Martin's version of the event, as recorded in New Orleans Police Department Report No. K-12634-63, dated Nov. 25, 1963.
5. Sam Newman, Affidavit, Jan. 24, 1967.
6. W. Hardy Davis, FBI interview, Nov. 27, 1963.
7. Jerry Phillip Stein, FBI interview, Nov. 25, 1963; Secret Service Report, December 13, 1963 (describing telephone calls from Stein and Donald Mitchell); Alec Gifford (WDSU), FBI interview, Nov. 25, 1963; David Ferrie, FBI interviews, Nov. 25, 1963, and Nov. 27, 1963; Jack S. Martin, FBI interview, Nov. 25, 1963; and G. Wray Gill, FBI interview, Nov. 27, 1963.
8. The police, who knew Martin, ignored his call, but television news director Bill Reid sent two representatives to David Ferrie's apartment. They began making inquiries in the neighborhood after learning from Ferrie's house guest that Ferrie was gone. Reid also contacted Ferrie's employer, attorney G. Wray Gill, and informed him about Ferrie's "possible involvement" with Oswald (Reid, FBI interview, Nov. 25, 1963; Martin, FBI interview, Nov. 27, 1963; Ferrie, FBI interview, Nov. 25, 1963; Gill, FBI interview, Nov. 27, 1963).
9. Jim Garrison and Pershing Gervais had been the object of a lawsuit filed by Martin the previous summer, which Martin later withdrew.
10. Jack Martin reached Herman Kohlman at home. (Martin insisted that his name be withheld, and Kohlman honored this promise at first, until he was pressed by his superior. Kohlman also was forced to reveal Martin's identity to the Secret Service.) A meeting was convened at Tulane and Broad to decide what should be done. Garrison wasn't there but "was kept informed." According to Kohlman, the local Secret Service didn't seem concerned about Martin's "information" until Kohlman called Dallas Homicide Chief Will Fritz. Kohlman later learned that a Dallas FBI police liaison contacted Washington concerning the information. After that, Kohlman said, the local FBI and Secret Service representatives were suddenly interested (Kohlman, telephone conversation with author, July 29, 1996).
11. New Orleans Secret Service Field Office Report, regarding investigation in New Orleans during period of "Nov. 24–29, 1963," dated Dec. 13, 1963, pp. 1–3. Herman Kohlman's telephone call to the Secret Service at 11:10 P.M. on Nov. 24, 1963, is described in this report. While Jack Martin told the FBI he spoke to Kohlman on Saturday, Nov. 23, it is clear from the Secret Service chronology of calls from Kohlman, Jerry Stein and Donald Mitchell, and the FBI interview with Stein, that Martin did not reach Kohlman until Sunday, Nov. 24, 1963, sometime after 10 A.M. (see also CD 87, item 61).
12. A number of people remembered Ferrie being in court on Nov. 22, 1963, including the presiding judge, Herbert W. Christenberry, FBI agent Regis

NOTES

Kennedy, and attorney G. Wray Gill (Herbert W. Christenberry, Jr., telephone conversation with author, Aug. 16, 1997; HSCA Vol. 10, p. 105). Also, in early 1967 William Gurvich was told by a federal marshal present at the trial that Ferrie was there.

13. At least a week before, Alvin Beaubouef had suggested going ice skating. He was a near-championship-class roller skater but had never been on ice skates and Ferrie had promised him that, at the conclusion of the trial, they would go ice skating (Ferrie, FBI interview, Nov. 25, 1963; Beaubouef, interviews by New Orleans D.A.'s office, Dec. 15, 1966, and Dec. 28, 1966; Melvin Coffey, FBI interview, Nov. 29, 1963; Beaubouef, interview with author, Sept. 5, 1993 [hereinafter Beaubouef Interview]).

14. Chuck Rolland, FBI interview, Nov. 28, 1963 (Ferrie's call to the skating rink); Ferrie, FBI interview, Nov. 25, 1963; Beaubouef Interview.

15. Ferrie, FBI interview, Nov. 25, 1963; Gill, FBI interview, Nov. 27, 1963.

16. Brener, *The Garrison Case*, p. 51; Ferrie, interview by New Orleans D.A.'s Office, Feb. 18, 1967.

17. Alvin Beaubouef, telephone conversation with author, July 9, 1998; Fenner Sedgebeer report (signed by Raymond Comstock) to Joseph I. Giarrusso, Superintendent of Police, Nov. 25, 1963, describing arrest of Beaubouef, Martens and Ferrie. The police also recovered from Ferrie's apartment "a page from a yellow pad" said to detail Ferrie's flying Carlos Marcello from Guatemala (where he had been unceremoniously deported by the U.S. government) "back into the United States." This was turned over to the FBI (Comstock, telephone interview with author, March 27, 1996).

18. New Orleans Secret Service Field Office Report, regarding investigation in New Orleans during period of "Nov. 24–29, 1963," dated Dec. 13, 1963, p. 4; Fenner Sedgebeer report, p. 2. Herman Kohlman would later tell FBI Agent Regis Kennedy that "an unknown police officer," reportedly in the Civil Air Patrol with Oswald, had said "that Ferrie knew Oswald" and "because Ferrie must have known Oswald and because it appeared [Ferrie] had lied when he denied knowing Oswald, Ferrie was arrested." But when the "unknown police officer," Vice Squad detective Frederick O'Sullivan, was interviewed that same day by the FBI, he said he thought Oswald had attended CAP meetings during the same time-frame that Ferrie was Squadron Commander but "could not say for certain that Oswald ever met Ferrie" (Fred O'Sullivan, FBI interviews, Nov. 25, 1963, and Nov. 26, 1963).

19. Ferrie, FBI interviews, Nov. 25, 1963, and Nov. 27, 1963; Ferrie, Secret Service interview, Nov. 25, 1963, described in Secret Service Report dated Dec. 13, 1963. Ferrie said that "to the best of his knowledge Oswald was never a member of the CAP Squadron in New Orleans during the period he was with that group." Shown some photographs of Oswald, Ferrie stated "that the profile view . . . has a very vague familiarity to him but the full face and full length photographs of Oswald are not familiar to him." When he was arrested, David Ferrie's New Orleans Public Library card # M.L. 89437 was among his personal items placed in the police department property room. It was returned to him when he was released and he showed it to the FBI agents who interviewed him on Nov. 27, 1963.

20. The manager of Winterland Skating Rink, Chuck Rolland, said that he and Ferrie "had a short general conversation" but denied that they discussed "the cost of equipping or operating an ice skating rink" (Rolland, FBI interview, Nov. 28, 1963). But Melvin Coffey told the FBI that Ferrie did talk to the "owner" of the rink about the cost of "installation and operation" (Coffey, FBI interview, Nov. 29, 1963).

21. Jack Martin also outlined his version of how it all came about, how he had seen rifles in David Ferrie's home; had heard on television that Oswald was in the CAP; and knew that Ferrie had been in the CAP too. Martin, the agents wrote, "after turning all these thoughts over in his mind" telephoned the D.A.'s office "and told his story as though it was based on facts rather than on his imagination" (Martin, Secret Service Interview, Nov. 29, 1963).

22. Jack Martin claimed that his speculation about David Ferrie began that Saturday evening when he saw the television program that revealed Oswald had been in the CAP with Ferrie. But Martin saw that broadcast *after* he and Hardy Davis had already engaged in their initial conjecture about Ferrie. After Davis went home, Martin telephoned "and told him that he heard a television program which had tied Ferrie in as Civil Air Patrol instructor with Lee Harvey Oswald" (Hardy Davis, FBI interview, Nov. 27, 1963; Martin, FBI interview, Nov. 25, 1963).

23. Gill and Ferrie, himself, both ventured explanations for Martin's actions, but neither of them had any way of knowing about the beating. Gill said "that Ferrie and Martin were once close friends, until they got involved in an 'ecclesiastical' deal." When Martin did not get a job he wanted with "the Holy Apostolic Catholic Church of North America," he blamed Ferrie and had "slandered" him "at every opportunity" (Gill, FBI interview, Nov. 27, 1963). Ferrie said that in June of 1963, at Gill's direction, he had "put Martin out" of Gill's office in an "undiplomatic" manner, and since then Martin had "bedeviled" him "in every manner possible" (Ferrie, FBI interview, Nov. 25, 1963).

24. Edward Stewart Suggs, FBI information sheet, June 21, 1968; FBI Memorandum, "Jack S. Martin also known as Edward Stewart Suggs," dated March 22, 1967, forwarded to the White House on March 24, 1967; "Informative Note," dated March 10, 1967, attached to FBI Airtel dated March 8, 1967, from SAC New Orleans to the Director; Jack Martin, Mercy Hospital records, dated Dec. 23, 1956, to Jan. 28, 1957. "[Jack Martin] had a way of breathing up stories and being very positive about things," Pershing Gervais said. "He would concoct things about someone and then he would talk to that someone" and construct a story "that would kind of jibe." Martin was "pretty good at that." When asked about Martin's reliability, Gervais laughed. "He couldn't be reliable if he intended to be" (Gervais, telephone conversation with author, Sept. 3, 1993).

25. Ferrie, FBI interview, Nov. 25, 1963.

26. Prentiles M. Davis, interview by New Orleans D.A.'s office, March 9, 1967; Memorandum by Louis Ivon re information from Joe Oster on March 6, 1967; R. M. Davis, FBI interview, Dec. 5, 1963. Dean Andrews referred to Davis in his Warren Commission testimony as "Preston M. Davis"; "R. M. Davis," the name in his FBI report, is used in this book.

27. Andrews, Clay Shaw trial testimony, p. 132.
28. *Ibid.*, p. 131.
29. WC Vol. VII, p. 329; WC Vol. III, pp. 85–86. On Saturday, Nov. 23, 1963, Oswald asked the president of the Dallas Bar Association, H. Louis Nichols, for help engaging Abt on his behalf; that same day Oswald made the same request of Ruth Paine.
30. Dr. J. B. Andrews, FBI interview, Dec. 5, 1963. The doctor said that Dean Andrews was under heavy sedation the first four days, i.e., Nov. 20 to Nov. 24, 1963.
31. The dialogue was reconstructed from Eva Springer's FBI interview of Dec. 5, 1963. Dean Andrews would later remember receiving the Bertrand telephone call between 6:00 and 9:00 P.M. that Saturday. But Eva Springer said Andrews's call to her about representing Oswald occurred "shortly after four" in the afternoon, and she tied her recollection to her marketing, which she had just completed. (Andrews also had no recollection of his investigator's visit to the hospital that same day.) Since Eva Springer's recollection, which places the Bertrand call prior to four o'clock, is more reliable, the reconstruction in this chapter is based on it. Since the call from Eugene Davis to Andrews occurred *after* R. M. Davis departed (at 3:30 P.M.) and *before* Andrews phoned his secretary (at 4:00 P.M.), the call could only have occurred between 3:30 and 4:00 P.M. (R. M. Davis, FBI interview, Dec. 5, 1963; Andrews, FBI interview, Dec. 5, 1963.)
32. Dean Andrews later told the FBI that the "first independent recollection" he had of his stay in the hospital was the evening of Saturday, Nov. 23, 1963, watching a television program about Oswald's life in New Orleans (Andrews, FBI interview, Dec. 5, 1963, p. 2).
33. Andrews, Clay Shaw trial testimony, p. 132.
34. The dialogue was reconstructed from Sam "Monk" Zelden's FBI interview of Nov. 25, 1963, and the following: Andrews, FBI interview, Dec. 3, 1963; WC Vol. XI, p. 337. Sometime that day, R. M. Davis again stopped by to see Andrews and during that visit Andrews told Davis about the call from "Clay Bertrand" (R. M. Davis, FBI interview, Dec. 5, 1963).
35. In 1969 Milton Brener, who knew and interviewed Dean Andrews, was the first to go on record suggesting that Andrews's Oswald-was-my-client story was bogus. "Circumstances strongly suggest that Andrews may never really have laid eyes on Oswald," Brener wrote (Brener, *The Garrison Case*, p. 58).
36. Secret Service Report, regarding interview with Andrews, Dec. 6, 1963; Andrews, Clay Shaw trial testimony. Andrews told Warren Commission attorney Wesley Liebeler that Oswald had wanted to institute citizenship proceedings for his wife (WC Vol. XI, p. 327), which is contrary to what we know was going on in the Oswald marriage. Even today, Marina Oswald Porter is not an American citizen. Moreover, if Oswald had had a relationship with Andrews, Oswald most likely would have contacted him on Aug. 9, 1963, when he was involved in a street scuffle in New Orleans (while handing out Fair Play for Cuba leaflets) and arrested; to his dismay, Oswald was forced to spend the night in jail.
37. The companions who supposedly accompanied Oswald to Dean Andrews's office are entirely inconsistent with what we know about Oswald's life and his

lifestyle. While in Russia Oswald was more social, but in this country he was a loner. No one else has described him going about with any sort of crowd, much less a group of overtly homosexual men. Not one scrap of paper, nor any credible testimony was ever produced to support this tale. Andrews probably peopled his Oswald fantasy with gay men because that was the clientele Andrews was accustomed to representing. Like any good storyteller, Andrews stayed with what he knew.

38. Dean Andrews's uncontrollable loquaciousness was part of his defense at his later perjury trial. If Lee Harvey Oswald, this infamous man-of-the-hour, whose life story was being trumpeted on television, had actually been in Andrews's office the previous summer, Andrews would have talked about it that weekend to everyone who entered his hospital room—the doctors, the nurses, the person who emptied his trash. *Lee Harvey Oswald: I know that cat!* But he didn't even tell his investigator, his secretary, or Monk Zelden. When he called Eva Springer on Saturday he didn't say, *You won't believe this: Lee Harvey Oswald consulted me last summer; the accused presidential assassin sat in my office, not once, but several times telling me his problems!* He said not one word about it. When his investigator visited earlier that same day, they discussed Andrews's political campaign. On Sunday when he called Monk Zelden, Andrews was still mute about it. The next day Andrews again failed to inform his investigator. The story first surfaced on Monday, Nov. 25, 1963, when Andrews called the FBI and the Secret Service, twenty-four hours *after* Oswald was shot and killed. (In 1967, in an apparent effort to help Andrews in his difficulties with Garrison, investigator Davis would make statements to the D.A.'s office that conflicted with his earlier FBI interviews and with statements made by Andrews himself to the Warren Commission regarding Davis's knowledge about the alleged Oswald visits. See Prentiles M. Davis, Jr., interview by New Orleans D.A.'s office, March 9, 1967.)

39. Andrews, FBI interview, Nov. 25, 1963; Secret Service Report, regarding interview with Andrews, Dec. 5, 1963.

40. Andrews, FBI interview, Dec. 3, 1963. Investigator Davis told the FBI that "he has no doubt that Andrews is now convinced that the call he received at the hospital was a dream" (R. M. Davis, FBI interview, Dec. 5, 1963).

41. WC Vol. XI, pp. 326, 338.

42. Ibid., pp. 334, 337. Dean Andrews told Wesley Liebeler that Bertrand was "about five feet eight inches" tall, "sandy hair, blue eyes, ruddy complexion"; on Dec. 3, 1963, in his statement to the FBI, Bertrand had been six feet one inch to six feet two inches tall, with "brown hair"; and on Nov. 25, 1963, in Andrews's earliest description to the FBI, Bertrand had been "youthful," twenty-two to twenty-three years old, five feet seven inches tall, with blonde crew-cut hair.

43. WC Vol. XI, p. 334.

44. The claim by some that Dean Andrews told Mark Lane about "Bertrand" is not supported by the record. According to Lane, in March 1966 Andrews refused to be interviewed on the subject because he had been threatened (*New Orleans Times-Picayune*, March 29, 1967).

45. Report of the President's Commission on the Assassination of President John F. Kennedy (Washington: U.S. Government Printing Office: 1964), p. 325. The

paragraph, most of which was devoted to the alleged consultations with Oswald, pointed out that "Andrews was able to locate no records of any of Oswald's alleged visits, and investigation has failed to locate the person who supposedly called Andrews on Nov. 23, at a time when Andrews was under heavy sedation." The name "Clay Bertrand" was not mentioned.

CHAPTER FOUR

1. James Kirkwood, *American Grotesque: An Account of the Clay Shaw-Jim Garrison Affair in the City of New Orleans* (New York: Simon and Schuster, 1970), p. 527.
2. Brener, *The Garrison Case,* p. 61. Brener gives the date of the first dinner as Oct. 27, 1966. In a damage suit Andrews filed against Garrison on April 18, 1967, Andrews specified the date as Oct. 29, 1966 (*New Orleans Times-Picayune,* April 19, 1967; Dean Andrews, NBC Interview, Metropolitan Crime Commission transcript [hereinafter Andrews NBC interview], undated).
3. Andrews NBC interview; Edward Jay Epstein, *Counterplot* (New York: The Viking Press, Inc., 1969), p. 93.
4. An article in *New Orleans* magazine claimed the Long–Garrison conversation occurred in Nov. 1966 ("The Garrison Investigation: How and why it began," April 1967). But the earliest recorded reference to the conversation is Sen. Long's statement that it occurred "last Oct. [1966]" (*New Orleans Times-Picayune,* Feb., 22, 1967). This supports Andrews's claim that his first dinner with Garrison was in October.
5. David Chandler, "The Devil's D.A.," pp. 90–91 (the article); Chandler Interview (the reaction). Before writing it, Chandler had visited Garrison and told him what he had been hearing but Garrison gave no credence to it. Chandler told this writer he wrote the piece to try to bring Garrison to his senses.
6. David Chandler, "The Assassin's Trail," *Westword,* Nov. 25–Dec. 1, 1992.
7. John Connally stated that he was hit by a bullet fired *after* the first one that struck the president. Since the time available was insufficient for Oswald to have fired the second shot that hit Connally, a second gunman was implicit.
8. Richard J. Whalen, "The Kennedy Assassination," *The Saturday Evening Post,* Jan. 14, 1967, pp. 22, 69.
9. "The Garrison Investigation: How and why it began," *New Orleans* magazine, April 1967, pp. 8, 50–51; Epstein, *Counterplot,* p. 41.
10. Andrews NBC Interview; Epstein, *Counterplot,* pp. 93–94.
11. Garrison, *On the Trail of the Assassins,* pp. 31–32; Jack Martin, interview with Pershing Gervais and Louis Ivon, at the Fontainebleau Motor Motel (hereinafter Martin Fontainebleau Interview), transcript, December 13, 1966 (AARC); Martin, "Statement" to Jim Garrison, December 26, 1966; see also cassette tape recording (contents unknown) labeled "Martin interview by J. Garrison," December 14, 1966.
12. Garrison, *On the Trail of the Assassins,* pp. 39–40. Garrison's memoir is stunningly unreliable but this admission of Martin's influence is supported by other documents that have survived (see notes 11 and 13, and chapter 16, note 10). That often-heard refrain, "Garrison must have something" applies here. He *did*

have something he withheld: his secret meetings with Martin. While Garrison was listening to Martin and, according to Louis Ivon, paying only Martin's "expenses" (Ivon, interview with author, Feb. 27, 1996), Garrison was denying to the press that he was doing either (Merriman Smith, "JFK Plot Quiz: Seamy Suspects," *Los Angeles Herald-Examiner*, March 5, 1967).

13. One of Martin's assignments was to establish liaison with Houston law enforcement (see undated handwritten letter on "Bellemont Motor Hotel" stationery from Martin to "Jim and Lou," i.e., Garrison and Ivon). Another job was to telephone certain people and, in part, elicit damaging statements while recording the call. The newsmen didn't bite ("We don't buy information," local reporter Richard Townley said over and over) and Aaron Kohn's lament, wearily repeated time and again, was for Martin to "stop playing games" and "finally tell the truth" (Jack Martin, telephone conversations with Aaron Kohn [7], Richard Townley [7], Walter Sheridan [1], Steve Plotkin [1], Anthony Garrich [1], Richard Robey [1], and Louis Ivon [1], transcripts, May 25, 1967 to Nov. 22, 1967).

14. Beaubouef Interview.

15. David Ferrie, interview with Asst. D.A. John Volz, December 15, 1966.

16. Epstein, *Counterplot*, p. 92. In Jack Martin's Fontainebleau Interview, when Pershing Gervais asked if Sergio Arcacha Smith was "a Latin type kid with a crewcut" (apparently fishing for information about the "Mexican" invented by Dean Andrews who supposedly accompanied Oswald everywhere), Martin replied, "that's [Morris] Brownlee"; "he's Jewish but he looks Latin American and speaks Spanish." This perhaps explains why Garrison pursued Brownlee so relentlessly.

17. Chandler, "The Devil's D.A."; Chandler, "The Assassin's Trail"; Chandler Interview. The "mutual acquaintance" was photographer Matt Herron.

18. Chandler, "The Assassin's Trail," p. 18.

19. Chandler Interview. Chandler recalled Billings's arrival date as December 7, 1966, and tied his recollection to Pearl Harbor; but Billings remembered the date as December 14, 1966 (Tom Bethell, "Excerpts from a Diary kept while working in the district attorney's office during the investigation of Kennedy's assassination" [hereinafter Bethell Diary], p. 42).

20. Chandler, "The Assassin's Trail," p. 19; Chandler Interview.

21. Chandler, "The Assassin's Trail"; Chandler Interview.

22. Chandler, "The Assassin's Trail"; Chandler Interview.

23. Edward F. Wegmann, address at dedication of Clay Shaw's Spanish Stables memorial in 1975; "Biographical Sketch of Clay L. Shaw" (hereinafter Shaw Biographical Sketch), three pages, undated; Phelan-Shaw Interview; Brener, *The Garrison Case*, p. 63; Kirkwood, *American Grotesque*, pp. 18, 19; the *New Orleans Times-Picayune*, Feb. 28, 1994; Dymond et al. Interview.

24. Shaw Biographical Sketch; Phelan–Shaw Interview; Dymond, et al. Interview. Shaw saw the non-profit Trade Mart as more than an opportunity to promote foreign trade through the Port of New Orleans. The war had instilled in him a concern for world peace. That could be strengthened, he believed, by closer relations between nations; understanding each other was the key, and trade was one way to bring that about (Kirkwood, *American Grosteque*, p. 18).

NOTES

25. Shaw Biographical Sketch; Phelan–Shaw Interview; "Carter," teletype to *Newsweek*, March 2, 1967.
26. Brener, *The Garrison Case*, pp. 61–62, vii (Gonzales narcotics charge); Memorandum, "Dean Andrews/Richard Townley," regarding April 19, 1967, conversation between Robert A. Wilson, Charles R. Carson, Richard Townley and Dean Andrews at the New Orleans Press Club; Andrews NBC Interview; Epstein, *Counterplot*, p. 94. Garrison believed that Gonzales appeared in pictures taken of Oswald as he handed out Fair Play for Cuba leaflets on Canal Street ("Carter," teletype to *Newsweek*, March 2, 1967).
27. Shaw Journal, pp. 3–5; Shaw, NBC interview, Metropolitan Crime Commission transcript (hereinafter Shaw NBC interview), undated; Brener, *The Garrison Case*, p. 64; Kirkwood, *American Grotesque*, pp. 19, 20.
28. Gurvich Conference, p. 14. The two newsmen Gurvich named—to whom Garrison exonerated Shaw—were "Bill" at WWL in New Orleans and Joe Wershba in New York.

CHAPTER FIVE

1. "Carter," teletype to *Newsweek*, March 2, 1967; "Dick Billings[,] personal notes on consultations and interviews with Garrison" (hereinafter Billings Personal Notes), p. 5 (AARC).
2. Tom Bethell, Memorandum to Garrison, Feb. 16, 1968 (living together); Brener, *The Garrison Case*, pp. 67 ("psychiatric" reasons), 69, 75, 85, 119; FBI, Memorandum to Mildred Stegall, The White House, March 24, 1967, David Lewis attachment, p. 2 (plastic gun); Lewis, NBC interview, undated transcript (Martin's urging).
3. *Los Angeles Times*, Feb. 23, 1967; David Lewis, interview with David Chandler, Jan. 21, 1967; Lewis, Statement to D.A.'s office, Dec. 15, 1966, Q & A transcript attached; James and Wardlaw, *Plot or Politics?* p. 49; *Los Angeles Herald-Examiner*, Feb. 23, 1967.
4. *Los Angeles Herald Examiner*, March, 5, 1967 (reporter declined); James and Wardlaw, *Plot or Politics?* p. 49 (primary witness); FBI, Memorandum to Mildred Stegall, The White House, March 24, 1967, Martin attachment, p. 3 ("information 'made up'": Martin's statement was reported by Ray Berg, president of Pacesetter Publishing Co.); Carlos Quiroga, interview with Jim Garrison, Jan. 21, 1967; Sergio Arcacha Smith, statement to the press, April 1, 1967 (denied it); Garrison, memorandum, "Investigative Assignments," Jan. 7, 1967, p. 2.
5. Gurvich Conference, Tape #2, p. 21.
6. Ibid., pp. 17–18; Kirkwood, *American Grotesque*, p. 538.
7. Chandler Interview.
8. *New Orleans States-Item*, "'M'Keithen Agent,' Chandler Tells Judges," Nov. 8, 1967 (subpoena); James and Wardlaw, *Plot or Politics?* p. 50; Chandler, "The Assassin's Trail" ("Get yourself a lawyer"); Chandler Interview (two factions). In addition to Malcolm McCombs (a "legendary *Life* editor"), Chandler named two other *Life* journalists who supported his position: Russ Sackett, "at the time an editor at the same level as Billings, working in New York, and Sandy Smith who at that time

was a contract hire from Chicago who specialized in organized crime." Both men came in and out of New Orleans, Chandler said, "to monitor things and [they] did not report to Billings."

9. James and Wardlaw, *Plot or Politics?* pp. 33–34 (James–Garrison conversation); James Phelan (quoting Rosemary James), interview with author, June 8, 1993 (hereinafter Phelan Interview); Rosemary James, filmed interview with Stephen Tyler, "He Must Have Something," 1992 ("print it"); Nicholas C. Chriss, "New Orleans Paper and DA at Odds Over Assassination Story," *Los Angeles Times*, Feb. 21, 1967 ("Go ahead": quoting *New Orleans States-Item* Managing Editor Walter G. Cowen).

10. *New Orleans Times-Picayune*, Feb. 18, 1967 ("unprintable phrase"); Nicholas C. Chriss, "New Orleans Paper and DA at Odds Over Assassination Story," *Los Angeles Times*, Feb. 21, 1967 ("substantially correct": quoting *New Orleans States-Item* Managing Editor Walter G. Cowen).

11. David Snyder, teletype to Time, Inc., Feb. 24, 1967 (AARC); Snyder, interview with author (hereinafter Snyder Interview), Sept. 4, 1993.

12. Dr. Ronald A. Welsh, interview with author, Dec. 1, 1993 (hereinafter Welsh Interview). Dr. Welsh stated that the microscopic slides showed that in addition to vessel perforating there was "scar tissue indicating that Ferrie had had another bleed, a small one, previously . . . at least one or two of them at least two weeks before he died. This is a common occurrence with berry aneurysms," Welsh said, "people have one or two before they blow out completely. . . . His headaches were from the . . . early bleeds."

13. Snyder Interview; *New Orleans States-Item*, Feb. 18, 1967; *New Orleans Times-Picayune*, Feb. 19, 1967, Feb. 23, 1967. Ferrie went a step further the following day— to another reporter he said Garrison's investigation was "a big joke."

14. Kirkwood, *American Grotesque*, p. 530 ("best defense": Aaron Kohn quoting Jim Garrison); "Garrison Predicts Success for Probe," *New Orleans Times-Picayune*, Feb. 19, 1967; "Oswald Didn't Act Alone, DA Says," *Los Angeles Times*, Feb. 19, 1967.

15. *New Orleans Times-Picayune*, Feb. 20, 1967.

16. *New Orleans Times-Picayune*, Feb. 21, 1967.

17. Aaron Kohn, managing director of the Metropolitan Crime Commission, who knew Garrison well, said about him: "He's a man who easily feels threatened. No matter how unreal it might look to other people, to him he is alarmingly threatened. And it may well be that he engages in extravagant diversions when he's threatened" (Kirkwood, *American Grotesque*, p. 530).

18. Garrison claimed the Ferrie surveillance "was secured" at 11:00 P.M., after Ferrie went to bed, but James Alcock said he and Louis Ivon were there "all night," and that is the reason they were the first ones on the scene from the district attorney's office the next day (James Alcock, interview with author, Dec. 3, 1993 [hereinafter Alcock Interview]). Alcock's account fits with George Lardner's statement that Ferrie's light was on when he arrived at midnight.

19. David W. Ferrie, Autopsy Protocol, Orleans Parish Coroner's Office, Feb. 22, 1967; Welsh Interview.

20. When Garrison learned about Ferrie's association with this church, he developed an expansive theory about the use of fringe religions as fronts by the CIA and sug-

gested the CIA might have corrupted "legitimate churches" as well (Garrison, Memorandum to Louis Ivon, Feb. 6, 1968, re "Old Churches & CIA File").

21. HSCA Vol. 10, note 66, p. 117.

22. By one account, the official basis for Ferrie's dismissal was his failure to pass his regular physical examination. But Ferrie's physical fitness was not the focus of the investigations conducted on behalf of Eastern Airlines and by the FAA. They focused on the molestation charges and Ferrie's "Moral Character." (See letter from Carl F. Maisch, Chief, FAA Investigations Division, to James Clatterbuck, Dec. 13, 1963, and FAA report of same date by Richard E. Robey.)

23. George Lardner, Jr., interview with David Ferrie, in cable from "Angeloff" to "Lang for Orshefsky" (hereinafter Lardner–Ferrie Interview), Feb. 22, 1967 (AARC); Perry Russo, interview with Bill Bankston, *Baton Rouge States-Time*, Feb. 24, 1967.

24. Brener, *The Garrison Case*, pp. 48–49. Cuban expatriate attorney Carlos Bringuier, disturbed by what he had been hearing about Ferrie, insisted on meeting him. When Sergio Arcacha Smith took Bringuier to Ferrie's apartment, they found him in the company of two young boys. The two men left immediately and Bringuier urged Smith to stop seeing Ferrie. In Bringuier's opinion Ferrie was not the sort of man who could do their cause any good. Two years later, on Nov. 25, 1963, Ferrie told the FBI that he was associated with Smith's organization from "approximately Nov. 1960 until Aug. 1961." Ferrie said he "collected food, money and medicine for it and gave talks to citizens groups" but had had no contact with "any" anti-Castro organization since Aug. 1961, though he had "social" contact with Smith (Ferrie, FBI interview, Nov. 25, 1963). Smith's organization was CIA supported but there is no evidence of any contact between that agency and Ferrie.

25. Welsh Interview. Welsh said that since Ferrie suffered from high blood pressure, and because anxiety and stress "make the blood pressure rise," that "being harassed and in fear of being arrested" could certainly have brought on the stroke.

26. David and Barbara Snyder, conversations with author, Sept. 4 and 5, 1993.

27. Lardner–Ferrie Interview ("to give him some rest"). See also note at p. 216.

28. Snyder, teletype to Time, Feb. 24, 1967.

29. Snyder Interview; Snyder, teletype to *Time*, Feb. 24, 1967; *New Orleans Times-Picayune*, Feb. 23, 1967.

30. George Lardner, statement to New Orleans district attorney's office, Feb. 22, 1967; Lardner–Ferrie Interview.

31. Alcock Interview.

32. The former letter began, "To leave this life is, for me, a sweet prospect," and closed, "If this is Justice, then Justice be damned." The latter, addressed "Dear Al," began, "When you receive this I will be quite dead, so no answer will be possible."

33. Secret Service Memorandum, from Donald L. Hughes, to Special Agent in Charge, New Orleans, Feb. 23, 1967 (this outlined the pressure Garrison put to Dr. Chetta "to find a suicide angle"); Welsh Interview. That Proloid could be fatal under any circumstances is unlikely but, if possible, the experts say it would require massive doses over a prolonged period. Garrison questioned

Ferrie's taking this medication at all and stated in his memoir that Ferrie had no condition requiring it. But he did (see Appendix A, item #28).

34. *New Orleans Times-Picayune*, Feb. 23, 1967; Alcock Interview; Garrison, *On the Trail of the Assassins*, pp. 137–140.
35. Lardner–Ferrie Interview.

CHAPTER SIX

1. Perry Russo, interview with Edward F. Wegmann, F. Irvin Dymond, and William Gurvich, transcript, April 16, 1971 (hereinafter Russo-Wegmann et al. Interview), p. 1 (from the files of William J. Wegmann).
2. *New Orleans Times-Picayune*, Feb. 25, 1967; "The Garrison Investigation: How and Why It Began," *New Orleans* magazine, April 1967. Truth and Consequences founders were: Joseph M. Rault, Jr., president of Rault Petroleum Company, Willard E. Robertson, a Volkswagen dealer, and Cecil Shilstone, owner of a chemical firm. Members named: real estate executive Harold E. Cook, attorney Eberhard Deutsch, Aviation Board member John Mmahat, Homestead President Edmond G. Miranne, and bank president Lawrence Merrigan.
3. *New Orleans Times-Picayune*, Feb. 25, 1967.
4. Perry Russo had written a letter to Jim Garrison and mailed it the same day Garrison declared Ferrie "one of history's most important individuals." It said, essentially, "I had occasion to meet Ferrie and some of his friends and I'm willing to tell you what I know about them." When told in 1994 that Garrison claimed he never received the letter, Russo seemed surprised (Russo, interview with author, Feb. 7, 1994.) His reaction supports the view that Garrison withheld the letter because its contents were so innocuous.
5. Bill Bankston, "Local Man Reports Ferrie Threat on Life of Kennedy," *Baton Rouge State-Times*, Feb. 24, 1967. Russo also told Bankston Ferrie had said Castro was "not such a bad guy and that he could be an ally of the United States" (Bankston, WWL-TV interview, undated transcript).
6. Andrew Sciambra, Memorandum to Jim Garrison, Feb. 27, 1967, re Perry Russo Interview on Feb. 25, 1967 (hereinafter Sciambra Memorandum); Layton Martens, WWL-TV interview, June 27, 1967, pp. 10, 11; *New Orleans Times-Picayune*, March 2, 1967; Brener, *The Garrison Case*, pp. 92–93.
7. Sciambra Memorandum.
8. Perry Russo, interview with William Gurvich and Leonard Gurvich, partial transcript, Jan. 29, 1971 (hereinafter Russo-Gurvich Interview), pp. 9–12 (from the files of James Phelan).
9. Andrew Sciambra, trial testimony, Feb. 12, 1969 (session following afternoon break), p. 19; Perry Russo, interview with William Gurvich, F. Irvin Dymond, Edward F. Wegmann, and Salvatore Panzeca, partial transcript, March 1971 (hereinafter Russo-Defense Team Interview), p. 12 (from the files of James Phelan).
10. Dr. Arthur Cho, Professor of Pharmacology at UCLA, telephone conversation with author, Nov. 21, 1994 ("inhibitions"); *New Orleans Times-Picayune*, March 4, 1967 (Dr. Gallant).

NOTES

11. Andrew Sciambra, Memorandum, "Interview with Perry Raymond Russo at Mercy Hospital on Feb. 27, 1967" (hereinafter Russo Hospital Interview). This memorandum, according to Sciambra's testimony at Clay Shaw's trial, was dictated jointly by Sciambra and Al Oser; it is written in the first person singular and bears only Sciambra's signature.

12. Russo–Defense Team Interview, p. 10. Russo said this conversation took place either on Saturday, during his first meeting with Sciambra in Baton Rouge, or the following Monday in New Orleans. According to Russo, when he couldn't supply Clay Shaw's name, Sciambra said, "Is his name Bertrand?" "I'm not sure," Russo said, "is that his name?" "That's the name he went as," Sciambra replied.

13. Russo Hospital Interview. In another echo of the Bankston article, Russo said "this was not the first time that Ferrie had talked to him about how easy it would be to assassinate a president." "In September and October of 1963," Ferrie became "obsessed with the idea that he could pull off a perfect assassination."

14. Richard Billings, "Garrison's Star Witness: Heard 'Plot' Plans," Miami Herald, April 23, 1968, p. 12A. Billings, present at the dinner, also recounted Russo's statement to Edward Epstein (Counterplot, p. 58).

15. Russo–Gurvich Interview, pp. 11–17.

16. Russo–Defense Team Interview, p. 7.

17. Ibid., p. 8. Garrison discussed this homosexual-thrill-killing theory, which made headlines in one of the tabloids of the period, with members of his staff and various journalists, including Richard Billings, James Phelan and Nicholas Chriss (Gurvich Conference, tape #2, p. 18; Billings Personal Notes, pp. 16, 18, 28; James Phelan, Scandals, Scamps, and Scoundrels [New York: Random House, 1982] pp. 150–151; Nicholas Chriss, "New Orleans: Melodrama, but the Plot Is Obscure," Los Angeles Times, Opinion, Section G, March 26, 1967, p. 2).

18. Russo–Defense Team Interview, p. 8; Perry Russo, preliminary hearing transcript, p. 76; Phelan–Shaw Interview.

19. Billings Personal Notes, March 3, 1967, p. 18.

20. Memorandum (untitled, unsigned, five-pages), by Edward F. Wegmann, "Jan. 27, 1971," describing interview with Perry Russo on Jan. 26, 1971 (hereinafter Wegmann Memorandum), pp. 1, 4. This interview took place in F. Irvin Dymond's office. Present were Perry Russo, F. Irvin Dymond, Edward F. Wegmann, and William J. Wegmann (F. Irvin Dymond, interview with author, Nov. 2, 1995).

21. James Phelan, memorandum, "Discrepancies and Contradictions in Russo's Story" (undated), item 25, p. 6 (Russo admitted this to Phelan on May 28, 1967).

22. Brener, The Garrison Case, pp. 64–65; Epstein, Counterplot, pp. 95–96.

23. James Kirkwood, "Surviving," Esquire, Dec. 1968.

24. Russo–Gurvich Interview, pp. 30–33; Wegmann Memorandum, p. 1.

25. New Orleans Times-Picayune, March 3, 1967; James and Wardlaw, Plot or Politics? p. 53; Brener, The Garrison Case, p. 113; Gurvich Conference, tape #2, pp. 12–13.

26. Milton Brener, telephone conversation with author, Feb. 7, 1994. Brener's information was obtained from William Gurvich. The date and time of the

FALSE WITNESS

hypnosis session is found in the preliminary hearing testimony of Dr. Fatter (transcript, p. 385).

27. Charles B. Clayman, ed., *Encyclopedia of Medicine* (Chicago: American Medical Association, 1989) p. 559.

28. Kirkwood, *American Grotesque*, p. 152 (citing an affidavit obtained from Dr. Spiegel by Clay Shaw's defense team). In 1967 Dr. Spiegel was Assistant Clinical Professor of Psychiatry and Director of courses in Hypnosis at Columbia University's College of Physicians and Surgeons, and Assistant Attending Psychiatrist, Presbyterian Hospital in New York.

29. For Dr. Fatter's technique, see "First Hypnotic Session," transcript labeled "Exhibit F," March 1, 1967. Courts in some states, California for one, do not allow testimony that has been influenced by hypnosis. Guidelines necessary to assure that posthypnotic testimony would be "taken seriously" were well known in 1967 and stipulated in a 1981 New Jersey criminal case, State v. Hurd (*The New Yorker*, Oct. 5, 1991, p. 116). Far from working "independently of either side," Dr. Fatter was working solely for District Attorney Jim Garrison; whatever information Fatter received beforehand was not recorded; Russo did not give Fatter "the facts" as he remembered them "before the hypnosis"; and, instead of "only the hypnotist and the witness" being present, five others were in attendance. Andrew Sciambra actually took over the questioning at one point (transcript, p. 10).

30. *The New Yorker*, Oct. 5, 1991, p. 116.

31. James Phelan, memorandum, "Discrepancies and Contradictions in Russo's Story," undated, item 20.

32. Russo–Gurvich Interview, pp. 42–43, 46; Wegmann Memorandum, p. 2; Russo, interview with author, Feb. 7, 1994; Russo–Wegmann et al. Interview, p. 2.

33. Wegmann Memorandum, pp. 1–3; Russo-Wegmann et al. Interview, p. 2. Russo said the arrangement between *Life* and Garrison was in the form of "written contracts"; he also claimed that as of 1971 Garrison owed him about $3,000 in per diems which had never been paid.

34. Perry Russo, interview with author, Feb. 7, 1994.

35. Don Jordan, television interview, undated transcript, p. 12.

36. New Orleans Police Department, Report, re pre-employment screening of Perry Russo, Aug. 10, 1970.

37. Don Jordan, television interview, undated transcript. At the Clay Shaw trial, Russo denied he had cut his wrists. Another Russo friend stated that he had told her about the "split personality" diagnosis (Sandra Moffett, television interview, undated transcript).

38. Russo–Gurvich Interview, p. 50; Wegmann Memorandum, p. 2.

39. *New Orleans Times-Picayune*, March 3, 1967; "Justice Admits Error in Shaw-Bertrand Tie," *Washington Post*, June 3, 1967.

40. Director, FBI, communiqué to The Attorney General, regarding Clay Shaw's attorney, Edward F. Wegmann, and the alleged FBI investigation of Clay Shaw, March 10, 1967. At the bottom of this document is the following internal Bureau "NOTE": "On March 2, 1967, Attorney General Clark made remarks to the press which the press had interpreted as stating that the FBI had investigat-

NOTES

ed Clay Shaw in New Orleans in Nov. and Dec., 1963. This of course is not true. We did not investigate Clay Shaw in connection with our investigation of the assassination. . . . The Attorney General contacted Mr. DeLoach 3/3/67 . . . [and] stated he had been misquoted by reporters." Clark was not misquoted, however, as the transcript of his press conference establishes ("CBS Interview with Ramsey Clark after his nomination hearing, March 2, 1967").

41. "Justice Admits Error in Shaw-Bertrand Tie," *Washington Post*, June 3, 1967. All the fault does not appear to lie with Ramsey Clark. The record suggests that the FBI's communications with Clark on March 2, 1967, contributed to his confusion and may have been the principal source of it. That day in an early morning telephone conversation, FBI Deputy Director C. D. DeLoach, responded to Clark's inquiries about Garrison's arrest of Clay Shaw the previous day by telling Clark that Shaw's name "had come up" in the FBI's 1963 investigation, a reference to the Bureau's search for "Clay Bertrand," which was specifically mentioned in the conversation. DeLoach also told Clark that "it had been alleged that this was an alias used by Shaw." This may have sounded to Clark as though that allegation was made in 1963 but the comprehensive memorandum sent to Clark that same morning by J. Edgar Hoover clearly stated that the allegation about Shaw using the alias was received by the FBI on February 24, 1967, from two sources. If it had come from fifty sources, it would be just as meaningless. For the allegation originated in Jim Garrison's office. Garrison had been saying it for at least two months, since December 1966 when he proclaimed it to David Chandler. (The rumor was so widespread that, as noted earlier, Shaw himself heard it on February 26, 1967.) As for Shaw's name having "come up" during the 1963 search for "Bertrand," Hoover's March 2, 1967, memorandum makes no mention of it. But Hoover's memorandum, in describing the Bureau's knowledge (dating from 1954) of Shaw's homosexuality, provides an explanation for why Shaw's name might have surfaced in the Bureau's 1963 search for Clay Bertrand—the Bureau knew Shaw's sexual orientation fit Bertrand's alleged profile (and the first name was the same). Those, of course, were two of the factors that had led Garrison to jump to the conclusion that Shaw *was* Bertrand. (C.D. DeLoach, Memorandum, to Mr. Tolson, March 2, 1967; J. Edgar Hoover, memoranda, concerning Garrison-Shaw matter, March 2, 1967 and March 3, 1967 [attachments to letter from Hoover to Dir., Bureau of Intelligence and Research, State Department, dated March 9, 1967].)

42. Two erroneous ideas are being promulgated by pro-Garrison writers: (1) that the FBI actually *was* investigating Clay Shaw in 1963; and (2) that the FBI was investigating "Clay Bertrand" prior to Dean Andrews's telephone call to the Bureau. Neither of these claims is supported by any evidence. Even if Clay Shaw's name *came up* in 1963 that does not mean he was being investigated. The notion of a pre-Andrews Bertrand inquiry is based on a gross misreading of the trial testimony of FBI Agent Regis Kennedy. If Kennedy *had* acknowledged investigating Bertrand earlier, as one monograph being circulated indicates, the prosecution would have made a major issue of it at the time.

43. Chandler Interview; Shaw Journal, pp. 32–33.

44. In Sept. 1967 *Life* published a series of three articles "detailing activities of

organized crime in Louisiana and the New Orleans area" (*New Orleans States-Item*, Nov. 8, 1967). These articles marked the final rupture of Jim Garrison's relationship with *Life* magazine (Chandler Interview).

45. Chandler Interview. How Jim Garrison first heard that *Life* was backing off is unknown. He apparently had supporters at the Miami dinner and one of them may have telephoned him; Garrison probably heard the news before Richard Billings did. Whatever the source of Garrison's information, David Chandler insisted that Garrison was informed prior to his contacting Phelan on March 3, insisted that Garrison contacted Phelan *because* of it.

CHAPTER SEVEN

1. Kirkwood, *American Grotesque*, p. 76.
2. Phelan Interview; Phelan, *Scandals*, p. 138.
3. Phelan Interview.
4. *New Orleans Times-Picayune*, March 3, 1967; Phelan Interview.
5. *New Orleans Times-Picayune*, March 3, 1967. This statement was made by Guy Johnson, who assisted in the early stages of Shaw's defense.
6. *New Orleans Times-Picayune*, March 9, 1967.
7. James Phelan, "Rush to Judgment in New Orleans," *The Saturday Evening Post*, May 6, 1967; Phelan Interview. Phelan left New Orleans on Friday, March 3, and checked into the Dunes in Las Vegas after midnight on the fourth. His hotel bill, which was entered into evidence when he testified at Shaw's trial, indicated he departed March 7. Jim Garrison had been planning the trip prior to Clay Shaw's arrest (Billings Personal Notes, Feb. 25, 1967, p. 14), and didn't alter his plans because of it.
8. Phelan, *Scandals*, p. 145; Phelan Interview.
9. Phelan Interview. Garrison told Phelan, among other things, "that the air [in Las Vegas] was better." According to David Chandler, Garrison liked Las Vegas "because the gangsters treated him like a king" (Chandler Interview).
10. James and Wardlaw, *Plot or Politics?* p. 72 (not alone); Phelan Interview.
11. Phelan, "Rush to Judgment"; Phelan, *Scandals*, pp. 145–146; Phelan Interview.
12. Garrison described to Phelan a nightclub entertainer named Breck Wall, tying him into the conspiracy because Wall, like Ferrie, had traveled to Galveston the weekend of the assassination and, while there, had received a telephone call from Jack Ruby. Garrison knew that Ruby's call and Wall's trip to Galveston were somehow linked to Ferrie's brush with that city and to Kennedy's murder. Yet Ruby and Wall, a union representative, had given the FBI the same explanation for the call. Ruby had closed his club out of respect for the fallen president and was upset and complaining to Wall because the competition hadn't followed suit.
13. Phelan Interview; Phelan, *Scandals*, p. 149.
14. Phelan, *Scandals*, p. 150.
15. *Ibid.*; Phelan Interview.
16. Phelan Interview; Phelan, *Scandals*, p. 151.
17. *Ibid.*

NOTES

18. Phelan Interview.
19. Phelan, *Scandals*, p. 154. A combination of factors contributed to Phelan's quick grasp of the documents. He was married to a clinical psychologist "familiar with the use of hypnosis"; he had researched and written about the Bridey Murphy past lives regression under hypnosis phenomenon; and he had flown to Copenhagen in 1959 and covered the "landmark" Palle Hardrup trial that centered on the "misuse of hypnosis" (Phelan Interview; Phelan letter to author, May 18, 1994).
20. Phelan Interview.
21. At the Desert Inn Phelan called Robert Maheu, former CIA employee and major-domo to billionaire Howard Hughes, who owned the place. This later became the subject of conspiratorial speculation by pro-Garrison researchers, who also challenge Phelan's motives for making the trip to Las Vegas. As a journalist who sometimes wrote about Hughes, Phelan's acquaintance with Maheu was unremarkable. They met in 1962 when Maheu unsuccessfully tried to persuade Phelan to kill a story he was writing about a loan Hughes made to Richard Nixon. Phelan's call to Maheu that morning was a simple matter of proximity and expediency: Copying machines in those days were scarce (Phelan Interview).
22. Phelan, *Scandals*, p. 155.
23. Ibid., pp. 155, 156.
24. The *Las Vegas Review-Journal* published the details about Garrison's stay in that town, which was noted in the *New Orleans Times-Picayune* on March 16, 1967.
25. "Statement of 2 on 'Plot' Doubted," *New York Times*, June 21, 1967; "NBC Tactics on Garrison Inquiry Hit," *Los Angeles Times*, June 21, 1967; Sgt. Edward O'Donnell, Report to Jim Garrison, regarding Perry Russo Interview (which refers to the test administered by Roy Jacob), dated June 20, 1967 (Appendix B in this book); Brener, *The Garrison Case*, p. 109; Leonard Gurvich, telephone interview with author, April 2, 1996. The Jacob polygraph examination occurred on March 8, 1967.
26. Brener, *The Garrison Case*, p. 110. At this point Russo had been hypnotized three times, in Chetta's office on March 1, 1967, in Asst. D.A. Ward's office on March 9, 1967, and again in Chetta's office on March 12, 1967. (Eventually, according to what Russo told this writer, he may have been hypnotized five times.) Transcripts of only two of these hypnosis sessions have survived.
27. "2nd Hypnotic Session" (actually the third), "Taken March 12, 1967," labeled "Exhibit G."
28. Ibid.
29. Russo–Wegmann et al. Interview, p. 3.
30. Russo–Gurvich Interview, p. 24.

CHAPTER EIGHT

1. Shaw Journal, p. 1.
2. Clay Shaw, nineteen-page narrative, "PH" (hereinafter Shaw Narrative), p. 7; Shaw Journal, p. 60; The *Chicago Tribune*, March 16, 1967.

3. Gurvich Conference, tape #2, p. 19.
4. Phelan, "Rush to Judgment in New Orleans."
5. Perry Russo, preliminary hearing transcript, p. 58; *New Orleans Times-Picayune*, March 15, 1967.
6. Shaw Journal, pp. 61-62; Perry Russo, preliminary hearing transcript, p. 76.
7. Perry Russo, preliminary hearing transcript, p. 96; Shaw Journal, pp. 64–65.
8. Perry Russo, preliminary hearing transcript, pp. 112–114, 182, 184–185, 206, 223–224.
9. *Ibid.*, pp. 190–191, 197, 202, 203, 205.
10. *Ibid.*, pp. 293, 311–313.
11. Dr. Esmond Fatter and Dr. Nicholas Chetta, preliminary hearing transcript, pp. 408, 423 (Fatter), 339, 372, 321–322 (Chetta).
12. Edwin A. Weinstein, M.D., "Truth Serum," *The Washington Post*, March 27, 1967. In WWII Weinstein was Chief of the Fifth Army Neuro-psychiatric Center in Italy where they used sodium Pentothal "to treat combat stress casualties."
13. Vernon Bundy, Jr., interview at Orleans Parish Prison, by William Gurvich, Charlie Jonau, and Cliency Navarre, March 16, 1967; Gurvich, interview on WWL-TV, June 27, 1967; *Times-Picayune*, March 18, 1967.
14. James Kruebbe, telephone interviews with author, Nov. 30, 1993, Dec. 2, 1993, and Dec. 3, 1993 (hereinafter Kruebbe Interviews); James Kruebbe, Work Report, dated March 18, 1967, regarding Bundy's polygraph examination (in the files of James Kruebbe). Kruebbe said Bundy's "polygrams and related data were given to Mr. Garrison to retain." Edward O'Donnell testified later in federal court that he too was present during Kruebbe's verbal report to Garrison (Christenberry transcript, p. 301).
15. *New Orleans Times-Picayune*, March 18, 1967. Bundy's polygraph occurred around noon and he took the stand at 2:30 P.M. on Friday, March 17, 1967.
16. Vernon Bundy, preliminary hearing transcript, pp. 431, 433–436, 441.
17. *New Orleans Times-Picayune*, March 18, 1967. In the official preliminary hearing transcript the summations, or "Arguments," are indicated as "Not Transcribed." William Wegmann recently explained that "not transcribing summations was customary in those days."
18. Shaw Journal, pp. 61, 68–69.
19. *Los Angeles Times*, June 28, 1967.
20. Sam Angeloff, memorandum, "summary of the day's findings," to Richard Billings, March 21, 1967 (O'Hara's statement to *Life*); Phelan, *Scandals*, p. 158 (Judge Bagert); Dymond et al. Interview ("done deal"); Wegmann Memorandum ("cut and dried").
21. Phelan Interview; Jerry Cohen, "Garrison Records on Russo Tend to Discredit Investigation," *Los Angeles Times*, April 24, 1967.
22. Phelan Interview.
23. *Ibid.*; James Phelan, memorandum, "Discrepancies and Contradictions in Russo's Story."
24. Phelan Interview.
25. *Ibid.* Garrison didn't try to explain the hole in Russo's story. He never addressed it. Thirty years later that still baffled Phelan.
26. Phelan Interview; Phelan, *Scandals*, p. 159; Kirkwood, *American Grotesque*, p. 165.

NOTES

Matt Herron never corroborated James Phelan's account publicly but he did so privately to members of Garrison's staff (Bethell Diary, pp. 34–35). Richard Billings, who was present when Sciambra orally briefed Garrison on the Baton Rouge interview, later said Sciambra did not mention the plot party at that briefing, and that he specifically told Garrison that Russo had seen Shaw twice—at Ferrie's service station and the Kennedy rally (Epstein, *Counterplot*, pp. 57, 58, 67; Billings, letter to Edward F. Wegmann, Jan. 8, 1969 [in the files of James Phelan]).
27. Russo–Wegmann et al. Interview, p. 3.
28. Phelan Interview.

CHAPTER NINE

1. Clay Shaw, quoted by Warren Rogers, "The Persecution of Clay Shaw: How One Man ruined Another and Subverted Our Legal System," *Look*, Aug. 26, 1969.
2. Alvin Beaubouef, interview with Louis Ivon, Dec. 28, 1966, transcript, p. 13 (Beaubouef was also interviewed by Ivon and Asst. D.A. John Volz on Dec. 15, 1966).
3. Billings Personal Notes, p. 36.
4. Hugh Exnicios and Lynn Loisel, "Telephone Conversation," two-page transcript, March 10, 1967; Report to Joseph I. Giarrusso, Supt. of Police, from Presly J. Trosclair, June 12, 1967 (hereinafter Trosclair Report); Billings Personal Notes, pp. 36–38; Brener, *The Garrison Case*, pp. 163–164.
5. Hugh Exnicios, Lynn Loisel, and Al Beaubouef, "Conference," twenty-nine-page transcript, March 10, 1967; Brener, *The Garrison Case*, pp. 165–171.
6. Dymond et al. Interview.
7. FBI Special Agent in Charge, New Orleans, airtel, to Director, May 5, 1967, "Letterhead Memorandum," attached, quotes Aaron Kohn about Langridge (Jim Garrison, FBIHQ Main File 46-55913).
8. Trosclair Report, p. 11.
9. Ibid.
10. Mutual Protective Association, Inc., Polygraph Examination Report, regarding Alvin R. Beaubouef, to "Mr. Fred Freid," May 10, 1967.
11. Among the Garrison material recently unearthed in his old office files in New Orleans are five lengthy transcriptions of several of the entirely innocuous Phelan-Russo conversations. Garrison never made them public because Phelan never said anything inappropriate ("First Interview Between Phelan and Russo," May 24, 1967 [transcript dated June 16, 1967]; "Second Interview Between Perry Russo and James Phelan," May 25, 1967; "Interview Between James Phelan and Perry Russo," May 27, 1967; "Fourth Interview Between Perry Russo and James Phelan," undated; "Interview with Perry Russo and James Phelan," May 28, 1967).
12. Phelan, memorandum, "Discrepancies and Contradictions In Russo's Story; Kirkwood, *American Grotesque*, p. 168–169; Phelan Interview.
13. Phelan Interview.
14. Phelan, memorandum, "Discrepancies and Contradictions in Russo's Story";

Kirkwood, *American Grotesque*, pp. 169–173.

15. Phelan, memorandum, "Discrepancies and Contradictions in Russo's Story"; Kirkwood, *American Grotesque*, pp. 169–173; Phelan Interview.

16. Billings Personal Notes, pp. 85, 86.

17. Sgt. Edward O'Donnell, report to Jim Garrison, regarding Perry Russo Interview, June 20, 1967 (Appendix B in this book). Perry Russo told Edward O'Donnell that "if he had to give a yes or no answer" as to whether Shaw was at the assassination party, "he would have to say no"; at the preliminary hearing he had intended to testify that he didn't know whether or not Shaw was there but changed his mind because Dymond's question about God had "turned him on"; the conversation at the party didn't sound like a real "plot" but "a bull session"; he would like to meet Clay Shaw to see if he was the sort of person that would be involved in such a plot; and he would like to know Garrison's "complete case against Shaw" in order to "help him come to a decision."

18. Edward O'Donnell, telephone interviews with author, July 28, 1993, Sept. 7, 1993, Nov. 14, 1993, March 18, 1996 (hereinafter O'Donnell Interviews). O'Donnell's account of the meeting in Garrison's office later was substantiated by Russo who said O'Donnell was "completely honest"; Russo, himself, referred to the "terrible scene" with Garrison and his aides over O'Donnell's report (Wegmann Memorandum; Russo interview with author, Dec. 4, 1993).

19. Gurvich Conference, p. 15. (The Alcock–Garrison conversation about arresting Sheridan is also mentioned in the Bethell diary.) On July 10, 1967, William Gurvich took a polygraph test administered by John E. Reid whose report stated that Gurvich "was telling the truth" about the fifteen questions he was asked. One of those questions was, "Did Garrison order the arrest, handcuffing and physical beating of Sheridan and Townley? Answer: Yes" (John E. Reid and Associates, Chicago, Illinois, Laboratory Report, July 10, 1967).

20. Posner, *Case Closed*, p. 441.

21. Niles Peterson and Sandra Moffett, the two friends Russo claimed were with him at Ferrie's party where the conspiracy was hatched, both appeared on the broadcast and, as they had in the past, denied it. Peterson remembered a party but saw neither Oswald nor Shaw there nor anyone resembling them. Sandra Moffett repeated what she had said initially: that she didn't meet David Ferrie until 1965.

22. Since Miguel Torres and John Cancler were both in jail at the time, they had nothing to gain and ran a considerable risk by telling their story and challenging Jim Garrison.

23. "Statement of 2 on 'Plot' Doubted," *New York Times*, June 21, 1967; "NBC Tactics on Garrison Inquiry Hit," *Los Angeles Times*, June 21, 1967.

24. "Statement of 2 on 'Plot' Doubted," *New York Times*, June 21, 1967; "NBC Tactics on Garrison Inquiry Hit," *Los Angeles Times*, June 21, 1967; Brener, *The Garrison Case*, p. 147. For his protection, the identity of the "real" Bertrand (Gene Davis) wasn't announced, but narrator McGee described him as a well known New Orleans businessman and homosexual whose name had been turned over to the Justice Department.

25. *New York Times*, June 20, 1967.

NOTES

26. Recently, in an effort to minimize William Gurvich's role, the charge has been made that he was not Garrison's "chief" investigator. But he was repeatedly referred to as such by the press at the time; treated as such by Garrison; and so identified in the earliest book on the case, *Plot or Politics?* by Rosemary James and Jack Wardlaw, at p. 149.
27. *Newsday*, June 23, 1967.
28. *Los Angeles Times*, June 24, 1967. The article also said Gurvich "strenuously denied" telling Kennedy that Garrison's case was "a hoax," a story that was circulating. The source of the "hoax" quote was an FBI informant at *Newsday* (FBI New York Field Office teletype to Director, June 21, 1967). Gurvich later told James Kirkwood that his exact words to Robert Kennedy were "Senator, Mr. Garrison will never shed any light on your brother's death" (Kirkwood, *American Grotesque*, p. 541).
29. *Los Angeles Times*, June 24, 26, and 27, 1967; *Los Angeles Herald Examiner*, June 26, 1967.
30. *Newsday*, June 23, 1967.
31. *Los Angeles Herald-Examiner*, June 26, 1967.
32. Gurvich also told a reporter at the *Los Angeles Times* that he decided to quit after Garrison pulled the name of his latest suspect from a letter written by a Texas woman. She wanted Garrison to help her locate her wandering husband who had a scar over his left eye. "Garrison has always thought that a man with a scar over his left eye was a companion of Lee Harvey Oswald," Gurvich said. "So now this man became his suspect. It was so absurd I figured Garrison had gone completely nuts" (*Los Angeles Times*, June 29, 1967).
33. Los Angeles *Times*, June 26, 27, and 29, 1967.
34. Judge Haggerty, quoted by James Kirkwood, *American Grotesque*, pp. 645–646; Gurvich Conference, Tape #3, p. 6.
35. Grand jury transcript, March 29, 1967 (Perry Russo).
36. Those testifying before the grand jury who preceded William Gurvich included: Aaron Kohn; former FBI agent and writer for *Ramparts* magazine, William Turner; NBC affiliate WDSU-TV news director Ed Planer; *New Orleans States-Item* reporter Ross Yockey; Eugene Davis; and Dean Andrews.
37. On July 12, 1967, Gurvich appeared again before the grand jury. He said he probably never would have made any public statements if, on the day he returned from New York, Garrison had seen him. Gurvich handed out copies of the lie-detector test administered to him by the well-known Chicago firm (described in note 19) which indicated his earlier statements to the jurors were true. Gurvich told the jurors of Garrison's plans to raid the local offices of the FBI, and about Vernon Bundy's polygraph. Garrison accused Gurvich of being paid and Gurvich called Garrison "a damn liar." Gurvich also detailed the pressure put on burglar John the Baptist (John Cancler) to break into Shaw's home (Grand Jury transcript, July 12, 1967, pp. 7–11, 22, 24, 65).
38. *New Orleans States-Item*, June 29, 1967.
39. At the same time Andrews fired off a shot of his own: a $100,000 damage suit against Garrison claiming he deprived Andrews of his civil rights. Andrews charged that Garrison, using Andrews's sworn testimony to the Warren Commission, had "compelled" him to answer questions before the grand jury "designed to trap him, full knowing that [Andrews] had no knowledge of any

conspiracy or any facts material to a conspiracy to murder John F. Kennedy."
In the pleading, Andrews stated that he had told Garrison "that there was no
connection between Clay Shaw and Clay Bertrand." Andrews called Garrison's
belief that Shaw and Bertrand were the same person, arbitrary, capricious and
not founded on any fact (*New Orleans Times-Picayune*, April 19, 1967). This suit
was later dropped.

40. Epstein, *Counterplot*, p. 34.
41. *New Orleans States-Item*, July 6, 1967.
42. *New Orleans States-Item*, Aug. 12, 1967.
43. *Los Angeles Times*, June 29, 1967; *New Orleans States-Item*, June 29, 1967; Brener, *The Garrison Case*, p. 148. Two entries in the Billings Personal Notes track the Andrews-Garrison struggle and support Andrews's version. One says that Andrews told Garrison Clay Bertrand didn't exist (Feb. 23, 1967, p. 13). The other, two days later, says that Garrison had spoken to Andrews but he wouldn't change his story (Feb. 25, 1967, p. 14). That same entry also says that Garrison had decided to pursue Shaw.
44. *New Orleans States-Item*, Aug. 17, 1967.
45. As Richard Billings wrote in his Personal Notes (May, 24, 1967, p. 85), Garrison would employ any method to obtain statements from key witnesses.
46. O'Donnell Interviews.
47. Leonard Gurvich, telephone interview with author, April 2, 1996; Gurvich Conference, Tape #2, p. 14.
48. "Playboy Interview: Jim Garrison," Oct. 1967; *The Tonight Show*, NBC, Jan. 31, 1968; "Garrison Says, 'Now Our Government Is Lying!'" *Los Angeles Free Press*, Nov. 17, 1967 (transcript of Garrison's Nov. 14, 1967, address to the Radio and Television News Association of Southern California); Clay Shaw, notes (hereinafter Shaw Notes) Jan. 31, 1968, p. 24.
49. Bethell Diary, pp. 27–30. According to Bethell, the letter-writer from Van Nuys who fingered Edgar Eugene Bradley was a man residing in the home of a woman involved in a lawsuit with Bradley. This woman reportedly identified a photograph of one of the so-called tramps arrested in the railroad yards at Dealey Plaza on November 22, 1963, as Bradley. But another picture taken from a different angle clearly established the tramp wasn't Bradley.
50. United Press International, interview with Jim Garrison, Nov. 1, 1967.
51. Shaw Journal, p. 69; Shaw Notes, Oct. 9, 1967, October 11, 1967, October 6, 1967.
52. Bethell Diary, p. 25.
53. Alcock Interview.

CHAPTER TEN

1. Kirkwood, *American Grotesque*, p. 301.
2. The report described the findings of four medical experts who examined the president's clothing, X-rays and photographs and confirmed the Warren Commission findings that he was shot from behind. Garrison's office had been trying to obtain the same material since May 1968 but had indicated it wasn't

essential to the state's case. Now Alcock said it was and the prosecution could not go to trial without it.

3. *New Orleans States-Item,* Feb. 6, 1969; Jim Garrison, opening statement, trial transcript, Feb. 6, 1969, pp. 3, 7, 35. Earlier, Judge Haggerty granted a defense motion requesting production of the Beaubouef bribery tape (but it was never produced); and denied a defense motion (opposed by the state) to obtain the testimony of Perry Russo's former girl friend, Sandra Moffett (Kirkwood, *American Grotesque,* p. 199).

4. F. Irvin Dymond, opening statement, trial transcript, Feb. 6, 1969, pp. 4, 5, 7, 20.

5. The trial testimony of twelve witnesses (among them Vernon Bundy, Charles Spiesel and Eugene Davis) was never transcribed. Why is unclear. The answer may lie in Judge Haggerty's "special" arrangement whereby court reporting firm owner Helen R. Dietrich (now deceased) was granted "all publication rights" in return for her firm transcribing the entire trial. (One stenographer "would not agree" to this and refused to sell Dietrich his notes, though he did participate in the transcription of some testimony.) Dietrich's son-in-law, William Griffin, suggests that because Dietrich received few orders for the full transcript, and perhaps received no specific orders for the testimony of some witnesses, she may have chosen to leave the latter untranscribed for financial reasons. Fortunately, the two local newspapers provided detailed daily descriptions of the proceedings, and the *New Orleans States-Item,* in many instances, published verbatim accounts of the testimony. Also, writer James Kirkwood (*American Grotesque*) sometimes used quotations directly from the proceedings. (Jonathan Blackmer, HSC memorandum to Robert Tanenbaum, "The Mysterious Clay Shaw Trial," Dec. 12, 1976; telephone conversations with William Griffin, June 16 and July 7, 1998, and Dave Snyder, June 16, 1998.)

6. *New Orleans Times-Picayune,* Feb. 8, 1969; *New York Times,* Feb. 8, 1969; Kirkwood, *American Grotesque,* pp. 231–233.

7. Dymond et al. Interview.

8. *Los Angeles Times,* Feb. 8, 1969; Dymond et al. Interview. Because Tom Bethell leaked the prosecution witness list to the defense shortly after the trial began, it has long been assumed by Bethell and others that the list enabled Shaw's attorneys to obtain the information they used to demolish Charles Spiesel. But the list actually was of little help to the defense.

9. Charles Spiesel led the jurors into a building at 1323 Dauphine which was next door to Shaw's home at 1313, but with no success; then Spiesel led the parade around the corner into a place on Esplanade where they visited three more apartments, including two that Shaw once owned. "I don't think he found anything," Irvin Dymond commented to the trailing newsmen, "but we saw a couple of pretty girls" (*Los Angeles Times,* Feb. 9, 1969).

10. Alcock Interview.

11. Tom Bethell, "Conspiracy to End Conspiracies," *National Review,* Dec. 16, 1991. James Alcock recently acknowledged that he was the one who "conducted the initial interview with Spiesel in New York." He also claimed that "everyone was taken by surprise by Spiesel" at the trial (Alcock Interview).

12. Perry Russo, trial transcript, February 10, 1969, pp. 30, 67–68, 129–120.

13. Ibid., pp. 154, 198; February 11, 1969, pp. 315, 257.

14. Ibid., March 11, 1969, pp. 382, 417–420, 447–450.

15. Ibid., pp. 502–503.

16. New Orleans States-Item, Feb. 12, 1969; Kirkwood, American Grotesque, p. 298. Later efforts by the prosecution to enter testimony about Russo's hypnosis sessions into the court record failed when Judge Haggerty sided with the defense and refused to allow Dr. Fatter to testify about them. When Haggerty ruled that the hypnosis transcripts, like the sodium Pentothal memorandum, were inadmissible as well, the defense abandoned its plan to present expert testimony regarding the inappropriately suggestive questions posed during the hypnosis interviews.

17. Andrew Sciambra, trial transcript, February 12, 1969, pp. 59, 26–27.

18. Ibid., pp. 20, 17, 42–44.

19. According to James Phelan, Garrison believed the 1963 FBI investigation of David Ferrie uncovered some inculpatory information that the bureau withheld, but Ferrie's FBI file is now available and Garrison was wrong.

20. James Hardiman, trial transcript, Feb. 12, 1969, p. 6, Feb. 13, 1969, p. 25; Kirkwood, American Grotesque, p. 308.

CHAPTER ELEVEN

1. Garrison, interview, Playboy magazine, Oct. 1967.

2. Abraham Zapruder, trial transcript, Feb. 13, 1969, pp. 80–82; Kirkwood, American Grotesque, 311–314.

3. Once in Jim Garrison's office the film was permanently "liberated." In Los Angeles a man using the name "Hervé Lamarr" appeared with a print in his possession, copies were struck, and soon the large body of interested parties in the area were viewing it, often under makeshift conditions—a sheet hung on a living room wall in the absence of a screen, for instance. (The illegality of possessing the film was a concern; those obtaining it were told to say, if asked, though no one ever did, that it arrived from parts unknown in their mailbox inside a plain manila envelope with no return address.) These bootlegged copies quickly proliferated and over time the quality deteriorated dramatically as copies were struck from copies. This led to some significant misinterpretations of the film.

4. New Orleans States-Item, Feb. 14, 1969.

5. Kirkwood, American Grotesque, p. 311.

6. Buell Wesley Frazier, and Lyndel Shaneyfelt, trial transcript, Feb. 14, 1969, pp. 11 (Frazier), 82, 78 (Shaneyfelt); New Orleans States-Item, Feb. 14, 1969.

7. Trial transcript, James Simmons, Feb. 15, 1969, pp. 8, 10; William Eugene Newman, Jr., Feb. 17, 1969, p. 11; Billy Joe Martin, Feb. 14, 1969, pp. 51–54; Roger Craig, Feb. 14, 1969, pp. 75–81; Richard E. Carr, Feb. 19, 1969, pp. 17–18, 20; Mrs. Elizabeth Carolyn Walton, Feb. 14, 1969, pp. 94–95.

8. Dr. John Marshall Nichols, trial transcript, Feb. 17 and 19, 1969, pp. 33–35, 40, 43–44, 45, 50–57.

9. New Orleans Times-Picayune, Feb. 20, 1969 (Mrs. Jessie Parker); Kirkwood, American Grotesque, pp. 348–350.

10. Garrison claimed a local television reporter was at fault for the publicity sur-

rounding the fingerprint card. Garrison supposedly locked up the records after Shaw's arrest and the matter of the alias on the card was forgotten until July of 1968 when Habighorst told his story on television and released a copy he had kept of the card. But an internal investigation by the Police Superintendent revealed the truth: Habighorst's televised interview was cleared by Garrison's office (*New Orleans States-Item*, Feb. 20, 1969). Why did Garrison do it? Perhaps he realized the judge would disallow the card as evidence under any circumstances, and that even if admitted, Habighorst's story would be discredited. By putting Habighorst on television, Garrison insured that his constituents—the potential jury pool—knew about Habighorst's story and heard only his version of it.

11. Trial transcript, Feb. 19, 1969, pp. 53, 69 (Aloysius J. Habighorst), 79, 82–84, 99–101 (Louis J. Curole), 109–111, 121 (Jonas J. Butzman), 124–125, 128–129 (John N. Perkins, Jr.), 132–135, 144 (Edward F. Wegmann), 147, 148 (Salvatore Panzeca), 155–157, 167–169 (Clay Shaw); Kirkwood, *American Grotesque*, pp. 353–359.

12. Judge Edward A. Haggerty, Jr., trial transcript, Feb. 19, 1969, pp. 179–180; *Los Angeles Times*, Feb. 20, 1969.

13. *New Orleans States-Item*, Feb. 21, 1969.

14. The testimony regarding the consistent ninety-degree temperature in the Clinton area has been challenged and probably rightly so. Gerald Posner in *Case Closed*, for instance, cited records of the U.S. Weather Bureau indicating that the daily temperature occasionally dropped into the eighties.

15. Robert A. Frazier, trial transcript, Feb. 21–22, 1969, pp. 49, 68–69.

16. Col. Pierre A. Finck, trial transcript, Feb. 24, 1969, pp. 11, 40.

17. Ibid., pp. 71 ("higher"), 48 ("in charge"), 117–120 ("not to," "probe") 17 (exited), 125 ("major bones"), 196–197, 207, (Feb. 25, 1969) 30–32 (rectangular structure), 137 (metallic fragments), 24–25, 192, (Feb. 25, 1969) 22, 28 (three inches too high). The *New Orleans Times-Picayune* (Feb. 25, 1969, p. 17, col. 3) reported Finck's description of the throat wound's exit point as "at the approximate level of the tie knot." The trial transcript (p. 17) contains the word "know" instead of "knot."

18. Following the trial, in a memorandum he submitted to Shaw's attorneys, Dr. Finck addressed several of the issues that had given him difficulty on cross-examination. One was "why the neck wound was not dissected." Finck wrote: "An attempt was made to probe this wound; however, the president had been transported from Dallas, Texas, to Washington, D.C., in a position other than that at the time he was shot and rigormortis had congealed the muscles in a manner different from the position at the time the bullet track or the missile track was made and this accounts for the inability to probe the wound." A new item Finck mentioned was the backward movement of the president's head at the time of the fatal shot. He wrote: "The Zapruder film shows the president extending back following the head wound. Some have used this as evidence that he was struck from the front. A better explanation is that (due to the severance of his brain from his spinal cord as described in the autopsy report) he experienced decerebrate rigidity due to loss of cerebral control" (six-page memorandum, undated and unsigned [from the files of William J. Wegmann]).

19. Dean Andrews, trial transcript, Feb. 25, 1969, pp. 3, 7, 11.

20. Ibid., pp. 8, 11, 13–16.

21. Ibid., pp. 17–34, 52, 55, 123, 126.
22. Ibid., pp. 127–128, 138, 130, 132, 131.
23. Ibid., pp. 132, 137.
24. Ibid., pp. 138, 147, 149, 157, 160, 148. During his direct examination by Dymond, Andrews said, "I believe my office investigator came to visit me and we talked about whether or not he remembered Lee Oswald," and Andrews placed the investigator's visit *after* the call to his secretary. But this conflicts with the earliest 1963 statements of Andrews and his investigator both as to the timing of the visit (it *preceded* the call to the secretary) and the content of their discussion (they talked about the upcoming election in which Andrews was running for a judgeship).
25. Kirkwood, *American Grotesque*, p. 395.
26. Charles A. Appel, Jr., trial transcript, Feb. 25, 1969, pp. 30–31.
27. Lt. Edward O'Donnell, trial transcript, Feb. 26, 1969, pp. 8, 7.
28. Clay L. Shaw, trial transcript, Feb. 27, 1969, pp. 5–6, 14–15, 7–8, 19–23; 15–17.
29. Ibid., pp. 11–12, 24–28.
30. Shaw referred to a letter dated Sept. 11, 1963, from the representative of the Columbia Basin World Development Conference in Portland, Oregon, confirming arrangements for him to speak there on Nov. 26. The Bermúdez letter soliciting the San Francisco speaking engagement was dated Nov. 11, prompting a telephone conversation between Shaw and Sullivan. Sullivan recalls that Shaw placed the call but Shaw's recollection was that Sullivan initiated it. Shaw's custom was to travel by train and he did so on this occasion. He stayed in Los Angeles from Nov. 18 to Nov. 20, 1963, and took the overnight Lark to San Francisco. He arrived there on the Nov. 21, left on Nov. 23, and traveled to Portland. The conference there was canceled but the sponsors arranged for him to address the Rotary Club (trial testimony, Feb. 27, 1969, pp. 24–25, 30–32; Monroe Sullivan, telephone conversation with author, June 21, 1995).
31. Clay L. Shaw, trial transcript, Feb. 27, 1969, pp. 55–56, 59, 42–43.
32. *New Orleans Times-Picayune*, Feb. 28, 1969; Kirkwood, *American Grotesque*, pp. 413–414.
33. Mr. and Mrs. Nicholas M. Tadin, trial transcript, Feb. 27, 1969, pp. 12–13, 10, 18–19, 29–31; Kirkwood, *American Grotesque*, p. 417.
34. Dr. John Marshall Nichols, trial transcript, Feb. 28, 1969, pp. 4–8, 35–41.
35. Kirkwood, *American Grotesque*, p. 423; Elizabeth McCarthy, trial transcript, Feb. 28, 1969, pp. 86, 92.
36. Jim Garrison, closing statement, trial transcript, Feb. 28, 1969, pp. 138–141; 146; 157. (Page 150 is missing in the available transcript but the text of it may be found in Kirkwood's *American Grotesque* at p. 458.)
37. Kirkwood, *American Grotesque*, p. 301.
38. Ibid., pp. 550, 557; *New Orleans Times-Picayune*, March 2, 1969; "Press Interviews of the Jury Immediately Following the Acquittal of Clay A. Shaw on March 1, 1969," eight-page memorandum (from the files of Edward F. Wegmann).
39. *New Orleans Times-Picayune*, March 2, 1969.
40. Kirkwood, *American Grotesque*, pp. 492–493.

NOTES

CHAPTER TWELVE

1. Perry Russo's statement to this writer that he may have been hypnotized as many as five times is supported by the charges Dr. Fatter billed to Garrison's office for his services. (See Daniel J. Jones, Christenberry transcript, p. 411.)
2. Jim Garrison, Christenberry transcript, p. 235.
3. Ibid., p. 226.
4. Ibid., pp. 246–247.
5. Ibid., pp. 269–270.
6. Ibid., pp. 275–276 ("a warm feeling"); p. 272 ("I cannot").
7. F. Irvin Dymond, interview with author, Nov. 2, 1995.
8. Christenberry transcript, p. 23.
9. Willard E. Robertson, Christenberry transcript, pp. 50, 51.
10. Nor did the founders of T & C have any information about Governor McKeithen's two $5,000 contributions. But when the news reached the governor that his generosity had been revealed in Christenberry's courtroom, McKeithen admitted to inquiring reporters that his donation had come from public funds; and that information was presented to the citizens of New Orleans in a banner headline.
11. William Gurvich, Christenberry transcript, pp. 337–346, 354.
12. Clay Shaw, Christenberry transcript, p. 465.
13. Perry Russo, interview with author, Dec. 4, 1993.
14. F. Irvin Dymond, interview with author, Nov. 2, 1995; Wegmann Memorandum; Russo–Defense Team Interview; Russo–Gurvich Interview; Russo–Wegmann et al. Interview.
15. Perry Russo, interviews with author, Dec. 4, 1993, Feb. 7, 1994.
16. Judge Christenberry's opinion, May 27, 1971, *Clay L. Shaw v. Jim Garrison*, Civil Action No. 71-135, 328 F.Supp. 390–404. Louis Ivon had confirmed that a *Life* magazine photographer took Shaw's picture unbeknownst to him through a two-way mirror (Christenberry transcript, pp. 443–444).
17. *New Orleans States-Item*, Aug. 15, 1974.
18. Edward O'Donnell, Confidential Report, to Joseph I. Giarrusso, Superintendent of Police, Aug. 10, 1970.
19. Conversation with David Snyder, Aug. 15, 1995.
20. Shaw Journal, pp. 37, 1; David Snyder, "The Ordeal of Clay Shaw: Character Assassination," *New Orleans Times-Picayune*, July 28, 1996.
21. Shaw Journal, pp. 106, 71; David Snyder, "The Ordeal of Clay Shaw: Character Assassination," *New Orleans Times-Picayune*, July 28, 1996.
22. HSCA Report, pp. 142; G. Robert Blakey and Richard N. Billings, *The Plot to Kill the President* (New York: Times Books, 1981), p. 46.

GARRISON EXPOUNDS ON THE ASSASSINATION

1. *New Orleans Times-Picayune*, Feb. 25, 1967; Nicholas C. Chriss, "Melodrama, but the Plot is Obscure," *Los Angeles Times*, March 26, 1967; Paris Flammonde, "Why President Kennedy Was Killed," *Evergreen*, Jan. 1969, p. 73 (citing the Associated

Press and the *Washington Post* of Feb. 25, 1967, and the *Washington Sunday Star* of Feb. 26, 1967).

2. *Newsweek*, March 20, 1967, citing *Paris-Match* quoting Garrison.

3. Nicholas C. Chriss, "Melodrama, but the Plot is Obscure," Los Angeles *Times*, March 26, 1967.

4. *Baton Rouge Morning Advocate*, May 22, 1967, citing Garrison interview with Bob Jones on WWL-TV.

5. *Baton Rouge Morning Advocate*, May 24, 1967, and *New Orleans States-Item*, May 23, 1967, both citing Associated Press interview with Garrison.

6. *New York Times*, July 17, 1967, describing Garrison's July 15, 1967, speech on NBC television.

7. Garrison, letter to Bertrand Russell, Aug. 27, 1967 (included in transcript of Assassination Records Review Board hearing in New Orleans on June 28, 1995, pp. 78–79).

8. Garrison, interview, "Mike Wallace at Large," NBC, Sept. 26, 1967.

9. Paris Flammonde, "Why President Kennedy Was Killed," *Evergreen*, Jan. 1969 (quoting Garrison interview on WFAA-TV in Dallas, Dec. 9, 1967), p. 76; Brener, *The Garrison Case*, p. 223 (citing the *New Orleans Times-Picayune*, Dec. 19, 1967).

10. *New Orleans Times-Picayune*, Dec. 27, 1967.

CHAPTER THIRTEEN

1. Dymond et al. Interview.

2. *Ibid.*

3. Salvatore Panzeca, interview with author, Nov. 30, 1993.

4. Jim Garrison, filmed interview, 1989, in Richard Cohen and Carol Kachmer's *Rough Side of the Mountain*, a documentary work-in-progress begun in 1971 about the Clinton witnesses.

5. Edwin Lea McGehee later (after Marina Oswald testified that Oswald could not drive, owned no car and that she had never been to the Clinton area) tried to disassociate his "Oswald" from the old car and its female passenger. He speculated to this writer that the "black car" with those other men inside could have been parked around the corner from his barber shop, out of sight. Yet, although McGehee never said he saw "Oswald" exit the car, in his earliest statement to the D.A.'s office and in his trial testimony McGehee clearly indicated that he believed Oswald arrived in it. Also, the car and the woman passenger were reportedly seen at the home of Reeves Morgan as well. Both were an integral part of the Oswald-in-Clinton story, at least in the beginning.

6. Kirkwood, *American Grotesque*, p. 612–613.

7. Director of the FBI, letter to the Attorney General, Feb. 10, 1969.

8. Richard H. Kilbourne, Sr., interview with author, Dec. 6, 1993.

9. John Manchester, trial transcript, Feb. 6, 1969, p. 69; William Dunn, trial transcript, Feb. 7, 1969, pp. 19–20.

10. Manchester, trial transcript, Feb. 6, 1969, p. 59; Palmer, trial transcript, p. 85.

NOTES

11. Manchester, trial transcript, Feb. 6, 1969, p. 72; Corrie Collins, trial transcript, Feb. 6, 1969, p. 118.
12. Garrison, On the Trail of the Assassins, pp. 108–109; Garrison also recited the Oswald-record-switching explanation in the documentary film, Rough Side of the Mountain (see note 4).
13. Anne Hundley Dischler, field notes (hereinafter Dischler Notes), entry dated May 18, 1967.
14. The message in the Dischler Notes reads: "People in St. Francisville few months [ago?]—Oswald—tried reg. to vote—tried to work at hosp.—in company of Shaw and Ferrie—Cadillac Henry Earl Palmer—Registrar of Voters 504-683-5171—Clinton, LA." The word "Jackson" appears after Palmer's name, but a line has been drawn though it (Dischler Notes, entry dated May 18, 1967). The meaning of the reference to St. Francisville, which is about twenty-five miles from Clinton, is unclear. But it is the home of Judge John Rarick (see note 28).
15. Jack Rogers had his own relationship with Jim Garrison, as seen in this Dischler notation dated Aug. 29, 1967: "Spoke to Jack Rogers by phone—said he is going to [New Orleans] this P.M.—needs to see Garrison. . . ."
16. The following entry in the Dischler Notes suggests that susceptibility to Garrison's rhetoric among Clinton's black community may have been a factor in their cooperation with him: "CORE people decided this year not to vote for [Clinton] Alderman [Willie Joe] Yarbrough because of his connection with Shaw (relative) who was mixed up with Oswald, so they may be of more help." (Dischler Notes, entry dated Aug. 15, 1967). Yarbrough was married to Doris Shaw, Clay Shaw's first cousin.
17. Anne Dischler, interview with author, Feb. 2–3, 1994 (hereinafter Dischler Interview); Billings Personal Notes, entry dated May 23, 1967, p. 81.
18. Dischler Interview. Dischler, who had earlier explained that many of Garrison's files had been stolen, said if I didn't find this picture that it might have been among those that "came up missing."
19. Dischler Interview; Dischler telephone conversation, Feb. 4, 1994.
20. Ibid.
21. Corrie Collins said the car stayed there "10 or 15 minutes" (Dischler Notes, Oct. 3, 1967). But the other testimony placed it in that spot for five hours; at the trial Collins retreated, saying he could not recall how long it was parked there.
22. In the Dischler Notes the name "Morgan" is accompanied by a question mark and then in parentheses: "(Is Zip Morgan related to Estus?)." That is followed by: "Note: This man may not be a Morgan — refer to Henry Earl [Palmer]" (Dischler Notes, Oct. 3, 1967).
23. The identification of the man "in white" as Winslow Foster was provided to Dischler by Henry Earl Palmer (Dischler Notes, entry dated Oct. 3, 1967; Dischler Interview).
24. Richard Stevens, telephone interview, April 8, 1995; Barney Lea, telephone interview, April 7, 1995.
25. Nellie Louise Morgan, telephone interview, March 31, 1996. (She and Estus Morgan were married three years and had two sons.) Morgan's birth and military information are found in his hospital employment records.

26. Andrew Sciambra, Memorandum to Garrison, June 1, 1967, re interview with Henry Earl Palmer on May 29, 1967.
27. Bethell Diary, Oct. 2, 1967, p. 10.
28. In Henry Earl Palmer's May 29, 1967, interview he stated that Judge John Rarick "may have been with him" when he saw the black car and that it "could have been" Judge Rarick who ran the license check on it. Notably, at that time John Manchester, who later provided the definitive identification of the car and its driver, was not yet a firm witness. This reference to Rarick suggests the role he might have played if Manchester had not firmed up. An ardent segregationist later elected to the U.S. House of Representatives, John Rarick's support of Jim Garrison is not widely known. But in 1971, when Garrison was under indictment on bribery charges, Rarick reportedly entered remarks into the Congressional Record supporting him. Described recently by a lifelong Clinton resident as "the spiritual leader" of the Ku Klux Klan, Rarick's 1963 rulings from the bench exacerbated the local strife. Then and later (while he was in Congress), Rarick reportedly maintained an extremely active interest and influence over all aspects of the Clinton community, especially East Louisiana State Hospital, and at least two of the Clinton witnesses had close ties to him: Palmer was regarded as Rarick's protégé, and barber McGehee in 1993 was still cutting Rarick's hair. It may be relevant that Rarick resides in St. Francisville, the first location mentioned in the initial tip about the black Cadillac (see note 14).
29. In a memorandum dated Oct. 26, 1967 (thirteen days after Frugé and Dischler were removed from the case), Andrew Sciambra advised Jim Garrison that he had a tape recording of an interview with Collins and that Collins remembered seeing the black Cadillac. Conspicuously missing from this October memorandum by Sciambra is any reference to the occupants of the car. The two men—one in white, the other (possibly) in blue jeans—that Collins told Frugé and Dischler he saw exiting the car, had vanished permanently from Collins's testimony. Sciambra wrote that a transcript of the Collins tape recording would be done "later"; it has never surfaced. The story that Collins would tell at Shaw's trial began to emerge in a memorandum Sciambra wrote to Garrison on January 31, 1968, describing an interview with Collins conducted by Sciambra and James Alcock. At this point, the two men exiting the car had become one man, and Collins positively identified a picture of him. In this January memorandum, Sciambra also specifically disassociated Estus Morgan from the car and from Oswald, stating that Collins said he knew Morgan and saw him in the registration line, but was uncertain whether or not it was the same day.
30. The trial testimony concerning Oswald's visit to East Louisiana State Hospital also materialized on Andrew Sciambra's watch. Maxine Kemp's claim that she saw Oswald's job application first appeared in a memorandum Sciambra wrote to Garrison two months after Frugé and Dischler were dismissed. Bobbie Dedon's claim that Oswald asked her for directions to the personnel office first appeared in another Sciambra memorandum written six days later, supposedly recapping an interview conducted on Aug. 4, 1967. But the Aug. 4, 1967, entry in the Dischler Notes describing that interview said only that Dedon found

NOTES

Oswald's picture "very familiar" (she said the same about Shaw's), and made no mention of Dedon having seen or spoken to Oswald. (Andrew Sciambra, Memorandum to Garrison, regarding Guy Broyles, Personnel Manager, ELSH, Jan. 23, 1968; Sciambra, Memorandum to Garrison, regarding interview with Bobbie Dedon on Aug. 4, 1967, dated Jan. 29, 1968; Dischler Notes, Aug. 4, 1967.)

31. The Committee members apparently accepted without question the statements made by Francis Frugé. But Frugé misled the Committee in several particulars: (1) Frugé said he was "detailed to work on the Garrison investigation in 1968." In fact, he was assigned to the case in February 1967, when he and Dischler looked into the Rose Cheramie matter. The Dischler Notes on the Cheramie investigation, which are quite extensive, start on February 25, 1967, and begin "Garrison—New Orleans—called Frugé in connection with one Rose Cheramie . . ." (2) When asked "what trail" led to the Clinton witnesses, Frugé said that Andrew Sciambra "would know best," that Sciambra had provided the list of "forty-five-plus potential witnesses." In fact, the "tip," as outlined in this chapter, went to Frugé and Dischler from the Sovereignty Commission. As for the names of potential witnesses, they were obtained by Frugé and Dischler in the course of their investigation. Many, perhaps most, appear to have come from Palmer's list of registrants. (3) Frugé told the Committee "one of the most believable" Clinton witnesses was Andrew Dunn, who died "in a jail cell before he could testify." Dunn, an alcoholic, who was found hanged in his cell in the Clinton jail and ruled a suicide, was regarded by Anne Dischler as quite credible. But Dischler told me Frugé disagreed, claiming that Dunn's alcoholism hurt his reliability, and Dunn was never slated to testify. Frugé touting Dunn to the HSC was odd since Dunn's story was quite different from the official one told in court. He claimed, for example, that there were four men in the Cadillac, one of them Banister, and they "got out of the car and stretched their legs" (Frugé, HSCA Outside Contact Report, Dec. 19, 1978; Dischler Interview; Sciambra, memorandum to Jim Garrison, July 18, 1967, re July 17, 1967, interview with Andrew H. Dunn; Andrew H. Dunn Affidavit, July 13, 1967).

32. Joe Newbrough, a private detective who worked for Guy Banister, described the building's layout on the television program, Frontline, Nov. 16, 1993 (transcript, p. 12). Reporter David Snyder recently verified that the Lafayette Street offices were not linked interiorly with those at 544 Camp.

33. Gurvich Conference, tape #3, p. 4.

34. Jack Martin tried to share the blame for the library card story with his friend Hardy Davis, telling the FBI that during several telephone conversations with Davis the two of them "may have come to the conclusion that Oswald had used or carried Ferrie's library card" (Martin, FBI interview, Nov. 27, 1963). David Ferrie categorically denied the library card story at its 1963 inception. At that time his card was in the New Orleans Police Department's First District property room, having been confiscated with the rest of his personal effects when he was arrested following his ice skating trip to Houston (Ferrie, FBI interviews, Nov. 25 and Nov. 27, 1963). Ferrie was so baffled by the story that he paid a visit to Oswald's former New Orleans apartment in a futile effort to resolve the mystery (Mrs. Jesse Garner, deposition, June 14, 1978, pp. 19–24,

33–37, 39–41). But the explanation, which follows, was buried in the files of the FBI, and wouldn't be released to the public for many years: Jack Martin passed the library card story on to Hardy Davis. Davis repeated it to Ferrie's employer, Attorney G. Wray Gill. Gill repeated it at least twice, to Ferrie's roommate, Layton Martens, and to Ferrie himself (Hardy Davis, FBI interview, Nov. 27, 1963; Gill, FBI interview, Nov. 27, 1963). But the Committee's references to the story begin and end with Gill, which is rather like omitting the first two acts of a three-act play (HSCA, Vol. 10, p. 113; HSCA Rpt., p. 144). By omitting Martin's role as author of the story, and Davis's as conduit of it, the Committee created the impression that Gill's knowledge came from some mysterious, authoritative source. This curious presentation, cutting it off from its false roots, made the story sound like an *authentic possibility* instead of what it actually was—one of the most effective falsehoods Martin ever told.

35. HSCA outside contact report, Nov. 22, 1977; HSCA Vol. 10, pp. 130, 131.
36. Richard Billings, letter to Garrison, April 22, 1968; Garrison, letter to Billings, April 29, 1968; Billings, letter to Edward F. Wegmann, Jan. 8, 1969 (in the files of James Phelan).

CHAPTER FOURTEEN

1. Sgt. Edward O'Donnell, report to Jim Garrison, June 20, 1967, regarding "Perry Russo Interview," conducted June 19, 1967. O'Donnell's report is included in this book as Appendix B, and discussed in chapter 9. The test by Roy Jacob, which is mentioned in O'Donnell's report, was administered on March 8, 1967, and is discussed in chapter 7.
2. Garrison, On the Trail of the Assassins, p. 152.
3. Garrison interview, Playboy, Oct. 1967, p. 64.
4. Ibid.
5. Garrison, On the Trail of the Assassins, p. 156.
6. Kruebbe Interview; Kruebbe's Work Report, dated March 18, 1967, regarding Bundy polygraph administered March 17, 1967 (in the files of James Kruebbe); Edward O'Donnell, Christenberry transcript, p. 301; Jim Garrison, Christenberry transcript, p. 247.
7. Hugh Exnicios, Lynn Loisel, and Al Beaubouef, "Conference," twenty-nine-page transcript, March 10, 1967; Hugh Exnicios and Mrs. William C. Super, Christenberry transcript, pp. 118–119 (Exnicios), 131–132 (Super); Trosclair Report; see also: Billings Personal Notes, pp. 35–38; New Orleans States-Item, May 10, 1967; New Orleans Times-Picayune, May 11, 1967; Hugh Aynesworth, "The JFK 'Conspiracy,'" Newsweek, May 15, 1967; Exnicios, letter to the Louisiana State Bar Association, May 9, 1967.
8. Garrison, On the Trail of the Assassins, p. 162; Trosclair Report. While the tape itself has not survived, a number of people heard it, among them two of Shaw's attorneys, the U.S. Attorney in New Orleans, the D.A. in Jefferson Parish, Deputy Superintendent of Police Trosclair, and Mrs. William C. Super, the court reporter who made a verbatim transcription of it (Dymond et al. Interview; Hugh B. Exnicios, Jr., letter to Louisiana State Bar Association, May 9, 1967; the Trosclair

NOTES

Report; Mrs. William C. Super, Christenberry transcript, pp. 131–132). A copy of that document is today available in the JFK Collection at the National Archives (Hugh Exnicios, Lynn Loisel, and Al Beaubouef, "Conference," twenty-nine-page transcript, March 10, 1967).

9. Garrison, On the Trail of the Assassins, pp. 131–132.
10. "Garrison Predicts Success for Probe," New Orleans Times-Picayune, Feb. 19, 1967; "Oswald Didn't Act Alone, DA Says," Los Angeles Times, Feb. 19, 1967. Both of these Sunday articles describe the news conference Garrison held the day before.
11. Shaw Journal, p. 105; Shaw Notes, Oct. 2, 1967; Steve Dorril, "PERMINDEX: The International Trade in Disinformation," Lobster #2, 1983. Garrison pretends that the Permindex information was discovered after Shaw's trial. It wasn't. It was published in the New Orleans States-Item and the New Orleans Times-Picayune on April 25, 1967, two months after Shaw's arrest and two years before the trial.
12. Shaw's contacts with the CIA's Domestic Contact Service were summarized in a memorandum released by that agency in 1992; some of the reports based on Shaw's information were released in 1994. Shaw was first contacted by the CIA's New Orleans office in December 1948; between 1949 and May 25, 1956 (when Shaw ceased to be a contact), he was contacted a total of thirty times. Eight reports were written based on Shaw's information. Six of those were "on hand" and described in the 1992 memorandum. Three concerned a trip Shaw made in March through May, 1949, to the West Indies, Central America, and Northern South America; and a fourth concerned a 1951 trip to Central and South America and the Caribbean area. The fifth report advised that Shaw had leased to the "CSR government" space for merchandise display in New Orleans for one year beginning in April 1949. The sixth, in March 1952, concerned a letter to the public relations director of the International Trade Mart from a trade consultant to the Bonn Government (CIA document, "Subject: Clay L. Shaw [201-813493]," "Enclosure 21"; "Approved for release 1992 CIA Historical Review Program").
13. The CIA report reads: "Shilstone, Cecil Maxwell. May have had contact with DCS, New Orleans. (Inquiry being made) Member of group of New Orleans businessmen supply Garrison with funds."
14. Victor Marchetti, quoted by Mark Lane in Plausible Denial (New York: Thunder's Mouth Press, 1991), p. 222; HSCA notes on Clay Shaw's CIA file, referring to "2/10/69–TWX #0002 to contacts/Washington, 10/13/67" (Record No. 180-10143-10221, CIA Segregated Collection, Box 19).
15. Garrison, On the Trail of the Assassins, pp. 82–83.
16. Ibid., p. 186. The witness was Richard Case Nagell.
17. Ibid., pp. 188–190.
18. Ibid., p. 202. Jim Garrison's earlier assertions of Oswald's innocence prompted James Alcock to say that "Garrison had 'pulled our overt act out from underneath us.'" (Bethell Diary, p. 11.)
19. Garrison, On the Trail of the Assassins, pp. 101–103. Garrison arrived at this notion when he discovered that the Warren Commission deleted from its exhibit 1365 an erroneous motorcade map (published the morning of the assassination in the Dallas Morning News), which showed the motorcade traveling down

Main Street instead of turning onto Houston and then onto Elm. This is one of those peculiar leaps that characterize Garrison's thinking.

20. The motorcade route was published in both newspapers on Nov. 19, 1963 (WR p. 40).

21. Iris Kelso, "Garrison's book on JFK's slaying," *New Orleans Times-Picayune*, Jan. 12, 1989. (For additional reviews see Jack Wardlaw, "Retrying a losing case," *New Orleans Times-Picayune*, Jan. 15, 1989; and Ronnie Dugger, "Reverberations of Dallas," *The New York Times Book Review*, Jan. 29, 1989.)

22. Edward Jay Epstein, "The Second Coming of Jim Garrison," *Atlantic Monthly*, March 1993; Prouty, *JFK: The CIA, Vietnam, and the Plot to Assassinate John F. Kennedy*, p. xvii. Oliver Stone's introductory essay to Prouty's book ("Oliver Stone Discusses His Film JFK and Introduces the Real 'Man X,'") reveals that Prouty "worked on" Garrison's manuscript "before its publication," and that he and Garrison were "well acquainted" through a long-standing correspondence.

23. Scheer, "Oliver Stone Builds His Own Myths."

CHAPTER FIFTEEN

1. Phelan Interview, June 8, 1993.

2. Richard Dodds, "Plot thickens: Garrison may shine in movie," *New Orleans Times-Picayune*, Feb. 5, 1991; "Director Oliver Stone tells why he tackled the big story of his time," *Dallas Morning News*, April 14, 1991.

3. Frank Beaver, *Oliver Stone: Wakeup Cinema* (New York: Twayne Publishers, 1994); Stephen Schiff, "The Last Wild Man," *The New Yorker*, Aug. 8, 1994; Oliver Stone, interview with Charlie Rose, *The Charlie Rose Show*, KCET, Sept. 25, 1997; "Oliver Stone: Biography/'JFK'" (in JFK press kit); David Baron, "Oliver's Story," *Lagniappe* (the New Orleans Times-Picayune Entertainment Guide), May 24, 1991; Stephen Talbot, "60s Something," *Mother Jones*, March–April, 1991; Robert Scheer, "Oliver Stone Builds His Own Myths," *Los Angeles Times, Calendar*, Dec. 15, 1991.

4. Oliver Stone, interview with Hugh Hewitt, "Life and Times," KCET, Dec. 16, 1993.

5. "Director Oliver Stone tells why he tackled the big story of his time," *The Dallas Morning News*, April 14, 1991; Stephen Talbot, "60s Something," *Mother Jones*, March–April 1991; Sean Mitchell, "Stone's Sixties," *USA Weekend*, Feb. 22–24, 1991.

6. Beverly Oliver is an example. She claimed to be the so-called babushka lady, the unidentified woman wearing the scarf and holding a camera who appears in some Dealey Plaza photographs. Oliver said she photographed the assassination but authorities confiscated her film. While few took her seriously, Stone did, and included her character in his story. He also seems to have included Ricky White's story (which was thoroughly discredited) that his father, a former Dallas Policeman, was the shooter on the knoll, and the man who later shot Officer Tippitt. The phony Ricky White story was peddled to Stone by Larry Howard, an admitted huckster (and co-director of the JFK Assassination Information Center in Dallas); Stone was so impressed that he hired Howard

NOTES

(and two colleagues) as "Consultants" and paid them $80,000.

7. Dymond et al. Interview; conversation with Harry F. Connick, Feb. 26, 1996.

8. Alcock Interview.

9. The contemporary story line actually begins with a scene in which a blond woman, who was known by the alias Rose Cheramie, is shoved from a moving car. Later she is seen being treated in a hospital where she says the president is going to be assassinated, and later still her dead body is shown lying alongside a Texas road. What is really known about Cheramie, real name Melba Christine Marcades, is that she was a prostitute, heroin addict, and sometimes mental patient known to exhibit "psychopathic behavior." She supposedly had fore-knowledge of President Kennedy's assassination and revealed it to a doctor at East Louisiana State Hospital and to Louisiana State Policeman Francis Frugé. She also allegedly claimed that she worked for Jack Ruby, the killer of Lee Harvey Oswald; that she saw Oswald with Ruby at his nightclub; and that Oswald and Ruby had been homosexual lovers for years. Cheramie's story did not surface until Jim Garrison's investigation of the assassination began. Francis Frugé, who was pro-moting the Cheramie story, was working for Garrison at the time, and searching for evidence to support Garrison's theories. Eventually Frugé, a controversial fig-ure, was forced to resign from the State Police.

10. David Ferrie, interview with Asst. D.A. John Volz, transcript Dec. 15, 1966, p. 12. In a 1996 interview with this writer, Louis Ivon made the startling claim that, during his evening at the Fontainebleau with Ferrie, Ferrie admitted he knew Oswald and Shaw. (Ivon Interview, Feb. 27, 1996; and telephone conver-sation with author, June 28, 1996.) Ivon's claim conflicts with every other statement Ferrie made about Oswald (Shaw was not yet an issue), both before and after that night at the Fontainebleau. Ferrie's denials began in 1963 with the New Orleans Police Department, the Secret Service, and the FBI; they con-tinued in 1966 with John Volz, in 1967 with David Snyder, and ended with George Lardner the night Ferrie died. Moreover, Jim Garrison never mentioned this crucial "admission" to the media, or, later, in his book, though Garrison trumpeted information to the press about Ferrie, and in his memoir wrote about the Ferrie-Ivon evening at the Fontainebleau. Nor did Garrison ever refer to Ferrie's "admission" in connection with the perjury charges he filed against Shaw, though it bore directly on those charges. Apparently, Ivon, who testified at both Shaw's trial and the Christenberry hearing, first went public with Ferrie's alleged admission when he spoke to Oliver Stone.

11. Alcock Interview.

12. Frank Minyard, interview with Stephen Tyler, documentary film, *He Must Have Something*, 1992. Minyard, who has endorsed this bizarre notion, described a bruise "on the inside of [Ferrie's] lip" that Minyard theorized was caused by "something that was traumatically inserted into [Ferrie's] mouth," citing the absence of any physical markings on the "outside" of Ferrie's body. But Dr. Ronald Welsh, who conducted Ferrie's autopsy, told me that an injury to the *outside*, from a fall, for instance, would manifest itself primarily on the *inside*. And he dismissed the bruise (described in the autopsy report as a "somewhat red-dish brown" three-quarter-inch "area of dryness" with "no deep hemorrhages or swellings") as entirely immaterial insofar as the cause of death was con-

FALSE WITNESS

cerned (Welsh Interview; David W. Ferrie, Autopsy Protocol, Orleans Parish Coroner's Office, Feb. 22, 1967, p. 1).

13. Oliver Stone, "Stone's *JFK*: A Higher Truth?" *Washington Post*, June 2, 1991; Ray LaFontaine and Mary LaFontaine, "First Look at Dallas' JFK Files," *Houston Post*, Feb. 2, 1992; George Lardner, Jr., "FBI Questions 'Tramps' at JFK Slaying Site," *Washington Post*, March 4, 1992.

14. George Lardner, "On the Set: Dallas in Wonderland," *Washington Post*, May 19, 1991. "Almost all of Boxley's nuttiness was feedback," Harold Weisberg told Lardner. "He'd go out and make up the evidence to suit Garrison's theories."

15. According to Stone, O'Keefe was a composite of three homosexual witnesses against Shaw: David Logan, Raymond Broshears, and Perry Russo. But Logan and Broshears played no part in the actual case. Only Russo counted.

16. David Logan's statement was not stolen. (For details, see item 25, Appendix A in this book.)

17. Stone, "Oliver Stone Talks Back," *Premiere*, Jan. 1992, p. 69. On at least one occasion Stone showed the pictures to a reporter. Stone also cited the pictures in a footnote to his screenplay. (*JFK: The Book of the Film*, pp. 511 [the reporter], 81 [the screenplay].)

18. Both Garrison and Shaw's attorneys investigated the pictures and Robert Brannon, who died in 1962, was positively identified by Mrs. Lawrence Fischer, who had been at the party, and Robert Cahlman, of Radio Station WYES, who knew Brannon well. Mrs. Fischer had in her possession some fourteen additional photographs from the party, as well as the one of the Brannon–Shaw group published May 12, 1967, in *The Councilor*. The pictures were taken around 1949 (before David Ferrie moved to New Orleans) by photographer Miles De Russey at a party given by a Tulane University student. Jeff Biddison was shown the "Ferrie" picture by a Garrison aide "about the time" of the preliminary hearing (March 1967), and Mr. and Mrs. Fischer were interviewed by Garrison's investigator sometime prior to May 23, 1967 (report on "Citizens' Council Newspaper The [Councilor]," regarding investigation conducted May 18, 19, and 23, 1967, on behalf of Shaw's attorneys; memo, "re Bob Brannon," by "CLS" [Shaw], undated).

19. Epstein, "The Second Coming of Jim Garrison." Epstein explains that the *New York Times* briefly took the book seriously because Dial Press, as part of the joke, had listed it as a non-fiction work.

20. Shaw, trial transcript, Feb. 27, 1969, p 7.

21. Carl Oglesby, *The JFK Assassination* (New York: Signet, 1992), pp. 286, 292.

22. Rosemary James, "Letters," *New Orleans Times-Picayune*, June 20, 1991.

23. David Ehrenstein, "JFK—A New Low for Hollywood: Oliver Stone's Film Is Fueled by Jim Garrison's Homophobia," *The Advocate*, Jan. 14, 1992.

24. David Baron, "Oliver's Story," *Lagniappe, New Orleans Times-Picayune*, May 24, 1991.

25. Roger Ebert, "Interview with Oliver Stone," Dec. 17, 1991, in *JFK: The Book of the Film*, p. 252.

26. Robert Sam Anson, "The Shooting of JFK," *Esquire*, November 1991, p. 174.

27. David Baron, "Oliver's Story," *Lagniappe, New Orleans Times-Picayune*, May 24, 1991.

28. Ehrenstein, "JFK—A New Low for Hollywood."

NOTES

CHAPTER SIXTEEN

1. Scheer, "Oliver Stone Builds His Own Myths."
2. Phelan–Shaw Interview.
3. New Orleans Times-Picayune, Nov. 20, 1983.
4. Jim Garrison, letter to Jonathan Blackmer, regarding Thomas E. Beckham, July 18, 1977.
5. Jim Garrison, memo to Cliff Fenton, regarding Shaw's trip to San Francisco on Nov. 22, 1963, undated.
6. New Orleans States-Item, May 12, 13, and 17, 1967; Brener, The Garrison Case, pp. 203–205.
7. Nicholas C. Chriss, "Melodrama, but the Plot Is Obscure," Los Angeles Times, March 26, 1967; Max Lerner, "New Orleans' Carnival Duo: Mardi Gras and Shaw Trial," Los Angeles Times, Feb. 12, 1969; James Phelan, telephone conversation with author, Aug. 5, 1995.
8. Nicholas C. Chriss, "Melodrama, But the Plot Is Obscure," Los Angeles Times, March 26, 1967; Bethell Diary, p. 11.
9. Pershing Gervais, telephone interview, Sept. 3, 1993 ("absolutely crazy"); Hugh Exnicios, Lynn Loisel, and Al Beaubouef, "Conference," twenty-nine-page transcript, March 10, 1967 (Loisel: "sack of roaches"); Billings Personal Notes (didn't trust; lied), pp. 2, 4.
10. Jack Martin's close relationship with Garrison continued until the latter part of 1967, when a break occurred. It was probably precipitated by an odd and revealing document Martin filed with the Recorder of Mortgages for the Parish of Orleans (in Book No. 2126) and with the Louisiana Secretary of State (in Book 8, Folio 83) entitled, "Articles of Incorporation of 'Garrison-Intelligence-Agency.'" The purpose of this "independent intelligence force" was "to render and give aid to Jim Garrison, and to otherwise support him in his efforts." "Dear Jim," Martin wrote, in his letter sending a copy of the articles to Garrison, "Well, I've done as you wanted." Martin described his preparation and filing of the papers for the entity "otherwise known as 'Garrison's Guerrillas,' just as we've talked about." He had "kited a couple of checks (cause we were broke)," Martin said, "to get these papers filed." Written in the upper right-hand corner of Martin's letter in Garrison's hand is this: "Spoke to J.M. [Jack Martin] 12/3/67. Must be abolished."
11. Russo–Gurvich Interview, pp. 56–59. This draft-dodging scheme involved a false theft charge filed by the "victim," a woman, followed by the young man's arraignment. While the case "rolled a while" the draft board was advised of the charges through a "regular form letter."
12. New Orleans Times-Picayune, March 30, 1967.
13. Nicholas C. Chriss, "New Orleans: Melodrama, But the Plot Is Obscure," Los Angeles Times, March 26, 1967.
14. Gurvich Conference, tape #2, pp. 19–20; Pershing Gervais, telephone conversation with author, Aug. 22, 1993; David Ehrenstein, "JFK—A New Low for Hollywood," The Advocate, Jan. 14, 1992; Warren Rogers, "The Persecution of Clay Shaw," Look, Aug. 26, 1969.

15. Jim Garrison, interview, *Playboy,* Oct., 1967, p. 70.
16. Jack Anderson, "Jim Garrison Accused of Molesting Boy, 13: Crime Commission Asks Grand Jury to Probe," Bell–McClure Syndicate, Feb. 23, 1970. The content of Anderson's conversation with William Krummel was repeated by Anderson to a representative of the *New Orleans Times-Picayune* and included in that newspaper's file on the story (from the files of David Snyder).
17. Ibid.
18. Telephone interview with the victim of the fondling episode, Dec. 7, 1993; interview with the victim's older brother, Dec. 15, 1993.
19. Chandler Interview.
20. This was not the only mention of drugs in connection with Garrison. A New Orleans physician pointed out that Garrison's "facial expression manifested what we call a flat affect," meaning that it didn't reflect the intensity of the moment which, he said, is characteristic of a drug abuser. Since Garrison had a back problem he could have been abusing a prescription drug.
21. FBI memorandum, describing Frank W. Manning's statements to a Bureau representative, dated March 6, 1967, and letter of same date transmitting memorandum to the White House (FBIHQ Main File No. 67-446884, James Carothers Garrison). The Manning investigation was instituted at the time of the judges' defamation charge against Garrison. It was never made public, nor completed—it was dropped when the Supreme Court ruled in Garrison's favor. Manning offered his file to the FBI, suggesting that the Bureau complete the investigation, but the Director declined.
22. Paul Hoch, *Echoes of Conspiracy,* vol. 1, 1986, p. 10; Garrison, letter to Ted Gandolfo, April 14, 1986.
23. *New Orleans Times-Picayune,* Sept. 13, 1965 (O'Hara); Warren Rogers, "The Persecution of Clay Shaw," *Look* magazine, Aug. 26, 1969, p. 54.
24. Kirkwood, *American Grotesque,* pp. 527–528 (Kohn); Brener, *The Garrison Case,* p. 226.
25. Robert Hare, *Without Conscience* (New York: Pocket Books, 1993), pp. 25, 29, 34–56, 75, 102–123.
26. Ibid.
27. Iris Kelso, "Final Judgment," *New Orleans Times-Picayune,* Oct. 25, 1992.
28. Hare, *Without Conscience,* pp. 46–49.
29. Ibid., pp. 38, 45.
30. Bethell Diary, p. 9.
31. Brener, *The Garrison Case,* p. 269.
32. Kevin Walsh wrote to Oliver Stone on April 25, 1991, and to George Lardner and Oliver Stone on June 21, 1991, calling on both to use their "stature" to obtain the release of the files

CHAPTER SEVENTEEN

1. David Lifton, "Is Garrison Out of his Mind?" *Open City,* May 31–June 6, 1968. This represents corrected text; the original contained printing errors—dropped lines and transpositions.

NOTES

2. A 1996 newsletter published by one of the pro-Garrison groups linked James Phelan and *Washington Post* journalist Bob Woodward in a way so obscure it was incomprehensible. Attesting to Woodward's suspicious background, the author quoted a writer who noted that Woodward had attended Yale where the CIA is "encouraged to recruit" ("Star Reporters or Government Flaks?" *Probe,* Jan.–Feb., 1996).

3. James Phelan's three (Random House) books are, *Howard Hughes: The Hidden Years* (1976); *Scandals, Scamps and Scoundrels: The Casebook of an Investigative Reporter* (1982), which contains a long chapter on Jim Garrison; and *The Money: The Battle for Howard Hughes's Billions* (1997), written with Lewis Chester. Phelan also assisted in the production of a fourth book, *Hoax, The Inside Story of the Howard Hughes-Clifford Irving Affair,* by Stephen Fay, Lewis Chester, and Magnus Linklater (New York: The Viking Press, 1972).

4. Garrison's supporters make the following charges about Phelan: (1) That he turned the Sciambra memorandum over to the CIA when he had it copied at the Desert Inn, the Las Vegas turf of Robert Maheu. (Phelan was interested only in Maheu's copying machine and didn't even see him that day.) (2) Fabricated the story about Garrison's "homosexual thrill-killing" theory. (William Gurvich told Shaw's attorneys about it in 1967; Russo recited the "theory" in his 1971 statements to them and said it came from the D.A.'s office; several references to it, tied directly to Garrison, including at least one direct quote, are found in the Billings Personal Notes; and journalist Nicholas C. Chriss connected it to Garrison [See chapter 6, note 17].) (3) Was some sort of FBI groupie because he reportedly briefed that agency on his Garrison information two weeks before it was published. (The evidence suggests this didn't happen: Phelan had no recollection of it; it would have been uncharacteristic of him; one of the FBI agents supposedly involved denied to Phelan that he dictated the memo ascribed to him; and the information transmitted to the FBI contains errors Phelan would not have made. Phelan briefed a large number of *Post* attorneys and staffers about his Las Vegas trip; any one of them could have passed the information to the FBI, and if the Bureau had reason to protect the real source, the obvious person to identify would have been Phelan. [FBI Memorandum, from R. E. Wick to Mr. DeLoach, April 3, 1967; FBI Memorandum, dictated by R. E. Lenihan, April 5, 1967; FBI Airtel, from the Director, dictated by R. E. Lenihan, to the New Orleans field office, April 12, 1967.])

5. George Lardner, Jr., "On the Set: Dallas in Wonderland," *The Washington Post,* May 19, 1991.

6. James Bates, "Garrison Estate Files Lawsuit Over JFK Net Profits," Los Angeles *Times,* Nov. 18, 1995.

7. Cynthia Wegmann, testimony, Assassination Records Review Board public hearing in New Orleans, June 28, 1995.

8. Shaw Journal, p. 40.

9. *Ibid.,* p. 3.

10. *Ibid.*

11. Clay Shaw, letter to Sylvia Meagher, July 8, 1968; Sylvia Meagher, letter to Clay Shaw, June 1, 1968.

12. Telephone conversation with Tom Samoluk, July 15, 1997.

13. Steven Tilley, telephone interview with author, July 20, 1998.

14. The first hypnosis session (on March 1, 1967) began with Dr. Fatter telling Russo to visualize a television screen. The second and third sessions (on March 9 and 12, 1967) began with Fatter telling Russo to visualize a descending staircase. Garrison's composite begins with the descending staircase, followed by the television set. Fatter gave Russo the post-hypnotic suggestion at the end of the third session; it appears at the end of Garrison's "A" document. (Fatter, preliminary hearing transcript, pp. 409–422; Garrison Memo; Russo hypnosis transcripts, March 1, 1967, March 12, 1967.)
15. For example, Jim Garrison's document made Dr. Fatter's leading questions seem unimportant, and it obscured the timing and intent of the post-hypnotic suggestion Fatter gave Perry Russo.

CHAPTER EIGHTEEN

1. Shaw NBC Interview.
2. Leonard Gurvich, telephone interview with author, April 2, 1996. Since then Gurvich expressed his views in a letter to the New Orleans Times-Picayune on April 28, 1996.
3. Posner, Case Closed, p. 446.
4. In 1993 I informed Steven Tilley, the archivist in charge of the JFK Collection, about the Christenberry proceeding, and he ordered a copy of the transcript for the Collection.

PRESS CONFERENCE, MARCH 2, 1967

1. Steven Tyler, documentary film, He Must Have Something, 1992.

SELECT BIBLIOGRAPHY

Many of those I interviewed provided documents from their personal files that proved to be invaluable. I also drew extensively on government records, and data generated by Jim Garrison, those assisting him, and others caught up in his investigation. I used the full range of media sources, in particular the two New Orleans newspapers. The interviews I conducted, and other material not included here, are cited as they appear in the source notes.

BOOKS AND ARTICLES

"A Matter of Reasonable Doubt." *Life*, November 25, 1966.

Anson, Robert Sam. "The Shooting of JFK." *Esquire*, November 1991.

Beaver, Frank. *Oliver Stone: Wakeup Cinema*. New York: Twayne Publishers, 1994.

Bethell, Tom. "Conspiracy to End Conspiracies." *National Review*, December 16, 1991.

Blakey, G. Robert, and Richard N. Billings, *The Plot to Kill the President*. New York: Times Books, 1981.

Brener, Milton. *The Garrison Case: A Study in the Abuse of Power*. New York: Clarkson N. Potter, Inc., 1969.

Chandler, David. "The Devil's D.A." *New Orleans*, November 1966.

———. "The Assassin's Trail." *Westword*, November 25–December 1, 1992.

Clayman, Charles B., ed. *Encyclopedia of Medicine*. Chicago: American Medical Association, 1989.

Crowdus, Gary. "Personal Struggles and Political Issues: An Interview with Oliver Stone." *Cineaste*, vol. 16, no. 3, 1988.

Ehrenstein, David. "JFK—A New Low For Hollywood." *The Advocate*, January 14, 1992.

Epstein, Edward Jay. *Counterplot*. New York: The Viking Press, Inc., 1969.

———. "The Second Coming of Jim Garrison." *Atlantic Monthly*, March 1993.

"The Garrison Investigation: How and why it began." *New Orleans*, April 1967.

Garrison, Jim. *A Heritage of Stone*. New York: G.P. Putnam's Sons, 1970.

———. *On the Trail of the Assassins: My Investigation and Prosecution of the Murder of President Kennedy*. New York: Sheridan Square Press, 1988; Warner Books, 1991.

———. *The Star Spangled Contract*. New York: McGraw-Hill Book Company, 1976.

Hare, Robert D. *Without Conscience: The Disturbing World of the Psychopaths Among Us*. New York: Pocket Books, 1993.

James, Rosemary, and Jack Wardlaw. *Plot or Politics?: The Garrison Case and Its Cast*. New Orleans: Pelican Publishing House, 1967.

JFK: The Book of the Film. Compiled by Jane Rusconi. New York: Applause Books, 1992.

Kennedy, John F. *Profiles in Courage*. Memorial Edition. New York: Harper & Row, Publishers, 1964.

Kirkwood, James. "Surviving." *Esquire*, December 1968.

———. *American Grotesque*. 2d ed. New York: Simon and Schuster, 1970.

Lane, Mark. *Plausible Denial: Was the CIA Involved in the Assassination of JFK?* New York: Thunder's Mouth Press, 1991.

FALSE WITNESS

Lifton, David S. *Best Evidence.* New York: Macmillian Publishing Co., Inc., 1980.
———. "Is Garrison Out of His Mind?" *Open City,* May 31–June 6, 1968.
Marrs, Jim. *Crossfire: The Plot That Killed Kennedy.* New York: Carroll & Graf Publishers, Inc., 1989.
Oglesby, Carl. *The JFK Assassination.* New York: Signet, 1992.
Phelan, James. "The Vice Man Cometh." *The Saturday Evening Post,* June 1963.
———. "A Plot to Kill Kennedy? Rush to Judgment in New Orleans." *The Saturday Evening Post,* May 6, 1967.
———. "Clay Shaw." *Penthouse,* November 1969.
———. *Scandals, Scamps and Scoundrels: The Casebook of an Investigative Reporter.* New York: Random House, 1982. Chap. 8, "Jim Garrison v. Clay Shaw."
Posner, Gerald. *Case Closed: Lee Harvey Oswald and the Assassination of JFK.* New York: Random House, 1993.
Prouty, L. Fletcher. *JFK: The CIA, Vietnam, and the Plot to Assassinate John F. Kennedy.* New York: Carol Publishing Group, 1992.
Report of the President's Commission on the Assassination of President John F. Kennedy, and twenty-six volumes of Hearings and Exhibits. Washington: U.S. Government Printing Office, 1964.
Report of the Select Committee on Assassinations, U.S. House of Representatives, and twelve volumes of Hearings and Appendices, 1979.
Roberts, Gene. "The Case of Jim Garrison and Lee Oswald." *The New York Times Magazine,* May 21, 1967.
Rogers, Warren. "The Persecution of Clay Shaw." *Look,* August 26, 1969.
Stone, Oliver. "Oliver Stone Talks Back." *Premiere,* January 1992.
Scheer, Robert. "Oliver Stone Builds His Own Myths." *Los Angeles Times,* Calendar, December 1991.
Schiff, Stephen. "The Last Wild Man." *The New Yorker,* Aug. 8, 1994.
Talbot, Stephen. "60s Something." *Mother Jones,* March–April 1991.
Thompson, Josiah. *Six Seconds In Dallas.* New York: Bernard Geis Associates, 1967.
———. "The Cross Fire That Killed President Kennedy." *The Saturday Evening Post,* December 2, 1967.
Weisberg, Harold. *Oswald In New Orleans.* New York: Canyon Books, 1967.
Whalen, Richard J. "The Kennedy Assassination." *The Saturday Evening Post,* January 14, 1967.
Williams, Harry T. *Huey Long.* New York: Vintage Books, 1981.
Wise, David. "Secret Evidence on the Kennedy Assassination." *The Saturday Evening Post,* April 6, 1968.
Yarbrough, Jeff. "Heart of Stone." *The Advocate,* April 7, 1992.

COURT TRANSCRIPTS

Clay L. Shaw, Arrestee. Criminal District Court For The Parish of Orleans, State of Louisiana, No. M-703. 1967 transcript.
State of Louisiana v. Clay L. Shaw. Criminal District Court, Parish of Orleans, No. 198-059. 1969 transcript.
Clay L. Shaw v. Jim Garrison. United States District Court, Eastern District of Louisiana, New Orleans Division, No. 71-135. 1971 transcript.

ACKNOWLEDGMENTS

James Phelan was the first and staunchest champion of this work. He shared with me his knowledge of the case, his files, his unique writer's eye, his wisdom, and his friendship. David Snyder's information was invaluable and his assistance ongoing. William Wegmann answered all my questions with fine humor and steered me to the Christenberry hearing. Irvin Dymond provided indispensable insights. Salvatore Panzeca's recollections inform the pages of this book. Cynthia Wegmann shared with me her father's papers and her memories of Clay Shaw and that difficult time.

Edward O'Donnell provided a copy of his report on Perry Russo's polygraph test and recalled his meetings with Garrison about it. David Chandler contributed firsthand knowledge of Garrison's personal life and his arrangement with Life magazine. Leonard Gurvich provided insights into Garrison and the personalities in his office, as well as details concerning Perry Russo's first polygraph. Hugh Aynesworth described his experiences with Garrison and sent a batch of useful material. Barbara Snyder recalled her impressions of David Ferrie and their conversations during his final days. James Kruebbe recounted his polygraph examination of Vernon Bundy and the scene in Garrison's office afterwards, and shared the report he wrote concerning all of it.

Richard Kilbourne enlightened me on the Clinton witnesses. Richard Kilbourne, Jr. enlightened me on the history and culture of that region. Meeting the remarkable Anne Dischler was one of the highlights of my research; I am indebted to her for sharing her records and recollections. Aline Woodside (who directed me to Anne Dischler) and Dr. Frank Silva filled in missing pieces of the puzzle surrounding East Louisiana State Hospital.

Herbert W. Christenberry, Jr. (whom I contacted after this book was written) passed on information about his father. Harry Connick's cooperation was generous, and his description of his meeting with

Oliver Stone was revealing. Dr. Edwin Weinstein informed me about the nature of sodium Pentothal. Raymond Comstock supplied useful information. It was gracious of James Alcock to speak to me.

Over the past five years, Paul Hoch has been a trusted touchstone on all matters concerning this book; he also read all the revisions. Tom Dardis has been a valuable and ongoing source of guidance. Terry Nixon made a contribution to my earliest effort. Milton Brener offered valuable practical advice. Bill Lambert, Shirley Warmuth, and Joe Warmuth also read the manuscript and provided helpful comments.

Steve Tilley and his staff at the National Archives answered my inquiries, kept my orders filled, and helped make my time there productive. David Lifton loaned me his Garrison clippings. Gus Russo shared his amazing personal directory. Amalie Phelan and Ginger Liebovitz provided insights in their field. A conversation with my nephew Terry Brossett caused me to embark on this book.

John Diamond kept the project afloat and my spirits up. Dr. Daniel Reeves kept me physically intact. The encouragement of friends and family kept me on an even keel. I am especially indebted to Mike Billings, Shirley Warmuth, Vicki Bleak, Marguerite Edelstein, Ginger Beattie, Amalie Phelan, Don Bleak, Joe Warmuth, Karen Beattie, Maurice Edelstein, Jeannette Billings, Pat Jacobs, Jesse Billings, and Lois Lambert. Without the confidence and support of my husband, this book would not have been written.

To all those at M. Evans and Co. who were enthusiastic about the manuscript and have helped to launch it into the world, I extend my deep appreciation. A special thanks goes to Rik Schell for his splendid work, which made this a better book.

I am grateful to George deKay for his faith in it—and for changing his mind.

INDEX

Abt, John, 32
Alcock, James L.
    as an assistant D.A., 96n
    and Andrews, 121n, 150
    and autopsy report, 314-315n2
    and Bradley, 124
    and civil action trial, 167
    and Clinton, 180n, 196-197
    and Ferrie, 64, 65, 302n18
    and Garrison, 325n18
    and Garrison, 54
    and Haggerty, 145-146
    and investigation, 53n
    and JFK (film), 214-215, 216
    and preliminary hearing, 102
    and request for continuance, 127
    and Shaw, 6, 8n, 125, 154
    and Spiesel, 134, 134n,
      315n11
Alford, William, 170
"A Matter of Reasonable Doubt"
    (Billings), 41, 46
American Bar Association, 161
Anderson, Jack, 225, 232
Andrews, Dean
    and Bertrand, 32, 34-36, 36n,
      37, 40, 50, 279, 297n31,
      298n42
    and Davis, 297n31, 297n34
    description of, 37
    and Garrison, 39-40, 50, 75,
      176, 205, 285, 313-
      314n39, 314n43
    and gay community, 31
    and grand jury trial, 120-121,
      313n36

    interview with Liebeler, 36-37
    and NBC White Paper, 116
    and Oswald, 31-34, 34n, 36n,
      40, 297n32, 297-298n37,
      298-299n45
    and parole action, 43, 43n
    and perjury trial, 121-122,
      298n38
    and phone calls, 34, 297n31
    portrayal of in JFK (film),
      216n, 216-217
    and press conference, 120-121
    resignation of, 121
    and sedatives, 297n30
    and Shaw, 50, 74-75, 216-217,
      284
    testimony of, 318n24
    and Warren Commission, 47n,
      150, 297n36
    and weekend of the assassina-
      tion, 31-34
    as witness for defense, 149-
      151
Andrews, J.B., 297n30
Anson, Robert Sam, 291n3
Anti-Castro Cubans. See Cuban con-
    nection
Appel, Charles A., 151-152, 156
Arresting officers of Shaw, 8n. See
    also specific individuals
Asner, Ed, 213, 215
Assassination
    according to JFK (film), 220
    and autopsy report, 127, 148,
      314-315n2, 317n18
    and exit wounds, 317n17

INDEX

Braniff, Matthew S., 95
Brannon, Robert, 191, 219, 219n, 328n18
Brener, Milton, 20, 69, 112n, 239, 297n35
Bribery attempt, 109-111, 112n, 172, 202n, 202-203, 315n3, 324n8. See also Beauboeuf, Alvin
Bringuier, Carlos, 63, 303n24
Brooke Army hospital, 13
Broshears, Raymond, 328n15
Broussard's restaurant, 39, 43
Brownlee, Morris, 45, 300n16
Bundy, Vernon, 99-101, 103n, 116, 132, 167, 202, 310n15
Bush, George, xvii, 243

Cahlman, Robert, 328n18
Calhoun, Algonquin J., 151
Califano, Joseph A., xvii
Camp Street address, 43, 278-279, 323n32
Cancler, John, 116, 284, 312n22
Candy, John, 216
CAP (Civil Air Patrol)
  and Ferrie, 68,
  and Ferrie/Oswald link, 28, 28n, 44n, 61n, 295n18, 295n19
  and Martin's story, 25, 296n21
  and Oswald, 25n
Carr, Richard Randolph, 144n, 159n
Case Closed (Posner), 248-249, 249n
Castro, Fidel, 51n
Chandler, David
  criticism of Garrison, 40-41
  and Ferrie, 46-47
  and Garrison, 19, 45n, 45-46, 299n5
  on Garrison, 55-56, 293n19
  and Garrison's case, 47
  on Garrison's sexuality, 236

and Life magazine's deal with Garrison, 43
  on Life split, 55-56, 82-83
  and Shaw, 49-50
  threatening of, 55
  and On the Trail of the Assassins, 281
Charity Hospital, 24
Cheramie, Rose, 323n31, 327n9
Chetta, Nicolas J., 60, 64, 71, 76, 80, 99
Child's Night Dream, A (Stone), 212n
Christenberry, Herbert W.
  and civil action trial, 170-171, 174-175, 332n4
  death of, 262
  description of, 168-169
  on Garrison's case, 165
CIA
  and Ferrie, 25, 25n
  and Garrison's theories, xiii, 45, 203, 277, 302-303n20
  and Martin, 294n10
  and Shaw, 203-206, 204n, 285, 325n12
Ciravolo, John, 61
Civil action trial, 165-172, 171n, 174-175, 332n4
Civil Air Patrol. See CAP (Civil Air Patrol)
Clark, Ramsey, 81-82, 127, 148, 306-307n40, 307n41
Clinton/Clinton witnesses. See also specific witnesses
  challenges to, 147
  and Dischler's findings, 190-197
  documentary about, 185
  first mention of, 129
  inquiry into, 197
  and jury, 163
  and Ku Klux Klan connection
  and M. Oswald, 147
  narrative of, 185-186

INDEX

INDEX

INDEX

INDEX